In this study James Simpson examines two great poems of the later medieval period, the Latin philosophical epic, Alan of Lille's *Anticlaudianus* (1181–3), and John Gower's English poem, the *Confessio amantis* (1390–3). Simpson locates these works in two traditions of literary humanism: the absolutist, whose philosophical mentor is Plato, whose literary model is Virgil and whose concept of the self is centred in the intellect; and the constitutionalist, whose classical models are Aristotle and Ovid and whose concept of the self resides in the mediatory power of the imagination. Both poems are examples of the *Bildungsroman*, in which the self reaches its fullness only by traversing an educational cursus in the related sciences of ethics, politics and cosmology; but as this study shows, there are very different polities behind their conceptions of selfhood and education.

CAMBRIDGE STUDIES IN MEDIEVAL LITERATURE 25

SCIENCES AND THE SELF IN
MEDIEVAL POETRY

This series of critical books seeks to cover the whole area of literature
written in the major medieval languages – the main European vernacu-
lars, and medieval Latin and Greek – during the period *c*. 1100–*c*. 1500.
Its chief aim is to publish and stimulate fresh scholarship and criticism on
medieval literature, special emphasis being placed on understanding
major works of poetry, prose and drama in relation to the contemporary
culture and learning which fostered them.

A complete list of titles in the series is given at the end of this volume

SCIENCES AND THE SELF IN MEDIEVAL POETRY

Alan of Lille's *Anticlaudianus* and John Gower's *Confessio amantis*

JAMES SIMPSON

University of Cambridge

CAMBRIDGE UNIVERSITY PRESS

Published by the Press Syndicate of the University of Cambridge
The Pitt Building, Trumpington Street, Cambridge CB2 1 RP
40 West 20th Street, New York, NY 10011-4211, USA
10 Stamford Road, Oakleigh, Melbourne 3166, Australia

First published 1995

Printed in Great Britain at the University Press, Cambridge

A catalogue record for this book is available from the British Library

Library of Congress cataloguing in publication data

Simpson, James, 1954–
Sciences and the self in medieval poetry: Alan of Lille's *Anticlaudianus* and John Gower's
Confessio amantis / James Simpson.
p. cm. – (Cambridge studies in medieval literature, 25)
Includes bibliographical references and index.
ISBN 0 521 47181 8 hardback
1. Alanus de Insulis d. 1203. *Anticlaudianus*. 2. Literature, Comparative – Latin (medieval
and modern) and English (Middle) 3. Literature, Comparative – English (Middle) and
Latin (medieval and modern) 4. Epic poetry, Latin (medieval and modern) – History and
criticism. 5. Gower, John, *c.* 1330–1408. *Confessio amantis*. 6. Poetry, medieval – History
and criticism. 7. Literature and science – Europe–History. 8. Poetry, medieval –
classical influences. 9. Philosophy, medieval, in literature. 10. Self in literature.
11. Love in literature. 12. Humanists. I. Title. II. Series.
PA8240.A5A657 1995
871'.0409–dc20 94–26520 CIP

ISBN 0 521 47181 8 hardback

Per carissima Luisella

Contents

Acknowledgements

I owe an immense debt to Alastair Minnis, whose warm encouragement and bracing criticism has marked every stage of this book's development. I should also like to thank Sarah Kay, who early on understood what I was doing. Winthrop Wetherbee and David Benson both generously offered penetrating comments on one chapter, just as many colleagues and students in Cambridge have provided intellectual stimulus (particularly Juliet Dusinberre, Anne Fernihough, Jeremy Dimmick, Jill Whitelock and Ad Putter). I benefited from the comments of anonymous readers at Cambridge University Press, while Pier-Maria and Franca Brunetti provided inestimable support of many kinds.

The substance of some chapters first appeared as articles (chapters 2 and 3 in *Traditio*, 47 (1992), pp. 113–60; chapter 6 in *Mediaevalia*, 16 (1993), pp. 159–95; and the Alanian material in chapter 8 in *Interpretation: Medieval and Modern*, The J. A. W. Bennett Memorial Lectures, eighth series, edited by Piero Boitani and Anna Torti (Cambridge, 1993), pp. 167–87). I register my thanks to the publishers of those articles for permission to re-use this material. Chapter 5 has vestigial connections with an article that first appeared in *Neophilologus*, 72 (1988), pp. 617–32.

Girton College, Cambridge

Abbreviations

Aa	*Ars amatoria*
AHDLMA	*Archives d'histoire doctrinale et littéraire du moyen âge*
BGPTM	*Beiträge zur Geschichte der Philosophie und Theologie des Mittelalters* (*Beiträge zur Geschichte der Philosophie des Mittelalters* in the case of fascicules before 1930)
CCCM	Corpus Christianorum, Continuatio Mediaevalis
EETS	Early English Text Society
GCARR	*Gower's 'Confessio Amantis': Responses and Reassessments*, edited by A. J. Minnis (Cambridge, 1983)
HTCWP	*A History of Twelfth-Century Western Philosophy*, edited by Peter Dronke (Cambridge, 1988)
MED	*Middle English Dictionary*, edited by Hans Kurath (Ann Arbor, 1956–)
PL	*Patrologia Latina*, edited by J.-P. Migne (Paris, 1844–64)
Ra	*Remedia amoris*
RF	*Romanische Forschungen*

CHAPTER I

Introduction

This book is partly about the different ways in which 'scientific' knowledge is presented in the two poems of my title. This sentence immediately raises the question as to why one should go to poetry for such knowledge. Surely we should instead go to properly 'scientific' texts produced in the periods of these two poems (*Anticlaudianus*, 1181–3, and 1390–3 for the *Confessio amantis*)? There we will be able to consult works of psychology, ethics, politics, and cosmology, for example (throughout this book I use the word 'scientific' to denote the entire range of academic disciplines available to a given writer). This objection is clearly not without force – a tradition at least as old as Plato has dismissed poetry as having at very best only a secondary philosophic value. Scientific information is best sought where it properly originates, in the academic works of trained philosophers.

Or is it? Certainly if we understand 'information' in its modern sense, then the objection might stand: clear expositions of scientific theory by professional academics, in whatever discipline, are the obvious place to look for scientific information. There is no shortage of such works in the respective milieux of both Alan and Gower – Alan, indeed, wrote works at the forefront of late twelfth-century ethics and theology himself.[1] But for both Alan and Gower the word 'information' is not half so dull as its modern descendant. A good deal of the argument of this book hinges on this very rich concept, and there follows, accordingly, an account of its semantic range.

'ENFORMACIOUN', *INFORMATIO*

I begin with the English text. It is true that 'information' in the modern sense of the word is offered by the *Confessio amantis*. Genius

[1] See chapter 2, n. 38.

I

explicates the sense of eighty or so stories (ostensibly providing moral information). Equally, he makes long expositions on various abstract philosophic matters, especially in the *divisio philosophiae* that occupies the whole of Book VII. And there are also 'scientific' expositions outside Book VII: in Book III, Genius gives a philosophical presentation of homicide; he lists the inventors of sciences in Book IV; and in Book V he gives a detailed exposition of the religions of the world. But this encyclopaedic material is by no means the essential 'information' of the poem; in the *Confessio* philosophic information (taken as denoting the actual content of a given philosophical doctrine), is, rather, intrinsically part of, *and subject to the distortions of,* a nexus of 'informations' – literary, pedagogic, and psychological. Understood in this broader sense, the word 'information' refers less to inert bodies of knowledge, and more to the action of transmitting and receiving knowledge.

There are two principal ways in which we might understand the 'information' of the *Confessio amantis*. On the one hand, the word denotes the artistic shaping both in and of the poem (i.e. Genius's act of shaping stories for Amans, and Gower's act of giving literary form, or shape, to the poem as a whole).[2] On the other, we should understand the word as referring to the act of transmitting knowledge in and by the poem (i.e. both Genius's act of teaching Amans, and Gower's act of teaching us).[3] One sense is artistic (specifically literary), the other pedagogic.

In Book VII of the *Confessio* God is represented as an artist, or as one who gives form, both to primary elements and to the human soul. Genius relates that 'hyle' (amorphous matter) pre-existed God's formation, 'as soun tofore the song is set':

> Riht so the hihe pourveance
> Tho hadde under his ordinance
> A gret substance, a gret matiere,
> Of which he wolde in his manere

---

[2] Throughout this book I shall use the word 'form', with reference to works of literature, to refer to both the style and structure of a given work (what thirteenth-century theorists called the *forma tractandi* and the *forma tractatus* of a work).

[3] The distinction between the learning processes represented *in* poems, and the learning processes activated in readers *by* poems is critical to my whole argument. It is a distinction rarely made in criticism of 'scientific' poetry, but see Green 1967, p. 9, n. 7, for the distinction I am making: Green distinguishes between the 'subjective dimension' of allegory, which is designed 'to bring about subjective realization of the truth', and the 'objective dimension', which is designed to provide 'knowledge of doctrinal truth'.

These othre thinges make and forme.
For yit withouten eny forme
Was that matiere universal,
Which hihte Ylem in special.
Of Ylem, as I am enformed,
These elementz ben mad and formed.   (VII.209–18)[4]

The essential opposition in this passage is between 'matiere' (along with its semantic cognates 'substance', 'Ylem') and 'forme', used as both noun and verb. It is clear that in this act of artistic formation God produces not merely an external shape or form, but also that he gives the elements their distinctive, proper form, the quality by which they are defined. God's information of the elements involves bringing the elements to their fullness, or perfection.[5] And just as God informed the shapeless mass of prime substance into elements, so too did he give form, or perfection, to the human soul, according to a divine, rather than a natural exemplar:

And thus nature his pourveance
Hath mad for man to liven hiere;
Bot god, which hath the Soule diere,
Hath formed it in other wise.
That can noman pleinli devise;
Bot as the clerkes ous enforme,
That lich to god it hath a forme,
Thurgh which figure and which liknesse
The Soule hath many an hyh noblesse
Appropred to his oghne kinde.   (VII.490–9)

God informs the soul as an artist shapes his matter, using a divine exemplar to reproduce an imitation of the divine (a 'figure and ... liknesse'). It is this quality which gives the soul its essential definition, those qualities which are 'appropred', proper to, the soul's ideal state.

If God operates as an artist, giving form to matter, this is equally true of Genius as artist, since Genius informs the matter of his stories. The tale of the false bachelor, for example, is introduced in this way:

---

4 All citations of the *Confessio amantis* are from Macaulay 1900–1.
5 See *MED*, 'forme', sense 14a (a) 'The archetype of a thing, or class of things, as it exists in the mind of God; the Platonistic "idea" which serves as the pattern for a created thing', and 14b (a) 'The essence of a thing, the formative principle, that which causes a thing to be what it is'.

> And forto speke of this matiere
> Touchende love and his Supplant,
> A tale which is acordant
> Unto thin Ere I thenke enforme.
> Now herkne, for this is the forme.   (II.2496–500)

In this small introduction Genius's informing activity is literary, since the object of his information here is the tale itself. Of course the pedagogic value of the story is implicit, since it is being informed for Amans's attention ('acordant / Unto thin Ere'), but Genius is not simply passing on 'information' passively; he is instead actively informing a tale concerning the matter of supplantation in love. The word play provoked by the rhyme on 'enforme' and 'forme' points to the nature of Genius's literary information: in the first place, the the word 'form' here must mean 'shape', or 'outer form', with reference to the tale which follows.[6] But the passage as a whole focuses a philosophical sense of the word 'form', since the 'form' of the tale is linked with the 'matter' concerning supplantation in love. This standard philosophical pairing (of form and matter) implies the notion that matter is shaped by a form, or exemplar: within the general 'matter' of supplantation in love, that is, Genius will 'inform' a tale according to the form, or exemplar, of a moral idea.[7] And if the notion of 'information' can be applied to Genius as a literary artist, as he shapes stories for Amans, then it has an obvious application to Gower's own activity as an artist, shaping the poem as a whole for his readers. Discussion of the 'information' of the *Confessio*, then, is not in the least restricted to the blocks of philosophical matter in the poem. On the contrary, consideration of the poem's 'information' will embrace discussion both of the principles by which the poem takes its own shape, and of Genius's role as a shaper, or informer, of stories for Amans.

So the primary meaning of 'information' is artistic, or literary (denoting the act of giving form to matter). What of the secondary, pedagogic, meaning? In the passages about God's information of the elements and of the human soul cited above (VII.209–18;

---

[6]   See *MED*, 'forme', sense 1a (a) 'The physical shape of something, contour, outline'.

[7]   See MED, sense 11 (a) 'Model of life or conduct, example to be imitated'. *MED*, under 'enfourmen', lists *Confessio amantis*, II.2499, under 5 (c), 'to tell (a story)'. But Genius says he is 'informing' a tale, rather than telling it; the sense should rather be the philosophical sense of 6 (a), 'to give form to (matter, in the Aristotelian sense)'. 'Platonic' would serve equally for 'Aristotelian' here.

490–9), Gower uses the verb 'forme' of God's activity, and expands its implications by the word 'enforme': the pedagogic activity of 'clerkes' imparting knowledge about God's creative information of the world is described as itself an 'information' ('as the clerkes ous enforme'). One kind of information (God's) gives rise to another (the clerks'). The role of shaper, or informer, is shared by Genius, since he informs stories to bring them to an ideal, proper form: Genius's literary information is a parallel activity to divine information, since both are designed to bring their objects to a kind of perfection. But in practice Genius's literary act of informing stories is designed to teach, or inform, Amans, and so the act of literary information shades into a pedagogic sense. Thus at the end of the story of the false bachelor in Book II Genius points to the pedagogic value of the tale, saying to Amans

> that thou thee miht avise
> Upon this enformacioun
> Touchende of Supplantacioun.   (II.2782–4)

'Information' is clearly being used in a more positive sense than the neutral, modern sense of the word: here the information of Genius is something by which Amans might be instructed, or morally informed. The word 'enformacioun' designates not so much a body of knowledge, that is, as its instructive effect – it denotes not a thing, but an action.[8] And so it has a verbal form, whose most frequent meaning is 'teach', as in this example (Amans asking Genius about jealousy):

> Wherfore I wolde you beseche,
> That ye me wolde enforme and teche
> What maner thing it mihte be.   (V.449–51)

To 'enforme', however, is not simply to teach, but to teach according to an ideal pattern, with the aim of forming the recipient of the teaching. We can see this in the example cited above (VII.490–9), where the 'clerkes' are said to 'enforme' us about the form of the soul, shaped directly by God. This pedagogic information not only reveals the form of the soul, but more especially brings the soul, through self-knowledge, to that proper, ideal form – the 'hyh noblesse / Appropred to his oghne kinde'.

---

[8]   See *MED*, 'informacioun', sense 1(a) 'instruction, direction, teaching'.

Very often the instruction of Genius is designated by the noun 'enformacioun', and his activity by the verb 'enforme', with the words used at pivotal points, at the borders of particular discussions, summarizing or promising instruction.[9] And very often both these senses (literary and pedagogic) are implicit in Gower's usage, with one predominating. Thus in the following example, the pedagogic sense of the word 'enforme' predominates, even if the artistic sense of 'forme' as 'exemplar', or 'model', is implicit in the parallelism of 'after the forme' and 'after the reule':

> Forthi, my fader, what is more
> Touchende to this ilke lore
> I you beseche, after the forme
> That ye pleinly me wolde enforme,
> So that I may myn herte reule
> In loves cause after the reule. (I.1337–42)

In this passage the 'forme' or 'reule' relating to 'love's cause' is a source of pedagogic information, impressing itself upon Amans's heart. In the following example, the pedagogic value of moral 'information' is certainly present, but the literary sense (of informing a tale from a 'matter') predominates:

> Bot if ye wolde in eny forme
> Of this matiere a tale enforme,
> Which were ayein this vice set,
> I scholde fare wel the bet. (I.1973–6)

Already we can see a range of senses which converge in the words 'enformacioun' and 'enforme': the exemplar of a moral idea informs a tale to produce a literary form or shape, the combination of which in turn informs, or teaches, the soul of the listener for whom the matter is designed.

And we have two kinds of 'information': the artistic information of verbal artefacts, and the instructive, informative effect of those artefacts. These two kinds of information are related: 'information' implies a process (either artistic or educative), tending towards a state of perfection, achieved when the story and the recipient of the story have received their ideal state, or form. Indeed, the ideal

---

9   Pickles and Dawson 1987 list thirty-nine instances of 'enformacion' and 'enforme'; sixteen of these refer to Genius's teaching of Amans, and, in all but two of these examples, the word appears finally in the line. Where the words appear as part of a narration, they tend to appear within the line, rather than finally.

form of the story can be defined by its effect of producing the ideal (human) form in its recipient. Referring to the 'information' in and of the *Confessio* will now suggest less that it is an encyclopaedic poem, and more that it is a *Bildungsroman*, where the literary form of the poem is designed to bring its readers to an ideal form. And the literary 'information' of the poem, I will suggest, is correlative with the form of the soul: the literary form of the poem follows the soul's contours; as the soul reaches its own perfection, so too does the poem draw to a close. Because the poem aims at human ful-filment through an educative process, so too is the poem's shape controlled by that end. The *Confessio*, like the *Anticlaudianus*, is a person-shaped poem.

Gower, as will be argued in chapter 7, writes within an Aristotelian frame. The semantic range he exemplifies in using the word 'enforme' derives, as one would expect, from Latin usage, particularly that of scholastic writers working within Aristotelian traditions. In the writings of Thomas Aquinas (*c.* 1224–74), for example, we find almost exactly the same range of usage in the word *informare*: the word can either mean to 'give a thing its essen-tial or substantial form or its accidental fashion', or, as a second sense, 'to establish, prepare, inform'. As with Gower, the primary sense is philosophical, dependent on the creative notion of form, and this produces a secondary, pedagogic sense.[10] The same is true, unsurprisingly, of the senses of '*informatio*': the first sense is the cre-ative sense of the word ('formation, i.e. providing with a form'), whereas the second denotes 'instruction'.[11]

What of twelfth-century Latin, and particularly of Alan's usage of the words *informatio* and *informare*? We have observed with regard to the *Confessio amantis* that discussion of the poem's 'information' directs us primarily to principles of literary shaping (by both Genius and Gower) on the one hand, and on the other to the peda-gogic process in and of the poem. Might the same be true of the *Anticlaudianus*?

---

[10]   See Deferrari and Barry 1948–9, *informo*, senses 1 and 2.

[11]   See Deferrari and Barry 1948–9, *informatio*, senses 1 and 2. The *Thesaurus Linguae Latinae* (Leipzig, 1900–), under *informatio*, lists sense 1 as *creatio*; sense 2(a) is *adumbratio, definitio, demonstratio*; and sense 2(b) is *instructio, doctrina*. Senses 1 and 2(b) are late classical. In classical Latin the word is of fairly low philosophical status: C. T. Lewis and C. Short, *A Latin Dictionary* (Oxford, 1879) give under *informatio* sense 1, 'an outline, sketch, first draft', and sense 2, 'an idea, conception'.

Alan's usage of the words *informare* and *informatio* covers the same range as Gower's, although it is true that he uses the words themselves rather sparingly in his literary works. In Book V of the *Anticlaudianus*, Fronesis[12] is described as following the *puella poli* in this way:

> Ulterius producit iter Prudencia, gressum
> Informans gressu comitis... (V.373–4)[13]

Prudence proceeds upon her journey, shaping her own step by that of her companion.[14]

Informare here clearly has the formative sense we have already seen in Gower: Fronesis shapes her own step according to the pattern of her companion's. Given that Fronesis is learning from the *puella poli* here, the pedagogic sense lies immediately behind the formative sense demanded by the poem's allegorical fiction of a journey.[15] This same oscillation between the formative and the pedagogic senses is found in Alan's earlier work, the *De planctu Naturae* (*c.* 1160–70), where, near the end of the work, Genius is represented in the artistic act of forming images of human perfection and imperfection with his right and left hands. Truth and Falsehood stand by, personifying the act of right and left hand respectively. Whatever images of human perfection are produced by Truth are defaced by Falsehood: 'quicquid illa conformiter informabat, ista informiter deformabat'.[16] The fiction of the poem is representing the formative processes of Nature, and so the artistic sense of *informare* has real force here. Equally, these images of human perfection are instructive; the pedagogic sense lies in wait behind the artistic.

In much humbler, non-literary contexts, Alan uses the word *informatio* in the sense of 'education', 'instruction', very often. In, for example, his preaching manual (the *Ars praedicandi*), he says that

---

[12] For the sake of convenience and consistency, throughout this book I shall use the name 'Fronesis' for the figure whom Alan calls indifferently 'Fronesis' and 'Prudentia'.

[13] All citations from the *Anticlaudianus* are from Bossuat 1955.

[14] The translation is from Sheridan 1973, p. 146; all future page references to this translation will be cited in the body of the text.

[15] For other uses of *informare* in the *Anticlaudianus*, see also VII.395–6 ('...simplex gracia mentis / Informet munus'), and VIII.70–1 ('Quod Natura creat, recreat noua gracia, formant / Mores, informat uirtus'), both of which are clearly drawing on the philosophical concept of form.

[16] Häring 1978, XVIII.111–2, p. 877. See Ziolkowski 1985, p. 28 for discussion of Alan's use of the word *forma*.

the 'final cause and utility of preaching is the instruction of men' ('informationi hominum deserviens, significatur causa finalis, sive utilitas praedicationis').[17] The word designates here, as it does in Gower, a particular, normative kind of teaching. And this is true of the word's usage in the twelfth century generally. John of Salisbury (*c.* 1115–80), for example, says that his own grammar teachers followed the model (*forma*) of Bernard of Chartres: 'Ad huius magistri formam preceptores mei in gramatica ... suos discipulos aliquandiu informaverunt',[18] where the etymological force of *forma* (embedded in the word *informare*) is activated.

Were it the case that Alan uses the words *informare* and *informatio* only quite rarely in his literary works, we might think the words had little purchase on them. But Alan, as I will argue in the following chapter, is writing within an intensely Platonistic philosophical culture, in which the concept of form plays a cardinal role. And as with John of Salisbury in the citation immediately above, Alan's sense of the word *informatio* is inextricably woven into the senses of the word *forma*. We can see this explicitly in his *Liber in distinctionibus dictionum theologicalium* (a kind of theological dictionary), where Alan gives eight acceptations of the word *forma*. The last of these senses is the educative sense we have already observed: he says that *forma* should be defined as *informatio*, whence it is said that the bishop 'informs' his flock by his good example: 'Praelatus est forma gregis, id est subditos informare debet bono exemplo.'[19] The 'information' of the bishop here is not of a neutral kind, but normative: he 'informs' by his good example, which serves as an ideal model.

But the word *forma* has other, creative senses, which might open the way for understanding other aspects of the poem apart from the teaching represented in it. The first sense of the word *forma* given by Alan in the *Liber in distinctionibus dictionum* concerns the outer, corporeal shape of a thing: 'proprie', he says, form 'idem est quod figura, scilicet illa proprietas quae consideratur secundum dispositionem lineamentorum' ('properly, form is the same as shape, that is, that property (of a thing) which is perceived according to the contour of its outlines'). This sense in turn leads to another definition, the philosophical concept of form, by which the form of a thing is its definition, or essential property: 'forma ...

---

[17] PL 210, cols. 111–198 (col. 112).
[19] PL 210, cols. 685–1012 (col. 796).
[18] Webb 1929, I.24, 856a, p. 57.

dicitur proprietas rei' ('form is said to be the definition of a thing').
Both these senses ('physical shape' and 'definition') are ultimately
dependent on the fifth definition given by Alan, which is the
Platonic sense of the word: 'forma ... dicitur sapientia divina, illa
scilicet paeordinatio sive praeconceptio quae fuit in mente divina
ab eterno de rebus creandis' ('form is defined as divine wisdom –
that preconception which existed in the divine mind from eternity
concerning the creation of things').[20]

So the word *forma* has many senses beyond its pedagogic sense,
all to do with the shaping of things, and to do with the essential
properties of things as determined by their formation. When considering the making of an object, *forma* designates many aspects of
its being: its outer shape, or figure; its essential properties, or definition; and, at the deepest level of its existence, the divine idea on
which it is modelled. As will be argued in chapters 2–4 of this
book, Alan is clearly aware of, and often exploits, all these senses
in the *Anticlaudianus*. But already we can see that understanding the
'information' of Alan's poem will involve consideration of at least
two things: of the teaching and learning processes represented in
(and provoked by) the poem on the one hand, and of formal
aspects of the poem's shape on the other. As with the *Confessio*, I
will be arguing that the form of the poem (its artistic information)
is intimately tied to its teaching process (its pedagogic information).
As the soul seeks to realize its own form, or ideal state, so too do
these poems take *their* shape. The narrative of both poems comes to
an end only with the education and integration of the soul; as the
soul gains knowledge, so too does its desire diminish, and so too
does the narrative of the poetry draw to a close.

DISCIPLINARY AND PSYCHOLOGICAL HIERARCHIES

The one thing, curiously, which the word *informatio* does *not* mean is
'information' in the modern sense – i.e. the actual content of a
body of knowledge or teaching. All the exposition so far would suggest that I will not in fact discuss that at all. I seem to be suggesting
that this book will be about the teaching processes of these poems
(rather than about *what* is taught), and about the formal structures
which serve those teaching processes. I seem, that is, entirely to

[20] Ibid.

have sidestepped discussion of the disciplinary content of these works – their philosophic 'information' in the modern sense. Such an evasion would find itself in a long critical tradition. From at least the fourteenth century poetic theorists have looked askance at explicitly philosophical poetry, regarding true poetry as a form of discourse which avoids the procedures of the philosopher.[21] Even where poetry is explicitly philosophical, the standard move has been to regard it not as knowledge, but as the non-affirmative representation of learning processes. Thus Croce (perhaps the most powerful twentieth-century exponent of this tradition) has it that what is significant about the philosophical content of Dante's *Commedia* is not what Dante learns, but what the experience of learning feels like.[22] By placing my emphasis on the teaching and learning experience designated by the word 'information', I seem about to join this tradition: I would seem, that is, to be giving secondary status to the content of what is learned, and to be focusing on that content simply for the experience to which it gives rise.

In fact I do think both these poems offer knowledge of a distinctive and original kind. And I will be talking about the philosophical content – 'information' in the modern sense – of both poems. How might these literary works offer real philosophical knowledge?

[21] This does not necessarily imply an opposition between poetry and philosophy. The essential distinction is between discursive mode. Thus Boccaccio, in the *De genealogia deorum* (*c.* 1360–3):

> For though their [the poets'] destination is the same as that of the philosophers, they do not arrive by the same road. The philosopher, everyone knows, by a process of syllogizing, disproves what he considers false, and in like manner proves his theory, and does all this as obviously as he can. The poet conceives his thought by contemplation, and, wholly without the help of syllogism, veils it as subtly and skilfully as he can under the outward semblance of his invention. (XIV.17; Osgood 1956, p. 79)

> For a similar argument, see Sidney's *Apology for Poetry* (Enright and DeChickera 1962, lines 657–713, pp. 20–1). See Greenfield 1981, and Hathaway 1962, pp. 65–80 for the development of attitudes towards explicitly philosophical poetry. See also Burrow 1993; Burrow 1982, pp. 18–23 and notes, offers a succinct discussion. For the tradition of 'scientific' poetry in antiquity, see Hardie 1986, pp. 5–32.

[22] He says this about the philosophical passages in the *Paradiso*, for example:

> Poesia didascalica, già è detto, ma poesia, in quanto cioè, diversamente che nella prosa, il motivo che vi domina non è l'indagare e l'insegnare che la mente opera, ma la rappresentazione dell'atto dell'indagare e insegnare, la virtú di quest'atto, che si compiace e gioisce di sé stessa e che delle cose insegnate si vale appunto come di materia per asserire sé stessa. (Croce 1921, p. 150)

> Croce's hostility towards 'scientific' poetry is shared by many influential schools of twentieth-century Anglo-American criticism as well (Leavisism and New Criticism, for example), for which see Graff 1970.

Both poems, I will argue, operate within a given hierarchy of the
sciences (the so-called 'Aristotelian division'), which separates philosophy into a theoretical and a practical division. I will explicate
this hierarchy of the sciences in chapter 2, but for the moment I
want only to remark that both poems reveal extremely subtle inter-
relations between the sciences, more subtle than those merely
asserted by medieval academic treatments of how the sciences
relate to each other.[23] In particular, I want to show how these
poems reveal the ways in which an ethics is dependent on a politics, which in turn is dependent on a cosmology. Both these poems
expose the pull from one discourse to another – from ethics, to politics, to cosmology. And in both poems politics is the science to
which others point. Both, I will argue, are concerned to imagine,
and to inform a philosopher–king, by revealing the subtle inter-
relations between ethical and political experience on the one hand,
and the structure of the cosmos on the other.

This, for the *Anticlaudianus*, is a new argument; all criticism which
has treated the poem at length this century has seen its essential
burden to reside in the movement through the cosmos, generated
by the Arts and culminating in the theological experience of Book
VI. The formation of the New Man through the courtly and ethical
virtues in Books VII–IX has been seen as a rather anti-climactic
appendage to the journey of Fronesis in Books I–VI.[24] I will be arguing, on the contrary, that these last three books, concerned as they
are with ethics and politics, exert a considerable weight and force in
the conception of the poem as a whole. For Gower, there have been
studies which have treated the political as a theme in the *Confessio*,
certainly;[25] but no study has, to my mind, properly understood the
subtle relations of the ostensible subject of the poem (the amatory
concerns of Amans) with this political theme. No study, that is, has
seen the political interest of the *Confessio* as predicated by the ethical
discussion between Genius and Amans in the way I propose here.
So this book will also offer a new reading of the *Confessio amantis*, a
reading which sees the structure of the poem as informed by, *and
itself a commentary on*, the structure of the sciences, and in particular
the relations between ethics, politics and cosmology.

---

[23] For medieval divisions of the sciences, see chapter 2, nn. 27–36.
[24] See chapter 2, n. 18.
[25] See particularly Coffman 1945; Fisher 1964, pp. 185–283; Peck 1978.

But how might these poems comment on the structure of the sciences? How might poetry provide original and distinctive forms of philosophical knowledge? I return to my earlier point that these poems are examples of the *Bildungsroman*, fables of the individual soul's education, in which narrative dynamic is a function of the soul's desire to realize its fullness. The premise of this point is that we are dealing, in both poems, with the representation of *one* soul, one person. This is a cardinal perception for the argument with regard to both poems: both are psychological allegories of the individual soul. And any knowledge gained by the individual soul will be modified by the psyche's passionate desires for and resistances to that knowledge. My point is very close to that made by Boethius's *Philosophia*; with regard to those who doubt the possibility of certainty in science, she says this:

And the cause of this errour is that of alle the thingis that every wyght hath iknowe, thei wenen that tho thingis ben iknowe al only by the strengthe and by the nature of the thinges that ben iwyst or iknowe. And it is al the contrarye; for al that evere is iknowe, it is rather comprehendid and knowen, nat aftir his strengthe and his nature, but aftir the faculte (that is to seyn, the power and the nature) of hem that knowen.[26]

Any 'information' we receive is invariably subject to the powers of the psychological faculty by which we receive it. Both poems are structured around a psychology, and both imply a very subtle psychology of learning, which profoundly modifies the scientific content of either poem.

It is central to the argument of the whole book, then, that both poems are coherent psychological allegories, anatomizing and representing the education of a *single* soul. Of course this will require some attention to the psychological hierarchies on which Alan and Gower draw. But so too, in the case of both poets, does attention to psychological hierarchies also direct us to disciplinary hierarchies. The soul's education not only modifies the knowledge it receives, but it also reveals the very structure of the disciplines. Alan and Gower are working within humanist traditions where the soul's fulfilment can only be achieved through cognitive as much as moral formation; accordingly, both poems incorporate a philosophic curriculum. 'Scientific' knowledge and selfhood are inti-

---

[26] Bk V, prose 4. Cited from Chaucer's translation (Benson 1988, lines 132–41, p. 463).

mately related for both these poets, and so the desire for psychic reintegration necessarily entails a movement through the sciences. The inter-relation of the sciences themselves (from an ethics, to a politics, to a cosmology) is experienced through the individual soul's movement towards 'information', towards being fully informed or perfected. And knowledge is not forced on the soul, but, in an essentially humanist tradition, it is the soul which generates the sciences, and which reveals their true relations. The sciences and movement through them are rooted in the structure of the human psyche. Movement through the sciences, from ethics, to politics, and to cosmology, is premised on the capacities and desires of the soul itself (i.e. a psychology).

Because the curriculum is being encountered as the formation of an individual soul in these poems, then its presentation is by no means flat and predictable. Both works register the resistances and desires of the soul in its formation, especially its attachment to particular stages in its development, and its unwillingness to progress beyond those stages (in the *Confessio* a comically extended unwillingness). But in both poems narrative movement is generated by the soul's desire for integration through 'scientific' information.

THE READER'S INFORMATION

Unlike the procedures of the academic treatise, then, the mode of these works is by no means straightforward pedagogically, given that they present bodies of knowledge as a function of the individual soul's desire for that knowledge. But there is a further dimension to the psychology of learning presented by these poems, which is to do with the psychology of reading. Neither the *Anticlaudianus* nor the *Confessio* provide from within their narratives wholly reliable authority-figures who make sense of those narratives. And both poems, I shall be arguing, are characterized by profound structural incoherences, which provoke intriguing difficulties for a reader. In attempting to understand the sense behind these incoherences, we as readers are invited to participate in the construction of meaning, and to participate ourselves, therefore, in the processes of learning represented in the poems. The ultimate aim of both Alan and Gower is not so much to represent the formation of the soul, but to enact that formation in the reader. The meaning of both works is to be located less in their represented narratives, than in the sense of those narratives, a sense which is understood only through the reader's act of interpretation. Their mode of meaning is, in short, literary rather than discursive. So although they both provide philosophic and educative 'information' in the more neutral sense of that word, that is not their prime function; the essential and, I think, intended effect of these literary structures is to inform the soul of the reader – to bring the soul of the reader to its own ideal state, or 'form'. Both poems seek to realize a self-knowledge in the reader through the reader's act of interpretation.

So a good part of the argument of this book is literary-critical; of course I will be explicating the actual structures and hierarchies of knowledge which these poets receive, but a fundamental principle by which my argument is directed is that an understanding of literary shaping is the premise of understanding the philosophical meaning of a work. An appreciation of the creative 'information' of a literary work is logically prior to understanding its philosophical 'information'. As we shall see, Alan and Gower draw, to a certain extent, on the same philosophical materials. But these materials are set into literary structures, and it is to the sense of those literary structures that the argument of the book is ultimately directed.

It may already be clear from what I have said that a poetics is implicit in the philosophico-poetic culture within which Alan and Gower are both writing – a poetics which gives a powerful place to poetry in the long-standing opposition between poetry and philosophy. Both poems might be working within divisions, and hierarchies of the disciplines; but they are both, in my view, equally claiming a serious place for poetry within these disciplinary hierarchies. After chapters offering new interpretations of the *Anticlaudianus* (chapters 2 to 4) and the *Confessio* (chapters 5 to 7), I shall explicate aspects of the poetics of creative information which is implicit (and occasionally explicit) in both these poems (chapter 8).

TWO KINDS OF HUMANISM

Earlier I argued that both the *Confessio* and the *Anticlaudianus* were concerned to imagine the philosophical information of a ruler, and to produce a philosopher-king; in the last few pages I have been arguing that the aim of both poems is to promote self-knowledge in their readers. This might seem contradictory: how can the focus of these poems be at once the ideal ruler and the everyman reader (I

use the word 'every*man*' advisedly)?[27] I do not think that these possibilities are in fact contradictory in the case of the *Confessio*; for
Alan's poem the New Man is indeed the ideal reader, but that
reader is also a young king. Both poems do, of course, have a specific political context, and are both addressed to young kings –
Philip Augustus and (in Gower's first recension) Richard II. In
chapter 9 I shall consider the relationship between the royal and the
more general readership of both poems. Apart from sketching the
specific political context of these works, most of this chapter will be
devoted to a comparison of the actual nature of the politics implicit
in both poems – I think Alan's politics are Platonic, Virgilian, elitist,
and rooted in the practice of the highest of the soul's faculties (the
intelligence); Gower's politics are Aristotelian, Ovidian, much less
strictly elitist, and rooted much 'lower' down in the soul, at the
point where the imagination and physical desire meet.

Why, though, a reader might object, should the *Anticlaudianus*
and the *Confessio*, and only these poems, be yoked together? In
answer to this question, I readily concede the many different direc-
tions this book might have taken from a base in the *Anticlaudianus*:
it could, for example, have investigated the place of the
Anticlaudianus within twelfth-century poetics generally. Or it could
have moved from the *Anticlaudianus* to other vernacular contexts
which can, I am convinced, be illuminated by a deeper understanding of Alan's poem. In particular the context of romance writing contemporary with Alan has profound connections with Alan's
philosophico-poetic world: for there too we find an ethics, a politics, and a cosmology mediated by a psychology; there too (in the
works of Chrétien de Troyes, for example) we find a connection
between personal wholeness and literary integration; and there too
we find a poetics of *conjointure* which has intimate connections, I
think, with the poetic of the *Anticlaudianus*. Similarly, it is time the
relations between the *Divine Comedy* and the *Anticlaudianus* were re-
examined; in both these works we find fundamentally the same
structural blocks – a narrative, that is, framed around a pagan

---

[27] Throughout this book I will use the word 'man' to designate the intended student of
both Alan's and Gower's poems. I do this because, however much these humanist works
propose themselves as directed towards 'human' integration, that is in fact a code for
'male' integration: both works address themselves to the ideal ruler, but that ruler is conceived of as male. The case of Gower is much more complex here, since the poem does
seriously engage with female desire and female victimization by male desire. This is a
large and fascinating topic which remains open.

ethics (in both poems associated with an infernal confrontation), coupled with, and constrained by, an intellectual ascent through the spheres, aided by grace. And both poems are centrally directed towards political renovation on earth.

I will touch cursorily on these possibilities in the progress of this book; but the main comparative text will be Gower's *Confessio amantis*. I have made this decision for two reasons, one directed by interpretative clarity, the other by a concern with the cultural history of humanism.

Interpretative clarity: when the *Confessio* has been set in its twelfth-century context, it has been compared with its more obvious counterpart, the *De planctu Naturae*;[28] given the presence of Genius in both poems, this comparison is both inevitable and illuminating. (Indeed, I make it myself in chapter 6 of this book.) But comparison between the *Confessio* and the *De planctu* disguises the fundamental interests of Gower in the *Confessio*: whereas the *De planctu* is essentially ethical in focus, the *Anticlaudianus* and the *Confessio* are, as I have already suggested, primarily political. Of course the *Confessio* is narrower in its 'disciplinary' scope than the twelfth-century poem – Gower pays only marginal attention to the theoretical sciences (in Book VII). And whereas Alan is concerned to set a politics in its true relation with the speculative sciences, Gower is more concerned with the subtle inter-relations and disruptions between ethics and politics. The education of Alexander in Book VII certainly includes education in the speculative sciences, but the weight of the work falls on achieving a reciprocity between ethics and politics.

But however much Gower's 'disciplinary' scope is less broad than Alan's, it remains true, I will be suggesting, that the principles underlying Gower's poem are best understood with reference to the optimistic, humanistic, philosophico-poetic culture of the twelfth century. And Alan's *Anticlaudianus*, rather than the *De planctu Naturae*, is the fullest and most revealing manifestation of that culture for the *Confessio*. Principles of reading one poem illuminate the other, since in both poems psychological hierarchies interact with disciplinary hierarchies – in both poems, that is, a range of the soul's powers is activated as the soul is informed by a range of disciplines.

[28] See, for example, Economou 1970.

So although the argument of this book will be fairly narrowly focused on these two texts, I hope, nonetheless, that its points of reference might provide bearings for mapping a larger territory of cultural history, and in particular for the history of humanism between the twelfth and the fourteenth centuries. Let me hasten to add that I am using the word 'humanism' in a broad sense, contravening Kristeller's plea that the word be reserved for the cultural and educational programme shaped in the Italian Renaissance by teachers whose range of expertise lay in grammar, rhetoric, history, poetry and moral philosophy.[29] Of course both Alan and Gower are deeply influenced by the study of ancient authors as promoted in medieval schools, and it was this educational milieu which gave rise to what Kristeller calls 'humanism'.[30] But it remains the case that we need a general term to describe the following range of cultural positions (found in very many Western European works written between the twelfth and fourteenth centuries): (i) a profound confidence in the powers of human reason, and in the capacity of reason to promote human perfection insofar as that is possible; (ii) a corresponding confidence in the constructive powers of human nature and Nature more broadly; (iii) a corresponding respect for and engagement with the texts of classical literature and philosophy; and (iv) a due recognition of politics as a pivotal, if not as the supreme science. Alan and Gower, along with many other 'medieval' writers, share all these characteristics, characteristics which I intend to designate by the word 'humanism'.[31]

But why, it might be asked, should these two poems in particular be chosen as points of reference in the mapping of humanist culture between the twelfth and fourteenth centuries? In my view, as I shall argue in chapter 9, these two poems are excellent representatives of two sharply *differing* forms of humanist culture. Alan's sympathies lie with Plato and Virgil; he writes explicitly for a very small elite; his Latin is difficult and highly mannered; his psychology is rooted in the supreme power of the soul, the intellect, whereas the body is for him a marginal phenomenon; and his

---

[29]   Kristeller 1979, pp. 22–3; Kristeller 1988.

[30]   For the importance of Northern European schools in the formation of Italian humanism, see Skinner 1978, p. 102; Kristeller 1988.

[31]   Southern 1970, p. 33 makes a similar claim for a medieval humanism; his characteristics overlap with mine.

politics are, accordingly, absolutist – all power is located in the philosopher–king. With Gower, each one of these choices is different: his sympathies lie with Aristotle and Ovid; he writes for 'Englandes sake' and for a wide audience;[32] he not only writes in the vernacular, but his English is plain and limpid; his psychology is rooted not in the intellect, nor even in the reason, but rather in the imagination, since it is the imagination which mediates between the sensual desires of the body and the reason; and, by analogy with this psychology, his politics are constitutionalist, recognizing at every point the necessity for mediation between the king and the rest of the body-politic. Gower, in short, is what might be described as a liberal humanist whereas Alan is a pure example of humanism's absolutist strain. The same kind of comparison could be made by putting either Jean de Meun or Chaucer beside Alan. Both these figures are powerful presences behind my understanding of Gower, since it seems to me that these three poets represent the liberal humanism of the thirteenth and fourteenth centuries in France and England in its most intelligent and subtle forms. Were there but world enough and time, this book would embrace discussion of all three vernacular writers. But even as it stands, the comparison of Alan's poem and the *Confessio* should serve not only to dispense with the myth that humanism begins in fifteenth-century Italy, but also to define some distinctive varieties of French and English literary humanism over the period 1180–1400.

ALAN OF LILLE AND JOHN GOWER

Alan was educated probably in either Paris or Chartres, probably in the 1240s: after *c.* 1150 he was active as a teacher in both Paris and Montpellier. In his old age he entered the Cistercian order at Citeaux, where he died in 1203.[33] Of Gower, born *c.* 1330, not

---

[32] In saying this I am referring to the self-presentation of the *Confessio*; when we consider surviving manuscripts of both works (*Confessio amantis*, 51; *Anticlaudianus*, 110) it would seem that Alan's poem was read more widely. For the manuscripts of the *Confessio*, see Macaulay 1900–1, vol. 1, pp. cxxxviii–clxvii, Fisher 1964, pp. 303–9, and Nicholson 1984b, p. 140, n. 2. A complete list will be available in *Descriptive Catalogue of the Manuscripts of the Works of John Gower*, edited by Derek Pearsall, Jeremy Griffiths and Kate Harris. For the manuscripts of the *Anticlaudianus*, see Raynaud de Lage 1951, pp. 184–6; Bossuat 1955, pp. 14–20, and Gibson and Palmer 1987.   [33] d'Alverny 1965, pp. 11–25.

much more is known: he was certainly a landowner in Kent; it
is possible that he held some legal office; and it is not unreason-
able to suppose that from about 1377 he was in residence at
St Mary Overeys in Southwark, and that he moved in the literary,
intellectual and bureaucratic circle which included Chaucer
and Ralph Strode. He seems to have received no patronage,
except from the future Henry IV. In 1398 he married, apparently
for the first time; he died in 1408.[34] Both the *Anticlaudianus* and
the *Confessio* are poems written by men past their middle age.
Both are written, or initially conceived, for young kings (Philip
Augustus and Richard II respectively). And both mark the culmination of each poet's literary career: Alan's other major literary
work, the *De planctu Naturae*, was written up to two decades before
the *Anticlaudianus*. Gower's other major works, the *Mirour de
l'omme* (written in Anglo-Norman, finished between 1376 and 1378)
and the *Vox clamantis* (written, in Latin elegiac couplets, substantially before 1386) are earlier than the *Confessio*, which appears to
have been composed from about 1385, being first published in
1390.[35]

That Gower knew the *Anticlaudianus* must be nearly certain: the
poem survives in many thirteenth- and fourteenth-century English
manuscripts;[36] it had a very high reputation in the late Middle

---

[34] Fisher 1964, pp. 37–69.
[35] I accept the arguments of Fisher 1964, pp. 70–134, with regard to the dating of Gower's works.
[36] Of the twenty-nine manuscripts of the *Anticlaudianus* currently in British libraries, eighteen are certainly of English provenance, and three others are either English or
Northern French. Of the eighteen manuscripts of English provenance, three are dated *c.*
1200; four from the beginning of the thirteenth century; two from the middle of the thirteenth century; two from the fourteenth century; and seven from the fifteenth century,
all in the first half of the century. See Gibson and Palmer 1987, p. 945. When we look to
the content of these manuscripts, we can see how some of them preserve 'integumental'
humanist texts in a coherent way. Oxford, Bodleian Library, Canonici Misc. 110, for
example, has the following contents: (1) *accessus* to Boethius, *De consolatione Philosophiae*,
imperfect; (2) commentary on the *Prologus* of *Anticlaudianus*, imperfect; (3) *Anticlaudianus*; (4)
De planctu Naturae; (5) Martianus Capella, *De nuptiis Philologiae et Mercurii* I–II; (6) Bernardus
Silvestris, *Cosmographia*. The manuscript is dated early fifteenth century, and is certainly
English (Gibson and Palmer 1987, item 18). One could also cite London, British Library,
Royal 8 A.XIII, of English provenance and dated to the first quarter of the fifteenth cen-
tury, where the *Anticlaudianus* is found beside *Moralium dogma philosophorum*, and Petrarch,
De secreto conflictu curarum mearum (Gibson and Palmer 1987, item 14), and Oxford, Balliol
College, 276 (*c.* 1442), where the main contents are as follows: (1) Geoffrey of Vinsauf,
Poetria nova; (2) *Anticlaudianus*; (3) *De planctu Naturae*; (4) Terence, *Comoediae*; (5) Matthew of
Vendôme, *Ars Versificatoria*; (6) Gervase of Melkley, *Ars poetica* (Gibson and Palmer 1987,
item 26).

Ages;[37] and Gower's friend, Chaucer, refers to 'Anteclaudian' (in the *House of Fame*) in such a way as to imply that his readers will certainly have read this seminal text.[38] But let it be said immediately that this study is not concerned with Gower's specific knowledge of Alan's text, for which I find no evidence; it is instead an exercise in comparative criticism, concerned to elucidate the ways in which a seminal text like the *Anticlaudianus* provides an extremely revealing frame for understanding a vernacular poet who follows almost exactly two hundred years later.

[37] For the continental reputation of the *Anticlaudianus*, see the introduction to chapter 1. It may be mentioned here that Brunetto Latini's *Li Livres dou Tresor* (definitely known by Gower) cites the *Anticlaudianus* by name (II.69, Carmody 1948, p. 246).

[38] Chaucer's explicit reference to Alan's *Anticlaudianus* is *House of Fame*, line 986; he refers to the *De planctu Naturae* in *Parliament of Fowls*, line 316. These are not by any means throwaway references, since both dream poems enter into dialogue with the poem of Alan to which each refers. See Dronke 1974b, for discussion of Chaucer's debt to twelfth-century cosmological poets. Dronke also makes the suggestive point that the *Parliament of Fowls*, in addition to its obvious and deep debts to the *De planctu*, is also indebted to the overall movement of the *Anticlaudianus*, since the cosmic concerns of Scipio's dream are brought into the political sphere in the birds' parliament (pp. 166–7). Although I do not have space in this book to take up this suggestion, it will be obvious from the arguments of chapters 4 and 7 (concerned with the importance of politics for both Alan and Gower) that I agree with it. Of course Alan's influence on English poetry did not stop in the late fourteenth century. Lydgate draws on the *Anticlaudianus* in his 'Balade in Commendation of Our Lady' (Norton-Smith 1966). Benedict Burgh, who in *c.* 1450 completed Lydgate's *Secrees of Old Philisoffres* after Lydgate's death, reveals a ready familiarity with at least the first six books of 'Anthyclaudyan' in the prologue to his continuation (lines 1492–1589); see Steele 1894, pp. 48–51. Spenser refers us to the *De planctu* in the *Mutability Cantos*, VII.9; Manitius 1931, p. 795 asserts that Milton drew on the *Anticlaudianus* in the invocation to Book III of *Paradise Lost* (lines 1–55). Manitius must have *Anticlaudianus* V.278–305 in mind. This connection seems to me to be at least plausible.

CHAPTER 2

The outer form of the Anticlaudianus

EXTRINSIC INTRODUCTION – THE RECEPTION OF THE
ANTICLAUDIANUS

Alan of Lille's *Anticlaudianus* was certainly one of the most widely
read literary texts of the later Middle Ages. Written between
1181 and 1183,[1] it was almost immediately accorded the status
of what Chaucer would call 'auctorite'. Alan's own pupil, Ralph
of Longchamps, wrote a commentary on the work in 1212–13.
In his prologue, Ralph says that he has written the commentary
for two reasons: in the first place he wishes to render 'the
Anticlaudianus of Alan, the memory of whose love and friendship
makes me weep, easier of access'; in the second, he wishes to exercise his own skill (*ingenium*).[2] Ralph implies a certain challenge in
meeting the work here, a challenge which was to be taken up by
several other commentators in the early thirteenth century. In the
changing intellectual climate of this period, Alan's poem was felt
to represent a still powerful voice from the humanistic, literary-
philosophical culture of the twelfth-century schools: not only did
William of Auxerre, and many other anonymous commentators,
produce both commentaries and summaries of the work,[3] but we
also have a wonderfully vivid and telling evidence for the status of
the poem in Henry d'Andely's *Battle of the Seven Arts* (written before
1236).[4]

---

[1] Hutchings 1924 and d'Alverny 1965, pp. 33–4 argue for 1182–3; Wilks 1977, p. 145, n. 39
   argues for a date not not later than 1181 on historical grounds.
[2] Sulowski 1972, p. 4.
[3] The fullest accounts of commentaries, glosses, *accessus* and summaries of the *Anticlaudianus*
   are Meier 1980, and Jung 1971, pp. 89–113. See also Kaske 1988, pp. 135–6. See
   Ochsenbein 1969 for the *Compendium Anticlaudiani*. I have not been able to consult Cornet
   1945, which also treats this material.   [4] Paetow 1914.

Henry pictures what is really a fight between Grammar, whose base is Orleans, and Dialectic, centred in Paris. The respective *auctores* of each city and each discipline confront each other in battle. Logic defeats the first attack of Grammar, whose assault troops are, by and large, classical poets. After the rout of this initial offensive, a group of 'grammar' texts with more philosophical thrust presents itself, and '*almost* captured Dame Logic' (line 349) before their final defeat. Amongst this group we find Martianus Capella, Bernard Silvestris and (named as a work) the *Anticlaudianus*. Despite his evident sympathy for humane letters against the victorious Dialectic, Henry nevertheless points to what he sees as the essential weakness of Grammar – its reliance on the fables of poetry; the authors defend themselves by wounding

> De caniveçons et de greffes,
> De longues fables et de beffes.
> Lor chastiaus fust bien deffensables
> S'il ne fust si garnis de fables;
> Qu'il enjoignent lor vanitez
> Par lor biaus mos en veritez.   (lines 252–7)

...with penknives and with styluses, with long fables and lies. Their castle would have been well defended, if it had not been so stuffed with fictive nonsense; for they palm off their trivia as truth, by means of fine phrases.

Henry's view of the defeat of humane letters does reflect a reality of the main currents of thirteenth-century academic interest and procedure;[5] it is nevertheless true that the philosophic culture of the twelfth century did survive in the teaching of grammar (which was largely constituted by the 'fables' of poets) and the writing of poetry. In France, Italy and England the great vernacular works of this tradition of philosophic poetry are, of course, *The Romance of the Rose, The Divine Comedy*, many of Chaucer's works, and the *Confessio amantis*; but this tradition of philosophic vision poetry is nourished by the reading of twelfth-century poetic

---

[5] This, the standard view, has recently been challenged by Alastair Minnis (Minnis and Scott 1988, p. 6). While it is true that scholastic thinkers did develop sophisticated literary theories, which then fed into vernacular poetic making, it remains true that their own procedures are dialectical rather than poetic. The discursive superiority they give to dialectical procedure above poetry is often explicit; for some examples, see Simpson 1989.

models, among which the *Anticlaudianus* stands high in later medieval estimation. Apart from the fact that Jean de Meun,[6] Dante[7] and Chaucer[8] all draw on Alan's epic, at much humbler levels we find the work mentioned as a standard grammar-text in schools by, for example, Everard the German in his *Laborinthus*;[9] manuscripts of the poem are given accompanying visual illustration;[10] versions of the poem are found in French and German abbreviations; and even a musical version exists.[11] The manuscript survival alone indicates an extraordinary and enduring popularity: 110 complete manuscripts survive, with almost an even frequency of copying between the thirteenth and fifteenth centuries inclusive.[12]

The very high status accorded the poem by readers and poets up to at least the fifteenth century corresponds with Alan's own claims for his work, made both in the prose and verse Prologues and in the body of the poem itself. In Book V, for example, as Fronesis is about to traverse the empyrean, Alan invokes God's inspiration (V.278–305); whereas the verse prologue had invoked Apollo for poetic inspiration, Alan introduces his invocation to God in Book V by signalling his adoption of the role of prophet above poet:

---

6   The most obvious borrowing from the *Anticlaudianus* is *Roman de la Rose*, lines 5921–6118. The topic of Jean de Meun's relationship to Alan's works is large and (apart from the use of Genius in both the *Roman de la Rose* and the *De planctu Naturae*, for which see Pelen 1987) largely unexplored.

7   The first treatment of this topic was Bossard 1885. Now see also Ciotti 1960; Curtius 1950; Dronke 1966; and Dronke 1986, pp. 8–14.

8   Chaucer's use of the *Anticlaudianus* is most obvious in the *House of Fame* (see above, chapter 1, n. 38). I am unconvinced by the arguments of Donovan 1957 that Chaucer drew on the *Anticlaudianus* in the *Franklin's Tale*. Minnis 1982, pp. 111, 119, 140 makes suggestive parallels between the Knight's astrological descriptions and those found in the *Anticlaudianus*.

9   Faral 1924, pp. 337–77 (p. 360): 'Septenas quid alat artes describit Alanus, / Virtutis species proprietate notat' (lines 661–2). (See Huber 1988 for a comprehensive account of the reception of Alan's works in German literature). Alan is numbered among the *auctores* in Henry of Ghent's *De Illustribus Ecclesiae Scriptoribus* (Cologne 1580), ch. 21, pp. 406–7, and by John of Garland, *Triumphus Ecclesiae* (Wright 1856, p. 74), where Alan is described as *Virgilio maior et Homero certior*. See Gibson and Palmer 1987, pp. 910–11, for the evidence from the manuscripts of the *Anticlaudianus* preserved in Britain, that the poem was used as a school text. Manitius 1931, p. 799 remarks that of the fifty-one medieval library catalogues known to him that mention the writings of Alan, forty-four list the *Anticlaudianus*.

10 Meier 1980 gives a detailed presentation of the ways in which the *Anticlaudianus* was illustrated.

11 See Bayart 1930, for the musical version (written probably 1284), and Creighton 1944 for a thirteenth-century French vernacular adaption. See also Jung 1971, pp. 89–113, for the adaptions of the *Anticlaudianus*.

12 See Raynaud de Lage 1951, p. 35, corrected by Bossuat 1955, pp. 14–15.

Hactenus insonuit tenui mea Musa susurro,
Hactenus in fragili lusit mea pagina uersu,
Phebea resonante cheli; sed parua resignans,
Maiorem nunc tendo liram totumque poetam
Deponens, usurpo michi noua uerba prophete.
Celesti Muse terrenus cedet Apollo,
Musa Ioui, uerbisque poli parencia cedent
Verba soli, tellusque locum concedet Olimpo.
Carminis huius ero calamus, non scriba uel a(u)ctor...   (v.265–73)

Thus far my Muse has sung in a gentle whisper; thus far my page has sported in fragile verse to the accompaniment of Phoebus's lyre of tortoise-shell. But abandoning things petty, I now pluck a mightier chord and laying aside entirely the role of poet, I appropriate a new speaking part, that of the prophet. The earthly Apollo yields to the heavenly Muse; the Muse gives place to Jupiter; the language of earth yields to and waits on the language of heaven, and Earth gives place to Olympus. I will be the pen of this poem, not the scribe or author. (p. 146, modified)

Alan is making extraordinary claims for his poem here: not only is he claiming originality for it (as he had in the verse Prologue), but he is also affirming that the poem now surpasses poetry in becoming inspired prophecy. In the epilogue to the poem Alan instructs the work not to attempt to rival ancient poets, but to tread humbly in their footsteps ('... nec antiquos temptes equare poetas, / Sed pocius ueterum uestigia semper adorans / Subsequere' (IX.412–14)). This, the more characteristic posture of medieval poets,[13] is however entirely uncharacteristic of Alan's self-presentation as poet and prophet throughout the work. Here he claims originality, inspiration, and an allegory open only to the highest perception.

The variety and depth of late medieval reception of the *Anticlaudianus* suggests that readers and poets until at least the fifteenth century took Alan's claim to *auctoritas* in earnest. In stark contrast to the enthusiasm of reception in those centuries, however, twentieth-century scholarship has almost consistently expressed disappointment with the work. C. S. Lewis's remark stands at one extreme: 'The *Anticlaudianus* ... is a work in every respect inferior to the *De Mundi Universitate*, and may be described as nearly

---

[13] The topos is derived, perhaps, from Statius, *Thebeiad* XII.816–19. See also Boccaccio, *Filocolo* V.97.5–8, and Chaucer, *Troilus and Criseyde* V.1791–2. Chaucer's line 'And kis the steppes where as thow seest pace' (V.1791), is much closer to Alan than to Boccaccio.

worthless except from the historical point of view.'[14] He goes on to describe how the reader's response moves from 'amused contempt' to 'something not far removed from a rankling personal hatred of the author'.[15] However refreshing in its candour, this is, as I say, an extreme and exceptional judgement. But even those who have been interested in Alan this century have tended either to focus on the *De planctu Naturae*, and/or to express a certain melancholy disappointment with the apparent incoherences of the *Anticlaudianus*. This is true, for example, of both Huizinga and Ochsenbein, who have both paid thoughtful, sustained and sensitive attention to the poem.[16] It is also true of a series of critics who admire the *De planctu*, but who treat Alan's mature work cursorily. Such critics will sometimes point to the essential problems of interpretation in the *Anticlaudianus*, without pausing to confront them.[17] I shall take Winthrop Wetherbee's remarks as an example of this sidelining of the *Anticlaudianus*, and as a convenient point of entry for my own argument.

INTRINSIC INTRODUCTION – *FORMA*

In his account of twelfth-century 'cosmologists', Wetherbee articulates an essential problem in the interpretation of the *Anticlaudianus*. He says that the major theme of the poem is 'the working out of the relation of the Arts to theology that culminates in Prudentia's vision of God'; given this, he argues that there is 'something gratuitous and anticlimactic about the ensuing *psychomachia* and the new earthly order to which it leads', especially when the 'virtues associated with the New Man are largely secular.' The conclusion to which these observations lead is ineluctable: 'Whatever its significance, the idealism of the "triumph of Nature", as Alan calls it, is difficult to reconcile

---

[14]   Lewis 1936, pp. 98–9.   [15]   Ibid., p. 100.
[16]   Huizinga 1932, pp. 51–4; Ochsenbein 1975, p. 192.
[17]   Thus Jung 1971, pp. 77–8; Wetherbee 1972, pp. 211–19; Lynch 1988, pp. 107–8. See also Lewis 1936, in a slightly more kindly temper with the *Anticlaudianus*: 'I do not say that he has effected a real reconciliation between the two ideals of the Middle Ages. The rift went deeper than he thought. He assumes, rather than makes, a peace' (p. 105). See Häring 1978, p. 802 for the evidence that the *Anticlaudianus* had much greater immediate success than the *De planctu Naturae*.

with the radical subordination of earthly knowledge in the central books of the poem.'[18]

A brief and necessarily bald summary of the action of Alan's poem will confirm the apparent justice of Wetherbee's remarks.

Book I Nature attempts to fashion a perfect soul. Failing, she convokes a council of her powers, who are described in the order Concordia, Copia, Favor, Iuventus, Risus, Pudor, Modestia, Racio, Honestas, Decus, Fronesis (sometimes called Prudentia), Pietas, Fides, Largitas and, finally, Nobilitas. Nature laments to her council that all her works are imperfect, and proposes to make a perfect man by way of recompensing past failures. Fronesis applauds the proposal, but is troubled by her knowledge that it does not lie within Nature's power to bring this work to its proper conclusion, since natural powers are unable to create a soul. She invokes the aid of Reason.

Book II Reason also favours the plan, and takes account of Fronesis's objection by proposing that God make the soul, looking favourably as he does on the prayers of Nature. An ambassador will need to be sent to God to propose the plan, and Reason nominates Fronesis. Fronesis wavers before the magnitude of such a mission, but finally accepts, persuaded by Concord. A chariot will need to be built by the Liberal Arts to transport Fronesis: Grammar begins this work by constructing the pole by which the chariot is to be drawn.

Book III The remaining arts of the Trivium (Rhetoric and Dialectic) make their contribution to the chariot. Then follow the first three arts of the Quadrivium, Mathematics, Music and Geometry, each of whom constructs a wheel.

Book IV Astronomy constructs her wheel, before the horses of the chariot, the five senses, are described. Reason, the charioteer, and Fronesis mount and take off, flying first into the sublunary atmosphere, before entering the planetary realms, where they traverse the sphere of each planet.

[18] Wetherbee 1988, p. 52. See also Wetherbee 1972, p. 217: 'But once the transformation (of human perception in heaven) has taken place these later events are wholly redundant. The real resolution of Alain's theme, in the *De planctu* and in the *Anticlaudianus*, takes place in heaven... The recovery of "erectness", of the dignity of the *imago dei*, and the psychological integration to which it testifies are the necessary climax of the allegory, and the "Illiad" of the final books is a concession to artistic pretentions which almost betray Alain's sure religious instinct.'

Book V They enter, and traverse, the starred heaven, before the horses baulk at entering the region of the empyrean. Here a *puella poli* appears, bearing crown and sceptre, whose garment is woven with the secrets of God. Fronesis relates her mission, and prays for her aid in proceeding further. The *puella poli* gladly offers her assistance, but directs that Fronesis must quit Reason and the chariot of the Arts and its horses, with the single exception of the 'horse' of hearing.

Book VI In the realm of the empyrean, Fronesis, dazzled and dazed by the extreme luminosity, falls into a lethargy. The *puella poli* calls on the aid of her sister (theological) Faith to restore Fronesis, which she does. Fronesis proceeds to the citadel of God, and makes her petition for a perfect soul, which is readily granted by God, who orders Noys to produce the model of a perfect soul. Fronesis bears the newly created soul back to Nature.

Book VII Fronesis is welcomed back; Nature sets to work on fashioning a body, and Concord oversees the joining of body and soul in the formation of the New Man. He is endowed with natural gifts by exactly the same series of virtues who answered Nature's summons in Book I. The last of these, Nobility, must ask the permission of Fortune to bestow nobility.

Book VIII Fortune grants nobility to the New Man; Rumour reports the creation of the perfect man throughout the world. Allecto hears of it and assembles the lords of Tartarus. She harangues the company of vices and incites them to war. The hero likewise prepares for battle.

Book IX The battle is described, in which the perfect man successively routs each vice. A golden age is established on earth.

When we consider the poem's action, even in this very bald summary, we can see the force of Wetherbee's objection: how do we correlate the championing of specifically theological perception above and beyond reason in Books I–VI with the subsequent presentation of the *natural* perfection of the New Man in Books VII–IX? This structural question leads immediately to philosophical questions implicit in the structure. What pattern of human perfection is being promoted by such a structure? A model by which humans are perfected through relation to a supra-rational God? Or is human perfection achieved through purely natural, human capacities? Is Alan championing the philosopher-cum-theologian, or the perfect courtier? There are other perplexing problems, too: who is the hero-figure of this epic poem – Nature, the *novus homo* or Fronesis;[19] who is signified by the *novus homo*?[20] I intend to answer all these questions in chapter 4. My investigation in this and the next chapter will be restricted to the structural question raised by Wetherbee. Questions as to the real hero of the poem, or as to the New Man's identity, are better focused by first answering this more profound question concerning the poem's structure, or form.

If Wetherbee's account of the broken structure of the poem is correct, then the work falls sadly short of Alan's own claims for it, which are very elevated indeed. In the prose Prologue, after warning the unlearned from attempting to understand his poem, Alan goes on to define the three levels of its appeal:

For in this work the sweetness of the literal sense will soothe the ears of boys, the moral instruction will inspire the mind on the road to perfection, the sharper subtlety of the allegory will whet the advanced intellect. (pp. 40–1)

In hoc etenim opere litteralis sensus suauitas puerilem demulcebit auditum, moralis instructio perficientem imbuet sensum, acutior allegorie subtilitas proficientem acuet intellectum. (Prose Prologue, p. 56)

He goes on to welcome those few who are capable of engaging with the real meaning of the work in this way:

Let those, however, who do not allow their reflexions to dwell on disgraceful imaginings, but have the courage to raise them to a view of forms above the heavens, enter the strait paths of my work. (p. 42)

sed hii qui sue rationis materiale in turpibus imaginibus non permittunt quiescere, sed ad intuitum supercelestium formarum audent attollere, mei operis ingrediantur angustias. (Prose Prologue, p. 56)

Wetherbee locates the 'theme' of the poem in the action represented by the poem (and only the action of the first six books) – the theme of 'the working out of the relation of the Arts to theology'. Alan himself, however, claims that the poem's meaning (and presumably the meaning of the *whole* poem) is to be discovered not so

[19] For the range of critical opinion on the matter of the real hero of the poem, Fronesis or the *novus homo*, see chapter 3, n. 10, and chapter 4, n. 34.
[20] For the range of critical opinion as to who is signified by the New Man, see discussion in Wilks 1977, and chapter 4, nn. 30–4.

much in its represented action, but through a 'a more acute subtlety of allegory', and he implies that the poem itself has 'a supercelestial form'. The meaning of the poem, that is, should not be understood referentially, in what the action depicts, but rather through the form of the work itself.

Some near contemporary readers of Alan's poem would disagree with me. Rather than defining the inner form, and rather than being interested in any formal qualities of the poem at all, they were instead concerned with the poem's 'information' in the modern sense of the word – i.e. with the poem's philosophical content. Thus Ralph of Longchamps, for example (the poem's first commentator), says in his prologue that the poem does not pertain to any particular branch of knowledge, but 'wanders through all parts of philosophy'.[21] And the actual practice of Ralph's commentary follows the lines established by his prologue, insofar as he touches on various disciplines, taking no account of the poetic form of the work,[22] and instead treats it as the occasion for a series of mini-excursuses on points of meteorology, psychology, astronomy and so on. His commentary stops, revealingly, at Book IV, where the cognitive course of the poem has been partly achieved, but fully prepared, with the completion of the chariot. Implicit in this partial commentary might be agreement with the view expressed by Wetherbee cited earlier: the really interesting part of this poem outlines a philosophical scheme (the relation of the Arts to theology); when that ends, the poem is effectively over. Implicit in Ralph's commentary is the idea that the poem's meaning is to be located at the level of its represented (noetic) action (its explicit educational 'information'), rather than in its poetic form as a whole.[23]

But, as we saw in chapter 1, the word *forma* has a variety of meanings beyond its pedagogic sense of *informatio*. For Alan it can denote both the outer form of an object ('the property of a thing which is perceived according to the contour of its

---

[21] Sulowski 1972, p. 20.

[22] Despite his discussion of the term '*theophania*' (Sulowski 1972, pp. 22–4), Ralph does not use this concept in his discussion of the poem.

[23] Ralph's treatment of the poem as a mini-encyclopaedia is repeated in some modern discussions of the *Anticlaudianus*. This is true of John M. Trout, *The Voyage of Prudentia: The World View of Alan of Lille* (Washington, 1979). Similar characterizations of the poem can be found in Raynaud de Lage 1951, p. 52, and Bossuat 1955, p. 14. See Ochsenbein 1975, pp. 75–7 for convincing arguments that the poem is not intended as an encyclopaedia.

outlines'),[24] and the inner form according to which it takes its outer shape – the inner form which he defines as the 'preconception which existed in the divine mind from eternity concerning the creation of things'.[25] It is these artistic and creative senses which might open the way for understanding the form, even the 'supercelestial form' of the poem as we are invited to by Alan. By understanding the way in which the poem itself is formed, we will be better placed to understand the educational 'information' it brings to its readers. Here and elsewhere in this book, I will proceed on the assumption that this formal, poetic enquiry is logically prior to any investigation of the poem's philosophical meaning.

Alan's definitions of the word 'form' offer us a schema by which to approach the poem itself. I will look first, in what remains of this chapter, at the outer form of the poem – its form in the sense of outer 'shape'. I will begin with the outer form of the noetic, or cognitive part of the poem (Books I–VI), and then move to the outer form of the ethical section of the poem (Books VII–IX).[26] In both cases, I will be concerned to show how each of these two parts of the poem gains its internal coherence by following through the structure of the sciences in the 'Aristotelian' division of philosophy. In themselves, Books I–VI and VII–IX are internally coherent and reflect intellectual developments of which Alan is near the forefront – a Neo-Platonic theology in Books I–VI, and a Stoic derived ethics and politics in the last three books. In the next chapter we will see how radically *incoherent* these two parts of the poem are when put together.

---

[24] *Liber in distinctionibus dictionum theologicalium*, PL 210, cols. 685–1012 (col. 796).

[25] Ibid.

[26] This division of the poem, into a noetic and an ethical part, was first explicated by Brinkmann 1964, p. 425. Ochsenbein 1975 refutes it (pp. 70–2), arguing firstly that Alan nowhere indicates such a division explicitly, and secondly that the division is not so clear in any case: Fronesis's journey presupposes ethical achievement, just as the ethical section of the poem involves theoretical arts (the gifts of Fronesis). Ochsenbein's resistance to this division is difficult to understand, since the commentary of his own book is divided up into a section dealing with the theoretical progress of Fronesis (pp. 78–114), and a section dealing with the virtues and vices (pp. 137–85). Of course he deals with other subjects, but these two discussions do cover the narrative of the poem, basically in the disposition suggested by Brinkmann. This chapter will argue that Alan is certainly drawing on a theoretical/practical division of sciences to shape the narrative of his poem. Ochsenbein's only strong point, that the theoretical part of the poem contains practical elements, and *vice versa*, will be answered in the following chapter.

OUTER FORM, BOOKS I–VI

The plot of the *Anticlaudianus* is, clearly enough, based on pedagogic structures; this is most obviously true of Books III–VI, where
the Arts first construct their chariot, which then traverses the heavens and leads Fronesis to a vision of God. But it is also true of the
last three books of the poem, where the New Man is, effectively,
instructed in moral and political wisdom. But what kind of pedagogic programme is Alan drawing on? Twelfth-century scholars
inherited three inter-related ways of organizing the field of knowledge (broadly called 'Philosophy'), from both classical and Patristic
sources. The main schemes are as follows:

(i) the Liberal Arts, leading to Sapientia. This scheme is originally
found in Varro (d. 27 BC), whose division of knowledge into nine
parts is reduced to seven by Martianus Capella (first half of 5th
century).[27] Transmitted in Christian pedagogy by many Patristic
and Carolingian figures,[28] it is found in a wide range of twelfth-
century texts, such as Adelard of Bath's *De eodem et diverso* (before
1116), Thierry of Chartres's *Heptateuchon* (1140s), and Honorius of
Autun's (*c.* 1080 – *c.* 1140) *De animae exilio*.[29]
(ii) The so-called 'Platonic' division, which divides Philosophy into
three parts, physics, ethics and logic. This system is a more
sophisticated version of the Liberal Arts, since physics is divided
into the Quadrivium, and logic into the Trivium (a division
authorized by the Greek senses of the word '*logos*', which
includes both 'word' (thus grammar and rhetoric) and 'idea'
(thus dialectic)). The real difference between this scheme and
that of the Liberal Arts is the inclusion of ethics, which does not
find a formal place in the scheme of the Arts.[30] This arrangement is first (probably erroneously) attributed to Plato by Cicero
(106–44 BC);[31] it passed into the Christian tradition on

---

[27] For the history of this division, see d'Alverny 1946 and Simone 1949.
[28] For a conspectus, see de Ghellinck 1948, Appendix 2, pp. 93–6.
[29] For Adelard's *De eodem et diverso*, see Willner 1903; for the prologue of Thierry of
Chartres's *Heptateuchon* (a work left incomplete by Thierry), see Jeauneau 1954; Honorius
of Autun, *De animae exilio et patria*, in PL 172, cols. 1242–6 (Honorius adds physics,
mechanics and economics to his scheme).
[30] For the 'Platonic' division, see Baur 1903, pp. 194–7; d'Alverny 1946, who points out that
the tripartite division was the most widely diffused until the twelfth-century (p. 250);
Gregory 1955, p. 272; and Weisheipl 1965. For the place of ethics in twelfth-century pedagogy, see Delhaye 1958.   [31] Cicero, *Academica*, I.5.19.

Augustine's (354–430) authority,[32] and is found in a wide range of late classical and early medieval writers; in the twelfth century it is used by John of Salisbury (*c.* 1115 – 1180).[33]

(iii) The so-called 'Aristotelian' division, according to which the field of philosophy is divided into two fundamental divisions, the theoretical and the practical. The theoretical sciences are physics, mathematics and theology, while the practical sciences are ethics (governance of self) economics (governance of a household) and politics (governance of a city or realm). The Liberal Arts are incorporated in this scheme by including the Quadrivial arts under mathematics, and by adding to the basic division a third category of the logical sciences (which are constituted by the Trivium). This classification passed into the twelfth century especially through Boethius (*c.* 480 – 524), but it is also brought to the West through Arab sources transmitted by Dominicus Gundissalinus's (d. after 1181) *De divisione philosophiae*.[34]

This scheme is by far the most important *divisio philosophiae* for the twelfth century: it is found in fictional narratives (e.g. the *Ordo artium*, or Godfrey of St Victor's *Fons Philosophiae* (1178));[35] as the basis of formal pedagogic programmes (e.g. Hugh of St Victor's *Didascalicon* (late 1120s));[36] and in the opening of commentaries, by way of placing the text commented on precisely within the constellation of the sciences. This is where and how it is found in, for example, the many twelfth-century commentaries on Boethius's *De trinitate*.[37]

The 'Aristotelian' division of philosophy is also behind the basic narrative divisions of the *Anticlaudianus*. In this section I focus on the theoretical sciences (which determine the progress of the narra-

---

[32] Augustine, *De civitate Dei*, VIII.4.

[33] Webb 1909, VII.5.645c, vol. 2, pp. 107–8, and Webb 1929, II.13.870b–871c, pp. 84–6, and II.15.872c, p. 88.

[34] For the Aristotelian division of the sciences, see Mariétan 1901; Baur 1903, pp. 196–202; Taylor 1961, pp. 161–2; and Weisheipl 1965.

[35] The *Ordo artium* is edited by Gompf 1966, who dates the manuscript to *c.* 1200; this text uses the 'Aristotelian' division of Sapientia, but adds three further divisions of knowledge: *eloquentia*, *poesis* and *mechanica*. This same scheme is found in the following: *Ysagoge in theologiam* (*c.* 1135–9) (Landgraf 1934); the commentaries attributed to Bernard Silvestris on the *Aeneid* (Jones and Jones 1977, p. 32) and the *De Nuptiis*, with the exception of *mechanica* (Westra 1986, VI. 1–90, pp. 130–2); Ralph of Longchamps's commentary on the *Anticlaudianus* (Sulowski 1972, chs. 28 and 29, pp. 39–41). For Geoffrey of St Victor's *Fons Philosophiae*, see Michaud-Quantin 1956.

[36] For the division of science in the *Didascalicon*, see Buttimer 1939, III.1, p. 48. Hugh adds the logical and mechanical arts to the basic division of philosophy.

[37] See n. 42 below.

tive up to Book VI); in the next I consider the way in which the
practical sciences inform Books VII–IX.

An account of the poem's plot in Books I–VI makes it clear how
the 'action' of the poem conforms with an educational programme.
Certainly the surface of the poem (its *sensus litteralis*, designed to
'soothe puerile ears') is couched in the narrative terms of a heroic
poem, with councils being taken, embassies being delivered, and so
on; but the personifications themselves leave us in no doubt that it
is an educational programme that is being described up to Book VI.
When we look across to Alan's other writings of speculative theology, we can see how the poem is keyed into pedagogic structures,
with regard to both the subjects studied and the psychological and
linguistic implications of such a cursus of study. We can also see
how the movement of Fronesis in this part of the poem is determined by a hierarchy within the theoretical sciences, with theology
at the top. In this hierarchization, as in the actual content of the
programme, Alan is at the forefront of a twelfth-century academic,
humanist pedagogy. The actual means of arriving at theology for
Alan are grounded in the physical sciences, and involve understanding the structure of the cosmos. And the content of theology
for Alan is not an understanding of the Bible, or of revelation history. On the contrary, Alan's is an intensely philosophical, Neo-
Platonic version of theology, according to which the highest science
requires the intellectual perception (open only to a very few) of
pure being. Alan was at the forefront of this concept of theology in
his other writings; he is, indeed, at the forefront of theology being
formed as an academic discipline itself – contrary to popular (even
to popular scholarly) opinion, theology as an academic discipline is
a new subject in the late twelfth century.[38]

The philosophical obstacle Nature faces, that she cannot understand the making of the soul, generates the noetic plot of the poem,
since it is the figure Fronesis who (aided by Reason) *can* understand
the nature of the soul's making by God, and is therefore entrusted
with the embassy to God. So the procreative action with which the
poem begins is arrested by a philosophical action, which begins
with Fronesis's objections, and which does not end until God com-

---

[38] For the development of theology as an academic discipline in the twelfth century, see
Evans 1980; and for Alan's place at the forefront of an intensely rational theology, see
Chenu 1935; Vasoli 1961; d'Alverny 1964; and Evans 1983.

mands Noys to fashion a soul in Book VI.[39] The conceptual ensemble with which the poem begins becomes delimited, then, to specifically noetic principles Ratio and Fronesis. We can see the range of their understanding in the description of Reason's mirrors at the end of Book I. Before Reason speaks, the poet describes the three mirrors she carries, each metallic, each superior to the one which precedes it. The mirrors represent the fundamental elements of creative and procreative activity: form (the informing essence of a given life) and matter, or the 'subject' of the form. Each mirror presents these elements in different relations. In the first (lines 454–5), to which Reason is said to give especial attention, she sees the union of form and matter. In the second, she sees the artificial separation of forms from the matter in which they normally exist; she sees subjects reverting to primordial chaos, and form rejoicing to rest in its own being ('Quomodo forma suo gaudens requiescit in esse', line 472). In the third, golden mirror, she sees the highest sources of life, the pure, archetypal forms themselves:

> Hic rerum fontem, mundi genus, orbis ydeam,
> Exemplar, speciem, causam, primordia, finem
> Conspicit et certis metitur singula metis.   (1.488–90)

Here she sees the fount of things, the genus of the universe, the idea, the exemplar, species, cause, first beginning and ultimate end of the world, and she measures each and every thing by definite boundaries. (p. 64)

The range of reflection indicated by these mirrors indicates that Ratio and Fronesis have within their conspectus the entire range of creative and procreative activity. This range of reflection is divided up along the lines of the theoretical sciences as they are described in the 'Aristotelian' division of the sciences, outlined above. The theoretical sciences in this scheme are, as I have said: physics, which considers form as it is joined to matter; mathematics, which considers formal categories as artificially abstracted from matter; and, at the highest level of abstraction, theology, which considers the creative models of life in their pure essence.[40] The most likely source of this division of science is Book II of

---

39 See Green 1967, p. 10 for an argument that Nature is shown to be presumptuous in attempting to form a perfect man by herself. I disagree – Nature's attempt implies the natural desire for divine understanding of the soul's origins, as will be argued below, chapter 4.   40 See n. 34 above.

Boethius's *De trinitate*, which would have been available to Alan in the many twelfth-century commentaries on this work. Theology, for Boethius, is not that extremely wide-ranging subject it was to become in the thirteenth century, covering metaphysics, anthropology and ethics. On the contrary, theology is limited in Boethius's usage to the investigation of pure being.

The perception of pure being makes particular psychological demands on a student, which Boethius discusses in Book II of the *De trinitate*. It is the intellect which must be brought into play in theology, since only through the intellect can we perceive pure form. In this study, he says, we are bound to use

intellectual concepts; and in Theology we should not be diverted to play with imaginations, but rather apprehend that form which is pure form and no image, which is very being and the source of Being.

in divinis intellectualiter versari oportebit neque diduci ad imaginationes, sed potius ipsam inspicere formam quae vere forma neque imago est et quae esse ipsum est et ex qua esse est.[41]

This is the very narrowly focused, intensely 'philosophical' concept of theology which was inherited and diffused by the *De trinitate* commentaries in the twelfth century, of Chartrian origin. Commentaries by Gilbert of Poitiers (1085/90–1154) and Thierry of Chartres (d. after 1156) survive; Alan is most likely to have been influenced by those of Gilbert.[42]

It is, then, the range of understanding comprehended by the sciences of physics, mathematics and theology which equips the psychological principles Ratio and Fronesis to travel to God, to ask for the creation of a new soul. Having delimited these psychological principles, and their instruments (the chariot constructed by the Arts and drawn by the senses), Alan follows through the logic of their combination from Book II to the moment when God orders the soul to be fashioned in Book VI.

---

[41] Stewart, Rand and Tester 1973, Bk II. p. 8, for text and translation. See Marenbon 1988a, pp. 338–40 for a discussion of how Gilbert of Poitiers receives these terms, particularly that of mathematics.

[42] For the commentaries by Gilbert of Poitiers, see Häring 1966. For those of Thierry of Chartres, see Häring 1971. See also the commentary by Clarembald of Arras, in Häring 1965, pp. 61–221. The first scholar to posit the pervasive influence of Gilbert on Alan's theological thought was Baumgartner 1896, *passim*. See also Marenbon 1988b, pp. 354–5 and notes. D'Alverny 1968, pp. 122–3, argues plausibly that Alan was at some stage a pupil of Thierry of Chartres.

The essential articulation of this noetic journey is that moment where Fronesis takes leave of Reason and the chariot constructed by the Liberal Arts (having successfully negotiated the journey through the atmosphere and the spheres up to the edge of the starred heaven). Whereas the Arts can provide philosophical knowledge of the cosmos, only Fronesis is capable of theological perception. This conceptual distinction is made in the action of the poem at the moment in Book V when Fronesis and Reason, along with the chariot, falter at the extremity of the starred heaven, as rational, philosophical knowledge is unable to gain any purchase. At this point, a maiden appears to Fronesis, who represents the highest stage of the Aristotelian division of the theoretical sciences, theology.[43]

This noetic passage in the poem is consistent with everything Alan says elsewhere about the movement from philosophical to theological knowledge. The moment of this passage is evidently one which greatly exercised Alan's energy and imagination, since it has institutional, psychological and linguistic implications, all of which are brought out both in the poem and in Alan's other writings. We can see his interest in it in purely practical, institutional terms in his *Sermo de clericis ad theologiam non accedentibus*. There he manipulates the topos of the *senex elementarius* to incite those who offer their best efforts to the Arts. The Arts are not to be damned, but employed as a way of leading to theology, and then left behind; just as in the poem the *puella poli* bears the *sceptrum regale*, marking her disciplinary pre-eminence over the Arts, so too is theology described by Alan in the sermon as 'heavenly queen':

the Liberal Arts are to be bidden farewell at the threshold; that is, after they have led us to the threshold of theology, to the entrance of the celestial queen, they are to be left behind in peace, not that we should stay our progress there, but rather that we should make a bridge.

---

43 The *puella poli* has been interpreted as theology by most modern commentators, including Huizinga 1932, pp. 34–5 (see especially d'Alverny 1964). Dronke 1986, pp. 12–13 is the only exception to this consensus, when he says that 'modern scholars ... have mostly asserted (without argument) that this *puella* stands for Theology.' I hope that the following arguments will prove conclusively that in every respect the characteristics of the *puella poli* coincide with those of theology as Alan conceived it. At the same time it should be recognized that for Alan a move to theological understanding is not simply a matter of moving through the curriculum: it involves profound psychic and linguistic resources.

salutande liberales artes a limine, id est, postquam nos perduxerint ad limen theologie, ad ianuam celestis regine, relinquende sunt in pace; non ut ibi figamus pedem, sed ut faciamus pontem.[44]

The movement to theological understanding is not, however, open to all; both in the poem and consistently in his theological works, Alan underlines the difficulty of the theological enterprise, and its accessibility only to a gifted few. In the poem the solitariness of this kind of understanding is suggested at the moment Fronesis falters at the edge of the starred heaven:

> Difficilis conscensus ad hanc facilisque recessus,
> Accessus paucis, casus patet omnibus, in quam
> Vix aliquis transire ualet, ualet omnis ab illa
> Declinare uia, que paucis peruia multis
> Clauditur, arta nimis uirtuti, larga ruine.   (v.57–61)

The ascent to this [light] is difficult, to slip back is easy; the approach is open to few, mishap awaits all; scarce anyone can cross to it, everyone can deviate from that path which offers passage to few but is closed to many, is very narrow even for the virtuous and wide open for ruin. (p. 139, slightly modified)

A passage of this kind not only echoes the statements in Alan's prose Prologue about the difficulty of his work and his warnings against those unprepared to understand it; it can also be placed in the larger context of Alan's works of speculative theology, where the same warnings, couched in the same terms, are made to the inexpert. Thus in the Prologue to the *Quoniam homines* (probably written in the same period as the *Anticlaudianus*),[45] Alan discusses the passage from *naturalibus ad theologica*; he first warns against improper understanding of the Liberal Arts, where the ignorant,

not taking prior consultation from the Arts, not guided by their true charioteering, while climbing to ineffable realms, descend unutterably ruined into various errors.

liberalium artium non preconsulentes scientiam, non earum recta aurigatione deducti, dum ad ineffabilia conscendunt, in varios errores ineffabiliter ruinosi descendunt.[46]

This change of academic discipline also has psychological concomi-

---

44   d'Alverny 1965, pp. 274–8 (p. 275).   45   Ibid., p. 37.
46   Glorieux 1953, Prologue, p. 119.

tants, present as much in the poem as explicated in Alan's theological works. In the *Regule celestis iuris* (also probably of the *Anticlaudianus* period),[47] Alan defines two kinds of theology, the rational and the intellectual; the rational considers *terrena*, through natural philosophy, and does not push man to pass beyond his own capacities. Ecstatic theology, on the other hand, causes man to pass beyond his own natural capacities; this transgression can be either good or bad, upwards towards intellectual contemplation, or downwards to vice, 'et talis excessus dicitur extasis, sive metamorphosis, quia per huiusmodi excessum excedit statum proprie mentis uel formam'. He goes on to elaborate the psychological aspect of this *extasis*:

This positive ecstatic state is called 'apotheosis', or 'deification', which occurs when man is taken up into the contemplation of divine things. And this comes about through the mediation of that power of the soul which is called 'intellectuality', through which we understand divine things.

Excessus autem superior dicitur apotheosis, quasi deificatio, quod fit quando homo ad diuinorum contemplationem rapitur. Et hoc fit mediante illa potentia anime, que dicitur intellectualitas qua conprehendimus diuina.[48]

This scheme of the *Regule*, whereby man can be deified through intellectual contemplation of the divine, is given a further nuance in the *Quoniam homines*. There the highest stage of perception is divided into two stages: on the one hand, through the intellect, angels and souls are contemplated; on the other, through the intelligence, man 'intuits' the Trinity:

But there are two kinds of positive ecstatic state: one is called 'intellect', through which man beholds spiritual things (as angels and souls), and through which man becomes a spirit, moving beyond himself. The other is called 'intelligence', through which man intuits the Trinity. By this a man becomes God, since through this speculation man is somehow deified.

Sed superioris due sunt species: una que dicitur intellectus, qua homo considerat spiritualia, id est angelos et animas; secundum quam homo fit spiritus, et ita supra se fit. Alia est que intelligentia dicitur, qua homo trinitatem intuetur; secundum quam homo fit homo deus, quia per hanc speculationem quodammodo deificatur.[49]

---

[47] D'Alverny 1965, p. 37.   [48] Häring 1981, Rule 99, p. 204.
[49] Glorieux 1953, Bk I.2, p. 121. See n. 38 above for accounts of Alan's concept of theology.

This is the structure of knowledge represented in the poem: the reason leads up to the limit of natural philosophy, and is supported by knowledge supplied by the senses, whereas Fronesis (representing the intellect) is capable of being led beyond the senses (except hearing) to contemplation of pure forms unrelated to matter. The entry into the realm of the *intellectus* is marked by the meeting with the *puella poli* in Book V; the moment in Book VI at which Fronesis faints and is revived by Fides marks the entry into the realm of the 'intelligence'. This is the moment for which Alan reserves the word *extasis*:

> Sic sopor inuasit uigilem, sic somnus adulter
> Oppressit Fronesis animum, sompnoque soporans
> Extasis ipsa suo, mentem dormire coegit.   (VI.6–8)[50]

Thus drowsiness overcame the alert mind of Fronesis and false sleep weighed it down: the trance bathing the mind in drowsiness forced it along the path to sleep. (p. 156)

Finally, and most importantly, perhaps, the change from human philosophy to theology as it is conceived by Alan involves linguistic changes. The essential feature of the decoration on the dress of the *puella poli* marks the way in which linguistic practice must be radically changed in theological discourse. 'What the tongue cannot tell, the picture declares' (V.118),

> Quomodo Nature subiectus sermo stupescit,
> Dum temptat diuina loqui, uiresque loquendi
> Perdit et ad ueterem cupit ille recurrere sensum,
> Mutescuntque soni, uix barbutire ualentes,
> Deque suo sensu deponunt uerba querelam...   (V.119–23)

How language, subject as it is to Nature, is dumbfounded when it tries to express things divine, loses its power of communicating and tries to take refuge in its old meaning. Sounds die into silence, scarce able to lisp, and words stop quarrelling about their connotation. (p. 141, modified)

This description of the changes to the values of words is near the heart of Alan's Boethian concept of theology. The linguistic distinctiveness of theological language derives, unsurprisingly, from the ontological distinctiveness of God. Earlier I referred to Boethius's division of speculative sciences, in which he defines theology as

---

[50] See Dronke 1966, for the motif of *letargo* as used in poetic traditions.

that science which treats 'ipsam ... formam quae vere forma neque imago est et quae esse ipsum est et ex qua esse est'.[51] This reference to the idea of pure form gives rise in Boethius's discussion to an account of the way in which the word 'form' should be used. Everything owes its being to a form. A statue, for example, is a statue not because of the brass of which it is made, but because of the form given to that matter. So nothing is said to exist because it possesses matter, but according to its distinctive form (*sed secundum propriam formam*). In this respect God is ontologically exceptional, since, Boethius says, 'divina substantia sine materia forma est atque ideo unum et est id quod est'.[52]

So whereas the essence of all other things is predicated by pre-existing forms, the essence of God is predicated by nothing but its own being. For Alan, as for other twelfth-century writers dependent on Boethius's concept of theology, this ontological distinctiveness has linguistic implications. When something is named, the naming designates that which is named, but presupposes something (a form) from which the thing can be named. Because God is not informed by any pre-existing form, then neither can he be properly named. God can only be named metaphorically. Alan makes this point, fundamental to his theology (and to his poetry), in the *Quoniam homines*:

> for where names arise in matters concerning the realm of Nature, there is the thing named on the one hand, and that from which it is named on the other; for example, there is a white thing on the one hand, so named from whiteness, and the whiteness on the other, from which the naming is made. Naming has no purchase on God, however, since God is 'God-ness' itself... Metaphor, but not literal naming, has purchase in naming the divine.

> in naturalibus enim ubi denominationes fiunt, aliut est quod denominatur, aliut a quo denominatur; verbi causa aliud est album quod denominatur ab albedine, aliut albedo a qua fit denominatio. In Deo vero non habet locum denominatio quia Deus est ipsa deitas... Transnominatio locum habet in divinis, sed non denominatio.[53]

It is precisely this linguistic change which occupies Alan so much

---

[51] Stewart, Rand and Tester 1973, Bk II, p. 8.   [52] Ibid., p. 10.

[53] Glorieux 1953, Bk I, pt I, 9b, p. 143. Behind this view is a 'grammatical Platonism', according to which the names of things are dependent on the ontological reality of the things to which they refer. For a conspectus of examples, see Jolivet 1966; for the most explicit proponent of this in the twelfth century, Thierry of Chartres, see Dronke 1988, pp. 372–3. For Alan's views of theological language, see Vasoli 1961, pp. 178–84; Chatillon 1980; and Evans 1983, pp. 29–41.

in the formulation of his *Regule*; rules 17 to 47 are formulations of the ways in which the meanings produced by grammatical rules are transformed when applied to God.

With regard to the noetic section of the poem as a whole, then, we can say that Alan enacts, in the narrative of the poem, precisely the programme of philosophical and theological education which he describes in his purely discursive works of speculative theology. Fronesis passes from perception of forms joined to matter (physics), to forms abstracted from matter (mathematics) and, finally, to the perception of pure form in God. And not only are these books working within a particular *divisio philosophiae*, but we can also see that the narrative movement is generated out of a hierarchy within that division of science: theology as the highest science draws Fronesis on through the empyrean, by means of theological faith, to perception of God in his purest essence. The narrative of this section of the poem does not end until the highest science has been reached and traversed – knowledge and movement in the *Anticlaudianus*, as in Dante's *Commedia*, are correlative. Stasis, therefore, presupposes 'scientific' perfection. The poem is closely following out a *reductio artium ad theologiam*, albeit within the particular Boethian, Porretan model of theology within which Alan is working, and which, in his works of Euclidian theology, he was pioneering.[54] Following d'Alverny, we can even say that Alan significantly rearranges the disciplinary hierarchy in the *Anticlaudianus*: the 'Aristotelian' division of the sciences is a division of *philosophy*; theology is a subdivision of that larger field of wisdom. Hugh of Saint Victor, for example, discusses *sacra pagina* and theology in two different parts of his *Didascalicon*. Alan, on the contrary, preparing for the disciplinary pre-eminence of theology in the thirteenth century, gives crown and sceptre to theology itself.[55]

OUTER FORM, BOOKS VII–IX

The first six books of the *Anticlaudianus* take their shape, then, from the theoretical sciences in the 'Aristotelian' division of philosophy. Not only this, but the narrative movement in those books is determined by a disciplinary hierarchy, whereby

---

[54] See n. 38 above.
[55] D'Alverny 1964. Hugh treats theology at II.2 of the *Didascalicon*, and *sacra pagina* in Books V and VI.

Fronesis reaches her destination only through the highest science, theology. Can the same kind of points be made for the last three books, Books VII–IX inclusive ?

I think they can. The last three books treat of the practical sciences, for here the moral and political endowments of the New Man are described. This section of the poem has been regarded as fundamentally incoherent, but when we look at it more closely, we can see how it is broadly informed by the structure of the practical sciences in the 'Aristotelian' scheme (ethics, economics and politics). And just as Alan's presentation of the theoretical sciences reveals him to be at the forefront of theology in the late twelfth century, so too with his presentation of the practical sciences: this is also striking for its humanist, classically derived coherence and confidence.

The creative and procreative action of the poem (i.e. the creative action of God in ordering a soul to be fashioned, and the procreative action of Nature in joining body and soul) occupy relatively small space in the poem. God orders the soul to be made at Book VI.429; by Book VII, line 74, the *novus homo* is physically formed. From this point on he is endowed with the gifts of the virtues (Concordia, Copia, Favor, Iuventus, Risus, Pudor, Modestia, Racio, Honestas, Decus, Fronesis (plus the Liberal Arts and (again unnamed) Theology), Pietas, Fides, Largitas and Nobilitas). And from this point until the establishment of the *aetas aurea* near the end of the poem (IX.379), the moral battle between Allecto's forces and the New Man is prepared for and fought. So what occupies the bulk of the action in the poem's last three books is in fact the enumeration of the New Man's moral qualities, and the enactment of those qualities in the battle, where they meet with, and defeat, their opposites.

With the exception of Ochsenbein, critics have agreed that the last three books are intellectually incoherent.[56] Is this true? Alan begins his treatise the *De virtutibus et de vitiis et de donis spiritus sancti*

---

[56] See Ochsenbein 1975, pp. 168–9 for a conspectus of views all agreeing on the fundamental incoherence of the ethical section of the poem. Among the citations he adduces, the following speak for the general view: Huizinga 1932, p. 74: 'Je mehr Figuren aufgezählt werden, desto weiter scheint der Sinn dieser Allegorie sich von jeder christlichen Grundlage zu entfernen und sich ins vage und bloss Rhetorische zu verflüchtigen... Nur eine seichte dichterische Phantasie, welche ihre klassischen Muster, die selbst schon stark rhetorisch waren, gedankenlos übernimmt und weiterführt, hat hier das Wort'; or Jung 1971, p. 80: 'Alain de Lille ne semble pas suivre un système défini. Ne cherchons pas la cohérence là où on ne saurait la trouver.'

It is one of the great merits of Ochsenbein 1975 to have given a largely convincing

by defining virtues as natural powers inherent in a rational creature from its creation: 'Sunt enim virtutes naturales potentie rationali creature a creatione indite.'[57] This Stoic derived idea of the
inborn quality of virtue makes sense of the essential action of the
endowment of the New Man by the virtues: after all, these virtues
are being bestowed at precisely the moment of birth, when the soul
of the New Man has been created by God, and joined to a body by
Nature.

The passage from the *De virtutibus et vitiis* that defines virtue as a
gift of Nature also clarifies the action of Books VIII and IX. For the
virtues bestowed naturally at birth are not virtues as such, but
potential virtues, whose endowment does not in itself make a person virtuous. Instead, one can be said to be virtuous only through
the exercise of virtue:

> Although a man should possess these powers by nature, with the coming
> of age he is not accordingly called brave, just, and temperate, since these
> words derive rather from the activation of a power than from the power
> itself.

> Sed quamuis homo a natura habeat has potentias, tamen adueniente etate
> non denominatur ab eis fortis, iustus, temperatus, quia huiusmodi denom-
> inationes potius sumuntur ab usu potentie quam a potentia.[58]

This simple distinction between the natural presence of potential
virtues, and the actuality of virtue which derives from exercise is
surely at the base of the poem's division of action: the virtues are
bestowed naturally at the moment of creation in Book VII, and
then made actual in the fight against the forces of Allecto in Books
VIII and IX.

The *De virtutibus et vitiis* as a whole is, however, of only limited
application to the *Anticlaudianus*. Alan is presenting a Christian
ethics in the tract, while in the poem his ethical system is purely
classical. The *De virtutibus et vitiis* itself makes the key distinction
here, between 'political' virtues (which non-Christians possess) and
'catholic' virtues. Alan says that virtue consists in two things: in the

---

account of the coherence of this section of the poem (pp. 137–85). My discussion is
indebted to his in important ways; I signal one point of disagreement in note 77 below,
rather than the many points of agreement, in the notes which follow.
57 Lottin 1960, ch. 1, art. 1, p. 47. My whole account of Alan's concept of virtue is indebted
to Delhaye 1963.   58 Lottin, 1960, ch. 1, art. 1, p. 48.

end to which it is directed (its *finis*) and in the correctness of its act according to the institution of the Church (its *officium*). A man might be chaste, not for God but for human praise; such chastity cannot be called a virtue, since it lacks a proper end. Another man might be chaste for God, but in a state of mortal sin at the same time (a homicide for example), in which case his act lacks its due *officium*. For, Alan argues, the *officium* of the Christian religion is a fitting act of each person according to the customs and decisions of the Church. These direct that the act of a person be directed to God and performed in a state of charity. So the chastity of the homicide cannot be defined as a virtue, since it lacks a virtue's proper *officium*.[59]

This definition of a virtue, according to its proper *finis* and *officium*, opens the way for Alan to define what he calls 'political' virtues – virtues which are directed to the proper end, but which lack a proper *officium* by existing outside the *mores et instituta* of the Church. He uses the example of non-Christians here, saying that the Jews might seem to practise virtues, but are really only practising 'political' virtues, since they lack the proper *officium* to be called virtues in any absolute sense.[60] One of the derivations given for this name 'political' virtue concerns its relevance, unsurprisingly, to the practice of civic government, since, as Alan says, the word *politica* derives from *polis*, or city, and pagans as much as Christians practised civic virtues.[61]

When we look to Book VII of the *Anticlaudianus* with this distinction (between 'political' and 'catholic' virtues) in mind, we might be surprised to see how insistently Alan stresses the 'political', as opposed to the 'catholic' nature of the virtues. Unlike his practice in the *De virtutibus et vitiis*, he rigorously excludes any specifically 'catholic' virtues (with the single exception of theology, which will be discussed later). This sequence of the poem is built around a concept of purely natural virtue. The endowment of the New Man with (or by) such virtues, and his victory over sin through them, implies the remarkable optimism of this section of the poem with regard to the capacities of nature. These virtues are not informed

---

[59] Ibid., pp. 48–9.   [60] Ibid., p. 50. See also Häring 1981, Rule 75, pp. 183–4.
[61] Lottin 1960, ch. 1, art. 1, p. 50. Alan's use of the concept 'political' virtue may have its origin in Macrobius's *Commentary on the Dream of Scipio* (Stahl 1952, 1.8, pp. 120–2). See Lottin 1949, pp. 103–15, for the use of the term 'political virtues', especially p. 106, n. 1.

by grace, and their contents are determined by reference to social relations, rather than by relations to God. There is no reference to penitence whatsoever here; rather than a morality concerned with one's personal relationship to God, here is a morality concerned wholly with life in society, and with the way in which personal and social qualities interpenetrate. The institution implied by these virtues is not the cathedral school or the monastery, but rather the court, where personal (ethical) and political qualities are required.

Fides, for example, appears in a quite different light here from the appearance of theological Faith to Fronesis in the Empyrean; here Fides makes no reference to biblical models, but instead endows the New Man with purely social virtues:

> Illa docet uitare dolos, contempnere fraudes,
> Fedus amicicie, fidei ius, pignus amoris
> Illesa seruare fide, nec nomine falso
> Pseudo uel ypocritam simulare latenter amicum. (VII.347–50)

She teaches him to avoid deceit, to despise fraud, to keep with inviolate loyalty pacts of friendship, the law of trust, the plight of love, not to hide under a deceptive name the role of false friend or hypocrite. (p. 184)

In the *De virtutibus et vitiis* Alan specifically calls the kind of faith described here a 'political' virtue, to be distinguished from the informed, 'catholic' virtue of faith. In article two, concerning the Cardinal Virtues, Alan defines *fides* as a species of *religio*, itself a species of justice. He defines *fides* as '... the perception of truth with assent, but without knowledge of causes'. He immediately goes on from here, however, to say that this definition is too general, covering as it does both 'catholic' and 'political' faith:

But this definition of faith is too broad, pertaining to both faith informed and faith uninformed [by grace], as much to catholic as to political faith.

Sed hec descriptio fidei nimis generalis est, tam informate quam informi fidei conueniens, tam catholice quam politice.[62]

And he continues by giving a more specific definition of Christian faith as 'perceptio ueritatis rerum inuisibilium ad christianam religionem pertinentium'. What we clearly have in Book VII of the *Anticlaudianus* is a political, rather than a theological virtue.

---

[62] Lottin 1960, ch. 1, art. 2, p. 54.

The *De virtutibus et vitiis*, then, provides us with ideas of natural, potential and 'political' virtues, all of which serve to focus the ensemble of virtues we find in Book VII of the *Anticlaudianus*. But because the tract is a work of Christian ethics, it can be of no further use in elucidating the ethical and political scheme of the poem. Here we must have recourse to classical, Stoic ethics.

Alan's presentation of the virtue Honestas suggests a close correlation between the ethical section of the poem and works of Ciceronian inspiration like the *Moralium dogma philosophorum*, possibly by William of Conches (*c.* 1085 – after 1154).[63] The virtue Honestas teaches the New Man

> Vt uicium fugiat, Naturam diligat, illud
> Quod facinus peperit damnans, quod praua uoluntas
> Edidit, amplectens quicquid Natura creauit;
> Non homines sed monstra cauens et crimina uitans.   (VII.208–11)

...to flee vice, love Nature, condemning what villainy has spawned or an evil will has brought forth and embracing whatever Nature has created, guarding not against men but against monsters and shunning reproach. (p. 179)

The logic of this passage implies the Stoic idea that Nature and virtue are coterminous, or at least largely overlapping: fleeing vice and loving Nature are registered as identical actions in the first line, and this emphasis is deepened in the admonition to embrace whatever Nature created. The implications of this point are followed through in the following line, where it is clear that to be a human is to follow nature, and, as such, virtue, whereas those who do not follow nature can no longer be called men, but are monsters.

Given that all the virtues are giving the gifts of Nature, we can see that the gifts of Honestas are essentially expressive of what each of the virtues gives separately. To give Honestas priority in this way makes sense only in the frame of Cicero's division of virtue into *honestum* and *utile*, where that which is *honestum* is concerned with what is morally right or wrong, while that which is *utile* is con-

---

[63] Over ninety manuscripts of the the *Moralium dogma* survive, and about forty manuscripts of the translation into Old French. For this information, and the likely attribution to William of Conches, see Delhaye 1949.

cerned with that which is 'conducive to comfort and happiness in life, to the command of means and wealth, to influence, and to power, by which [men] may be able to help themselves and their friends'.[64] The author of the *Moralium dogma* (closely following the structure of Cicero's *De officiis*) distributes his discussion of *honestum* amongst the four Cardinal Virtues. It is this theoretical frame, whereby all the Cardinal Virtues are seen as constituting the *honestum*, which makes sense of Alan's presentation of *honestas* in Book VII, insofar as this virtue promotes the Stoic ethic of following Nature.

Many of the virtues in Book VII are species of the Cardinal Virtues. The virtues Risus, Pudor and Modestia in particular are closely derived from accounts of Temperance in the Ciceronian/Stoic tradition; Ratio derives from Prudence, while Pietas, Fides and Largitas are derived from accounts of Justice.

Consider, for example, Alan's Ratio, who in Books VII–IX is turned wholly to practical, rather than speculative ends. Just as the *Moralium dogma* defines Prudentia as '[discretio] rerum bonarum et malarum et utrarumque', and divides this virtue into species of prudential, practical wisdom (*providentia, circumspectio, cautio, docilitas*),[65] so too is Alan's Ratio devoted to action in the world, to the perception of what is *honestum*:

> Docet ergo repente
> Ne quid agat subitumue nil presumat, at omne
> Factum preveniat animo, deliberet ante
> Quam faciat, primumque suos examinet actus;
> Diuidat a falso uerum, secernat honestum
> A turpi, uicium fugiens, sectator honesti.   (VII.171–6)

She instructs him not to adopt any sudden course of action, to undertake no venture without preparation, to think over every action first, to take thought before he acts and first examine his projects, to separate the true from the false, to distinguish between the honourable and the base, fleeing vice and pursuing virtue. (p. 178)

The one Cardinal Virtue with which the New Man is not explicitly endowed is that of Fortitude. It could be argued, however, that

---

[64] Cicero, *De officiis* (Miller 1947, 1.3.9, p. 10).   [65] Holmberg 1929, I.A, p. 8.

the whole action of Books VIII and IX is itself an act of fortitude, in the fight against the vices. It can also be argued that the essentially public orientation of the virtues given to the New Man implies this virtue. In the *De officiis*, in his discussion of Fortitude, Cicero stresses the necessity of manifesting one's virtue through the exercise of public administration. Blaming those who retire from public life, he argues that those who have been gifted by nature for public affairs should without hesitation enter the magistracy and participate in governance of the republic. Otherwise, he says, neither the state can be ruled nor magnanimity of spirit be made manifest.[66] In the endowment of Alan's New Man, the necessity of his manifesting ethical qualities publicly is everywhere implicit, and often stressed explicitly. Honestas, for example, teaches

> In communue bonum ne lux abscondita parce
> Luceat et uirtus det fructus clausa minores,
> Interius sibimet ut pauci uiuat et extra
> Ut plures, intus sibi uiuens, pluribus extra.   (VII.212–15)

...not to let his light be hidden and shine grudgingly for the common good nor his virtue be confined and produce lesser fruits; to have an interior life of his own which few have and an exterior life which many have, living his interior life for himself and his exterior life for the many. (pp. 179–80)

And Fronesis, likewise, gives the gift of wisdom that (in a positive version of Virgil's Fama), 'nisi publica fiat, / Labitur, et multas uires adquirit eundo' (VII.240–1; cf. *Aeneid* IV.175). The New Man is nothing if not a ruler; the public manifestation of his virtue everywhere implies the magnanimity of Fortitude.

The Cardinal Virtues, then (in their uninformed, natural state), clearly provide the basic frame for the coherence of the virtues with which the New Man is endowed. Certain exceptions, however, remain. In Book VII qualities appear which we would not normally think of as moral qualities at all (i.e. Copia, Favor, Iuventus and Nobilitas). Peter Ochsenbein has given the most convincing account of the presence of these 'virtues'. He argues that these qualities can

---

[66] Miller 1947, I.21.71–2, pp. 72–4. Baron 1988 argues that the medieval readers of Cicero understood him to praise philosophic retirement from politics, whereas the 'civic humanists' of the Florentine Republic of the early fifteenth century recover the real Cicero – the Cicero, that is, who argues that the philosopher should be engaged in the active life. Alan's view squares with the 'real' Cicero.

be accounted for by referring the list of virtues to a rhetorical, rather than a philosophical tradition. He points to the classical traditions of praise and blame as defined in demonstrative rhetoric. This tradition distinguishes external circumstances, physical advantages and moral qualities as aspects of a person that require articulation.[67] In, for example, the *Rhetorica ad Herennium* (a work on which Alan may have made a commentary[68]), we find these three areas of praise elaborated on. External circumstances are concerned chiefly with ancestry, and also include education; whether or not the object of praise has used his bearing (*dignitas*) and beauty (*forma*), his strength and agility, and his good health to positive purpose are then to be treated under physical advantages. And finally, the treatise recommends a return to external circumstances, and to a consideration as to whether or not virtues of character (*animi virtutes*) have been exercised with regard to these. Here it is asked whether or not the person has been rich and worthy of fame; in discussion of his moral conduct, the praise is to be articulated within the Cardinal Virtues.[69]

The argument that the *Anticlaudianus* is working within this tradition is surely unquestionable; as Ochsenbein points out, the poem is, after all, answering Claudian's *In Rufinum*, which is itself a *vituperatio*.[70] Admittedly, Alan's presentation of the virtues, and his systematic opposition of virtue and vice, is much more philosophical than Claudian's presentation of vices. Not only are Alan's virtues more closely related to Ciceronian accounts of the Cardinal Virtues than anything we find either in Claudian's *vituperatio* or his panegyrics, but we might also note that Alan's treatment of nobility is deeply affected by the philosophical cast of his poem in ways uncharacteristic of praise poetry. Thus, in Alan's poem, Nobility comes last; her lack of beauty besides the other virtues is stressed from her first appearance – '... forme laude secunda' (1.46), and her gift of nobility can only be granted after a long digression in which she petitions the favour of her mother Fortune. Fortune insists that Nature has no need of gifts dependent on chance (VIII.77–105).

But even if Alan's account of the virtues is philosophic in ways uncharacteristic of Claudian's praise or blame poems, it remains

---

[67] Ochsenbein 1975, pp. 173–4, and Georgi 1969, pp. 8–20.
[68] d'Alverny 1965, pp. 62–5.
[69] *Rhetorica ad Herennium* (Caplan 1954, III.7.13–16, pp. 178–82).
[70] Ochsenbein 1975, pp. 172–3.

true that the tradition of panegyric does account for the particular
range of qualities that we find in Alan's poem. Copia, Favor,
Iuventus and Nobilitas are all important points of the panegyric
tradition. One might add to Ochsenbein's argument that the entire
action of Book VII, where Nature excels herself in her endowments
to one creature, is itself an extended play on a topos of the praise
tradition. Thus, in contemporary vernacular poetry, for example,
we find Chrétien praising Cligés thus:

> Si chevol resanbloient d'or
> Et sa face rose novele;
> Nes ot bien fet et boche bele,
> Et fu de si boene estature
> Com mialz le sot feire Nature,
> Que an lui mist trestot a un
> Ce que par parz done a chascun.
> En lui fu Nature si large
> Que trestot mist en une charge,
> Si li dona quanque ele ot. (*Cligés*, lines 2736–45)[71]

The tradition of praise as prescribed by demonstrative rhetoric
provides the single frame which accounts for the range of virtues
that endow the New Man. We should also observe how Ciceronian
ethical texts, in particular the *De officiis*, also provided a defence of
placing the qualities Copia and Favor among the virtues. As I
mentioned earlier, Cicero divides his ethical treatise the *De officiis*
into a discussion of the *honestum* and the *utile*, where the *utile* considers those qualities which may help us to win influence for both personal and the public good. Cicero's ethical system is focused on
those who aim to exercise public influence; his discussion of the
utile is directed to success in the public domain, and divides accordingly into the attainment of influence through glory on the one
hand and liberality on the other. Ochsenbein also points out that,
unlike his Stoic predecessors, Cicero makes a close, even inseparable connection between virtues which pertain to the realm of the
honestum and those which pertain to the *utile*.[72] This discussion, I
think, accounts for Alan's placing of Copia and Favor as the first
virtues after Concord to endow the New Man; the theoretical iden-

---

[71] Micha 1957. See Luttrell 1974, for parallels between Chrétien's and Alan's portraits.
[72] Miller 1947, III.4.19–20, pp. 286–8. Discussed by Ochsenbein 1975, pp. 179–81.

tification Cicero makes between the *honestum* and the *utile* also accounts for the fact that external goods are treated as virtues, at least in potential.[73]

The rhetorical tradition of panegyric, then, accounts for the overall pattern of these personifications, which include external goods along with moral virtues. Alan's treatment of the virtues is heavily indebted to the Ciceronian, largely Stoic ethical tradition, and this applies as much to moral virtues as to external goods which are used to virtuous ends. In this remarkably humanist ensemble, all the virtues are gifts of Nature, given as potential qualities which become virtues proper when exercised as a *habitus*; and all the virtues remain those of Nature, uninformed by Christian charity.

This is a satisfying account in itself, despite the fact that it provokes acute problems when set into the structure of the poem as a whole, and despite the fact that two virtues (Concordia and Fronesis) have not yet been accounted for in this series. I shall look to the problems provoked by the overall structure of the poem in the following chapter. By way of concluding the present discussion, I should like to focus briefly on the anomalies of Concordia and Fronesis.

Concordia is listed in the *Moralium dogma* as a species of justice; it is defined as a 'virtus concives et compatriotas in eodem iure et cohabitacione spontanee vincens'.[74] This political definition of concord is much narrower in scope than the virtue Concordia as it is presented in Alan's poem. There Concord is rather presented as a cosmic force, whose action of joining body and soul is parallel to her action in the universe more widely:

> Sic nocti lucem connectit et ethera terre,
> Sic diuersa tenent pacem, sic dissona litem
> Deponunt propriam nec iam caro bella minatur,
> Spiritui cedens sed non sine murmure multo.   (VII.62–5)

It is thus that she joins night and day, Ether and Earth. Thus contraries live in peace, discordants lay aside the contention natural to them and

---

[73] Alan diverges here from the author of the *Moralium dogma*, who treats the category of the *utile* with considerable suspicion, warning against pride in wealth or glory (Holmberg 1929, III, pp. 54–67). Alan, like Cicero, treats these benefits of (and means to) power with positive approbation. See Jaeger 1985 for a presentation of the social contexts (particularly episcopal contexts) which nurtured the curial virtues and manners we find represented in Alan's poem.   [74] Holmberg 1929, I.B, p. 27.

flesh no longer threatens war, as it yields to the spirit, though not without many a murmur. (p. 175)

Concordia is the first of the sisters of Nature to be named in Book I; given that each of those sisters is renamed in the catalogue of virtues who endow the New Man in Book VII, we must assume that Concord is formally one of the virtues. But her action is not so much one of endowing the New Man with a specific quality, as one of manifesting in his make-up the cosmic harmony which is elsewhere manifest in the universe. It is clear that the philosophical scope of Books VII–IX of the *Anticlaudianus* extends beyond the purely ethical scope of Cicero's *De officiis*. Alan is setting his ethical frame in the context of the cosmos more widely, and any satisfactory reading of the poem will have to make sense of Concordia's nature and place among the virtues.

Finally, we should not leave the grouping of virtues without observing the anomaly of Fronesis's place there. In both the *De officiis* and the *Moralium dogma* Prudentia (another name for Alan's Fronesis) is treated ambiguously: on the one hand, the virtue clearly represents a prudential wisdom which informs the rationality of all actions; on the other, it is discussed in such a way as to suggest that its field is that of the theoretical sciences. Thus in the *Moralium dogma* the compiler names the Cardinal Virtues before going on to point to the pre-eminence of Prudentia, since Prudence advises, whereas the other virtues act; advice must precede act.[75] But if Prudence is felt to precede the other virtues at this point, the same virtue is named as being posterior to the others in another part of the same treatise (and in this ambivalence the compiler is following Cicero). When it comes to the comparison and respective valuation of different Cardinal Virtues amongst themselves, the *Moralium dogma* repeats an imagined example from Cicero, of the learned man who will abandon his theoretical studies into the nature of the universe, once he is called to action in the service of the state. The conclusion of this example is that 'prudentia ergo posterior est tribus reliquis'.[76]

The ambivalence here is due, I think, to differing views as to the content of Prudentia: on the one hand, the virtue is regarded as the source of prudential counsel, and as such precedes the action of all

---

[75] Ibid., I, p. 8.　　　　[76] Ibid., I, pp. 52–3.

other virtues; on the other, it is the source of theoretical knowledge of the universe, and so follows, and is (in Cicero's view) qualitatively secondary to the other virtues. In the *Anticlaudianus*, we find both these aspects of Prudentia among the virtues: as pointed out above, the virtue Ratio teaches prudential action – the qualities of carefulness, caution, deliberation and constancy in all actions (VII.166–201).[77] Fronesis, on the other hand, endows the New Man with the tools of theoretical knowledge – the seven Liberal Arts plus theology. It is true that the wealth of wisdom provided by Fronesis is said to be directed to the public good: 'Clausa perit, diffusa redit; nisi publica fiat, / Labitur et multas vires adquirit eundo' (VII.241–2). But while all the other virtues are definitely turned towards action in the public sphere, those of Fronesis are in themselves theoretical, insofar as they teach the New Man the rules of the seven Arts.

But most surprising among the otherwise purely natural arts endowed by Fronesis is the presence of Theology. As in Book V, Theology is not named; but there can be no doubt, from the description given, that Theology is being designated. Following Astronomy, a further art is described thus:

> ...sed eum diuinius afflans,
> Ars divina poli, ueri uia, nescia falsi,
> Ars que sola fide gaudet subnixa nec arte
> Nititur, humane fugiens racionis asilum,
> Gracius arrisit.   (VII.316–20)

With a more god-like breath, however, the divine science of heaven, the way of truth that knows not falsehood, the science which, rejoicing in its dependence on Faith alone, relies on no art and refuses to take refuge in human reason, smiled charmingly on him. (p. 183)

The most remarkable aspect of this description is its emphasis on theology's supra-rational quality and its source in divine grace. Here the word *fides* is being used in its theological, 'catholic' sense. Of course this emphasis is unexceptional in a description of theology itself, as we saw in our discussion of Books I–VI. But in the context of all the other purely *natural* virtues, Theology's presence here

---

[77] Ochsenbein 1975, p. 170 suggests that *Prudentia/Fronesis* represents a Cardinal Virtue in the endowment of Book VII; surely *Ratio* better fits the definition of *Prudentia* as a Cardinal Virtue.

is apparently eccentric, just as her failure to participate in the battle against the vices is eccentric. A satisfying interpretation of the poem will have to account for these anomalies.

In following the outer form of the poem, we have seen how the two parts of the work are (with some exceptions in Books VII–IX) internally coherent, shaped as they are by the theoretical and practical sciences respectively. But this very observation of coherence merely serves to intensify the kind of objection made by Wetherbee about the structure of the poem, with which I began this chapter: Books I–VI present the model of intellectual development, through which the mind moves from knowledge of the natural cosmos through to a knowledge, born of grace, about the divine origins of the soul. Books VII–IX, on the contrary, champion the model of the urbane and courtly ruler, who draws his *virtù* from the powers of nature alone. After the 'working out of the relation of the Arts to theology', the triumph of the natural man is indeed, as Wetherbee says, 'difficult to reconcile with the radical subordination of earthly knowledge in the central books of the poem'.[78]

But it may be that an interpretation based on the poem's outer form alone has stopped short of fully understanding the workings of the narrative. By looking at the ascent of Fronesis to theology, we have observed the implications of this movement, implications elaborated by Alan within, as much as outside the *Anticlaudianus*. We have seen, that is, that theological understanding, within Alan's theological culture, involves disciplinary, linguistic and psychological demands open only to the very few to undertake. When we turn back to the prose Prologue, we observe that these are the very demands that Alan wishes us as *readers* to face. Just as those who have not yet mastered the Arts should not attempt theological understanding, so too are those who are still within the inferior disciplines warned away from the deepest meanings of this poem; just as it is the intellect which must be employed in theology, so too are we as readers invited to exercise our intellect on Alan's poem, whose 'acutior allegorie subtilitas proficientem acuet intellectum'. And just as only a few are capable of entering the realm of theology, so too are only a few capable of understanding the poem:

[78] Wetherbee 1988, p. 52.

Let those be denied access to this work who pursue only sense images and do not reach out for the truth that comes from reason, lest what is holy, being set before dogs, be soiled, lest the pearl, trampled under the feet of swine be lost, lest the esoteric be impaired if its grandeur is revealed to the unworthy. (p. 41)

Ab huius igitur operis arceantur ingressu qui, solam sensualitatis insequentes imaginem, rationis non appetunt ueritatem, ne sanctum canibus prostitutum sordescat, ne porcorum pedibus conculcata margarita depereat, ne derogetur secretis, si eorum magestas divulgetur indignis. (p. 56)

The implication of these close parallels between theological understanding and reading Alan's poem is that Alan wishes us to read his poem as if it were itself a theological artefact. It is only those who dare, he says, to raise their mind to 'the intuition of supercelestial forms' who should attempt to enter the 'narrow paths' of the work, which itself contains not only the rules of all the Arts, but also *theophanie celestis emblema*. If this is the case, then the poem's meaning should not be sought at the level of its represented, referential action, an action which provides educational 'information'; instead, Alan is directing us to meanings inherent in the form of the work itself. I should now like to approach the idea, or inner form of the poem – its *creative* 'information' – by pointing, in the following chapter, to problems which arise with regard to the poem's outer form.

CHAPTER 3

A preposterous interpretation of the Anticlaudianus

INTRODUCTION

The theoretical and practical parts of the poem are, then, each internally coherent (with the exception of Concordia and Theology's presence among the natural virtues). At the same time, each of these parts of the poem is consistent either with Alan's other writings (the noetic journey), or with works in Alan's context with which he was certainly familiar (the ethical and political endowment).

As I mentioned in the last chapter, Alan defines the levels of meaning in his poem, and the qualifications his reader will need to perceive these levels. Only, he says, the proficient student should attempt to approach the poem's 'more subtle allegory'. The qualifications needed to understand this 'more subtle allegory' are defined in fairly austere terms. He says that his work contains not only the rules of human arts, but also 'an abundance of celestial theophany' (*theophanie celestis emblema*); because of this, those people who do not 'extend the course of reason beyond the limits of sense' should not attempt to 'enter the narrow paths' of the work, but only those who 'dare to raise their mind to the intuition of supercelestial forms' ('rationis materiale ... ad intuitum supercelestium formarum audent attollere'). This is the reader whose 'proficient intellect' the 'more acute subtlety of the allegory' will sharpen ('acutior allegorie subtilitas proficientem acuet intellectum').[1]

But what allegorical meaning could this poem possibly have? An account of its plot, such as I gave at the beginning of the last chapter, gives little promise of the creative indirectness of allegory; instead, the action of the poem at its literal surface is intensely conceptual, and has the appearance more of the *product* of, than the

---

[1]   Bossuat 1955, p. 56.

occasion for, allegoresis. Immediately below the thinnest of veils (the poem's action) we can perceive an educational programme: an education in the speculative sciences in Books III–VI, and in the practical sciences in Books VII–IX. Many of the ideas expressed by the poem's action are quite startling in themselves, such as the affirmation of human perfection through natural resources in Book IX. But they are also perfectly clear, and do not suggest any way in which the poem itself might, through its form, contribute to, or modify the philosophical positions which seem evidently present in the plot. It is not evident, that is, how the information (or philosophical content) the poem contains might in any way be modified by the information (or shaping) of the poem itself. Prosopopeia is, after all, an extremely explicit literary procedure, designed for the maximum degree of clarity, quite unlike allegory proper, which 'says one thing and means another'. Given that Alan calls almost every one of his actors by a conceptual name,[2] the poem would appear not to permit us the liberty of taking the text to mean anything but what it says.

And, as I say, the poem does indeed look like the *product of*, rather than the occasion for an allegorical reading. In his commentary on Martianus Capella's *De Nuptiis*, (?)Bernard Silvestris (*c.* 1100–60) defines a tradition of the *Bildungsroman*:

There is imitation of an author, since he [Martianus] follows Virgil. For just as in Virgil's poem Aeneas is led through the infernal regions by the Sybil to Anchises, so too here Mercury is led through the regions of the cosmos by Virtue to Jove. Likewise in the *Consolation* Boethius mounts through false goods to the ultimate good with Philosophy as his guide. These three figures express almost the same thing. Thus Martianus imitates Virgil, and Boethius Martianus.

Auctoris vero imitatio est, quia Maronem emulatur. Sicut enim apud illum ducitur Eneas per inferos comite Sibilla usque ad Anchisem, ita et hic Mercurius per mundi regiones Virtute comite ad Iovem. Ita quoque in libro *De Consolatione* scandit Boetius per falsa bona ad summum bonum

---

[2]   There are some exceptions to explicit naming in the poem: none of the Liberal Arts in Books II–IV are named immediately, if at all; the *puella poli* is not named as Theology at v.83–177; Christ remains unnamed in v.521–43; Liberality is not explicitly named in VII.378–96. We should not, I think, make too much of these silences – in each case we are offered the smallest puzzle, which is immediately answered by the attentive reader. The only significant silence, perhaps, is the failure to name Christ, whose marginalization in Alan's almost wholly a-historical world-view is remarkable.

duce Philosophia. Que quidem tres figure fere idem exprimunt. Imitatur ergo Marcianus Maronem, Boecius Marcianum.[3]

But whereas in his *Aeneid* commentary (?)Bernard would have it (as he implies here) that Virgil's poem is a covert *Bildungsroman*, the plot of Alan's poem is all but an *explicit* story of the soul's education. Traditions of allegoresis (such as we find in the commentaries on Martianus and Virgil attributed to Bernard Silvestris) interpreted fabulous narratives as stories of the soul's education. Alan, it could be argued, fashions a narrative surface out of the *interpretations* of allegorical readings, much in the same way that Guillaume de Lorris constructs a narrative out of the psychological personification implicit in earlier romance. The story is turned inside out, the signified becomes the signifier.

This might make the narrative surface of the *Anticlaudianus* seem unproblematic, if dull. But when we look at the *juxtaposition* of the two educational 'blocks' of the poem (the speculative and the practical parts) then not only does the ethical part of the poem seem, in Wetherbee's formulation, 'gratuitous and anticlimactic', but the poem as a whole seems radically incoherent. I should like to isolate three problems in particular which strike us once we try to make sense of the progression from the first, noetic part of the poem, to the second, ethical part. Out of these problems we can formulate the ways in which the poem is *itself* allegorical, saying one thing and meaning quite another.

THE ORDER OF THE SCIENCES

In the order of the poem, the practical sciences follow, and are represented as the culmination of, the theoretical sciences. This is striking and odd. Alan's perfect man is not a philosopher withdrawn from the world, like, say, Hugh of St Victor's ideal student as outlined in the *Didascalicon*, but a ruler very definitely in, and governing, a society.[4] His practical education follows the representation of perfection in the theoretical sciences. This is unique in Alan's own schemes of knowledge, and in the Aristotelian scheme generally.

---

3 Westra 1986, II.114–20, p. 47.
4 Hugh describes the virtues of the ideal student in *Didascalicon*, III.6–19; Buttimer 1939, pp. 57–69.

Writers working within the Aristotelian division of sciences unequivocally place the practical sciences before the theoretical in the order of pedagogy. They also claim superiority for the theoretical sciences. William of Conches, for example, says this about the order of pedagogy in his commentary on Boethius's *Consolatio*:

One should ascend from the practical to the theoretical, not descend from the theoretical to the practical, unless for the sake of public duty. It will now be shown what are the steps of philosophy – that is, the order of ascending from the practical to the theoretical. Firstly a man should be instructed in morals through ethics, then in the control of his own household through economics, and afterwards in matters of government through politics. Then, when he has been fully exercised in these, he should pass to contemplation of those things which pertain to bodies, through mathematics and physics, moving up to the celestial realm; from there he should pass to contemplation of incorporeal things, moving to the creator, through theology. This is the order of philosophy.

A practica adscendendum est ad theoricam, non de theorica descendendum ad practicam, nisi causa communis utilitatis. Qui vero sint illi gradus philosophie, id est ordo ascendendi de practica ad theoricam, sic videndum est. Prius est homo instruendus in moribus per ethicam, deinde in dispensatione proprie familie per economicam, postea in gubernatione rerum per politicam. Deinde, cum in istis perfecte exercitatus fuerit, debet transire ad contemplationem eorum quae sunt circa corpora, per mathematicam et physicam, usque ad celestia; deinde ad contemplationem incorporeorum usque ad creatorem, per theologiam. Et hic est ordo philosophie.[5]

---

[5] Jourdain 1862, p. 35. The superiority awarded by William to the theoretical sciences derives immediately from Boethius. In the first prose section of the *De consolatione Philosophiae*, Boethius describes Philosophy's dress, on which the letters Π and θ are woven. The Π (shorthand for *practike*) is lower than the θ (*theoretike*), and joined by a ladder:

Atque inter utrasque litteras in scalarum modum gradus quidam insigniti uidebantur quibus ab inferiore ad superius elementum esset ascensus. (Stewart, Rand and Tester 1973, I, prose 1, 19–22, pp. 132–4)

See chapter 4, p. 97 for further discussion of this passage.

   William makes one exception to the rule that one should move from the practical to the theoretical sciences, *causa communis utilitatis*. This qualification would seem to derive from Cicero's *De officiis*, 1.43.153.

   Grabmann 1909, vol. 2, p. 37, cites a Bamberg manuscript from the second half of the twelfth century, which is clearly working in the same hierarchies of science as William. After outlining the Aristotelian division, the author goes on to discuss the order of the sciences:

Non enim quocumque ordine artes addiscende sunt. Ordo enim in omnibus tenendus est. Litera scilicet P, quam Boetius in inferiori parte vestis philosophie dicit depictam,

It is true that some twelfth-century writers do name ethics as the highest science (e.g. John of Salisbury), but such comments are rare, and are in any case made within the context of a different division of philosophy.[6] It would be particularly surprising to find Alan making such an affirmation, since he so rigorously defines the dignity of sciences according to the psychological faculty by which they are understood. And this method of organizing the sciences in order of superiority is in any case implicit in the Aristotelian division of the theoretical sciences, since one clearly passes from physics to mathematics to theology in ascending degrees of abstraction, drawing on increasingly profound psychological resources as one progresses.

And if a hierarchy of theoretical sciences is, as I say, implicit in the Aristotelian division of the theoretical sciences, twelfth-century writers working within the Boethian conception of theology often make the point about the resulting superiority of theology explicitly. Alan, drawing especially on Gilbert of Poitiers, says as much on many occasions. In the Prologue to the *Regulae*, for example, Alan defines the rules which pertain to each science before coming to theology; when he does come to theology, he defines the pre-eminence of the subject both

---

designat a practica esse incipiendum et per gradus interpositos ad T i. ad contemplationem sive theoricam ascendendum... In philosophia ut diximus auctoritate Boetii a practica incipiendum est. [Here he outlines the order of the practical sciences: ethics, ecomomics, politics. After outlining the first two steps of the theoretical sciences, which he, surprisingly, places in the order mathematics and physics, he goes on to the final stage of education]. Hinc ad theologiam pervenitur, que est cognitio rerum divinarum que solo intellectu capiuntur.

It should also be observed that such hierarchies were adduced in the interpretation of noetic allegories. Thus (?) Bernard Silvestris describes the cursus in his commentary on the *De nuptiis*; after having studied poesis and the Trivium, the student should approach philosophy, beginning with practical disciplines and moving to theoretical, and not *vice versa*:

Nam quamvis dignitate precedat accionem contemplatio, illa tamen ordine doctrine prior est. Vides enim que priora sunt natura, doctrina sunt tamen posteriora.

At this point he goes on to articulate the 'Aristotelian' division of the practical and theoretical sciences (Westra 1986, VI.1–90, pp. 131–2).

6 In his *Metalogicon*, John of Salisbury describes ethics as pre-eminent among the sciences:

Illa autem que ceteris philosophie partibus preminet, Ethicam dico, sine qua nec philosophi subsistit nomen, collati decoris gratia omnes alias antecedit.

(Webb 1929, I.24.854c, p. 55). John is working within the so-called Platonic division of the sciences, physics, logic and ethics.

according to the certainty of its rules, and according to the profundity of psychological level which it requires.[7]

But however much it would be surprising to find Alan describing an educative progression in which the theoretical sciences lead to the practical, this is, nevertheless, the schema presented by the poem. And it is not merely that the description of the practical sciences follows that of the theoretical, but the practical sciences seem to be given *priority* over the theoretical. In the endowment of the New Man, as we saw in the last chapter, psychological faculties capable of speculative science (Ratio and Fronesis) do play their part. But in Books VII–IX, represented as a climax of perfection, these psychological faculties either serve purely prudential, non-theoretical ends, or else they seem superfluous. Ratio, for example, is presented carrying the three mirrors in Book I, mirrors which represent, as I argued earlier, the three theoretical sciences. In Book VII, on the contrary, her role is devoted entirely to prudential reflection. She instructs the New Man in how he can consider proposed actions rationally before their execution, for example, or how to concentrate his energies on few projects in order that they be effective (VII.166–201). And although Fronesis's handmaidens (the Arts and theology) do provide the tools of, and inspiration to theoretical perception, they seem superfluous in the moral battle as it is depicted.

In short, then, it is as if all the Arts come down on the practical, courtly knowledge represented (albeit in debased form) by Polonius, against Hamlet's theoretical knowledge. Constancy, even, instructs the New Man in his hair style, lest by a too dishevelled appearance (like Hamlet) he show himself 'too much of a philosopher' (*Philosophum nimis esse probet*) (VII.152). Such a disposi-

---

[7] Supercelestis uero scientia i.e. theologia suis non fraudatur maximis. Habet enim regulas digniores sui obscuritate et subtilitate ceteris preminentes. Et cum ceterarum regularum tota necessitas nutet, quia in consuetudine sola est consistens penes consuetum nature decursum, necessitas theologicarum maximarum absoluta est et irrefragabilis quia de his fidem faciunt que actu uel natura mutari non possunt. Vnde propter inmutabilem sui necessitatem et gloriosam sui subtilitatem a philosophis *paradoxa* dicuntur quasi recte gloriose propter sui obscuritatem; *enigmata* propter internum intelligentie splendorem dicuntur; *emblemata* quia puriore mentis acumine conprehenduntur.

Cited from Häring 1981, Prologue, p. 122. For the relation between the terms used by Alan here to describe the excellence of theology and those used by Gilbert of Poitiers in his *De hebdomadibus* commentary, see Jolivet 1980, pp. 88–9.

tion of sciences is wholly at odds with Alan's sense of the structure of the sciences expressed consistently in his works of speculative theology. It is exactly as if Dante's *Inferno* (likewise based on a scheme drawn from the *De officiis*) had been placed *after* the *Paradiso*.

THE ORDER OF VIRTUE

The second problem that the order of Alan's poem poses concerns the order of virtue. The noetic progress of Fronesis does require the help of Fides in Book VI, where Faith is clearly an informed, theological virtue. Reason, says Alan, teaches nothing to this Faith:

> Ipsam namque Fidem Racio non prevenit, immo
> Ipsa Fides hanc anticipat Fideique docenti
> Obsequitur tandem Racio, sequiturque docentem
> Articulos Fidei... (VI.24–7)

For Reason does not come before Faith; rather Faith anticipates it and Reason finally obeys the dogmas of Faith and follows her as she teaches the Articles of Faith. (p. 156)

In the last, moral section of the poem, however, the *novus homo* is endowed with natural virtues, including the virtue of 'political' faith, which, as a political virtue, is given a purely natural definition concerned with social allegiance rather than with Christian belief. This ordering stands in contradiction to the way in which Alan conceives of the perfection of virtue in his other writings. In, for example, article three of the *De virtutibus*, Alan says that the natural virtues are not strictly speaking virtues until they have been informed by grace. The difference between gracious and natural virtues, for Alan, hangs not in their essence, but in the ends to which they are directed:

The difference between virtues of grace and natural virtues does not consist in their essence, but rather in the way in which they are practised. For when we practise virtues by the direction of nature alone, without the information of grace, they are to be called natural virtues. When however we practise the same virtues informed by charity, they are the virtues of grace.

Differentia autem que assignatur inter gratuita et naturalia non attenditur in essentiis, sed in utendi modis. Cum enim utimur naturalibus solo ductu nature, non informatione gratie, naturalia dicuntur. Cum uero eisdem caritate informatis utimur, gratuita nuncupantur.[8]

The 'political' virtues of the infidel are perfected, or brought to their ideal form, only by charity: 'ut temperantia uel prudentia uel fortitudo uel iustitia que prius erat in gentili informis consequenter recipiat formam'.[9] So it is the *informatio* of charity which perfects the uninformed natural virtues; this is the position of the theological writings (both the *De virtutibus* and the *Regulae*). The poem shows a reversed order, with the natural virtues following the informed virtues, and, the poem's order suggests, with the natural virtues *perfecting* man. Either Alan has changed his mind in a daring and quite extraordinary way about the relation of informed to uninformed virtues, or else we should seek some interpretation of the poem which makes sense of this ordering.

THE ROLE OF FRONESIS AND THE FUNCTION OF HER JOURNEY

Thirdly, and most puzzlingly, what function does the noetic part of the poem (Books I–VI) have in the formation of the New Man himself? Wetherbee would seem to be right in arguing that the major theme of the poem is the working out of the relation of the Arts to theology; apart from anything else, one might observe, this part of the poem receives six books as opposed to the three books devoted to the ethical formation of the New Man. But if the poem's climax and point is indeed the formation of a perfect man, then from one point of view it is the voyage of Fronesis which is apparently 'gratuitous', since the voyage is designed to receive the soul from God. The elaborate representation of human sciences leading up to the point of their own exhaustion, whatever its own interest, is in fact superfluous to what is apparently the essential plot of the poem, the formation of a perfect man by Nature, which begins in Book VII.

In asking this question about the function of Fronesis's voyage in the structure of the poem as a whole, one might rephrase it, by

[8] Lottin 1960, ch. 1, art. 3, p. 59. For Alan's understanding of the difference between natural and informed virtues, see Delhaye 1963, pp. 20–1.

[9] Lottin 1960, ch. 1, art. 3, p. 58.

asking 'who is being instructed here?' Is it the New Man himself? From the poem as it is presented to us, this is apparently not the case, since the New Man is born into the poem only in Book VI, and his information is by natural, practically directed, virtues and arts. If this is so, then are we to assume that perfection does *not* involve progress in the theoretical disciplines, and, especially, in theology? But even if this were so (and, given the discussion immediately above, concerning the order of the sciences, it would be extraordinary for Alan to suggest that it were), then we are still left with the question of what the function of Fronesis's noetic journey is. To whom is this instruction directed? If to Fronesis, then why is this poem ostensibly about the creation of human perfection as located in the New Man?

And related to this question about the role of Fronesis and her voyage is a question which has puzzled critics of the poem from the moment of its modern reception, concerning the real hero of the poem. In the epic of the *Anticlaudianus*, who is the epic hero? Who serves as the unifying centre of this poem? Is it Fronesis, as many critics have argued? Or is it the New Man, as the poem itself would seem to propose? Or should we agree with Jung in his statement that the fault of the poem is the lack of *any* hero: 'un des défauts de l'*Anticlaudianus*: il manque au poème, qui se veut épique, un héros, autour duquel s'organise et se cristallise l'ensemble ... l'*Anticlaudianus* n'est pas une allégorie cohérente'?[10] Alan might be following the medieval reading of the *Aeneid* as a *Bildungsroman*, but if so, then where is Aeneas?

Is the chariot of Fronesis the chariot of the soul? This is what one would expect from a long iconographic tradition, originating with Plato, and certainly known to Alan (who uses it more than once elsewhere in his works). Again, the answer is 'apparently not', since, as Jung has argued, how could the chariot of Fronesis be the

---

[10] Jung 1971, p. 83. From the remarks cited by Wetherbee 1988, pp. 51–3, it would seem implicit that for him Fronesis is the heroine of the poem, as it would seem implicit in the argument of Green 1967, who reads the poem as an *ascensus mentis in deum*. Sheridan 1973 also supports this line: 'The epic figure that predominates is Phronesis' (p. 28). Jauss 1960 argues that the *iuvenis* is the key figure of the poem, even if his meaning, along with the allegorical form of the poem, remains hidden: 'Da der *iuvenis* zweifellos die Schlüsselfigur des *Anticlaudianus* darstellt, muss uns mit seiner Bedeutung auch der allegorische Sinn dieses Werkes verborgen bleiben' (p. 198). For a conspectus of views, see Meier 1977, pp. 252–3, to which should be added Chance 1983, who argues that the Artist is the epic hero of the poem. For fuller discussion, see chapter 4, n. 34.

chariot of the soul, when it is going to God precisely to ask for the making of the soul?[11]

So, even if the noetic and moral sections of Alan's poem are on the whole internally coherent and consistent with Alan's cultural milieu, serious problems arise when we consider their juxtaposition. The disposition of the poem, or its outer form – that *forma* defined by Alan as 'figura, scilicet proprietas que consideratur secundum dispositionem lineamentorum' – this outer form, taken as a whole, seems in fact to be radically incoherent, and poses a series of enigmas.[12]

A PREPOSTEROUS SOLUTION

At this point, I want to suggest an answer to these problems. I think we should read the poem in reversed order. I propose that the *real* order of this poem begins from the birth of the soul in Book VI, proceeds to the soul's moral education in Books VII–IX, and then to its theoretical education in Books I–VI, culminating in the perception of the soul's creation. At the very least, we can see how a reversed reading would resolve my three problems about the outer form of the poem: according to the reversed order, the theoretical sciences follow and provide a culmination of moral perfection within the limits of natural morality; the natural virtues are informed by grace; and the theoretical voyage of Fronesis is the theoretical voyage of the *homo perfectus*, in the chariot of his soul. According to a reversed order, the poem becomes an entirely coherent narrative from both an educative

---

[11] Jung 1971 is in fact more categorical in his negation: 'Or, pour nôtre propos, il importe seulement de retenir que le char allégorique d'Alain de Lille n'est pas un char de l'âme. Comment pourrait-il l'être, s'il doit précisément faire l'ascension du ciel pour y aller quérir une âme?' (p. 83).

[12] Ochsenbein 1975 concludes his work with a characteristically frank admission of what he sees as the fundamental lack of unity in the poem: 'weil die Dichtung – für den modernen Leser wenigstens – als ein sehr uneinheitliches Gebilde erscheint... Bedenken treten auf, ob sich der Anticlaudianus überhaupt als geschlossenes Ganzes erweisen lässt oder ob er nicht in einzelne Teile auseinanderfällt. Vor allem lässt sich zwischen dem ersten und zweiten Teil, also zwischen dem *consilium Naturae* und der Himmelsreise der Prudentia einerseits und der Gabenbeschenkung und dem Kampf andererseits, nur sehr schwer eine innere Beziehung herstellen' (p. 192).

and a theological perspective. An extremely positive view of nature nevertheless registers nature's limitations and gives way to a movement beyond natural capacities, and culminates in an essentially religious, if intensely intellectual version of human perfection.

An imagined reader may be remarking how tidy my solution to the poem's difficulties is, but how preposterous (in the modern sense of the word) at the same time. Literary critics simply are not allowed to take poems apart and put them together at will. In what remains of this chapter, I want to adduce the evidence that such a 'preposterous', or back-to-front reading is entirely consistent with what Alan says about the allegory of his poem, and that such a reading has very strong backing from within Alan's cultural milieu. A preposterous reading discovers Alan's allegory – through the way he orders his material, he does 'say one thing and mean another'.

I argued at the end of chapter 2 that we are invited by Alan's prose Prologue to read the poem itself as if it were a theological creation. I should like now to take up this invitation by developing the ideas of 'superessential form' and *intellectus*, since, as we have observed in the prose Prologue, the poem's 'more acute subtlety of allegory' will sharpen the reader's 'intellect', and only those readers who are prepared to raise their minds to the 'intuition of supercelestial forms' should attempt to perceive the poem's highest, allegorical sense. There will inevitably be some overlap in the ideas presented here and those elucidated in chapter 2, since in both discussions I am concerned to define Alan's concept of theology. In chapter 2 the discussion was directed to an understanding of theology as it was presented in the action of the poem; here, on the other hand, I am concerned to show how theological ideas are deployed by Alan as part of a poetics.

As we have seen, the word *forma* is used in many different senses by Alan. What he means by 'supercelestial form' is best understood by beginning from the word *supercelestis*. With this word Alan points us towards the highest kind of theological investigation; in the *Quoniam homines*, for example, he defines two kinds of theology, the subcelestial and the supercelestial. From the intellect arises the subcelestial, which concerns itself with spiritual creatures; from the intelligence arises the supercelestial that considers the divine nature, which is pure form.[13] The word 'supercelestial', then, in Alan's usage, leads us directly to the word 'form'.

For Alan the essential theological act is to move from the perception of outer to inner form. To recall the definition of *forma* in the *Liber de distinctionibus* cited earlier, for example, we see how Alan elaborates his Platonic definition of the word by reference to Boethius's *De trinitate*, Book II:

Form is defined as divine wisdom – that preconception that existed in the divine mind from eternity concerning the creation of things; thus Boethius: 'We should not be drawn to imaginary forms, but to eternal forms from which others derive.'

[forma] dicitur sapientia diuina, illa scilicet praeordinatio sive praeconceptio quae fuit in mente diuina ab eterno de rebus creandis, unde Boethius: 'Non opportet nos deduci ad imaginarias formas, sed ad formas aeternas ex quibus aliae sunt.'[14]

At the basis of this citation from Boethius is the idea that God is pure form; in the *De trinitate*, Boethius defines theology as the science which considers separable forms without change, 'since the substance of God is without matter or change'; for this reason, he says, 'in diuinis intellectualiter uersari oportebit neque diduci ad imaginationes, sed potius ipsam inspicere formam quae uere forma … est'. Boethius goes on to develop the idea of what is 'truly form' by distinguishing form which exists outside matter from the form we perceive in matter. Only that form which is without matter can be truly called form, whereas the form we perceive in an object should rather be called an 'image':

For from these forms which are outside matter come those forms which are in matter and produce a body. We misname the entities that reside in bodies when we call them forms, since they are mere images.

Ex his enim formis quae praeter materiam sunt, istae formae venerunt quae sunt in materia et corpus efficiunt. Nam ceteras quae in corporibus sunt abutimur formas vocantes, dum imagines sint.[15]

Boethius's idea that perception of pure form is the goal of theologi-

[13] Glorieux 1953, p. 121.
[14] PL 210, col. 796.   [15] Stewart, Rand and Tester 1973, Bk II, p. 12.

cal investigation is also at the centre of Alan's theology. In the *Regulae*, for example, he says this about God:

Since that which informs something else and is informed by nothing should truly be called 'form', what is more truly form than God, who informs everything and is informed by nothing?

Cum forma illud uere dicatur quod aliud informat et a nullo informatur, quid uerius forma quam deus qui omnia informat et a nullo informatur?[16]

From this he passes by a series of logical steps to the statement: 'Diuina enim forma a nullo informatur ut sit cum sit forma formalissima.'[17] (The divine form is informed by nothing in order to exist, since it is the essence of form.)

This conception of God as pure form has linguistic implications, which Alan develops, largely from Boethius, but also by deploying the concept *theophania*, drawn by Alan from Scotus Eriugena.[18] The essential step is that 'every name is given from its essential property, or form'; given this, words change their meaning when applied to God, since God is nothing but form, or essence – nothing can be predicated of God. Thus statements about God do not signify what they seem to, as in the statement, 'God is just', since God is rather justice than just.[19] Words about God must be understood not through their literal, but rather their metaphorical sense ('potius sensum ex quo fiunt verba quam sensum quem faciunt verba').[20]

We have seen how this overturning of linguistic procedure characterizes part of the poem's represented narrative in Book VI. But in asking us to perceive the 'supercelestial form' of his work, Alan is clearly asking us to consider his own poem as a theological artefact, and therefore to locate the poem's essential meaning not in the sense *quem faciunt verba* (its represented action), but rather in a prior sense, the sense *ex quo fiunt verba*. We are being asked, in Boethius's terminology, to move from consideration

[16] Häring 1981, Rule 13, p. 135.   [17] Häring 1981, Rule 16, p. 136.

[18] Alan discusses the concept *theophania* at length in two loci, the *Quoniam homines* (Glorieux 1953, Bk II, ch. 144, pp. 282–3), and the *Expositio prosae de angelis* (d'Alverny 1965, p. 205). In both instances he draws on Boethius's *De trinitate*, Book II, and in particular on the idea that 'cum de deo ratiocinamur non oportet nos deduci ad ymaginationes'. In my view, Alan's negative theology in matters of language derives its coherence fundamentally from Boethius's theological tractates; Alan exploits the coincidence of linguistic theory he finds in Boethius and Scotus Eriugena with the term *theophania*.

[19] Häring 1981, Rule 18, p. 137.

[20] Häring 1981, Rule 18, p. 137. See also Rule 36, p. 149, and the references in chapter 2, n. 38.

of the *imago* of the poem (its outer form) to its real form, the informing idea behind the poem which makes sense of its outer shape.

I am suggesting, then, that Alan is producing a Platonic poetics from within a Boethian concept of theology. Poetic theorists contemporary with Alan also, it should be noticed in passing, present the idea of a poetic 'archetype' which must precede poetic making, as if poetic making is modelled on divine creation. Geoffrey of Vinsauf's *Poetria nova* (*c.* 1200–2), for example, opens by describing the initial creative act as the formation of an idea, which then informs an outer poetic shape:

> Si quis habet fundare domum, non currit ad actum
> Impetuosa manus: intrinseca linea cordis
> Praemetitur opus, seriemque sub ordine certo
> Interior praescribit homo, totamque figurat
> Ante manus cordis quam corporis; et status ejus
> Est prius archetypus quam sensilis. Ipsa poesis
> Spectet in hoc speculo quae lex sit danda poetis.[21]

If a man has a house to build, his impetuous hand does not rush into action. The measuring line of his mind first lays out the work, and he mentally outlines the successive steps in a definite order. The mind's hand shapes the entire house before the body's hand builds it. Its mode of being is archetypal before it is actual. Poetic art may see in this analogy the law to be given to poets. (pp. 16–17)

It will have been noticed how often forms of the word *intellectus* have been used in the preceding discussion of form. Boethius, for example, says it is necessary to proceed *intellectualiter* in theology. In this discussion of what may be called Alan's theological poetics, the word *intellectus* also requires attention, since, according to Alan's Prologue, it is through the intellect that we perceive the 'supercelestial form' of the work, or its 'more subtle allegory'. What did Boethius mean by the word 'intellect', and how did twelfth-century thinkers understand his psychological definition?

The twelfth century inherited a coherent psychological system from different sources, one of the most influential of which was the list in Boethius's *Consolatio* and his *De trinitate*: sense, imagination, reason and intelligence, an ascending psychological progression

---

[21] Faral 1924, lines 43–9, p. 198. The translation is cited from Nims 1967, pp. 16–17. All future page references to this translation will be cited in the text.

arranged according to the degree of abstraction of which each level is capable.[22] We find this series presented in, for example, the *Glosae in Platonem* (1144–9) of William of Conches, where he lists *sensus, imaginatio, ratio* and *intellectus* (this last being an alternative for Boethius's *intelligentia*).[23] For writers working within a specifically Boethian tradition of theology, however, the concept of the intellect is deployed inseparably from their discussions of the theoretical sciences, and in particular of the psychological faculty required for the perception of pure form. These writers separate the highest of Boethius's faculties, intelligence, into two faculties. In his *Glosa* on Boethius's *De trinitate*, for example, Thierry of Chartres (d. after 1156) begins his commentary on Book II by discussing the psychological faculties. After discussing sense, imagination and reason, he makes a twofold division, between *intelligentia* and *intelligibilitas*. Intelligence he defines as that power of the soul that considers the single qualities and properties of forms, or those forms themselves, as they really are. He gives the example of perceiving humanity or a circle in their true being, whereby their nature is perceived in a way impossible when that nature is instantiated in a subject matter.[24] *Intelligibilitas* he defines as capable of perceiving pure being,[25] and in the same discussion he says, citing Plato, that such perception is accessible only to God and to very few men.[26]

Although he uses a slightly different terminology, Alan, too, divides the last of Boethius's faculties into two stages, as we saw in the last chapter. We observed there how the stages of theological progress were divided for Alan between *intellectus* and *intelligentia*. Through the *intellectus* man considers spiritual beings – angels and souls, for example; through the *intelligentia* man intuits the Trinity, and becomes 'in some sense deified' (*quodammodo deificatur*).[27] He

---

[22] For a conspectus of psychological thought in the twelfth century, see Michaud-Quantin 1949.   [23] Jeauneau 1965, para. 34, p. 100.

[24] Häring 1971, II.7, pp. 269–70. See Dronke 1988, pp. 365–7 for discussion of these terms in Thierry's usage. See Parent 1938, pp. 29–32 for a wider account of 'Chartrian' psychology.

[25] Thierry defines *intelligibilitas* thus:

> uis animae remouens ab his formis omnes terminos quibus inter se distincte erant atque quod de ipsis remanet solum esse atque entiam contemplans omnem pluralitatem inde absterret omniumque unionum simplicem contuetur unionem. (Häring 1971, II.8, p. 270)

[26] Häring 1971, II.9, p. 270.

elaborates this highest stage of perception with considerable freedom in many of his works. In, for example, the *Sermo de sphaera
intelligibili*, he describes the soul's powers as the four wheels of a
chariot, or as the rungs of a ladder; the fourth power of the soul is
intellectualitas:

Through 'intellectuality' ... the human soul drives its chariot as far as the
inmost bridal chamber of the ideas, where it contemplates the eternal
archetypes of things verdant in the flower of their eternity.

Per intellectualitatem ... ad penitiorem ydearum thalamum humana
anima aurigatur, ubi eterna rerum exemplaria in sue eternitatis flore
virentia contemplatur.[28]

Or in his *Sermo in die Epiphaniae*, he defines the gift of the third
Magus as the third and highest of the spiritual senses of Scripture:
'hanc offert intellectus, quia circa formas eius versatur intuitus'.[29] It
might be added that the word *intuitus* here designates the specific
act of the intellect. Alan uses this word in specifying the kind of
attention his poem requires from its reader, in saying that only
those readers should approach the 'narrow straits' of the work who
raise their mind 'ad intuitum supercelestium formarum'.

For writers in a Boethian tradition of theology, then, the intellect, and variations on the concept, are to be used for the perception, or intuition, of pure form, the province of theology. But Alan
is asking us, in the Prologue to the *Anticlaudianus*, to apply our intellects to the making of a poem. What does he mean by this? The
function of the intellect is to separate categories in ways they cannot be separated in reality. Thus Thierry of Chartres says that the
role of the intelligence is to perceive forms in their being, such that
they do not vary in the flux of matter; the role of *intelligibilitas* is to
perceive the pure being of a form, as when we might remove the
'term of being humanity from humanity' ('auferas ... terminum
essendi humanitatem humanitati').[30] When twelfth-century writers
come to explicating the role of the intellect, they do so precisely in
terms of separating things in ways they cannot in reality be separated. William of Conches, for example (again under Boethian

[27] Glorieux 1953, Bk I.2, p. 121. See chapter 4, nn. 52–62 for further reference.
[28] D'Alverny 1965, p. 303. See Dronke 1974a, ch. 5, for a discussion of this sermon. The
translation is drawn from this source (p. 150).
[29] D'Alverny 1965, p. 243.   [30] Häring 1971, II.8, p. 270.

influence) describes the role of the intellect as one of mentally taking apart previously joined things, or of joining disparate things, by virtue of its capacity to perceive the essential, intellectually separable essence of a thing. He says that the intellect has the capacity to see beyond the nature of things as they are presently constituted:

We say that the being of things exists in one way, the intellect and speech of men in another. For even if a substance is not able to exist except as this or that, it is however able to be understood intellectually as neither this nor that, since it is the role of the intellect to separate joined things and to join separate things.

Dicimus quod aliter habet se esse rerum, aliter intellectus hominum et sermo: etsi enim substantia esse non possit nisi hec vel illa, ita tamen potest intelligi quod non hec vel illa quia vis est intellectus coniuncta disiungere et disiuncta coniungere.[31]

William clearly has in mind intellectual activity as applied to words, when he says this:

Things can be signified and intellectually understood in diverse ways, which are not able to *be* different. For it is the function of the intellect and of speech to separate joined things and to join separated things. But sensual and bestial grammarians, being ignorant of this, are deceived in many matters through the existence of things.

Diuerse possunt significari et intelligi que non possunt diversa esse: vis enim intellectus et locutionis est coniuncta disiungere et disiuncta coniungere. Sed sensuales et bestiales gramatici, hoc ignorantes, in multis per existenciam rerum decipiuntur.[32]

---

[31] Cited from William of Conches, *Glosae super Priscianum*, Instit. II.18 (cited in Jeauneau 1965, p. 129, n. a). John of Salisbury also discusses the role of the intellect (for which he uses the word *intelligentia* interchangeably):

Verum si ad incorporea diuertendum est, ratione opus est et intellectu, cum absque intelligentia haec non ualeant comprehendi, et uerum non possit esse de his sine ratione iudicium. Intellectus itaque aliis deficientibus exerit uires suas, et quasi in arce animae constitutus omnia inferiora complectitur, cum ab inferioribus superiora nequeant comprehendi. Et nunc quidem res ut sunt, nunc aliter intuetur, nunc simpliciter, nunc composite, nunc disiuncta coniungit, nunc coniuncta distrahit et disiungit... Coniuncta vero disiungit, ut si formam teneat absque materia, cum tamen sine ea forma omnino esse non possit... Sed licet aliter quam sint, dum tamen simpliciter, coniuncta disiungat, non inanis erit conceptio, quae totius investigationis sapientiae expeditissimam parit uiam. Hic est enim totius philosophiae instrumentum, quod et mentem mira subtilitate exacuit et res singulas a se inuicem naturae suae proprietate distinguit.

Polycraticus, Webb 1909, vol. 1, Bk II, ch. 18, 437b–438a, pp. 103–4.
[32] Cited from William of Conches, *Glosae super Priscianum*, Instit. II.17.17 (cited Jeauneau 1965, p. 129, n. a).

We may assume, then, that Alan is also encouraging an 'intellectual' literary criticism in his dismissal of 'grammarians' who rest content with the outer surface of literary works. In his description of the pictures on Grammar's dresses, Alan says that only grammarians of worth are represented, whereas

> minime dignata fateri
> Gramaticos humiles, qui sola cortice gaudent,
> Quos non dimittit intus pinguedo medulle:
> Si foris exposcunt framenta, putamine solo
> Contenti, nequeunt nuclei libare saporem.   (II.509–13)

it disdains to recognize base grammarians who rejoice in mere husks, whom the richness of the marrow within does not set apart: if they seek chippings from the outside, content with mere shells, they cannot taste the flavour of the nut. (p. 90)

What we call literary criticism was included under the discipline of grammar in the twelfth century; here Alan is suggesting that a literary criticism which rests satisfied with the exterior of a text (its outer form) will end up with mere fragments; only, he implies, by understanding the inner sense of the work will it become coherent.

In summary, it is the intellectual part of the soul which can mentally join unjoined, and unjoin joined things, precisely by virtue of its capacity to perceive the archetypal form of a thing. When applied to verbal artefacts, such a theory of perception involves organizing one's perceptions less around the outer form, but rather around what the intellect perceives as its inner form, or essential 'idea'. We should consider not so much the sense which is made by the words, but the sense 'from which the words arise' (*sensum ex quo fiunt verba*). So when we return to the Prologue of the *Anticlaudianus*, and read that the allegory is designed to sharpen the intellect, and that only those readers should attempt to interpret the work who are capable of the perception of 'supercelestial forms', then we are being invited, in William of Conches's words, not to interpret the work according to its 'existence', but rather according to our perception of its informing idea. Very crudely, it could be said that we are being invited to 'take the poem apart', as it were – to 'unjoin joined things'.

RHETORICAL ORDER

This is a broad invitation, and one which is clearly attractive for my proposed reading, whereby we should, I suggest, take the *Anticlaudianus* apart, and read it not as it is, but rather as our intellect orders it. But however broad the invitation of rearrangement offered by the intellect might be, it is obviously not an invitation which leaves us open simply to rearrange the poem at will. But in defence of my proposed reordering, I should like to appeal to a standard rhetorical conception of organizing material.

Medieval rhetoricians and grammarians inherited from classical rhetoric two ways of ordering narrative, the natural and the artificial order.[33] Hugh of St Victor, to choose one among many possible twelfth-century writers who transmit this standard rhetorical notion, says in his *Didascalicon* that narration follows

according to an order which is twofold: that is, either a natural order, when an event is narrated in the order in which it happened, or an artificial order, when that which happened afterwards is related first.

secundum dispositionem, quae duplex est; naturalis videlicet quando res eo refertur ordine quo gesta est, et artificialis, id est, quando id quod postea gestum est prius narratur.[34]

Hugh's exposition here suggests that in any given work, an author will choose to order his material in one way or the other – either according to the natural order, in which events are related according to their historical sequence, or else according to an artificial order, in which historical sequence is inverted.

When we look to late twelfth-, or early thirteenth-century poetics, however, we find an implicit sense that the two orders can be somehow present in the one work. This is the way in which Geoffrey of Vinsauf, for example, describes the disposition of a poem in his *Poetria nova*:

> Ordo bifurcat iter: tum limite nititur artis,
> Tum sequitur stratam naturae. Linea stratae
> Est ibi dux, ubi res et verba sequuntur eumdem
> Cursum nec sermo declinat ab ordine rerum.

---

33 See, for example, *Rhetorica ad Herennium*, III.9.16–17. But the order specified there applies to oratory rather than narration. Alan may have written a commentary on the *Ad Herennium* (d'Alverny 1965, pp. 52–5). See Quadlbauer 1982 for a full conspectus of this tradition; see also Faral 1924, pp. 56–9, and Hunt 1972, pp. 332–4 for further references.
34 *Didascalicon*, Buttimer 1939, III.8, p. 58.

> Limite currit opus, si praelocet aptior ordo
> Posteriora prius, vel detrahat ipsa priora
> Posterius; sed in hoc, nec posteriora priori,
> Ordine transposito, nec posteriore priora
> Dedecus incurrunt, immo sine lite licenter
> Alternas sedes capiunt et more faceto
> Sponte sibi cedunt: ars callida res ita vertit,
> Ut non pervertat; transponit ut hoc tamen ipso
> Rem melius ponat. Civilior ordine recto
> Et longe prior est, quamvis praeposterus ordo.[35]

The material's order may follow two possible courses: at one time it advances along the pathway of art, at another it travels the smooth road of nature. Nature's smooth road points the way when 'things' and 'words' follow the same sequence, and the order of discourse does not depart from the order of occurrence. The poem travels the pathway of art if a more effective order presents first what was later in time, and defers the appearance of what was actually earlier. Now, when the natural order is thus transposed, later events incur no censure by their early appearance, nor do early events by their late introduction. Without contention, indeed, they willingly assume each other's place, and gracefully yield to each other with ready consent. Deft artistry inverts things in such a way that it does not pervert them; in transposing, it disposes the material to better effect. The order of art is more elegant than natural order, and in excellence far ahead, even though it puts last things first. (pp.18–19)

Geoffrey's description of the two orders here implies that the natural order is not effaced by the artificial, but that both orders retain their force when the artificial order is used: both orders change places willingly, in a playful manner, without one doing offence to the other. He also stresses that this order is by far the most sophisticated of the two orders. He makes the same point in his tract *Documentum de modo et arte dictandi et versificandi*, where he says that the natural order is uncultured and common-place: 'hoc genus principii dici potest agreste vel vulgare, quod cuilibet datum est sic incipere.'[36] (This kind of beginning

---

35   Faral 1924, lines 87–100, p. 200. It should be mentioned here that the *Anticlaudianus* was often copied with the *Poetria nova* in the same manuscript. Thus, of the twenty-nine manuscripts of Alan's poem in British libraries, no fewer than six also include the *Poetria nova*. See Gibson and Palmer 1987.

36   Faral 1924, I.2, p. 265. The notion that the artificial order is more sophisticated is of long standing; Faral 1924, p. 56 cites a commentary by Alcuin or by someone of his school on Horace's *Ars Poetica*, lines 42–5, which begins: 'Nam sententia talis est: quicumque promittit se facturum bonum carmen et lucidum habere ordinem, amet artificialem

can be said to be rustic or vulgar, since it is open to anyone to begin thus).

In Geoffrey's *Poetria nova*, then, we not only have the commonplace rhetorical idea of the artificial and the natural order. In elaboration of this traditional idea, Geoffrey also suggests that *both orders might be preserved in the one poem*, and that the artificial order is by far the most sophisticated. It might be objected that Geoffrey's *Poetria nova* is just a little too late (*c.* 1200–2) to enlist in support of an interpretation of the *Anticlaudianus*. In fact the temporal difference is by no means large, since Alan and Geoffrey are effectively contemporaries (Alan is supposed to have died in 1203), and in any case the rhetorical practice I am proposing was easily available to Alan writing in the 1180's. For this rhetorical model, applied in the sophisticated way suggested by Geoffrey, is certainly evident in the commentaries of twelfth-century grammarians. They use it in their interpretation of philosophico-poetic texts, as a way of penetrating and defining the deep philosophical sense of a work.

In the commentary attributed to Bernard Silvestris on the *Aeneid* (I shall continue here to use the name 'Bernard' for convenience), we can see how the two orders might be conceived of as inhering in the same work. According to Bernard, the *Aeneid* has two orders – an artificial and a natural order. In the beginning of his commentary, Bernard states the standard rhetorical theory concerning the disposition of a work – it can follow one of two orders:

a natural, that is, and an artificial order. The natural order pertains when the narration is disposed according to the series of events and times; this occurs when the narration occurs in the order in which it happened... But the artificial order pertains when we begin from the middle of the narration and return in an artificial manner to the beginning.

ordinem et spernat naturalem.' The tradition has a long future before it. Thus in the sixteenth century Ronsard directs a young poet thus:

Tu doibs sçavoir sur toutes choses que les grands poesmes ne se commencent jamais par la premiere occasion du faict, ny se sont tellement accomplis, que le lecteur espris de plaisir n'y puisse encores desirer une plus longue fin, mais les bons ouvriers le commencent par le milieu, et sçavent si bien joindre le commencement au milieu et le milieu à la fin que de telles pieces rapportées, font un corps entier et parfaict.

Ronsard, *Abregé de l'art poétique*, in *Ronsard, L'art poétique. Cinq préfaces*, edited by Jean Stewart (Cambridge, 1930), p. 9. I am grateful to Luiṣella Simpson for this reference.

naturalem scilicet et artificialem. Naturalis est quando narratio secundum seriem rerum ac temporum distribuitur, quod fit dum eo ordine quo res gesta est narratur ... Artificialis ordo vero est quando a medio narrationem incipimus artificio atque modo ad principium recurrimus.[37]

He goes on to say that Virgil follows the second of these orders in the *Aeneid*. But Bernard's handling of these orders makes explicit what Geoffrey of Vinsauf had implied – that is, that *both* orders are present in the one poem: 'Notandum est in hoc libro geminum esse narrationis ordinem.'[38] It is precisely this sense of a double order which allows Bernard to distinguish the poetic from the philosophical order in the poem, and, as a consequence, to elucidate what he takes to be the poem's philosophical meaning. In his description of the work's philosophical truth, he says that as a philosopher, Virgil used the natural order, as a poet, the artificial:

in describing this he used a natural order; he therefore observed both orders of narration – the artificial as a poet, and the natural as a philosopher.

Atque in hoc describendo naturali utitur ordine atque ita utrumque ordinem narrationis observat, artificialem poeta, naturalem philosophus.[39]

So, in Bernard's interpretation, both orders retain a certain coherence and force: the poetic order is artificial, insofar as it begins *in medias res*, and only in Book II returns to the fall of Troy; but below this poetic, artificial order, there is a natural, philosophical order, whereby each book represents the successive stages of growth in the human soul, from birth in Book I, to philosophical maturity in Book VI.[40]

How might these categories apply to Alan's poem? The *artificial*

---

37 Jones and Jones 1977, Prologue, pp. 1–2. Singerman 1986, pp. 1–25 provides a good account of the two orders as applied to the *Aeneid* in the tradition of interpreting that poem as an allegory of the ages of man. See Baswell (1995), ch. 3, for this tradition as represented in one English manuscript. I am grateful both to Christopher Baswell for his permission to read his fine book in typescript, and to the efficient offices of Katerina Brett of CUP in this matter.   38 Jones and Jones 1977, Prologue, p. 1.

39 Jones and Jones 1977, Prologue, p. 3. See Minnis 1988, p. 150, n. 151 for the Macrobian background to this tradition of Virgil as poet and philosopher.

40 The fact that Aeneas reaches philosophical maturity in Book VI, according to this interpretation, may be significant for my own interpretation of the *Anticlaudianus*, since, as will be argued below, it seems to me that Book VI of Alan's poem is also the apogée of philosophical/theological understanding. For the twelfth-century interpretation of the *Aeneid* as a *Bildungsroman*, see also John of Salisbury, *Polycraticus* (Webb 1909, Bk VIII, ch. 24, pp. 415–17), where the existence of a double order of narration is also implicit. It may also be relevant here to remark that in Book VI of the *Aeneid* (Anchises's speech, esp. lines 724–51), just as in Book VI of the *Anticlaudianus*, the soul's ultimate origins are treated.

order is the order followed by the plot of the poem as we read it – that outer form of the story by which we observe Fronesis in her ascent to God in search of the human soul. This is the order whose form I have followed in chapter 2, according to which the poem begins with the project of Fronesis's journey, and culminates in the *aetas aurea* at the end of Book IX with the moral victory of the New Man. According to this order, the poem moves from the theoretical to the practical sciences, after the birth of the perfect man. This is the order by which, to use Bernard's phrase, we 'return to a beginning' (*ad principium recurrimus*). The 'beginning' to which we return is the creation of the soul, whose growth we then follow through the last three books.

This much is clear, but what of the *natural* order of the poem? I suggest we invert the order of the poem to perceive its natural order. The birth of the soul, and its natural moral perfection in the last three books come before, and are presupposed by, the noetic journey of Fronesis in Books I–VI. The soul we see briefly being created mid-poem (in Book VI.428–65) marks the beginning of the poem's natural order. We witness the moral endowment and exercise of this soul, before (in an intellectual reading) we return to the opening of the poem and see the dissatisfaction of Nature at natural perfection. From this moment of dissatisfaction, we witness the continued 'information' of the New Man, this time through education in the theoretical sciences. The end of the poem's natural order lies in the moment at which Fronesis perceives the soul's beginnings, a perception which constitutes the highest form of self-knowledge in Alan's intellectual world.[41]

So the New Man *is* in fact present in Book I, even if his nature is dissatisfied by his soul's lack of perfection, given its lack of understanding about the origins of the soul. In the economy of this natural order, we can see, too, that Fronesis's journey to the heavens is in fact the noetic journey of the New Man in the chariot of his soul in search of the highest wisdom, led by his own intelligence (Fronesis). As the natural order ends in Book VI with perception of the soul's own creation, so too does the natural order of the poem begin. What Alan does is brilliantly to link the end of philosophical and theological enquiry with the birth of the soul in the poem: the

---

[41] For knowledge of the soul's origins being the highest form of knowledge in Alan's intellectual world, see chapter 4, nn. 41–9.

moment of the highest intellectual perception becomes the moment of creation.

In this reading, then, Alan creates two climaxes for his poem. The climax of the artificial order is the beautiful establishment of the *aetas aurea* at the end of Book IX, while the natural order culminates in the equally beautiful and climactic vision of the soul's creation in Book VI. The beginning of the poem, then, is not the beginning of the poem's action in time; it marks, instead, the middle of the action, and a critical point at which a purely natural ensemble registers its own lack of autonomy. Geoffrey of Vinsauf specifies eight ways of beginning if one is using the artificial order; Alan is following the second of these possibilities, according to which one can begin with the middle of the narration. After first showing how one might begin with the end of the story, Geoffrey goes on to declare that a poet may also begin with the middle of his narration:

> Primus apex operis non solum fulget ab ipso
> Fine, sed ipsius duplex est gloria: finis
> Thematis et medium. Trahit ars ab utroque facetum
> Principium, ludit quasi quaedam praestigiatrix,
> Et facit ut fiat res postera prima, futura
> Praesens, transversa directa, remota propinqua;
> Rustica sic fiunt urbana, vetusta novella,
> Publica privata, nigra candida, vilia cara.[42]

The place of honour at the beginning of a work does not reserve its lustre for the end of the material only; rather, two parts share the glory: the end of the material and the middle. Art draws from either of these a graceful beginning. Art plays, as it were, the conjurer: causes the last to be first, the future to be present, the oblique to be straight, the remote to be near; what is rustic becomes urbane, what is old becomes new, public things are made private, black things white, and worthless things are made precious. (pp. 19–20)

What does this interpretation have to recommend it? It will be immediately clear that this solution resolves my three puzzles: (i) according to the natural order of the poem, the theoretical sciences follow and provide a culmination for progress in the practical sciences; (ii) the natural virtues are informed by grace; and (iii) the noetic voyage of Fronesis is the voyage of the *homo perfectus*, in the

---

[42] Faral 1924, lines 118–25, p. 201.

chariot of his soul. Debates as to whether the *novus homo* or Fronesis is the hero/heroine of the epic poem are therefore beside the point: Fronesis is the intellectual faculty of the soul created in Book VI; she is the intellectual faculty of the *novus homo*. It will also be clear that this interpretation answers the frequently stated objection (exemplified in the remarks by Winthrop Wetherbee cited in the introduction to chapter 2) that the *Anticlaudianus* is an incoherent poem, in which the profoundly religious sense of the soul's origins is fundamentally unconnected with the natural triumph of the New Man in Book IX: the reading I propose here understands the triumph of Nature as an essential prelude to the noetic voyage in Books I–VI.

THREE SUPPORTIVE ARGUMENTS

In the next chapter, I want to suggest *why* Alan should so structure his poem. In particular I want to argue that Alan poses these two orders in the poem as a way of imagining the perfect ruler, who is a philosopher–king, on the model of Plato's ideal ruler. In the present chapter I shall restrict myself to arguing simply *that* Alan ordered his poem artificially. By way of concluding this chapter, then, I suggest three further arguments supporting the proposed interpretation.

First, as I argued in chapter 2, there is one virtue which stands completely outside the range of virtues presented in Book VII, and which plays no substantive part in the establishment of the Golden Age. This is the 'virtue' Fronesis, who endows the New Man with the Liberal Arts and with Theology.[43] In the fight against the vices, Fronesis certainly fights against the vices of the poor student, but there is no account of the Arts, let alone of Theology, engaging in the fight against the vices. Theology is exceptional in another way, too, insofar as she is specifically presented as a virtue informed by grace, as I argued earlier.

The fact that Theology was informed by grace, and the fact that

---

[43] I place inverted commas around the word 'virtue' with respect to Fronesis, since in the *De virtutibus et vitiis* Alan specifically denies that reason and intellect are strictly speaking virtues at all:

> Cetere etiam potentie que non habent uitia sibi opposita, ut ratio, intellectus, memoria uirtutes esse non possunt, quia ui non stant. Huiusmodi enim potentie operantur ad exercitium uirtutum; ordinante enim ratione uel intellectu surgit usus prudentie uel fortitudinis. (Lottin 1960, ch. 1, art. 1, p. 50).

she had no part to play in the fight against the vices, seemed incoherent in the frame of the ethical section of the poem. When set into the structure of the whole poem, as I am describing it, her place becomes clear: theological perception is given as a *potential* in the New Man by nature, but not fulfilled as an actuality in the poem in Books VII–IX; only with the continuation of the poem's natural order, in Books I–VI, are the Arts and Theology actualized, in the same way that the other virtues had been actualized in Book IX. It is significant, I think, that Theology is described as having smiled upon the soul when still in heaven, before its descent into the body (VII.316–28). The soul is imagined, that is, as retaining a vestigial, Platonic recollection of its divine source even when it enters the body. It is this vestigial recollection which ultimately produces the effort to transcend nature from Book I to Book VI. Theology is said to teach the New Man not only to control the impulses of passion (which he does in Books VII–IX), but also to ascend in mind to heaven:

> Illa docet celeste sequi, uitare caducum,
> Viuere lege poli, sursum suspendere mentem,
> Fastidire solum, celum conscendere mente.   (VII.324–6)

She teaches him to follow what is of heaven, avoid what is transitory, live by the law of heaven, direct his mind on high, shrink from the earth, ascend in mind to heaven. (p. 183)

In Books VII–IX we do not see this teaching enacted at all: the New Man lives entirely by the beautiful, rational, but limited world of Nature on earth, even if in an ideal form. Only in Books I–VI do we see the New Man perfected by his journey to the heavens, as he climbs the heavens in his mind (*celum conscendere mente*). Understood in the frame of the interpretation I propose, the role of the Liberal Arts and of Theology becomes entirely coherent.

Second, if Fronesis's journey were in fact the noetic journey of the New Man in his ascent to theoretical perfection, we would expect Fronesis to be represented as actually learning in her ascent to God. This is in fact how she is presented. Fronesis is chosen to seek out God not because she has the knowledge of the soul already, but because she has the *potential* to perceive the source of created things in the divine mind,

> Quomodo terrestrem formam celestis ydea

Gignit et in nostram sobolem transcribit abissum,
Mittit in exilium formas quas destinet orbi.   (1.495–7)

how the heavenly idea begets the earthly form, transforms chaos into the species we know, and sends abroad the forms which it destines for the earth. (pp. 64–5)

Fronesis's capacity for this kind of knowledge (a capacity with which the New Man has been endowed in Book VII, at his birth) qualifies her to take the prayer of Nature to God. But the knowledge she gains on her journey through the heavens is not merely a (long) digressive preliminary to her delivering her prayer to God for a perfect soul. The journey through the heavens, and the knowledge gained through that journey, more accurately *constitute* the 'prayer' to God, or at the very least qualify Fronesis to make the prayer. By understanding the structure of the cosmos as a necessary preliminary to theological perception of the soul's own origins, Fronesis is equipped to gain God's favour in the creation of a perfect soul.

Earlier I asked what the role of Fronesis's journey is (see p. 64). In the artificial order of the poem, we are uncertain as to what relation this journey has to the formation of the Perfect Man. For in the frame of the artificial order of the poem alone, it seems certain that the education of Fronesis is not the education of the New Man, since Fronesis seems to be going to heaven precisely to ask for the granting of a perfect soul. Now, in the preposterous interpretation offered here, we can see how the education of Fronesis is indeed the education of the New Man, in the highest point of his being, his intellect and intelligence.

Fronesis's journey is, after all, represented not merely as a display of her already achieved knowledge, but rather as a philosophical and theological formation, a process of perfection through the soul's understanding of the natural universe, and, ultimately, of itself. At each stage of her journey, the verbs which denote her responses to what she sees indicate an educative, formative experience. The identity of physical movement and intellectual formation is encapsulated in the way in which Fronesis 'informs' (a word Alan does not use lightly) her step by following the *puella poli*:

Vlterius producit iter Prudencia, gressum
Informans gressu comitis, tandemque labore
Magno, multiplici nisu, cognamine multo
Ascendit loca leticie...   (v.373–6)

Prudence [i.e. Fronesis] proceeds upon her journey, matching step for step with her companion. Finally, with great toil, repeated effort, numerous struggles, she made her way up to the realms of happiness. (p. 150)

The voyage of Fronesis is analogous to the journey of Nature in Bernard Silvestris's *Cosmographia*. There, too, Nature makes a journey through the heavens in search of Urania, or the principle of man's celestial existence, before descending to search out Physis, the principle of man's material existence. Nature's voyage is posed as a *prelude*, in the plot of the poem at least, to her fashioning man. But although man himself is strictly absent from this voyage (not having been created), it is nevertheless clear that the philosophical wisdom acquired by Nature through Urania and Physis is essentially constitutive of man's soul. In the garden of Gramision, after Nature's journey but before the creation of man, Noys promises Nature that man will have a wide range of knowledge – precisely that range which Nature has acquired on her journey:

Dii superi stelleque sibi celumque loquetur,
    Consilium Lachesi notificante suum.
Viderit in lucem mersas caligine causas,
    Ut Natura nichil occuluisse queat -
Aerios tractus, tenebrosa silencia Ditis,
    Alta poli, terre lata, profunda maris.
Viderit unde vices rerum, cur estuat estas,
    Siccitat autumpnus, ver tepet, alget hyemps.
Viderit unde suum Phebo iubar, unde sorori,
    Unde tremit tellus, unde marina tument,
Cur longis estiva dies extenditur horis,
    Parvaque contrahitur nox breviore mora.[44]

The heavenly powers, the stars, the firmament, will speak to him, and Lachesis reveal to him her deliberations. He shall behold clearly principles shrouded in darkness, so that Nature may keep nothing undisclosed. He will survey the aerial realms, the shadowy stillness of Dis, the vault of heaven, the breadth of earth, the depths of the sea. He will perceive whence things change, why the summer swelters, autumn blights the land,

---

[44] *Cosmographia, Microcosmos*, X, 33–44, in Dronke 1978, p. 141.

spring is balmy, winter cold. He will see why the sun is radiant, and the moon, why the earth trembles and the ocean swells. Why the summer day draws out its long hours, and night is reduced to a brief interval.[45]

This promise is made *before* the creation of man, but the range of knowledge outlined by Noys here has already been enacted in the poem by Nature's own journey to find Urania and Physis. A speech of Urania earlier affirmed, in fact, that precisely this range of knowledge has been observed by Nature herself, in her journey.[46] Nature's voyage, then, despite coming *before* the creation of man, is clearly in some sense *part* of that creation. That Nature will not be able to hide her secrets from man is because man's own creation has involved these very secrets. This is analogous to the fact that Fronesis's journey is ostensibly to ask for the creation of the perfect man, when in the reading I propose, her journey actually contributes to the achievement of that perfection. Timaean-inspired *involucra* seek to express the complex *synchronic* relations within systems (of the universe, of the body, of the constellation of the sciences); it is unsurprising, therefore, that they should manifest peculiarity in the *order* of their narration, since that order has no obvious historical pattern to follow.[47]

Unless Fronesis's education *were* in some way directed to the wholeness and perfection of the New Man, we would feel, as Wetherbee does (along with many other critics), that the poem is radically incoherent. We would also feel that the poem has, effectively, two hero figures. And we would, furthermore, feel that the poem offers two distinct and contradictory versions of human perfection – the natural perfection of the *aetas aurea* at the end of Book IX, and the intellectual perfection of Fronesis in Book VI. In the natural order of the poem, however, these problems point not to incoherence and contradiction, but rather to a fascinating wholeness and unity of conception. One can see, that is, how Fronesis's education contributes to the wholeness and perfection of the New Man, since Fronesis represents the intellectual resources of that naturally perfect soul. For the same reason, there is only one hero figure in the poem. Equally, the work ultimately offers only one version of human perfection, which is constituted by theological intuition of the soul's origins.

---

[45] Wetherbee 1973, pp. 113–14.
[46] *Cosmographia, Microcosmos*, VIII, in Dronke 1978, pp. 137–8; Wetherbee 1973, p. 109.
[47] See below, nn. 50–1.

It is essential that Alan should pose two models of perfection, the natural and the theological, at the two climaxes of the poem (Book VI.428–51, the creation of the soul, and Book XI.380–409, the establishment of the *aetas aurea*); it is not simply the case that the perfection of the natural man is a flimsy feint for man's real, religious perfection. On the contrary, both versions of perfection in the poem have their own coherence and force, as one climaxes the artificial order (the perfection of Nature) and the other climaxes the natural order (the perfection of the intellect). The perfection of Nature might lead us back to the perfection of the soul, but the perfection of the soul equally leads us forward to the perfection of Nature. But even if these two versions of human perfection are placed in tension, it remains the case that the kind of perfection promoted by the natural order of the poem – the theological perfection as Fronesis recognizes the origins of the soul in Book VI (lines 428–51) – is ultimately given priority. At the same time, it is clearly not the case that Alan wishes to place theological perfection at the expense of the new world order promised in the Golden Age of Book IX; the political *renovatio* promised in Book IX can only be fully achieved by the philosopher–king, who understands the ultimate status of Nature. Political perfection is not posed, I think, as a mere stepping stone on the road to theological understanding; it is precisely the understanding of the soul's origins in Book VI which underwrites the prophetic *renovatio* in Book IX.

And correlative with the proposition that there is only one hero-figure in the poem is the further point that the chariot of Fronesis is the chariot of the soul. I referred earlier to the arguments of Jung on this point, who argues cogently that the chariot of Fronesis cannot be the chariot of the soul, since Fronesis is voyaging in the chariot precisely to ask for a soul. But once we understand the poem in the order I suggest, the iconographic image of the chariot of the soul – an image which Alan uses in other works – regains its coherence: the chariot constructed by the Arts, drawn by the senses, and driven by Reason and Fronesis, is the chariot of the New Man's soul.[48]

---

[48] Alan was certainly familiar with the Platonic image of the chariot of the soul; he uses it in the *Sermo de sphaera intelligibili*, for example; see d'Alverny 1965, p. 302, and n. 41, for further examples. The image was celebrated through its appearance in Boethius, *De consolatione Philosophiae*, III, metre 9, lines 18–21. It was also available to Alan through Calcidius's commentary on the *Timaeus*, Waszink 1962, 41.E, p. 36.

The third and final supporting argument concerns the place of moral perfection in Fronesis's journey. An important aspect of my argument is that the moral narrative of the last three books in fact precedes (in the natural order of the poem) the noetic narrative of the first six books. Is there any evidence that the noetic progress of Fronesis in fact *presupposes* moral perfection of the kind we see represented in the poem's last three books?

I think there is. On the very border of the empyrean – on the verge, that is, of Fronesis's theological formation – Alan describes how the realm of the empyrean is difficult of access. One aspect of this difficulty is that even for the virtuous entry is not guaranteed: 'que paucis peruia multis / Clauditur, arta nimis uirtuti, larga ruine' (v.60–1) (which offers passage to few but is closed to many, is very narrow even for the virtuous and open for destruction (p. 139, modified)). It is clear that moral virtue does not guarantee entry into this paradise; it is, however, a necessary minimum. Alan continues by specifying the moral qualities which are necessary for entry; these are more restricted than the inclusive series of courtly virtues described in both Books I and VII. The list here describes the moral qualities necessary for the philosopher and theologian in particular, rather than a ruler: here there is no mention of Youth or Laughter. The conception of virtue here does not reject the courtly virtues of the last three books, but it does demand a spiritual detachment from the trappings of power:

> Non huc nobilitas generis, non gracia forme,
> Non gaze deiectus amor, non gloria rerum,
> Non mundanus apex, non uirtus corporis, audax
> Improbitas hominis, preceps audacia tendit,
> Sed solum uirtus animi, constancia mentis
> Factaque nobilitas, non nata sed insita menti,
> Interior species, uirtutum copia, morum
> Regula, paupertas mundi, contemptus honoris. (v.62–9)

Not nobility of lineage, not the charm of beauty, not the abandoned love of riches, not glory from accomplishments, not the highest worldly honour, not strength of body, not the presumptuous improbity of a man, not unrestrained temerity leads thither, but virtue of soul, constancy of mind, nobility attained not by birth but cultivated in the heart, interior beauty, a host of virtues, rule of life, poverty in worldly goods, contempt of position. (p. 139, modified)

When we compare this with the list of virtues that bestow their gifts on the New Man, it strikes us by the difference it implies: Concordia, Copia, Favor, Iuventus, Risus, Pudor, Modestia, Prudentia, Pietas, Fides, Largitas, Nobilitas. One set of virtues applies to the philosopher, another to the courtly ruler. But these virtues are not contradictory: they certainly stand in tension with each other, since the virtues required of the philosopher demand a dispassionate detachment from worldly grace, fame and riches. But if these two sets of virtues are placed in tension with each other through the double ordering of the poem, that tension is not debilitating or ultimately confusing: the point Alan is making is that a successful ruler necessarily requires courtly virtues; in important ways, these virtues *prepare* him for philosophical development (especially those virtues which derive from the Cardinal Virtues). But if these virtues are in important ways a preparation for philosophical and theological development, they must at the same time be reviewed and set at a distance (particularly the gift of nobility of blood). An ethics grounded in the *honestum* and *utile* (an ethics of honour) must be constrained by an ethics of conscience.

The argument of this chapter would clearly have it that Alan is consciously placing himself in the same tradition of noetic fiction defined by Bernard Silvestris in his *Aeneid* commentary. Bernard uncovers the philosophical sense of the *Aeneid* through his recognition that Virgil's work has a double order, one the order of poetry (the artificial order), the other the order of philosophy (the natural order). As in Bernard's sense of the *Aeneid*, in the *Anticlaudianus* there are two orders, the poetic and the philosophical, present in the single poem. The artificial, poetic order is perceived as the outer form of the poem, whereas the natural, philosophical order is organized around the poem's inner form, or shaping idea. The meeting point of these two orders is the moment when Fronesis perceives the making of the human soul:

> Ipse Deus rem prosequitur, producit in actum
> Que pepigit. Vocat ergo Noym, que preparet illi
> Numinis exemplar, humane mentis ydeam,
> Ad cuius formam formetur spiritus...   (VI.428–31)

God himself pursues the task and proceeds to realise his determination. Accordingly, He calls Noys to prepare for Him an exemplar for this divine being, an archetype of the human soul, so that the spirit may be made to conform to its form. (p. 170)

Perception of the '*ydea*' or archetype of the human soul, then, equally marks perception of the 'archetype', or informing idea, of the poem itself, since this moment is the hinge of the poem's natural order. This moment in which the soul's origins are understood is the fulcrum of the poem, the point of mediation between the theoretical development of Books I–VI and the practical development of Books VII–IX. An anthropology mediates, that is, a cosmology and a politics. Alan has created an artefact which offers an analogy to God's own making, and which, like God's handiwork, is animated by a 'supercelestial form' that we can perceive through the intellect. This enactment of the Platonic experience is at the heart of the poem.[49]

But whereas Bernard's own interpretation of the *Aeneid* might be unsatisfying in its arbitrary impositions of meaning, the 'more subtle allegory' of the *Anticlaudianus* seems to me remarkably coherent with the narrative which gives rise to it. In Bernard's interpretation of the *Aeneid*, there is nothing in the artificial order of the poem which provokes the reader to seek out the natural, philosophical order (or Bernard never demonstrates this, at any rate). On the contrary, in fact: the philosophic order of the poem is felt to be completely separate from the poetic, artificial plot. In Alan's poem, by distinction, the natural, philosophic order of the poem is not arbitrarily imposed on the artificial plot. Instead, the *Anticlaudianus* is entirely coherent in conception, insofar as the very problems posed by the artificial order of the poem provoke the reader to look for solutions to them. The troubling order of sciences, with the practical following the theoretical, provokes us to consider how else the the poem might be ordered; the troubling culmination of

---

[49] It is apposite here to remember what seems to me an exact and far-reaching statement by Huizinga. In section IV of his book on the relations between the poetic and the theological in Alan's works, Huizinga discusses Alan's uses of pictures; he says that through poetic pictures, Alan wants to express what his theology cannot, 'das zentrale Wunder der Erschaffung der Formen' (Huizinga 1932, p. 65). I shall develop this point in chapter 8.

My interpretation of the *Anticlaudianus* as itself a theological artefact, which requires a theological hermeneutics, may be relevant to the long-running debate in Dante scholarship about whether or not a human poet can presume to write in the manner of God; Alan most certainly does presume to model his making on God's.

the poem in the purely natural victory of virtue, unaided by grace, provokes us to think more deeply about the way in which moral development and human perfection is really imagined here. And the puzzling absence of the poem's hero for most of the poem provokes us to look again at Fronesis's voyage, and to recognize that in a profound sense the hero is not absent, but in formation, travelling to theological, intellectual perception in the chariot of his soul. Unlike the practice of much typological exegesis, and unlike the imposition of many moral and physical allegories on pagan fable in the twelfth century, Alan practises an allegory which is entirely coherent, and in which the poetic surface of the text has its own density and strength, rather than being simply tossed away as the exterior cortex of an inner form. Equally, Alan cannot be said to have written a noetic and ethical treatise in verse: the creative information of the *Anticlaudianus* ensures that the stabilities and certainties of the orthodox treatise are upset, and seen in a fresh light, providing, through poetry, a new philosophical 'information'.

It is in Timaean-inspired poetry that we should expect problems of ordering: the *Timaeus* represents a cosmos in which the essential relations are ones of position in a rational order, rather than sequence in time, synchronic rather than diachronic, structuralist rather than historical.[50] Understanding of the Timaean universe, as of a Timaean-inspired poem, depends above all on a sense of its synchronic wholeness rather than on its development through time. We can see this in the *Timaeus* itself, where Plato says that although the world soul is described after the body of the universe, we should not understand this to mean that the soul was created later in time than the body.[51] In chapter 8 I will show how Alan's concept of poetry as painting is derived from his cosmology – one sees a painting all at once, rather than reading it, as one reads a poem, sequentially. And in the next chapter we shall investigate the new, specifically poetic meanings which emerge through Alan's allegorical ordering. But for the moment, we can leave this chapter with the reflection that if Plato reorders narrative and historical time in

---

[50] See Stock 1972, p. 8 for a lucid distinction between the 'historical' and 'structural' approach to meaning: 'In the historical, the natural order was subordinated to historical genesis; in the structural, history was subordinated to rational order. According to the historical interpretation, the world had a beginning and, presumably, an end; in the structural, the world underwent transformations, but was in essence eternal.' These comments point to the profoundly a-historical consciousness of Alan in his literary works.

[51] Cornford 1937, 34B-C, pp. 58–9.

his account of the formation of the world, then so too does Alan reorder temporal sequence in his representation of educational formation. What is important is not so much the sequence, but the inter-relations of all the parts.

CHAPTER 4

Alan's philosopher–king

INTRODUCTION

In a fascinating aside to his exposition of the *involucra* of pagan philosophers in the *Theologia christiana* (1122–7), Abelard registers a possible objection from his critics. He has argued that pagan philosophical fables are foreshadowings of Christian truth; so, he imagines, his detractors will accuse him of having distorted the *real*, historical sense of pagan *integumenta* in order to make them conform to Christian orthodoxy:

> If, however, anyone should object that I am an unfit and destructive expositor, by arguing that I have twisted the words of the philosophers to agree with our faith by an exceedingly poor interpretation, and that I have imposed meanings on them which they did not intend at all...

> Si quis autem me quasi importunum ac violentum expositorem causetur, eo quod nimis improba expositione ad fidem nostram verba philosphorum detorqueam et hoc eis imponam quod nequaquam ipsi senserint...

He goes on to answer the charge by saying that the philosophers spoke better than they knew, unknowingly inspired by the Holy Spirit.[1] I relate this hermeneutic reflection here because I feel open to the same criticism as Abelard: just as he thinks that he might be accused of twisting the sense of the texts he interprets in order to make them conform to a present orthodoxy, so too, it could be argued, does my interpretation of the *Anticlaudianus* adjust the literal sense of the poem to make it square with an orthodoxy. Certainly I am on safer ground than Abelard, since the 'orthodoxy' to which I refer the poem is, if not dominant, at least contemporary with my author, and an orthodoxy to which he had open access – indeed, which he actively formed in his other writings.

---

[1] Buytaert 1969, I.117, p. 121.

But, it might still be argued, I have 'rewritten' the poem with the effect of reducing what seems most striking and daring to what is relatively orthodox. Alan presents a remarkably optimistic vision of natural achievement and human perfection in Book IX, with the Golden Age established through the purely natural, political virtues of the *novus homo*. My argument of the preceding chapter would have it that this culmination is only apparent: in the *real* (natural) order of the poem, the achievement of natural perfection is the prelude to, even the provocation to, a speculative journey to self-knowledge which ultimately requires grace. Practical knowledge precedes theoretical, nature precedes grace, and everything follows in an orthodox order. I seem, that is, to have flattened, even 'twisted' what appeared striking, daring and new about this poem back into a more familiar shape.

In this chapter, I want to refute this charge. Both orders, I shall argue, retain their coherence and force. There are two orders in the poem, not one 'real' order and one illusory veil. It is not the case that politics is merely a staging post on the way to theology; on the contrary, the poem as a whole presents the picture of a philosopher–king, whose political victory can be sustained only through a speculative self-knowledge, a self-knowledge which itself requires knowledge of the cosmos. But self-knowledge through cosmology is not an end point in itself – it leads back into a politics. Just as a politics calls forth a cosmology, so too does the cosmology point back to a politics. Something new is being realized in Alan's poem, of which strictly philosophical structures are incapable: the constellation of the sciences, both practical and theoretical, is being set into a reciprocal relation, and politics remains, I think, the essential focus of attention.

The division of argument in this chapter is as follows: I want first to develop the idea that politics and cosmology stand in a reciprocal relation in the poem; I will then give my answer to the question which has puzzled almost every reader, medieval and modern, of Alan's poem: who is the New Man?

NEO-PLATONIC COSMOLOGY AND POLITICS

In Plato's (*c.* 428–*c.* 348 BC) *Republic* the ideal king is also the ideal philosopher. The *Republic*, of course, was unknown by Alan as a full text, but the one Platonic text which was partially known by him was the *Timaeus*, Plato's cosmological fable.[2] However much the *Timaeus* is concerned with the making of the cosmos and of man, it is nevertheless closely keyed in with political questions and political texts. The dialogue begins, in Plato's fiction at least, on the day after the dialogue of the *Republic*. Socrates begins by summarizing certain aspects of the city-state imagined the day before, one element of which is the nature of the state's guardians, who must be (in the words of Calcidius's Latin translation), 'in tutela patriae ciuiumque ferociores, porro in pacis officiis religione sapientes' – 'both more fierce in protection of the state and its citizens, and, furthermore, wise through duty in peacetime offices'.[3] This conception of governance, as combining both political and philosophical values, constitutes the central ideal of the *Republic*, but it is clear from the positioning of the *Timaeus* that the philosophic wisdom of the ruler is not restricted to wisdom in political matters alone. For the cosmological narrative of the *Timaeus* is born out of, and designed to lead back into, exactly those questions of the state raised in the *Republic*.

After his recapitulation of the previous day's discussion, Socrates continues by saying that he would like to see this ideal city set in motion, but that both he, as a philosopher ignorant of war, and the poets who cannot imagine something unknown to them, are unable to bring such an ideal state to life. Only his guests, who are both philosophers and rulers, are capable of this. And so it is agreed that Timaeus should begin by accounting for the formation of the universe and of man, before Critias should take up these new made men, created by Timaeus and educated by Socrates, and 'bring them before our tribunal and make them fellow citizens ... In the rest of our discourse we shall take their claim to the citizenship of Athens as established.'[4]

The dialogue is unfinished, since only Timaeus speaks. But we might see two challenges to a poet implicit within this overture to the dialogue: on the one hand, a poet might take up the challenge to step into the visionary territory of which Socrates says poets are

---

[2]   Although the actual content of Plato's *Republic* was known only through repeated snippets, it was well known by reputation. See Klibansky 1939, pp. 21–31, and Dutton, 1983, pp. 79–119.

[3]   Waszink 1962, 18A, p. 8, lines 12–13. For the political conception of the *Timaeus*, see Hardie 1986, p. 71.

[4]   Cited from Cornford 1937, 27B, p. 20; Waszink 1962, 27B, pp. 19–20, lines 22–3.

incapable; on the other, a writer responding to Plato's text might complete it, by drawing the cosmological matter into line with the political narrative promised but unachieved in the ancient dialogue. I will argue that Alan meets both these challenges, but for the moment we can leave the *Timaeus* itself with the observation that the cosmological narrative is both the product of, and the prelude to, discussion of politics.

As with the one source of Greek cosmology with which Alan was familiar, so too with one of the main sources of Roman cosmology: following Plato, who ends the *Republic* with a reported vision of the afterworld, Cicero concludes his *De republica* (54–51 BC) with an account of the heavens, as witnessed by Scipio in his dream. This narrative, preserved in Macrobius's (fl. late 4th, early 5th century) commentary,[5] was in fact the only section of the larger work that survived in the medieval period. But however much the cosmology has once again been artificially truncated from the political setting to which it naturally belongs, the closeness of connection between the two fields of enquiry is evident from within the text. Macrobius recognizes that not all rulers will be capable of theoretical wisdom, but the ideal ruler, he implies, will combine practical with theoretical understanding. Both kinds of knowledge make a man blessed, and very occasionally they are found mixed in the same man:

> In an early part of this work we noted that men of leisure possessed some virtues and men of affairs others, that the former virtues befitted philosophers and the latter the leaders in public welfare, and that the exercise of both made one blessed. These virtues are sometimes separated, but they are occasionally combined when a man by disposition and training is found to have a capacity for both.[6]

> ...in superiore huius operis parte diximus alias otiosas, alias negotiosas esse virtutes, et illas philosophis, has rerum publicarum rectoribus convenire, utrasque tamen exercentem facere beatum. Hae virtutes interdum dividuntur, non numquam vero miscentur, cum utrarumque capax et natura et institutione animus invenitur.[7]

---

[5] For the nature and influence of Macrobius's commentary on Cicero's *Somnium Scipionis*, see Stahl 1952, pp. 9–11 and pp. 39–55, and Gersh 1986, vol. 2, pp. 493–5. For the twelfth-century reception of Macrobius's commentary, see Jeauneau 1960 (discussing William of Conches's commentary on the commentary of Macrobius). Hardie 1986, pp. 71–6, provides an account of cosmological-political relations in Cicero's *De republica*.

[6] Stahl 1952, II.17.4, p. 244.   [7] Willis 1970, II.17.4, p. 151.

The earlier part of the work to which Macrobius refers here is Book I.8, in which he confirms the justification for a cosmology within a treatise on politics. Cicero's text, in the person of Scipio Africanus, asserts that all those who have served the republic shall be saved, and that the vision of the afterworld should strengthen the statesman in his assurance of salvation. Macrobius confirms this by outlining the ways in which the purely philosophical spirit will be saved by the exercise of the cardinal virtues in rejection of the world,[8] whereas the ruler will be saved by the exercise of those same virtues in governance of the state. Like Alan, Macrobius specifically calls such virtues 'political'.[9] This is, essentially, the passage we find abridged in Chaucer's *Parlement of Fowls*:

> Thanne preyede hym Scipion to telle hym al
> The wey to come into that hevene blisse.
> And he seyde, 'Know thyself first immortal,
> And loke ay besyly thow werche and wysse
> To commune profit, and thow shalt not mysse
> To comen swiftly to that place deere
> That ful of blysse is and of soules cleere.   (lines 71–7)[10]

---

[8]   The cardinal virtues as exercised by the philosopher are similar to the virtues, both moral and intellectual, required of Alan's Fronesis as she ascends the heavens:

...prudence, that is, to despise the world and all that is in the world in contemplation of what is divine, and direct all the attention of the soul to divine things alone; temperance, to abstain from everything that the habits of the body seek, as far as nature will permit; courage, for the soul not to be terrified as it withdraws from the body, so to speak, under the guidance of philosophy, and have no dread of the dizzy heights of the complete ascension to the celestial realms; justice, to accept the only way to this mode of life, namely, obedience to each virtue. (Stahl 1952, I.8.4, p. 121)

[9]   As with the virtues required for theoretical perfection being very similar to those required by Fronesis, so too are the Cardinal Virtues, as exercised by a ruler, remarkably similar to the virtues required by the New Man:

To have political prudence one must direct all his [sic] thoughts and actions by the standard of reason... In prudence we find reason, understanding, circumspection, foresight, willingness to learn, and caution... Courage endows one with magnanimity, confidence, composure, nobleness, constancy, endurance, and steadfastness... Temperance is accompanied by modesty, humility, self-restraint, chastity, integrity, moderation, frugality, sobriety, and purity. To have political justice, one must safeguard for each man that which belongs to him. From justice comes uprightness, friendship, harmony, sense of duty, piety, love, and human sympathy. By these virtues the good man is first made lord of himself and then ruler of the state. (Stahl 1952, I.8.7–8, p. 122)

[10]   Benson 1988, lines 71–7, p. 386. (Unlike Alan, Chaucer does not, however, go as far as Macrobius, who asserts that the man who works for the common profit will become a god (Stahl 1952, I.9.6–10, pp. 125–6).)

So two of the main sources of cosmological theory for a twelfth-century writer consciously placed that cosmology within the context of political discourse, despite the fact that the accidents of textual transmission obscured the full force of that contextualization. Neither should we forget the *De consolatione Philosophiae* (*c.* 522–5) of Boethius here, which, although it is primarily speculative in interest, begins with an assertion of the wholeness of philosophy, in both its practical and theoretical branches. Philosophy's dress is decorated with the letters Π in the lower margin, with stairs ascending to θ in the higher.[11] The dress is torn, and Philosophy complains that different philosophical sects have torn off pieces, claiming to be in possession of the whole.[12] When Boethius begins to speak, it is clear that the essence of his problem is, in fact, an inability to see the wholeness of philosophy. He complains to Philosophy that he has ended up in prison precisely because he had followed Philosophy's own (Platonic) advice about philosophers engaging in politics:

Are these our rewards for obedient service to you? It was you who established through the words of Plato the principle that those states would be happy where philosophers were kings or their governors were philosophers.

Haecine praemia referimus tibi obsequentes? Atqui tu hanc sententiam Platonis ore sanxisti: beatas fore res publicas, si eas uel studiosi sapientiae regerent uel earum rectores studere sapientiae contigisset.[13]

But this charge against Philosophy has force only as long as Boethius thinks of the practical, especially political sciences, and the encouragement of Philosophy to practise them. Philosophy's strategy is to cure Boethius by giving him access to the speculative sciences. The treatment of the speculative sciences in this work only occurs as a complement to Boethius's enthusiastic but ultimately painful pursuit of the political good.

But if these essential sources of Neo-Platonic cosmology see politics and cosmology as intimately related, this connection remains unexplored in the main twelfth-century poetic response to the *Timaeus* prior to Alan. Thus in Bernard Silvestris's *Cosmographia* it is the creative and procreative action of the *Timaeus* which is devel-

---

[11] Stewart, Rand and Tester 1973, I, prose 1, 18–22, pp. 132–4.
[12] Ibid., I, prose 3, 10–30, pp. 140–2.　　　[13] Ibid., I, prose 4, 17–21, p. 146.

oped, largely cut off from a politics. Bernard develops the
idea of Nature as a coherent, inter-related, physical system deriv-
ing from the hand of a divine maker, but possessing its own
laws according to which the making of man mirrors the making
of the universe. The fundamental interests of this work are cosmological and anthropological.[14] It has been argued that Alan's original contribution to the elaboration of the Timaean model by
'Chartrian' thinkers is to have formally included a moral system
as part of the world of Nature: not only does anthropology, or
the make-up of man's soul and body, depend on and reflect
the make-up of the universe, but, in Alan's two literary works
(so the argument goes) an *ethical* system is also represented as
having a natural basis, and as belonging to a micro/macrocosmic
structure.[15]

I think this view is largely correct with regard to the *De planctu
Naturae*. But, as I shall now argue, the *Anticlaudianus* embraces a
much wider spectrum of interests. The focus of the *De planctu* is
indeed essentially ethical: the cosmology provides a frame, but the
accent of the work falls on moral regeneration. In the *Anticlaudianus*
on the other hand, the focus of the last three books is not only ethical, but also political. And the cosmology of Books IV–VI is presented not merely as the shadowy frame of political regeneration –
it is the necessary context of that regeneration, with its own coherence and force; its relations with the realm of the political are thoroughly reciprocal.

CONCORDIA

The inter-relation of cosmology and politics underlies the structure
of the whole poem, and we can see it especially clearly in the
role of Concord. As I argued in chapter 2, the presence of Concord
among the virtues who endow the New Man in Book VII is

---

[14] In his study of the idea of a tripartite society through Timaean traditions, Dutton 1983
remarks that Bernard passes over the political development of this idea: 'Thus while
Bernard knew various details of Calcidius's comparison of the body to the state and even
spoke of the body as a city, he preferred to use the latter to describe the former. He
moved directly from a description of the cosmos-state to the human body, bypassing the
image of the city-state and its orders of men' (p. 107).

[15] See Raynaud de Lage 1951, p. 73, and Ochsenbein 1975, pp. 126–8. Gregory 1958, pp.
144–9 makes the same point, though making clear that Alan's understanding of the relation of Nature and ethics has obvious Stoic influences.

anomalous as long as we consider the endowment of virtues only in the light of the practical virtues. In the *Moralium dogma*, as we have seen, Concord is given a purely political definition, as a part of justice: 'virtus concives et compatriotas in eodem iure et cohabitacione spontanee vincens'.[16] Certainly in the fight against the vices, it is this political aspect of the virtue which Alan stresses. The enemies of Concord are the first to attack, which appropriately places the emphasis of the whole battle on the political. Discord is beheaded by the New Man (IX.35–40) (reversing the making whole of the New Man's own body through Concord in Book VII), before her followers (Hatred, Contention, Anger, Rage, and Fear) are destroyed. So Alan does certainly present Concord here as a political value – Discord is, after all, described as the one through whom first arose the desire for war: 'primo conflictus et ire / Primeuique metus et belli prima cupido' (IX.39–40) ('at first conflict and rage, the first fears and the first desire for war' (p. 204)).

But despite this political presentation in Book IX, Concord remains an anomaly within the endowment of virtues in Book VII. For there she was described not as an ethical or political virtue, but rather as a cosmic force, who joins soul and body in the same way that she joins forces in the universe more generally:

> Sic nocti lucem connectit et ethera terre,
> Sic diuersa tenent pacem, sic dissona litem
> Deponunt propriam nec iam caro bella minatur,
> Spiritui cedens sed non sine murmure multo.　　　　(VII.62–5)

It is thus that she joins night and day, Ether and Earth. Thus contraries live in peace, discordants lay aside the contention natural to them and flesh no longer threatens war, as it yields to the spirit, though not without many a murmur. (p. 175)

If Concord's place in Alan's poem *were* anomalous, this would, after all, be all the more surprising in the very figure of Concord, who ties all things together with ingenious connectives: just as she joins soul to body with 'subtle adhesives' (*gunfis subtilibus*, VII.59), so too does she bring individual contributions to the chariot into harmony:

---

[16]　Holmberg, 1929, I.B.2, p. 27.

Apponensque manum supremam, fine beato
Concludens operam, sparsas Concordia partes
Ordine, lege, loco confederat, unit, adequat.
Ergo iunctura, clauis gumfisque ligate
Partes effigiant currum qui luce decoris
Preradians, facie propria demonstrat in ipso
Diuinam sudasse manum superumque Mineruam.   (IV.76–82)

Concord, applying the finishing touch, brings the work to a happy end, unites the scattered parts in order, binds them by law and fits them in place. With their articulations, nails and connections to unite them, they make a chariot which, as it gleams forth with the light of beauty, shows by its very appearance that a divine hand and Minerva from the gods above have toiled over it. (p. 120)

Concord's main function within the poem, then, is to promote integrity, a quality which, through the subtlety of its achievement, reveals a divine presence.

Does the poem become unhinged through its presentation of Concord? A poem which is so concerned in its represented action for the subtle unity of artefacts is surely unlikely to leave itself open to the charge of being incoherent. Although all critics have confessed themselves puzzled by the relation of the political renovation imagined in Book IX to the cosmological journey for self-knowledge in Books IV–VI, it is especially through the figure of Concord that their unity can be understood.[17] She remains an anomaly within the purely ethical and political endowment of the virtues only as long as we see this endowment separately from its place in the cosmological narrative of the first six books.

Concord first appears in Book I, leading the other virtues in response to Nature's call. But her first substantial contribution to the action is in Book II, as she mediates between Reason and

---

[17] All criticism which has broached the subject has confessed itself at a loss to account for the place of the ethical and political section of the poem (Books VII–IX) within its overall structure. The primary problem here was that critics until Ochsenbein could not perceive any coherence within the system of virtues in Books VII–IX, let alone see how they were related to Books I–VI. See Ochsenbein 1975, pp. 168–9 for a conspectus of views about the lack of coherence within the virtues. But Ochsenbein himself, who recognized the overall coherence of the virtues within themselves, does not see this part of the poem as coherently related to the narrative of Books I–VI (Ochsenbein 1975, p. 192). Wetherbee 1988, p. 52 and Wetherbee 1972, p. 217, make the same far-reaching criticism of the poem. Green (1967), does not broach the problem, laying the emphasis of his interpretation on Books I–VI.

Fronesis, Reason arguing that Fronesis should undertake the embassy to God, while Fronesis vacillates before the magnitude of the task. Concord's first contribution, then, is essentially one of *psychological* mediation, attempting to reconcile contradictory psychological impulses. I will return to this psychological point later in this chapter, but for the moment we should focus on the way in which her presentation there far exceeds the immediate needs of the narrative. Whereas the narrative action is one of psychological harmonizing, Concord is presented as a force of cosmic, political and ethical harmony.

Her body and dress are first described. On the dress are painted images of friendship – images of concord, that is, in the ethical or personal sphere: David and Jonathan, Theseus and Pirithous, Tydeus and Polynices, Nisus and Euryalus, Orestes and Pylades. In her speech (II.213–309), she enlarges these examples of personal concord by pointing to counter examples of both personal and political enmity. She begins by saying that if the world had once served her rules, or if it continued to serve them now, it would not have known internecine disasters. The examples she gives begin with familial slaughter (Atreus and Thyestes, Polynices and Etiocles, Progne and Tereus), but move to civil strife: she says that Troy would still be standing, before pointing to the terrible ends of the main players in the Roman civil wars – Crassus, Pompey, Caesar, Antony and Cleopatra. And from this account of civil strife, she enlarges her scope yet further by declaring that were it not for her power, the cosmos itself would experience internal chaos:

> Et nisi sponte meis obnoxia legibus essent
> Astra poli, celique uices, septemque planete
> Ordine, pace, fide, numero nexuque ligati,
> Omnia fortuitis ruerent incerta ruinis.
>
> (II.249–52)

If the stars in the sky, the alternations in the heavens and the seven planets were not the willing subjects of my laws and were not bound together by ties of order, peace, faithfulness, harmony and restraint, all of them without fixed direction would perish by chance crashes. (p. 77)

And, as the final part of the introductory statement of her case, she returns to her energies of harmonizing spiritual and physical powers within man:

> Ni mea corporibus animas iunctura ligasset,
> Dedignans habitare casas, ergastula carnis,
> Spiritus egrediens proprios remearet in ortus.   (II.253–5)

If my bond had not united souls to bodies, the spirit, refusing to live in a hovel, a penitentiary of flesh, would leave and return to its place of origin. (p. 77)

And from these introductory arguments, which have covered ethical, political, cosmic and psychological harmony, Concord broaches the essential petition of her speech, that Fronesis concur with the desires of Nature and the Virtues.

The ostensible object of this long speech is simply to persuade Fronesis to undertake the role of messenger to God. As I have said, the scope of the oration far exceeds its immediate petitionary object. But seen from the perspective of the whole poem, this speech provides an essential link between the noetic and the political parts of the poem: it is precisely the force for unity within the cosmos, the *polis* and the self which corroborates the psychological desire within the individual soul to undertake the noetic journey to God through the cosmos. And, equally, it is the same desire for concord which brings the soul back to earth to extend the harmony of the cosmos into the political sphere. Concord herself says, in the lines cited immediately above, that the soul would leave the body were it not for the principle of concord. The soul in this poem does return to its origins (*remearet in ortus*), but, given the principle of concord operating through the action of the whole poem, we should not imagine it as having definitively left the body and the human world behind. Cosmology, and an understanding of the cosmos, provoke (in the narrative of the poem) a return to the body and the world of human society. Cosmology and politics are, that is, intimately related; the soul, integrated in the body, achieves its fullness only through reciprocal understanding of both sciences.

IUSTICIA NATURALIS, IUSTICIA DIVINA

So Concord does appear as an essentially political value in the fight against Discord and her followers in Book IX; but this political presentation is intrinsically related to her role as the force which binds soul and body in Book VII, as it is to her role as the force which binds the universe as presented in Book II. Whereas, as I have mentioned, some twelfth-century poets (and I am thinking especially of Bernard Silvestris's *Cosmographia*) received the Timaeian model as primarily a pattern of cosmological and anthropological reflection, Alan restores the cosmology and anthropology of the *Timaeus* to its rightful place, as originating from, and leading back into, a politics.

In doing so, he was not, however, by any means alone: a coherent tradition of commentaries on the *Timaeus* insist on the intimate connection between cosmology and politics. But even here, we can see Alan's individual contribution. For Alan the ultimate sources of power are in a sense *un*natural and inaccessible to human reason, whereas the *Timaeus* commentaries, as we shall see, give an entirely rationalist, naturalist account of human justice.

Macrobius's placing of cosmology and politics, in his commentary on the *Dream of Scipio*, is relatively superficial: if a man works for the republic, then he will be rewarded in heaven; the vision of heaven is designed to strengthen the faith of the statesman. In the *Timaeus*, on the other hand, the connection is much closer – Socrates wants to set his ideal republic in motion, and to do so, Timaeus will recount the creation of the world and of man by way of producing 'new men' for the visionary republic. Twelfth-century commentators on the *Timaeus* were consistently alert to the intimacy of connection between politics and cosmology in the prologues to their commentaries. In particular, they stress how the treatment of positive justice in the *Republic* calls forth an account of natural justice, upon which positive justice is based. And natural justice can only be understood through a cosmology. There is much in these commentaries which suggests the *Anticlaudianus*; equally, I will argue, Alan takes issue with their purely naturalist accounts of justice.

Let us take, for example, the anonymous commentary preserved in Vienna, Nationalbibliothek, Latin 2376.2, excerpts of which have been published by Tullio Gregory. The commentator begins, as does the *Timaeus* itself, by treating the previous dialogue, that of the *Republic*. He says that Socrates had imagined (*adumbravit*) an ideal city to prove his point that justice helped especially the weak. Justice, says the commentator, is defined as 'giving to each that which is his', but it can be either positive or natural:

one kind [of justice] is positive, that is customary, pertaining to the ordinances of men, both written and non-written; the other kind is natural justice, which teaches us to show reverence to God and to our elders, dutifulness towards our parents, and love to those deserving of it. Positive justice instructs our moral sense to flee those actions which should be rejected, especially through fear – that is by weighing the punishments and rewards for our deserts. Natural justice is common to both God and men, and produces its effects rather through love.

alia species positiva, idest consuetudinaria, pertinens ad hominum instituta tam scripta quam non scripta; alia naturalis, que docet reverentiam deo et maioribus exhibere, parentibus pietatem, dilectionem diligendis communicare. Positiva spernenda fugere mores instruit, maxime ex timore, scilicet ex meritis penas pensans et premia. Naturalis deo communis et hominibus ex dilectione magis operatur.[18]

But these two species of justice are not, of course, unrelated. Therefore, the commentator continues, a representation of *positive* justice will call forth an account of natural justice, as the *Republic* calls forth the *Timaeus*:

Since, therefore, Socrates had taught in ten books that the imagined republic should be administered sometimes by natural justice, sometimes by other kinds, it remained to investigate natural justice, which is the source and origin of positive justice.

Cum ergo Socrates rem publicam adumbratam tum positiva iusticia tum aliis administrari decem libris docuisset, superesset vero naturalis inquisitio iusticie que fons est et origo positive.[19]

But this immediately requires a treatment of the cosmos more generally:

---

[18] Gregory 1958, p. 67. See Gregory 1958, pp. 59–73 (earlier printed in Gregory 1955) for examples of the way in which all the *accessus* stress the connection between cosmology and politics. He introduces the topic by commenting that 'negli *accessus* al *Timeo* torna insistentemente un motivo centrale: materia del dialogo è la *naturalis iustitia sive mundi creatio*, la cui conoscenza è indispensabile per fondare la *positiva iustitia* che della naturale deve essere trascrizione fedele' (p. 59). See Gibson 1969, p. 188 for a list of *Timaeus* commentaries. She comments that 'each is drawing on the same material for the same purposes in virtually the same manner' (p. 189). On p. 188 she remarks that the Viennese commentary which I cite here is also found in Germany, France and England, surviving in five manuscripts: 'It was in circulation in the mid- and later twelfth century.' See Jeauneau 1965, pp. 58–9, for William of Conches's treatment of the relation between cosmology and politics in the *accessus* to his commentary on the *Timaeus*. See also Jeauneau 1973, pp. 209–27 for relevant excerpts from Avranches, Municipal Library, 226. For the central importance of the distinction, as made in these *accessus* (and particularly in that of William of Conches), to the concept of positive law in legal discourse, see Gagner 1960, pp. 179–240, especially pp. 236–40. [19] Gregory 1958, p. 67.

And because Plato wished to treat natural justice in its entirety, he began with the creation of the world. In whose creation, by the disposition of the parts, and by the separation of the celestial and non-celestial, he showed the power of natural justice that the Creator manifested towards his creature, by granting, out of love alone, to each that which is his naturally.

Et quia Plato de naturali iusticia plene agere voluit a genitura sensilis mundi cepit. In cuius creatione, partium ordinatione et celestium et non celestium discretione, naturalis vim iusticie docuit qua creator erga creaturam usus est, ex sola dilectione tribuendo quod suum est cuique naturaliter.[20]

And, once the cosmos and man have been created according to the principles of natural justice, Plato instructs men in those very virtues:

Then, once men had been created, he instructed them in morals, and adorned them with virtues, thus showing when natural justice most flourishes in men, that is in their first age, and through all these things he invites us to the exercise of natural justice.

Deinde creatis hominibus moribus eos instruit, virtutibus exornat sic ostendens quando naturalis iusticia maxime viguit in hominibus, scilicet etate prima, et per hec omnia nos invitat ad naturalis exercitium iusticie.[21]

The structural principles of the *Anticlaudianus* (as I read it) are visible in this discussion of the *Timaeus*: although Alan is not concerned with positive law (as Gower is), the establishment of natural justice on earth requires an understanding of the basis of natural justice, which is perceived in the structure of the cosmos. Cosmology, morality and politics are conceived of as distinct yet profoundly inter-related fields. And all point, in the view of this, and other commentators of the *Timaeus*, towards the governance of the state. When this commentator goes on to account for the utility of the *Timaeus*, he says that according to some, Plato intends to teach us how we should learn to administer a republic from our reading of the work; its ultimate purpose is to seek out the 'fruit which Macrobius promises to govenors and administrators of the republic'. According to others, the accent is more on the natural justice of cosmic concord (and again one thinks of the importance of Concord for Alan):

[20] Ibid., p. 68.   [21] Ibid.

Or according to others the principal matter [of this work] is the generation of the physical world, in which natural justice is understood, through
which the gods concur amongst themselves, and by which this world and
those things which are of it are ruled harmoniously by the gods. For even
though the elements should have some contrary qualities, one never
makes an incursion into the office of another. According to these commentators, natural justice is a concord amongst all things.

Vel secundum alios principalis materia est generatio sensilis mundi in qua
investigatur naturalis iusticia per quam dii concordant inter se et hic
mundus et que sunt eius ab illis reguntur concorditer. Nam licet elementa
quasdam habeant contrarias qualitates, numquam tamen una transit in
officium alterius. Est autem secundum hos naturalis iusticia rerum
omnium concordia.[22]

So we find in this commentary (and it is representative of a
coherent tradition) confirmation that Alan's reading of (and 'completion' of) the *Timaeus* is by no means exceptional: to see the
establishment of natural justice through the ideal ruler of Book IX
as intimately connected with the cosmic journey is consistent with
the relations between politics and cosmology posited by all these
commentators.

But there are nevertheless critical differences between Alan and
the naturalizing thesis of these commentaries. For the commentators, justice (both natural and positive) in human affairs finds its
'*fons et origo*' in the natural justice of the cosmos. For Alan, on the
contrary, the natural justice in human affairs seeks its exemplar
ultimately in the divine rather than the natural. By way of concluding this discussion of the relations between cosmology and politics,
let me briefly elaborate these differences.

As I read the poem, the climax of natural perfection with
the establishment of the Golden Age at the end of Book IX can
only be a provisional victory. The poem seems to grant an astonishing primacy to politics and to human perfection through
the practical rather than speculative sciences. But if we read the
poem as having two orders, an artificial order (which we read) and
a natural order (which we perceive below the surface of the
artificial order), then we see that the image of natural perfection
is a prelude to a further, higher perfection through self-understanding. It is true, as I have argued, that the 'higher perfection'

---

[22]　Ibid.

of self-knowledge is itself a basis for political rule: relations between cosmology and politics are reciprocal. But it is equally true that the double order of the poem contains within it a *critique* of natural perfection and natural justice as being self-sufficient.

Once we read the poem's natural order as leading us from its apparent end in Book IX to its apparent beginning in Book I, the fact and nature of this critique become evident. Surely one of the conditions of my argument about the poem's preposterous order must be that the 'beginning' of the poem (in Book I) is a plausible continuation of its ostensible ending in Book IX. In fact the beginning and end of the poem are extremely similar.

Book IX ends with an *aetas aurea* established through the victory of the New Man, who has fought with the arms of the Virtues. The Virgilian scene[23] is described thus:

> Nec iam corrigitur rastro, nec uomere campus
> Leditur, aut curui deplorat uulnus aratri,
> Ut tellus auido, quamuis inuita, colono
> Pareat, et semen multo cum fenore reddat.
> Non arbor cultrum querit, non uinea falcem,
> Sed fructus dat sponte nouos et uota coloni
> Fertilitate premit. (IX.396–402)

No longer is the field brought to order by the hoe, or wounded by the ploughshare, no longer does it bemoan the scars inflicted by the curved plough to make it, however unwilling, obey the greedy husbandman and return the seed with high interest. The tree does not need the knife nor the vineyard the pruning-hook. They bear new fruit of their own accord and surpass in fertility the husbandman's prayers. (p. 216, modified)

The poem begins, in Book I, with a description of Nature's domain. It, too, depicts a *locus amoenus*, drawn from exactly the same traditions of the Golden Age as the description in Book IX:

---

[23] The scene of the Golden Age is indebted especially to Virgil's Fourth Eclogue, lines 37–45, not only for verbal borrowings, but also in its conceptual placing: in both panegyrics, the Golden Age will arrive with the maturity of a perfect ruler. Of course the Golden Age is also described in Ovid, *Metamorphoses* I.101–12. But Ovid's conceptual placing of the perfect time is utterly different from that of both Virgil and Alan: for Ovid the Golden Age is in the irretrievable past, whereas Virgil and Alan predict its coming. Claudian is relevant, here, too: see chapter 9, n. 11.

Iste parit, nullo vexatus uomere, quicquid
Militat aduersum morbos nostramque renodat,
Instantis morbi proscripta peste, salutem.
Non uulgus uerum, uerum miracula gignens
Sponte nec externo tellus adiuta colono,
Nature contenta manu Zephirique fauore,
Parturit et tanta natorum prole superbit.   (I.74–80)

Untroubled by the ploughshare, this land produces everything that wars
against disease and, banishing the bane of harrassing illness, restores our
health. Without the extraneous aid of husbandman, content with Nature's
hand and the favouring Zephyrus, the land bears and gives birth not
indeed to common produce but to things wondrous, and it prides itself on
a progeny so large. (p. 47)

Certainly, there are important differences between the two scenes:
in the first, the palace of Nature is described as being far from our
regions (though clearly not in heaven), and the Virtues as a group
are said only to tolerate (rather than enjoy) the unpleasantness of
the world (*tolerans fastidia mundi*), preferring the court of heaven. In
Book IX, on the contrary, the Golden Age is very definitely located
on earth ('Iam celo contendit humus, jam terra nitorem / Induit
ethereum'), and the virtues are said to set up camp willingly on
earth:

Virtutes mundumque regunt, nec iam magis illis
Astra placent sedesque poli quam terrenus orbis.   (IX.392–3)

The Virtues guide the world; the stars and the abodes at the poles are
now no more pleasing to them than the earthly sphere. (p. 216)

But what can the force of this final triumph on earth be when
the palace of Nature is itself fundamentally flawed? The ensemble
of virtues that aids the New Man in his fight against the vices is
exactly the same as the set that comes to Nature's council. There is
no new, extra force available to this set of virtues as they are represented at the end of the poem: just as in Book I, they represent the
powers of Nature individually, unaided by grace. And if this is true,
then how can we accept the triumph of Book IX as definitive and
stable? The poem begins, as we know, with Nature's desire for a
further perfection, and her recognition that, although some live
well, none live *in omni parte beate*. Although Nature does lament the
presence of sin on earth (as she does in section 8 of the *De planctu*),

it is important to note that there is an essential difference between the laments of Alan's two poems: in the *Anticlaudianus* Nature's complaint falls largely on *herself*, rather than on humans who have failed to achieve natural perfection.[24] After all, she is lamenting the fact that even those whom she has fashioned with her right hand (i.e. models of human, natural perfection) can level complaints against her skill (1.214–18).[25] The implication of this self-accusation is, I think, that even within the limits of natural perfection, there is still room for lament. And even if those who are naturally perfect can still accuse Nature of not providing perfection *in omni parte*, it is equally true that many fall well short of natural perfection anyway. But the burden of Nature's lament is not aimed wholly at sinful humans; it falls largely on herself, and only secondarily on humans:

> Heu! pudeat nostrum tociens errasse laborem
> Et tociens fructum male respondisse labori!
> Heu! pudeat nostra terris decreta silere,
> Quod nostri languescit amor, quod fama tepescens
> Torpet et a toto uiles proscribimur orbe. (1.256–60)

Alas! let us feel shame that our work so often missed the mark, and that the result was so often a poor return for our effort. Alas! let us feel shame that our decrees for the earth get no hearing beacause love for us grows cold, our waning reputation loses its power, we are exiled from the whole world as useless. (p. 56)

All the verbs in the last three lines of this passage imply that Nature *has* ruled on earth in the past, but that her power is failing. If this is the case here, then how can the reader have any confidence in the stability of the Golden Age of Book IX? The forces of Nature are clearly inadequate in Book I against the full force of vice. If, in Book IX, as we have seen, the New Man is empowered by exactly those courtly, purely natural virtues who come to Nature in Book I,

---

[24] I am indebted to Ochsenbein 1975, pp. 133–5 for the differences between Nature's lament in the *De planctu* and the *Anticlaudianus*.

[25] For the iconography of Nature's right and left hands, see *De planctu Naturae* XVIII, lines 64–85 (Häring 1978, pp. 875–6). If Nature's initial complaint in the *De planctu* puts the blame on humans, the presentation of Genius makes it clear that human defects also come from the natural endowments of men: Genius informs models of natural human perfection with his right hand, while his left produces deformed products (*De planctu Naturae*, XVIII.64–91 (Häring 1978, pp. 875–6)). In the *De planctu*, Nature is complaining only about those who are fashioned by the left hand; in the *Anticlaudianus* she complains on behalf of those fashioned by her right hand.

and no others, then how can the victory of Nature in Book IX be permanent? Nature's opening lament implies past victories of Nature which have now given way to the onset of disorder.

So the beginning of the poem as I read it contains the critique of its ending. A further critique of Nature and, therefore, of the victory in Book IX, is made on the walls of Nature's palace. There we find murals depicting human perfection within the bounds of Nature: images of Aristotle, Plato, Seneca, Ptolemy, Cicero and Virgil adorn the walls, representing perfection of human knowledge; beside them we find images of ideal men of action: Hercules, Ulysses, Titus, Turnus and Hippolitus. These images from the classical world point forward to the natural perfection of the New Man in Book IX. But Nature is incapable of procreating such models consistently; her powers are insufficient to sustain this level of perfection, and indeed allow for the procreation of negative models. For beside these images, on the most recently painted part of the wall, we find the following anti-types: two contemporary poets mocked by Alan, *noster Ennius* and Walter of Châtillon,[26] alongside the classical anti-types Nero, Midas, Ajax, Paris and Davus:

> Ergo Nature quicquid munuscula plene
> Percipit aut eius modicam subterfugit artem,
> Inscriptum calamis picture fabula monstrat. (1.184–6)

Whatever, then, receives in full the little gifts of Nature or avoids her moderate art the painting's story shows drawn by the pen. (p. 53, modified)

Nature is responsible equally for the natural perfection of human kind – for whoever, like the New Man in Books VII–IX, 'fully receives the small gifts of Nature' – and for those who fail to meet this standard. The diminutive *munuscula*, and the possible double sense of *modicam* in line 185 (both 'moderate' and 'small', 'modest') might be accountable for in terms of the serious qualification to natural perfection being made here: Nature's gifts are the smaller if she cannot ensure perfection within her own powers.

But the most powerful critique of any purely natural triumph comes from the very opening move of Book I, as Nature tries to fashion a perfect soul herself. The initial impulse of Nature reveals a profound desire *within the natural realm* to transcend the natural. Read as a sequel to the end of Book IX, the impulse of Nature is the impulse of the New Man to transcend the limits of the natural, to stabilize the Golden Age established in Book IX. I read Book I (Books I–VI, indeed) as a psychological allegory, in which the natural powers of the New Man respond to a natural impulse to move beyond the natural. When (as in any psychological personification allegory) we try to make coherent sense of the anatomized action, we discover that Alan is analysing the natural, psychological impulse within a human for perfection. Nature represents the ensemble of the New Man's moral powers, while Reason and Fronesis represent the highest powers of his soul, his reason and intellect. When Nature says that she wants to fashion a new and perfect soul, the sense of this is that the New Man wishes to perfect and renew his soul through understanding its divine origins. The ruler wishes to perfect his rule through self-understanding.

If this is the way we should read the opening of Book I, then we can see that, for Alan, Nature itself is unsatisfied with the purely natural. The impulse towards self-knowledge, through knowledge of the cosmos, but ultimately through perception of the soul's origin in God, is a natural desire. Insofar as it is, Alan is once again granting an extraordinary potency to nature: the very impulse to transcend nature, to search out the divine source of the soul through exploration of the cosmos, is itself a natural impulse. If this impulse is not obeyed, Alan implies, the soul is disordered, unformed, with its psychological powers in conflict (a conflict which is itself represented in political, or at least curial terms). It is here that the gift of Theology to the New Man, as an endowment of his birth in Book VII, is fully activated. Theology, we remember, taught the New Man to 'ascend the heavens in mind' (VII.326). In the fight against the vices this virtue, unlike all the other virtues granted in Book VII, remains dormant. Only now, at the beginning of Book I, is this gift actualized.

But if the New Man does desire to sustain his provisional victory of natural justice by seeking out the source of justice in the universe, then he must pass beyond the realm of the natural. The *Timaeus* commentaries have it that natural justice is the *fons et origo* of positive justice, and that for man to understand natural justice, he must seek out its model in the pattern of the cosmos. Fronesis does indeed investigate the pattern of the cosmos in Books III and IV, passing through the atmosphere before traversing the spheres. In each of the spheres she recognizes the astrological influence of the planets, but, in so recognizing them, and in passing through them, she transcends those influences. And in many spheres, she learns not only about the personal effects of different planets, but also about their political effects. The very language used to describe the relations of the planets is itself political. If, for example, a friendly star should align itself with Jupiter, the planets portend peace to men, as well as consorting as if in political relationship:

> Vel si forte Ioui societur stella salutis
> Nuncia, stella Iouis uultu meliore salutem
> Auget et euentus melioris dupplicat omen,
> Fedus amans pacisque sator, nutritor amoris,
> Extirpans iras, proscribens bella, furores
> Compescens, delens lites Martemque refrenans.   (IV.452–7)

Should it happen, though, that a star that heralds safety is allied with Jupiter, the star of Jupiter, with its more propitious aspect, further guarantees its protection and doubles the omen for greater success, since it loves agreement, cultivates peace, fosters love, uproots resentment, outlaws wars, restrains rage, terminates disputes and curbs Mars. (p. 134)

So Fronesis sees patterns of natural justice in the movements of the planets themselves, both as individually exemplified in some planets such as Jupiter, and in the overall concord of the planetary system. This system contains the violence of individual planets (Mars and Saturn, for example) in a cosmic pattern of stability. If this were all, then Alan's poem would conform to the purely naturalizing account of justice contained within the *Timaeus* commentaries. But the very impetus of Fronesis's journey is directed beyond the natural. It is precisely the momentum within the natural world, coupled with the potential of Fronesis as a psychological power, which propels her outside that purely natural system to its unnatural, divine source, which lies outside the system itself.

The first example of this change from natural to divine perception comes, as I argued in chapter 2, with the arrival of the *puella poli* at the beginning of Book V. And once Fronesis begins to travel with the *puella*, accompanied only by the sense of hearing (the one horse she takes beyond the chariot), she witnesses the paradoxical overturning of natural affinities and laws. Here too the language used to describe natural phenomena is essentially political, but the nature of these relationships is not open to rational investigation:

> Dum transit, miratur aquas, quas federat igni
> Indiuisa loci series, nec flamma liquorem
> Impedit, aut flamme certat liquor ille repugnans,
> Sed pocius sua deponunt certaminis arma.
> Nec iam natiuos querunt memorare tumultus
> Quos ligat assensus discors, discordia conchors,
> Pax inimica, fides fantastica, falsus amoris
> Nexus, amicicia fallax, umbratile fedus.   (v.311–18)

In her journey she wonders at the water united to fire by locations side by side without separation, while the flame does not interfere with the water nor the water, a contrary element, contend with the flame but rather they lay aside their battle gear. They no longer seek to remember their natural repugnance: they are bound by a dissenting assent, a concordant discord, a hostile peace, an unreliable reliance, a fictitious bond of love, a deceptive friendship, a shadow covenant. (pp. 147–8)

Alan consistently emphasizes the paradoxical, *un*natural, quality of physical relations in the Empyrean. And if there is an implicit critique of unaided nature in the opening of the poem, that critique becomes explicit here, as Alan points to the folly of philosophical understanding in matters of divine creation. He refers (v.344) to the stupidity of the philosopher who refuses to believe that the waters of the firmament hang above fire (a reference, almost certainly, to William of Conches, who initially refused to accept the Genesis account of the waters of the firmament, since it appeared to transgress the laws of nature). Alan's poem contains not only a critique of Nature, but also of the naturalism of Alan's 'Chartrian' predecessors.[27]

---

[27] The question of the waters above the firmament arises from Genesis 1.6–7 (Weber 1969, vol. 1, p. 4):

Dixit quoque Deus: Fiat firmamentum in medio aquarum: et dividat aquas ab aquis. Et fecit Deus firmamentum, divisivit aquas, quae erant sub firmamento, ab his quae erant super firmamentum.

This text clearly provides a point of controversy between those who wish to read Genesis literally, and those who, like William of Conches, wished to interpret the Bible within the limits of a Timaean-inspired physics, according to which this passage is understood allegorically. See Duhem 1914, vol. 2, pp. 487–501 for the history of the problem. For William's views, see Jeauneau 1964, pp. 847–9, and Gregory 1955, pp. 240–4. William's reading of Genesis on this point was also censured by (?)Bernard Silvestris, in his commentary on Martianus; see Westra 1986, 8.410–72, pp. 186–8.

But the most startling moment in which natural laws are directly challenged is in Book VI, where we see the images painted onto the gown of Fides. As I argued in chapter 2, this is clearly Fides in a Christian sense, rather than the purely political virtue who appears as one of Nature's powers. All the figures on Faith's gown are specifically Jewish or Christian. But their presentation is not in the least typological: the force of the exemplum is, in almost each case, to stress the *un*naturalness of human obedience to God. This is particularly true of the first and most extended image:

> Hic Abraham, nostre fidei pater, exuit actus
> Patris, dum summo Patri parere libenti
> Contendens animo, nato pater esse recusat,
> In quo discordes Natura Fidesque duellum
> Exercent unamque trahunt in dissona mentem;
> Nam Natura docet genitorem parcere nato.
> Econtra stat firma Fides que spernere natum
> Imperat, ut summo faueat Natura parenti.   (VI.38–45)

Here Abraham, the father of our faith, lays aside the role of father; hastening with obedient soul to obey his Father in heaven, he refused to be a father to his son. In him Nature and Faith at variance carry on a battle and draw one mind to irreconcilables. For Nature tells the father to spare the son. On the other hand Faith takes a firm stand and orders him to spurn his son in order that Nature may show deference to the Father in heaven. (p. 157, modified)

Alan chooses Abraham as his prime example of Faith; this is consistent with exegetical traditions, but Alan's interest in the Abraham story is not typological or historical.[28] Instead, he chooses this story because it marks the essence of the relations between reason and faith – or between faith as a political virtue and faith as a theological virtue. Far from having the natural jus-

---

I place inverted commas around 'Chartrian' in this sentence by way of alluding to the controversy about the importance of the school of Chartres. The main contributions are Dronke 1969, Southern 1979 and 1982. It is possible, but by no means certain, that Alan studied in Chartres.

[28] This is a convenient moment to note the radical differences between Alan's poem and the *Psychomachia* of Prudentius, with which the *Anticlaudianus* is often compared. Prudentius is at every point concerned to illuminate typological connections between abstract moral principles and biblical figures. Alan's almost wholly a-historical poem does not rely on typology at all, neither in Books I–VI, nor in Books VII–IX (where the comparison with the *Psychomachia* might seem strongest). The only thing Alan shares with Prudentius's poem is an epic style. See Jauss 1968.

tice of earth modelled simply on the natural justice of the cosmos,
Alan reveals how the system of Nature has its roots in the divine,
supra-rational world, where natural laws are turned on their heads.
Piety and faith (in the political senses) between parents and children stand near the heart of the moral and political renovation
Alan imagines in Books VII–IX; here, however, those relations of
natural justice are registered as having their source in a divine justice, whose rationale is closed to human reason. Christian faith has
priority over political and familial faith-keeping. Or, rather, obedience to the father of all things requires, paradoxically, abnegation
of earthly paternity.

In conclusion to this discussion of the reciprocal relations
between cosmology and politics, then, we can say that for Alan
these two realms of enquiry are intimately related: as with the
Timaeus, the *Dream of Scipio* and the *Consolation of Philosophy*, Alan
sets cosmology in a political context: discussion of the ideal republic leads to a cosmology, which in turn is designed to lead back into
reflection on politics. But this should not suggest an unqualified
'Chartrian' naturalism on Alan's part. The establishment of the
ideal king in Book IX leads inevitably to investigation of the cosmos
in Books I–VI. This in itself qualifies the political renovation imagined at the end of the poem: such a renovation requires a cosmology. But the daring and optimistic presentation of the triumph of
natural virtues at the end of the poem is more radically qualified,
since Alan is concerned to show how the realm of Nature has its
basis in supra-rational and supernatural divine sources. Despite the
apparent climax of the poem in the political triumph of the natural
man, the poem as a whole is concerned to reveal the provisional
nature of that triumph.

Of course Alan has left himself wide open to misinterpretation
(and this is, perhaps, why he is so defensive about the work in the
prose Prologue):[29] he might seem to have confirmed the naturalism
of his 'Chartrian' predecessors, in the presentation of the *aetas aurea*
as the apparent climax of the whole work. But understood according to the standard of a double order, Alan's optimistic praise of

---

[29] See Jung 1971, p. 73 for the plausible argument that the poem had been subject to attack,
which had then prompted Alan to add the (very defensive) prose Prologue. See Bossuat
1955, p. 24 and Gibson and Palmer 1987, pp. 925–6 for complementary evidence that the
prose Prologue was added later (but by Alan).

nature in Book IX is not unqualified. At the same time, the triumph of Nature in Book IX is not to be simply dismissed as illusory. In exactly the same way that an ironic statement retains a kind of force once its irony has been decoded, so too does the triumph of Nature register the value and provisional coherence of that moment. Like other humanist representations of Utopia (More's, for example), Alain's is presented playfully, granting such a vision a certain power, but setting it in a structure by which it is open to question.

THE INFORMATION OF THE READER

Medieval commentators, glossators and adaptors, as much as modern scholars, have been puzzled by the identity of the New Man. Among the medieval accounts, there is a clear division between those who see the New Man as Christ, and those who see him as a figure within the reach of human potential. In a text known as the *Compendium anticlaudiani* (of monastic provenance), for example, the New Man is interpreted unequivocally as Christ:

If we wish to understand the formation of this new man, the story should be shaped in this way: all the virtues entered the Blessed Virgin Mary and, with the co-operation of the Holy Spirit, made ready her body and soul for the conception of the new and most blessed man.[30]

A further set of medieval responses, however, places the perfection imagined by the poem within reach of the reader. This is true of the early thirteenth-century *Summarium* and of Ralph of Longchamps's readings, which both define the value of the poem as being self-knowledge for the reader. It is also true of a text known as the *Directorium breve*, an intelligent summary of the *Anticlaudianus* found in an Erfurt manuscript dated 1366, which begins by saying that Alan wrote the *Anticlaudianus* '...in order that

---

[30]   The Latin text (Ochsenbein 1969, 27.2, p. 107) reads:

Si volumus huius novi hominis plasmacionem intelligere, formetur hystoria sic: omnes igitur Virtutes beatissimam virginem Mariam intraverunt et corpus eius et animam spiritu sancto cooperante ad novi et sanctissimi hominis concepcionem habilitaverunt.

The earliest surviving manuscript of the *Compendium anticlaudiani* is either late thirteenth, or early fourteenth century (Ochsenbein 1969, p. 85, where thirty-one manuscripts of this text are listed). The provenance of this Christological reading is Cistercian; see also Meier 1980, pp. 480–3, and p. 508 for a listing of medieval Christological interpretations of the *Anticlaudianus*.

he could instruct and teach his students and listeners to follow a virtuous, careful and good life'.[31]

Twentieth-century scholarship is unanimous in its conclusion that the New Man is not Christ.[32] Even a moderately careful reading of the poem must recognize, after all, that Christ is unmistakeably referred to in the closing lines of Book V; Fronesis beholds the court of heaven, which is ruled by Mary and (although he is unnamed) Christ:

> Hic est qui nostram sortem miseratus, ab aula
> Eterni patris egrediens, fastidia nostre
> Sustinuit sortis, sine crimine criminis in se
> Deffigens penas et nostri damna reatus.   (V.540–3)

He is the one who, in pity for our fate, left the court of his eternal father, endured his aversion for our condition, fastening to himself, though innocent, the penalties of our lot and the damaging effects of our guilt. (p. 155)

It is true that, in Alan's *almost* entirely a-historical intellectual world, Christ is marginalized and nameless. But the poem does nevertheless register the atonement as an event which has happened. It produced its own Golden Age – at Mary's coming *redit etas aurea mundo* (V.505), but this is definitely in the past of the poem's action.

So scholars this century have, then, confessed themselves at a loss to account for the identity of the New Man, and have followed Huizinga's lead, when he says that there is a weakness in Alan's central theme, since the references which might suggest that the New Man is Christ are cancelled out by those which indicate that he is not. He concludes that Alan seems to 'have presented a poetic phantasy, for which there was no place in his theological system ... while on the other hand neither did the neo-Platonic cosmological doctrines offer any support'.[33] And a further result of this uncertainty has been a correlative doubt about the hero-figure of this

---

[31] '...ut discipulos vel auditores suos possit instruere et docere ad consequendum vitam virtuosam et morosam et bonam'. The *Directorium breve* is edited in Meier 1980, pp. 521–4 (p. 521). For the idea of self-knowledge in the reader as presented in Ralph of Longchamps's commentary and the *Summarium*, see below, nn. 41 and 42 respectively.

[32] See, for example, Huizinga 1932, pp. 51–4; Jung 1971, pp. 76–8; Ochsenbein 1975, p. 190; Evans 1983, pp. 148–52.

[33] Huizinga 1932, p. 54.

obviously epic work: is it the New Man?, Nature?, Fronesis?, the poet?, or, as some historians have argued, Philip Augustus?[34] Whatever choice a critic makes among these possibilities, he or she will nevertheless probably agree with Jung's complaint that a central weakness of the poem is its lack of a centre of gravity, an epic hero, 'around whom the ensemble organises and cristallises itself'.[35]

In the last two chapters I have attempted to define the form of Alan's poem; given the centrality Alan gives to questions of form for the meaning of artefacts, then any questions concerning the meaning of the poem should, I argued, be posterior to a definition of the poem's form. So it is in the light of those formal solutions that I should now like to broach the difficult question of the New Man's identity. For I think that the formal resolution I have offered also provides an epic hero, around whom the poem does find its coherence.

In the formal resolution to the poem offered in the last chapter, there are two orders in which the poem can be read. As long as we read the poem according to its artificial order (the order, that is, in which the poem is presented to us), then we are left with a variety of possible hero/heroine figures, at least three of whom can make a good claim for centrality. But the very fact that there are so many strong possibilities from within the poem (Nature, Fronesis or the New Man) itself indicates the inadequacy of any: by definition, the hero or heroine of a poem, especially an epic, is unquestionably its central figure.

Once we read the poem according to its natural order, then the poem begins to look much more coherent. The New Man is born into the poem with the creation of his soul directly by God in Book VI. His body is procreated by Nature in Book VII, where the soul is also endowed by the natural virtues. These potential virtues become actual in Book IX, as he fights against and defeats the vices. The *aetas aurea* is established, as the beautiful but provisional triumph of Nature. But the poem 'continues' according to its natural order – to that order which traces events in the order of their happening, and which traces the natural progression of the hero in formation. Within this order, the New Man's achieved Nature laments her inadequacy to create a perfect soul. The poem's alle-

[34] For the New Man as hero: Jauss 1960, p. 198; for Nature as the heroine: Raynaud de Lage 1951, pp. 59–88, esp. p. 88; for Fronesis: Sheridan 1973, p. 35 (Fronesis as heroine is also implicit in Wetherbee 1972 and 1988); for the poet as hero: Chance 1983; for Philip Augustus: Wilks 1977 and Marshall 1979.   [35] Jung 1971, p. 83.

gory would have it that Nature's lament is noetic, as Nature complains that a fully achieved Nature is still incapable of a perfection
which can only be achieved through understanding the soul's origins in God. The council between Reason, Fronesis and Concord
is a psychological personification allegory, in which the highest
psychological powers of the New Man, his reason and intellect, are
harmonized in concord (or by Concord), the principle within him
by which his soul and body are brought into peaceful relations.
And so the noetic action of the poem begins, as the chariot of the
New Man's soul ascends the cosmos in search of its own origins
and its own perfection. The culmination of this noetic voyage is the
moment in Book VI when God commands Noys to fashion a soul:
the king of Book IX becomes the perfect philosopher–king who perceives the origins of the soul. From this moment of theological
speculation, the poem's natural order begins again, as the movement of the narrative points again to political renovation.

So within this reading, we have one hero figure, who is born into
the poem in Book VI, and whose formation, both practical and theoretical, is traced to its culmination in Book VI, as the New Man
perceives the origins of the soul. This reading provides what Jung
desired in the poem – an epic hero. Nature is the principle of
nature as embodied in the New Man; Fronesis is the New Man's
fronesis, or intellect. There is only one hero figure, who is consistently present throughout the poem. As a mode, needless to say,
this kind of psychological personification allegory has a long tradition behind it, and a brilliant future before it: we need think only
of Augustine's *Soliloquies* or of Prudentius's *Psychomachia* to register
two very different late antique examples behind Alan, while
Guillaume de Lorris's *Roman de la Rose*, Langland's *Piers Plowman*,
and, I shall argue, Gower's *Confessio amantis* are three of the greatest
examples of very many late medieval fables of the soul, presented
as psychological allegories, which are to come after Alan.[36]

---

[36] The subject of medieval psychological allegory requires a coherent treatment unto itself.
The seminal works either treat this kind of allegory along with others (Lewis 1936), or
else treat a particular period (Muscatine 1953). See also Lynch 1988, many of whose
interpretations of individual works turn on the recognition of a work as psychological
allegory. Of particular interest is her reading of the *De planctu Naturae* as a representation
of the central figure's own psyche (pp. 77–112), an interpretation that conforms with the
reading of the *Anticlaudianus* proposed in this chapter. By contrast, compare Piehler 1971,
with reference to both the *Cosmographia* and the *Anticlaudianus*: 'The main action of these
epics concerns the efforts of such relatively accessible *potentiae* as Nature or Prudence to

We have a hero, then, whose representation conforms to a familiar medieval literary and philosophical convention. We have yet to account for his identity. But surely our placing of the *Anticlaudianus* within this literary/philosophic tradition also points us towards the identity of the New Man: as in any medieval psychological personification allegory, the hero is a model for the reader; the New Man is a model for ourselves. Of course there is an element of referentiality in such heroes – Will in *Piers Plowman*, for example, clearly refers in some ways to a personal biography (in my view as autobiography), but his primary function is to engage the reader in the theological and political problematic of the poem. The reader becomes the central locus of the poem, in which its strains are registered. Rather than being primarily referential, such poems are *enactive* – they draw readers into their action in such a way as to reproduce problems and/or experiences within the reader. It is through the reader's resolution of these problems and experiences – the reader's information – that the poems work most significantly. And it is precisely through their effects on readers that such works escape the charge of didacticism. Instead of being the passive transmitters of received ideas, such works become the locus in which received ideas are experienced anew through the reader's resolution of, or struggle with, those ideas. They are, that is, primarily enactive, rather than referential: their essential meaning is literary, where the force of ideas is less important than the way in which they are experienced. Or, as I would rather say, the force of received ideas is, through the reader's experience, in some way transformed in the great examples of this genre.[37]

ameliorate the condition of the natural world through the interposition of higher, celestial, *potentiae* such as Nous and Urania. When man finally appears he is presented from the outside as created and guided by the *potentiae*. These allegories thus depict man as seen through the eyes of the *potentiae*, a strange reversal of viewpoint, which provides an indication of the astonishing degree of imaginative reality these figures had acquired in this period, and some measure of the gulf which separates twelfth-century consciousness from our own' (p. 85). I agree with these remarks as applied to the *Cosmographia*, which is an account of the creation of the *first* man; my reading of Books I–VI of the *Anticlaudianus*, which is a narrative of man in educational formation (with a long tradition of human culture behind him) would put Piehler's remarks in exact reverse: the *potentiae* are seen from within one psyche.

37 Although Green 1967 gives no account of the place of Books VII–IX in the whole poem, my discussion of the reader's engagement with the narrative of the poem is close to his. He makes a distinction between the 'subjective dimension' of allegory, designed to bring about the subjective realization of the truth proposed by the 'objective dimension' of an allegory, which is designed to provide 'knowledge of doctrinal truth' (p. 9, n. 7). He says that interpretation of the poem 'exploits the mind's awareness of its own cognitive processes' (p. 9).

How might the meaning of the *Anticlaudianus* be described as achieved enactively through the experience of its readers? In what ways is the central action of this poem not so much the action represented, but rather the reader's understanding the sense of that represented action? How is the reader informed?

The first section of this chapter has been devoted to the relations between cosmology and politics. A politics requires a cosmology, and a cosmology leads back into a politics. Implicit in that discussion was a corresponding anthropology: we remember that Concord is the principle not only of cosmic and political harmony, but also of harmony within the microcosm of man. It is Concord who joins the soul to the body:

> Postquam materiem Nature dextra beauit
> Vultibus humanis, animam Concordia carni
> Federat et stabili connectit dissona nexu.
> Iunctura tenui, gunfis subtilibus aptat
> Composito simplex, hebeti subtile, ligatque
> Federe complacito, carni diuina maritat. (VII.56–61)

After Nature's right hand enriched the material with human features, Concord joins soul to flesh and unites discordants by a stable bond. By a subtle bond and rare cohesive she fits the simple to the composite, the subtle to the dull, binds them in an acceptable compact and weds the divine to flesh. (pp. 174–5)

And it is through the body's subjection to the natural virtues that the political renovation of Book IX is made possible. But the body's subjection to the rational control of the soul does not in itself represent the fullness of human being as Alan conceives of that perfection. Human perfection can, in Alan's eyes, only be achieved through the balancing of practical with speculative perfection. And for the fulfilment of speculative perfection, a psychology comes into play. The New Man has been endowed with Reason and Fronesis in Book VII; against the vices, only the practical, not the speculative potential of these psychological faculties has been activated. And Fronesis's gift of theological understanding (VII.315–28) has not been activated in its speculative aspects at all. Theology (*ars diuina poli*) endows the New Man with the capacity to investigate heaven:

Illa docet celeste sequi, uitare caducum,
Viuere lege poli, sursum suspendere mentem,
Fastidire solum, celum conscendere mente,
Corporis insultus frenare, reffellere luxus
Carnis et illicitos racioni subdere motus.   (VII.324–8)

She teaches him to follow what is of heaven, avoid what is transitory, live
by the law of heaven, direct his mind on high, shrink from the earth,
ascend in mind to heaven, check the violent outbursts of the body, com-
bat the excesses of the flesh and bring unlawful tendencies into subjection
to reason. (p. 183)

Certainly the moral teachings of theology are activated in the
fight against the vices in Book IX, but of the speculative potential
of Fronesis (theology is Fronesis's gift) we hear nothing. It is only
in Book I that we see the initial impulses of this gift's activation.
For the soul of the New Man to activate its own full potential,
it must achieve the speculative potential it has from birth. And,
as we see in Book I, that speculative potential can be achieved
only through the highest psychological powers of the soul, reason
and intellect. In the cosmic journey, we see the soul's powers
progressively exploited and exhausted: Reason draws on imagination and the senses in the passage through the atmosphere and
the spheres, up to the edge of the universe; from this point
on, only intellect is capable of progressing, with the sole sense
of hearing.

So just as a politics requires a cosmology, so too must
both be mediated by an anthropology, and in particular by a
psychology. Before the noetic action of the poem can come to
an end, the full potential of the soul must be realized. The plot of
the poem itself is a function of the soul's own dimensions: as the
soul is informed, so too, that is, does the poem's narrative continue.
Once the information of the soul is complete, then the narrative
of the poem comes to an end – the poem's own form is complete.
The same is true of all late medieval poems whose structure
is determined by the 'information' of the soul. The narrative
of Dante's *Divine Comedy*, for example, ends as Dante the pilgrim's
own desire is totally satisfied, turned as it is by the same cosmic
love which turns the universe:

All'alta fantasia qui mancò possa;
ma già volgeva il mio disio e 'l velle,
sí come rota ch'igualmente è mossa,
l'amor che move il sole e l'altre stelle.

(*Paradiso* XXXIII.142–5)[38]

And, just as Dante the pilgrim's soul is wholly satisfied in its vision of the divine sources of human perfection, so too does the natural order of the *Anticlaudianus* end with intellection of the divine source of the human soul: the highest power of the soul recognizes its own divine origins. Once Noys has prepared the perfect exemplar, God forms the soul:

Hanc formam Noys ipsa Deo presentat, ut eius
Formet ad exemplar animam. Tunc ille sigillum
Sumpsit, ad ipsius forme uestigia formam
Dans anime, uultum qualem desposcit ydea
Imprimit exemplo, totas usurpat ymago
Exemplaris opes, loquiturque figura sigillum.   (VI.442–7)

Noys herself presents this form to God to use as exemplar in forming the soul. He then took a seal and gives the soul a form along the lines of this archetype; he impresses on the pattern the appearance called for by the archetype. The image takes on all the powers of the exemplar and the figure identifies the seal. (p. 171, modified)

In the poem's represented action, then, we see the full development of human being: through the highest psychological power of intellect, the soul perceives its own origins. It is, in fact, this psychological action which gives dynamism to the poem's action as a whole: the realms of politics and cosmology are traversed by way of informing, or perfecting, the self. But what of the *reader's* experience of this formation? I will not recapitulate the arguments of the last chapter, but the essence of my argument is that the reader must equally exercise the full powers of his or her soul to understand Alan's poem. Just as Alan *represents* the soul's full potential, so too must the reader *enact* that potential. Just as Alan represents a theological (i.e. intellectual) perception *in* the poem, so too, I am arguing, is the reader afforded a theological experience *by* the poem. Alan transforms his theology into a theological poetics.

In order to understand the inner, 'supercelestial' form of the poem, we must exercise first our senses and imagination, then our

---

[38]   Singleton 1975.

reason, and, finally, our intellect. Alan himself, we remember, designates a triple reading of the poem in his prose Prologue: the delicacy of the literal sense will 'soothe the ears of boys' ('puerilem demulcet auditum'); the moral instruction will instruct the reason of those on the way to perfection ('perficientem imbuet sensus'); while the 'more acute subtlety of the allegory' will 'sharpen the intellect of the advanced' ('acutior allegorie subtilitas proficien-tem acuet intellectum').[39] In the reading I propose, we have three levels of reading which activate distinct psychological faculties. At the primary level of the story and its poetic expression, our sense of 'hearing' is pleased (or otherwise!) by the richness of verbal patterning, while our imagination is offered images characteristic of epic: councils, embassies, battles. Our reason perceives the speculative and practical models on which the action is based. But, faced with the difficulties of a purely rational reading of the poem, our intellects are activated to perceive the inner, archetypal form of the poem, the essential idea (of a double order) from which the poem takes its fundamental coherence, and without which it would remain a 'rag-bag poem', to use the insult Alan himself directs at a contemporary poet ('... pannoso plebescit carmine nos-ter / Ennius', 1.165–6). We are provoked to recognize the 'sense from which the words arise', as distinct from the sense 'which the words produce' ('potius ... sensum ex quo fiunt verba quam sen-sum quem faciunt verba').[40] And, we should note, the form of the poem turns on the moment at which we recognize the form of the soul: self-knowledge for the reader equally marks the moment at which the highest power of the soul is activated in our reading itself.

I am arguing, then, that the poem not only represents the pow-ers of the soul but also (more importantly for its literary meaning)

---

[39] Bossuat 1955, p. 56. Although the scheme is slightly different, it should be noted that Alan makes connections between levels of interpretation and the powers of the soul in his biblical exegesis also. See, for example, his *Sermo in die epiphaniae*, in d'Alverny 1965, pp. 241–5, where the three gifts of the Magi are said to represent levels of interpretation, which are in turn related to powers of the soul:

> Per myrram ... historia figuratur ... hanc offert ratio, quia circa historialia eius versatur consideratio. Per thus ... figuratur tropologia siue moralitas, que circa mores et hominum informationes vertitur ... hanc offert intellectus, quia circa formas eius versatur intuitus. Per aurum significatur anagoge, id est celestium consideratio... Hanc offert superior anime potentia, id est, intelligentia, que sola contemplatur diuina. (p. 243)

[40] Häring 1981, Rule 18, p. 137.

that it brings those same psychological powers into play as we read. The poem's primary 'meaning' is to be found not so much in its represented action, but rather in the self-knowledge it provokes in its reader. The implication of this is that the reader is the focus of the poem's meaning – the reader, as with the 'New Man', perceives the highest point of the soul's origins through his or her intellect. The *Anticlaudianus*, unlike the *Cosmographia*, is not a poem concerned with original creation, either of the universe or of man. It does represent the creation of the soul, but the action of the poem from that point on is concerned rather with formation than creation. And it is a formation by which the New Man, and, by implication, the poem's reader, come to self-knowledge.

'KNOW THYSELF'

Some medieval commentaries on the *Anticlaudianus* defined what they called the 'utility' of the the poem precisely in terms of its power to offer the reader self-knowledge. This implies, I think, that the reader is the central focus of the text (as we would expect, after all, from the thoroughly reader-centred poetic culture of the late Middle Ages). The poem's first commentator, for example, Ralph of Longchamps, describes the poem's 'final cause' in this way:

The utility or final cause [of the work] is that celestial proverb 'nothis elittos', that is, 'know thyself'. For it is of the highest value to have an understanding of one's origin.

Utilitas sive finalis causa est illud coeleste proverbium 'nothis elittos' id est 'cognosce teipsum'. Est enim maximum et perutile suae originis habere cognitionem.[41]

Likewise, the author of the *Summarium* (which appears in manuscripts from the beginning of the thirteenth century)[42] says rather the same thing – the utility of the work is *humane nature cognitio*.

Readings of philosophical narrative as providing the reader with self-knowledge are common in the immediate philosophico-poetic

---

[41] Sulowski 1972, p. 20.
[42] Bossuat 1955, p. 201. For the date of the *Summarium* as early thirteenth century, see Bossuat 1955, p. 24. Gibson and Palmer 1987, pp. 925–6 place the date just 'slightly earlier'.

tradition within which Alan is working. The commentary on the *Aeneid* attributed to Bernard Silvestris, for example, defines the utility of Virgil's poem as self-knowledge for its readers:

A man will derive a value from this work, which is an understanding of himself. For it is extremely profitable, as Macrobius says, for a man to know himself. On account of which it is said, 'From the heaven descended "nothis elitos", that is, know thyself.'

Utilitatem vero capit homo ex hoc opere, scilicet sui cognitionem; homini enim magna est utilitas, ut ait Macrobius, se ipsum cognoscere. Unde dictum est, 'De celo descendit nothis elitos', id est, cognosce te.[43]

Or, to consider another work which was regarded as a noetic allegory, twelfth-century commentaries on the *De Nuptiis* of Martianus Capella emphasize its value for the reader's self-knowledge. Commentators pause to explicate the moment where Mercury, having been rejected by Sophia and Mantice, wants to woo Psyche, daughter of Endelichia and the Sun. The anonymous Florentine fragmentary commentary, which Peter Dronke links to the presumed commentary of William of Conches on the *De Nuptiis*, interprets this moment at length; the commentator concludes in this way:

Whoever wins a knowledge of this soul at once knows himself to be godlike. Through the soul, he conceives a certain knowledge of the creator, so that what has been said to come down from heaven – 'know yourself' – may be fulfilled. For among the things that can be the subject of human cognizance nothing is found more difficult to comprehend than the soul.[44]

Huius anime cognitionem quicumque sortitur, statim se deo similem esse cognoscit. Per animam creatoris quandam concipit cognitionem, ut impleatur, quod dictum est de celo descendere, 'notisoliton', id est, cognosce te ipsum. Nichil enim difficilius comprehensione inveniri inter ea, que humane possunt subiacere notitie, quam ipsa anima.[45]

And behind these twelfth-century interpretations of fabulous narrative are sources fundamental to both Neo-Platonic and Hermetic traditions with which Alan was familiar. According to these traditions, one approaches God through knowledge of the

---

[43] Jones and Jones 1977, p. 3.
[44] Cited from Dronke 1974a, p. 118. For the connection between this fragmentary commentary and William of Conches's presumed commentary on Martianus, see Dronke 1974a, Appendix B, pp. 167–80.
[45] Cited from Dronke 1974a, p. 111 (p. 118 for Latin text). See Leonardi 1959 for a detailed survey of the survival of *De nuptiis* manuscripts.

soul's origin. Given the influence of the planets on the soul, and the community of elemental matter between the human body and the cosmos more generally, to know the soul requires knowledge of the cosmos. It is precisely the community of substance between the soul and the universe which makes the soul's knowledge of the universe possible and desired.[46] In his commentary on the *Dream of Scipio*, for example, Macrobius declares that

Philosophers whose views are correct do not hesitate to agree that souls originate in the sky; moreover, this is the perfect wisdom of the soul, while it occupies a body, that it recognizes from what source it came ... A man has but one way of knowing himself, as we have just remarked: if he will look back to his first beginning and origin ... in this manner the soul, in the very cognizance of its high estate, assumes those virtues by which it is raised aloft after leaving the body and returns to the place of its origin.[47]

Animarum originem manare de caelo inter recte philosophantes indubitatae constat esse sententiae: et animae, dum corpore utitur, haec est perfecta sapientia ut, unde orta sit, de quo fonte venerit, recognoscat ... Homini autem, ut diximus, una est agnitio sui, si originis natalisque principii exordia prima respexerit ... sic enim anima virtutes ipsas conscientia nobilitatis induitur, quibus post corpus evecta eo unde descenderat reportatur.[48]

While the 'pessimistic' tradition of Neo-Platonism and Christian Neo-Platonism define self-knowledge by a *rejection* of intellectual curiosity about the natural world,[49] the optimistic Neo-Platonist tradition in which Alan is writing places the burden of self-knowledge in speculative as much as moral perfection. The resources of human

---

[46] The tradition of 'know thyself' from Antiquity through to the twelfth century is presented by Courcelle 1974; but the tradition of self-knowledge in which Alan is working, that of 'cosmic religion', is most richly treated by Festugière 1944–54, vol. 2.

[47] Stahl 1952, I.9.1–3, p. 124.   [48] Willis 1970, I.9.1–3, p. 40.

[49] Festugière opens his treatment of cosmic religion by outlining two currents within it, one optimistic, the other pessimistic. In the optimistic current, the world and the universe is considered as a beautiful, whole entity. Such an order presupposes a maker, such that contemplation of the world leads naturally to recognition and adoration of that divine maker. The pessimistic current, on the other hand, is dualist, regarding the corporal as defective and disordered. God is utterly transcendent, and one cannot reach him through contemplation of the world. On the contrary, one must flee the material (Festugière 1944–54, vol. 2, pp. x–xi). Within the Christian tradition, this pessimistic form of Neo-Platonism produces a rejection of the world and of scientific knowledge in the search for self-knowledge. One ascends to God through moral rather than cognitive progress, and one requires grace to do so. For examples, see Courcelle 1974, pp. 149–50 (Augustine); p. 266 (St Bernard); and pp. 280–1 (the group of twelfth-century monastic texts around the *Meditationes piisimae*).

knowledge are therefore essential in the process of knowing oneself. Boethius's *Consolation* expresses these traditions most fully in the beautiful hymn *O qui perpetua* (III.m.IX), and *metrum* IV.I, which answers to that hymn. Whereas the hymn identifies the creative principles of both universe and soul, and expresses a prayer that the soul may return to its source, the first *metrum* of Book IV charts the course of that return to beginnings, by way of philosophic, cognitive perfection (the speaker is Philosophy). Having described the way in which the soul mounts towards heaven with the wings of philosophy, passing through the atmosphere and the spheres, the soul's arrival in heaven is described as a recognition of its origins:

> Hic regum sceptrum dominus tenet
> 　Orbisque habenas temperat
> Et uolucrem currum stabilis regit
> 　Rerum coruscus arbiter.
> Huc te si reducem referat uia,
> 　Quam nunc requiris immemor:
> 'Haec' dices, 'memini, patria est mihi,
> 　Hinc ortus, hic sistam gradum.'

Here the lord of kings his sceptre holds, / Controls the reins of the world, / And guides its swift chariot, though himself unmoved, / The shining master of the universe. / If the road bring you back, returning to this place, / Which you now seek, forgetful, / 'This I remember' you will say, 'is my native land, / Here I was born, here I shall halt my step.'[50]

But, my reader will surely object, how can the reader 'be' the poem's hero when the New Man is described so often as 'divine'? From the first, Nature declares the project of perfection as one of producing a divine creature:

> Non terre fecem redolens, non materialis
> Sed diuinus homo nostro molimine terras
> Incolat et nostris donet solacia damnis,
> Insideat celis animo, sed corpore terris:
> In terris humanus erit, diuinus in astris.
> Sic homo sicque Deus fiet, sic factus uterque
> Quod neuter mediaque uia tutissimus ibit.　　(I.235–41)

Through our efforts let a man not just human but divine inhabit the earth, a man with no odour of earthly dregs and let him console us for the

---

[50]　Stewart, Rand and Tester 1973, IV, metre 1, 19–26, p. 316.

damage we have done. Through his soul let him dwell in heaven, through his body on earth. On earth he will be human, in heaven divine. Thus he will become God and man, so becoming both that he is not just either, and he will tread with perfect safety the road between the two. (p. 55)

How, it might be argued, can this description possibly fit with my proposal that the reader is the poem's real hero? If the New Man is in some way a god, then this must surely imply that we should seek his identity outside the poem – if not in Christ, then in some visionary hero prophesied by the poem. In fact a reading of the poem as prophetic of a new, perfect king is not inconsistent with my interpretation, and such referential readings have been plausibly argued.[51] But even if the poem does have a single, visionary hero in mind (and I shall broach this more specific question in chapter 9), such a reading does not rule out the argument that the 'real' hero of the poem is the reader. For the notion of deification is central to Alan's own theology. The true theologian, argues Alan, is in some way 'deified'. Given this, then any reader who perceives the 'supercelestial form' of the work through the intelligence is, in Alan's terms, equally 'deified' in some way. To put it like this (particularly as I feel I offer a coherent interpretation of the poem) sounds ridiculously pretentious. But when we look to the way in which Alan conceives of theological experience, we can see that divinity, for him, is within reach of the human mind.

Alan states his doctrine of the deification of the theologian quite unambiguously. In his *Quoniam homines*, for example, he defines two species of 'superior' extasis:

one is called intellect, by which a man considers spiritual things (i.e. angels and souls). Through this a man becomes a spirit, and is accordingly taken above himself. The other extasis is called intelligence, by which a man intuits the trinity. Through this he becomes a 'man-god', since through speculation of this kind a man is in some way deified.

una que dicitur intellectus, qua homo considerat spiritualia, id est angelos et animas; secundum quam homo fit spiritus, et ita supra se fit. Alia est que intelligentia dicitur, qua homo trinitatem intuetur; secundum quam homo fit homo deus, quia per hanc speculationem quodammodo deificatur.[52]

---

[51]   See Wilks 1977 and Marshall 1979.
[52]   Glorieux 1953, I.2, p. 121. See also *Regulae caelestis iuris*, Rule 99, discussing the ways in which the soul can transgress its proper (rational) limits:

The most obvious source for such a notion within Alan's theological works is the writings of Johannes Scotus Eriugena, where the same idea is found.[53] But in the narrative content and structure of Alan's poem, it is the Neo-Platonic and Hermetic traditions which provide much closer and more convincing influences. All these traditions make an intimate connection between knowledge and divinization; but the Neo-Platonic and Hermetic traditions define this knowledge in terms much closer to Alan's representation in the *Anticlaudianus* – in terms, that is, of self-knowledge via knowledge of the cosmos.[54]

In the *De nuptiis*, for example, Philology is divinized by Athansia, or Immortality, and her mother Apotheosis immediately before her ascent through the spheres to a heaven populated by poets and philosophers.[55] We also find the idea of divinization in Macrobius's commentary on the *Dream of Scipio*: Cicero's Africanus tells Scipio to understand that he is a god (VIII.2). Macrobius comments on this passage by recounting that after Scipio was dissuaded from committing suicide to reach heaven, Scipio Africanus inflamed him for desire of heaven; Scipio learns about 'the nature, movements, and regulation of the sky and stars, and understood that these were to be the rewards of virtue'. After having been instructed to despise glory, Scipio had almost put behind him his mortal nature and purged his mind; and now, finally

·

Sed aliquando excedit homo istum statum uel descendendo in uicia uel ascendendo in celestium contemplationem. Et talis excessus dicitur extasis siue metamorphosis quia per huiusmodi excessum excedit statum proprie mentis uel formam. Excessus autem superior dicitur apotheosis quasi deificatio quod fit quando homo ad diuinorum contemplationem rapitur. Et hoc fit mediante illa potentia anime que dicitur intellectualitas qua conprehendimus diuina. (Häring 1981, p. 204)

See also *Sermo de sphaera intelligibili*: 'per intellectualitatem fit anima humana Deus' (d'Alverny 1965, p. 303).

53   For the Dionysian account of deification, see Roques 1954, pp. 117–31.
54   See Roques 1954, pp. 240–4, for an account of the differences between the Dionysian and Hermetic traditions:

Il parait donc certain que le langage et les schémas de la gnose, specialement hermétique, ont aidé Denys à prendre une conscience plus vive des caractères et des relations qui definissent la science et la sainteté. Mais en se situant dans ces traditions de pensée, il ne trahit pas les valeurs dont il se réclame. La science qu'il nous décrit et nous propose reste véritablement une science des Ecritures, une science d'Eglise, une science à transmission hiérarchique dans des cadres sacramentels. (p. 244)

55   See Lenaz 1975, II.139–42, pp. 146–8.

prepared to assume his true nature, he is here clearly told to realize that he is a god.[56]

Finally, it is also pertinent to mention Hermetic traditions here. Alan cites the *Asclepius*[57] often and with approval in his works of theology.[58] According to the *Asclepius*, God created first the world, and then man in order to govern the world and contemplate the beauty of the universe. The soul is created by God as a form of the divine likeness (*divinae similitudinis formam*):[59]

Thus he [god] formed man from the nature of spirit and body, that is from the eternal and the mortal, in order that the creature thus formed could satisfy its double origin, to admire and adore the celestial and to dwell in and govern the terrestrial.

Itaque hominem conformat ex animi atque corporis id est ex aeterna atque mortali natura, ut animal ita conformatum utraeque origini suae satisfacere possit, et mirari atque adorare caelestia et incolere atque gubernare terrena.[60]

The intimate relation between the divine nature of the intellect and God produces praise of man as himself divine:

So, Asclepius, man is a great marvel, worthy of reverence and honour. For he passes into the nature of god, as if he were a god … he despises the part of his nature which is only human, trusting in the divinity of the other part.

Propter haec, O Asclepi, magnum miraculum est homo, animal adorandum atque honorandum. Hoc enim in naturam dei transit, quasi ipse sit deus … hoc humanae naturae partem in se ipse despicit, alterius partis diuinitate confisus.[61]

---

[56] Stahl 1952, II.12.1–6. Willis 1970, II.12.5: 'Africanus igitur, paene exutus hominem et defaecata mente iam naturae suae capax, hic apertius admonetur ut esse se deum noverit' (p. 131).

[57] The *Asclepius* was a 'patristic translation of a lost Greek original' (Stock 1972, p. 102). The original was probably written in the second century (Festugière 1944–54, vol. 3, p. 1). For the diffusion of the text in the twelfth century, see Nock and Festugière 1960, pp. 267–9, and Stock 1972, p. 102, n. 59. For its influence on Bernard Silvestris, see Stock 1972, pp. 102–5 and *passim*.

[58] See, for example, *Quoniam homines*, which cites the *Asclepius* twelve times (Glorieux 1953, p. 366). It may even be the case that Alan playfully used 'Hermes Trismegistus' as an *alias* for his more adventurous theological works. The Basel manuscript of the *Regulae caelestis iuris* describes the author of the work thus: 'Iste auctor nuncupatur Mercurius, Alanus Porretanus, Trimegistus' (Häring 1981, p. 117).

[59] Nock and Festugière 1960, 7, p. 304.4.   [60] Ibid., 8, p. 306.2–7.

[61] Ibid., 6, pp. 301.18–302.5.

These texts form part of what Marrou calls the 'religion of culture' – an intensely intellectualist, optimistic, elitist cultural tradition in which divinity is assured for a select few through their intellectual achievement.[62] Of course this is essentially a classical,
non-Christian tradition, but it does survive into Christianity, and
survives in remarkably pure form in Alan's poem. In Book V
Fronesis is said to witness the saved in heaven:

> Hic habitat quem uita deum uirtusque beatum
> Fecit et in terris meruit sibi numen Olimpi.   (V.443–5)

Here dwells he whose life has made him a god, and whose virtue has
made him blessed, and who on earth deserved the divinity of Olympus for
himself. (p. 152, modified)

This description must be read as impersonal, referring to the saved
generally. This in itself suggests that the earth has *already* seen 'god-
men', and that the New Man is not unique historically. Alan distinguishes among the saved those who were saved through their
virginity, through martyrdom, or through the laurels of a teacher
(*uel doctoris sua laurea ditat*, V.461). Here other paths to salvation are
acknowledged, but it remains true that the entire narrative
is restricted to the divinization of the *doctor*. Alan is not heterodox;
he does not entirely neglect any account of Christ's saving power
in the poem (although Christ is marginalized, he is nevertheless
recognized in the narrative). But Alan must surely have incurred
the danger of being labelled heterodox by his presentation
of divinization essentially through natural impulses and intellectual
means, with no representation of co-operative divine grace in
Book I.[63]

So, Alan's New Man has very strong backing from within his
theological culture; Huizinga's conclusion that neither Alan's theology nor the Neo-Platonic doctrines of the cosmos offered any support for Alan's presentation of such a figure is simply wrong. But

---

[62] See Marrou 1958, pt. 2, ch. 1, pp. 146–7 for the 'religion of culture' in the classical and
Hellenistic periods. See also below, chapter 9, n. 14 for the intellectual elitism of this tradition.

[63] It has been argued that the unguent applied to the soul in Book VI.461–5 represents the
grace of Christian baptism (Ochsenbein 1975, p. 190). But, as Ochsenbein himself immediately goes on to point out, grace has no part in the victory of the virtues. Even if we do
accept this interpretation of Noys's ointment, it would remain true that prevenient grace
plays a marginal part in the ascent of Fronesis.

my essential point here is not to place Alan's presentation of the *nouus homo* within its cultural background, as a point of intellectual history. The thrust of my argument is rather that Alan's concept of the *homo-deus* is one that he puts in reach of human capacities. The fact that the New Man is divine is not evidence that it could not be within reach of human capacities; instead it reveals just how exalted Alan's conception of human capacities is. Certainly, access to the highest kinds of knowledge is represented in the poem as being open only to a few (V.57–69); but so too does the Prologue insist that understanding of the poem is open only to a few: only those who 'dare to lift their reason to the intuition of supercelestial forms' should enter the 'narrow straits' of the poem. But, as such a comparison between the New Man and the reader implies, those who *do* raise their minds to the intuition of supercelestial forms in their reading of the work will in effect 'become' the poem's hero. What has been *represented* in the poem will become *enacted* in its readers.

The *Anticlaudianus*, then, is working within an intensely optimistic current of humanism, with its roots deep in classical culture. Each branch of science in this tradition is inter-related: anthropology, and particularly psychology, provoke an understanding of cosmology; and a cosmology, in turn, provides the model for an ethics and a politics. The model which gives dynamism to Alan's representation of this inter-locking set of discourses is the whole human: the control of the body through ethics provokes a perfection of the mind through a cosmology; and a cosmology, in its turn, provides the source for a politics. Only through the human desire for integration, or *concordia*, can the full force of human nature be realized. The reader understands the degree to which these different branches of knowledge and experience are inter-related through experiencing, vicariously at least, the same ascent as the New Man. So understanding such a system also involves a hermeneutics, which I have outlined in the second half of this chapter. If this book were only about the *Anticlaudianus*, then this would be the moment to investigate further the poetics which is equally implicit in a such a world-view. But before we look at Alan's poetics, we should pause and look ahead to further developments of the humanist culture celebrated in the *Anticlaudianus*, and in particular to the way in which one late fourteenth-century English poem also imagines the philosopher–king.

CHAPTER 5

Ovidian disunity in Gower's Confessio amantis

INTRODUCTION

Once the creative information of the *Anticlaudianus* is understood,
its philosophical information (in the modern sense) looks very
different. The only way to make sense of the incongruences of the
poem's outer form is to read the poem in a different, artificial
order. Once one reads in this way, the peculiar outer form of the
poem can be explained by its inner form; equally, the inner form
produces a reading of the poem as the information, or education,
of a single soul. Understanding of the poem's artistic information
reveals that the poem represents a pedagogic information. And
this in turn modifies the evident philosophical content of the poem:
as the learning experience of a single soul, the *Anticlaudianus* reveals
how the soul both requires and structures knowledge for its
fulfilment. So far from being an encyclopaedic work, a mere
gathering of instructional matter, we have seen that the poem
represents the teaching (or information) of a single soul. A psychology underwrites a movement through an ethics and a politics to
a cosmology and a theology. Equally, the theology and cosmology
point back to a politics. The poem reveals the pull between
different discourses as the sciences are traversed by the individual
soul.

What possible value could this set of observations have for
understanding Gower's *Confessio amantis*, written a little over two
hundred years later? There are, certainly, blocks of 'scientific' matter in the English poem, notably the *divisio philosophiae* of Book VII,
but, my reader will object, the philosophic information of the
poem is relatively restricted in scope. Most of the poem represents
a learning process with matter of a very different kind, that of love,
in which Amans is

134

> curious
> Of hem that conne best enforme
> To knowe and witen al the forme,
> What falleth unto loves craft. (IV.923–6)

How might Gower's poem represent the information of a single
soul? And how might this pedagogic information reveal the inter-
relations between the sciences?

In the following two chapters I want to argue that the *Confessio*
does indeed represent a psychological unity, where Genius and
Amans are faculties of the same soul. Equally, I shall argue that the
poem, as the *Bildungsroman* of a single soul, reveals the very subtle
inter-relations of the sciences, particularly between ethics and politics. Like the *Anticlaudianus*, the *Confessio* is a humanist psychological
allegory, in which the soul requires philosophical knowledge to
achieve its information, or proper form. And like the *Anticlaudianus*,
politics in the *Confessio* is a pivotal science for the soul's understanding of itself.

All these points will be given substance in chapters 6 and 7. But
for the moment I should like to focus on the creative information
of the poem. For, as with Alan's poem, here too we see a radical
incoherence in the poem's outer shape, or form. As in our
approach to the *Anticlaudianus*, understanding of the philosophic
information of the *Confessio* should be approached via its creative,
or artistic information, the principles by which it takes its outer
form. Discussion of the formal dynamics of these poems is logically
prior to understanding their philosophical 'information'.

It will be recalled from the Introduction that the words
'enforme' and 'information' are used very often in the *Confessio* to
describe both Genius's activity and the learning process of Amans.
I suggested then that the *Confessio* was working within the philosophical, literary and pedagogic nexus of the word 'information'.
Both Amans and Genius describe Genius's activity as an act of literary information; this act is modelled on the divine act of informing matter; and it is designed to bring the soul of Amans to self-
knowledge, to its proper form, conforming Amans, as the will, with
the reason.

This account of the poem's 'information' suggests that the
Confessio amantis is an extremely coherent ethical and pedagogic
text. If the argument were accurate, it would confirm the main

lines of Gower criticism this century, by setting the pedagogic 'information' of Genius into its philosophical, psychological and literary context. For, although scholars have not focused on Genius's instruction as an act of 'information' as such,[1] they have, nevertheless, described it as an ideal model, and identified the instruction of the poem itself with that of Genius, whereby Genius is implicitly read as the Gower instructor figure.

In response to an earlier consensus, whereby Gower's poem was thought to be simply confused in its imposition of a moral, confessional frame on amatory matter drawn largely from Ovid,[2] a powerful consensus this century has argued instead for the entire, readily perceptible moral coherence of the work. C. S. Lewis makes the initial step, with his influential perception (drawn from Andreas Capellanus but applied to Gower) that, 'except on certain obviously untractable points, the virtues of a good lover were indistinguishable from those of a good man; the commandments of the god of Love for the most part were mere repetitions of the commandments of the Church'. So, Lewis argues, to pass from moralizing the sins of a courtly lover to moralizing *tout court* would produce 'no excessive strain on the fabric of the poem': 'Thus at one stroke the main problem is solved, and all the serious "sentence" can be dovetailed into a poem on love without discrepancy.'[3] J. A. W. Bennett's influential essay 'Gower's "Honeste Love"' provides an *expolitio* of Lewis's central perception; and he also explicates the point implicit in Lewis's argument – that Genius is the ideal moral instructor in the poem: 'If Genius's prime concern seems to be with a lover's faults and failings, we are never allowed to forget that these reflect vices common to all mankind.'[4] The argument leads Bennett where it must: 'The creed of Genius, then, is the poet's creed; and Amans accepts the ethics that Genius affirms.'[5] Later still, the same essential perception generates Alastair Minnis's account of the structural logic of the *Confessio*; but whereas Lewis traced the identity between

---

[1]   With the exception of Chance Nitzsche 1975, who briefly but trenchantly discusses Genius as a poet–philosopher figure, 'informing' Amans (pp. 128-30). I develop this suggestion in chapter 8.

[2]   See, for example, Macaulay 1900–1: 'With considerable merits both of plan and execution the *Confessio Amantis* has also no doubt most serious faults. The scheme itself, with its conception of a Confessor who as priest of Venus has to expound a system of morality, while as a devotee of Venus he is concerned only with the affairs of love ... can hardly be called a consistent or happy one' (vol. 1, p. xix).

[3]   Lewis 1936, p. 199.   [4]   Bennett 1966, p. 111.   [5]   Ibid., p.112.

a lover's sins and sins *simpliciter* to Andreas Capellanus, Minnis traces the connection to a different source, the moralized Ovids: 'Indeed, in the *Confessio* there is no distinction between lovers' virtues and Christian virtues, between lovers' sins and real sins: Gower manifests his conviction that virtue is virtue and sin is sin... In the *Confessio*, Amans and Confessor ultimately serve not the God of Love but the God of medieval Christianity.'[6]

In these three accounts, then, we can see how an initial perception draws others into it: Lewis's argument simply posits the identity of lovers' sins and 'real' sins; Bennett adds the implicit point that Genius is, therefore, the reliable moralizer, a spokesman for Gower in fact; and Minnis relates this to Gower's use of Ovid. Whereas Chaucer used Ovid with due recognition of Ovid's subversiveness, Gower rests safely within the terms of the 'medieval', moralized Ovid. In the way of literary critical orthodoxies, this inter-related set of arguments has pulled yet other areas of discussion into itself: thus the psychological figure of Gower's Genius has been described as a return to Alan's reliable figure in the *De planctu Naturae*, repressing the slippery complexities of Genius in Jean de Meun's *Roman de la Rose*; in a number of studies, he is seen to speak reliably for Gower as author.[7] Gower's use of political satire in the

---

[6] Minnis 1980, p. 214. Minnis 1991 (an excellent article) has since made it clear that he should not be taken to mean that there is no real discrepancy between the *'persona amans* and the *auctor sapiens'*; he points out that the tension between these two positions was 'culturally inevitable' (p. 55) and that Gower does not by any means come down unequivocally on the side of the *auctor sapiens*: 'In his Latin self-commentary he offered a final signified, which many parts of the *Confessio* supported; hence the conditions necessary for the assignment of authority were created. However, within the English text itself, or indeed within the work taken as a whole (English verse, Latin verse and Latin commentary), the brake is applied but does not hold, and the sparks fly; meaning cannot be halted, because aspects of *amor* and *auctoritas* were, within late-medieval culture, inevitably at odds' (p. 65). This frame for reading the *Confessio* is extremely suggestive, and consonant with the argument of this book; I develop the 'pro Amans' case here in chapter 9.

[7] I have already referred to Bennett 1966, p. 112, in this regard. The same argument (that Genius is an entirely reliable moral guide, implicitly speaking for Gower as author) can be found in Fisher 1964, p. 162; Schueler 1972, p. 250; Economou 1970; Chance Nitzsche 1975, pp. 125–30; and Copeland 1991, p. 205. More recently a wholly opposed view of Genius has emerged, which argues that he is an unstable, unreliable figure. Thus Hiscoe 1985; Hatton 1987; White 1988; and Simpson 1988. As I argue here and in the next chapter, Genius is indeed an unstable figure, but the arguments of Hiscoe and Hatton tend to see him only as hopelessly concupiscent; neither see him in sufficiently broad a psychology to accommodate the interesting mixture of irrational and rational 'information' (some relevant to love, some not) given by Genius. The next chapter will mediate between these two sets of views. Its position is close to the excellent articles by Baker

Prologue is, we are told, totally consistent with his treatment of love in the body of the poem;[8] and, more recently, it has been argued that Gower's deployment of academic glossing within the body of his text provides a firm interpretative base from within the poem itself.[9]

The consensus I am describing, then, implies a complete squaring of the literary form of the *Confessio amantis* with its pedagogic 'information': the poem is being presented as a coherent, efficient, moralizing structure. Here I should like to disagree. The interpretative solutions which I arrived at for the *Anticlaudianus* were provoked by my observation of the profound incoherence of the poem as it is presented to us. My whole discussion in chapters 2 and 3 proceeded on the critical principle of seeking the maximum degree of formal unity in a poem only by first recognizing the maximum degree of formal disunity. Those interpretations which can account for elements that most resist interpretation will be most satisfying. As for the *Anticlaudianus*, so with the *Confessio amantis*: there are deeply planted structural incongruences in this poem. Not only do I argue that these incongruences exist, but I also suggest that our understanding of them is inseparable from an understanding of Gower's extraordinarily intelligent and wide-ranging reading of Ovid. It is only once these Ovidian incongruences have been understood that we can begin to perceive how, at a yet deeper level, the poem is coherent.

So in this chapter I would like to take issue with the formidable consensus regarding the poem's unity; I want to argue that, through his use of Ovid especially, Gower constructs a literary structure in which there is no reliable authority figure from within the text. Far from being coherently, consistently and persuasively didactic, the poem involves its reader as an active participant in the construction of its meaning. In the *Confessio* (as distinct from his other major works), Gower is a poet working in the ironic traditions of Ovid, Jean de Meun and Chaucer, rather than an efficient moralizer and compiler of literary and philosophical materials.

1976 and Wetherbee 1986, and to the discussions in Lynch 1988, pp. 168–71, 182–5 and Olsson 1989 and 1992, pp. 52–62.

[8]   Thus Miller 1983; Peck 1978 implies a consistency between stories devoted to political and amatory ends.   [9]   Copeland 1991, pp. 202–20.

AMANS AND THE NARRATOR OF THE *AMORES*

The most striking formal incongruence of the *Confessio amantis* occurs in the shift from the Prologue to Book I. In the Prologue, the narrator's discourse is essentially political; of course this provokes historical discussion (the ages of the world) and anthropology (the analysis of man as a microcosm of the macrocosm), which, in its turn, necessarily involves ethical analysis concerning the source of moral instability. The narrator opens by arguing forcefully that what men call Fortune is in fact within our own souls; we are the masters of our destiny, and it is our moral choices which determine the response of our environment:

> And natheles yet som men wryte
> And sein that fortune is to wyte,
> And som men hold oppinion
> That it is constellacion,
> Which causeth al that a man doth:
> God wot of bothe which is soth.
> The world as of his propre kynde
> Was evere untrewe, and as the blynde
> Improprelich he demeth fame,
> He blameth that is noght to blame
> And preiseth that is noght to preise:
> Thus whan he schal the thinges peise,
> Ther is deceipte in his balance,
> And al is that the variance
> Of ous, that scholde ous betre avise;
> For after that we falle and rise,
> The world arist and falth withal,
> So that the man is overal
> His oghne cause of wel and wo.
> That we fortune clepe so
> Out of the man himself it groweth.   (Prol. 529–49)

This lucid account of the determining impulses of human action is turned towards politics: the narrator moves to an Estates Satire from this argument about Fortune, and his concluding prayer in the Prologue is for the emergence of a new Arion, a poet-figure who can heal the divisions between, and harmonize, all classes of society.

This, then, is a poetry directed towards the 'commune profit', and one which stands well with the impulse of writing the poem as it is presented fictionally, at least, from within the same Prologue: Gower presents himself (in the first recension of the *Confessio*)[10] as having chanced to meet Richard II on the Thames; from Richard he receives the charge to 'book' 'som newe thing'; and so, we hear, he is writing

> A bok for king Richardes sake,
> To whom belongeth my ligeance
> With al myn hertes obeissance
> In al that evere a liege man
> Unto his king may doon or can.   (Prol. 24–8)

The efficient cause of the book is (ultimately) the king; the matter (of the Prologue, at least) is political; and its final cause, it is implied, is, like Arion's, to heal social division.[11]

Book I puts a very sudden and unexpected brake on all this:

> I may not strecche up to the hevene
> Min hand, ne setten al in evene
> This world, which evere is in balance:
> It stant noght in my suffiance
> So grete thinges to compasse
> Bot I mot lete it overpasse,
> And treten upon othre thinges.   (I.1–7)

In some *Vox clamantis* manuscripts we find an illumination of Gower aiming his arrow at the globe, with an inscription beginning *Ad mundum mitto mea iacula*.[12] Here at the beginning of the *Confessio*, on the contrary, we are arrested by a sudden refusal to continue the political themes of the Prologue, which are indeed directed at the 'world' as a whole.

Certainly, we have in part been prepared in the Prologue for *some* change between the Prologue and the body of the work: the narrator has told us that the Prologue will concern wisdom, whereas

---

[10] There are three recensions, 1390, 1390–1, 1392–3. See Macaulay 1900–1, vol. 1, pp. xxi–xxviii. See Nicholson 1987 for a severe qualification to Macaulay's understanding that these recensions are in every respect authorial products.

[11] This paragraph is structured loosely around the 'Aristotelian' four-cause *accessus*, for which see Sandkühler 1967, pp. 30–41, and Minnis 1984, pp. 28–39.

[12] The image is reproduced in Macaulay 1902, *The Latin Works*, frontispiece.

This bok schal afterward ben ended
Of love, which doth many a wonder
And many a wys man hath put under.   (Prol. 74–6)

This way of putting it suggests that the discussion of love is related
to the discussion of 'wisdom' by way of negative exemplification: if
love puts the wise man 'under', then, presumably, we should relate
this back to the discussion of 'wisdom' in the Prologue. This is a
possible relationship between the Prologue's political 'wisdom' and
Book I's renunciation of it, a relationship between prologues which
has academic precedent for Gower. Alastair Minnis has drawn our
attention to the pattern of an extrinsic and an intrinsic prologue in
scholastic writing, where the extrinsic prologue was used to relate
the branch of philosophy relevant for a given text to the
Aristotelian hierarchy of sciences, and 'was followed by an "intrinsic" prologue in which *intentio* and *modus procedendi* were discussed'.[13]
Here, then, Gower describes wisdom in general, whereas the treatise which follows treats a specific branch of wisdom, the ethics of
human love.

I think Minnis is right. But I want to develop his point by showing how the text as it is presented to us actively resists the kind of
'scientific' subordination which he describes. If the study of ethics
treated in the body of the book can be related back to political wisdom, then who is to do the relating? It is certainly not the narrator
of Book I.

Medieval *accessus* to Ovid's *Amores* relate a tradition according to
which Ovid was ordered by Augustus to describe his war against
Antony, in five books. Ovid, however, was 'drawn away' by Cupid,
and made only three books, whose subject was his girlfriend and
his love for her.[14] Whatever the source of this story, we can see how
Ovid playfully presents the opposition between tragedy and love
elegy throughout his erotic poetry, but particularly in the *Amores*.
The book opens, indeed, with the invasion of Cupid into the territory of tragedy:

---

[13] Minnis 1983, and 1984, pp. 177–81.
[14] Huygens 1970, p. 36. This text is translated in Minnis and Scott 1988, p. 27. See also
Ghisalberti 1946, p. 12.

> Arma gravi numero violentaque bella parabam
> edere, materia conveniente modis.
> par erat inferior versus – risisse Cupido
> dicitur atque unum surripuisse pedem.   (*Amores* I.1.1–4)[15]

Arms, and the violent deeds of war, I was making ready to sound forth –
in weighty numbers, with matter suited to the measure. The second verse
was equal to the first – but Cupid, they say, with a laugh stole away one
foot. (p. 319)

The narrator (Ovid the poet) complains about this formal and discursive invasion (what, he asks, if Venus should seize the arms of
Minerva?), but to no effect: Cupid as patron registers his power as
he bends his bow, and commands Ovid to take this apolitical subject for his theme. Cupid's authority occludes and subverts that of
Augustus; and Ovid the poet becomes the lover–narrator, subject
of the text through subjection to Cupid:

> Me miserum! certas habuit puer ille sagittas.
> uror, et in vacuo pectore regnat Amor.   (*Amores* I.1.25–6)

Ah, wretched me! Sure were the arrows that that boy had; I burn, and
Love reigns in my deserted heart. (p. 321, modified)

Throughout the *Amores* the defeat of tragedy, or rather the comic
subversion of tragedy, recurs as a metatextual leitmotif: the second
book opens with Ovid's recollection that he had begun to sing of
the wars of heaven, but that, as his lover closed her door,

> ego cum Iove fulmen omisi;
> excidit ingenio Iuppiter ipse meo.   (*Amores* II.1.17–18)

I let fall Jove with his lightning; Jove's very self dropped from my
thoughts. (p. 381)

And in the opening of Book III Ovid recounts his vision of Tragedy
and Elegy personified, debating their respective claims. Tragedy
with her regal sceptre attacks Ovid for the worthlessness of his
poetry – *materia premit ingenium*, she says (III.1.25). Elegy responds by
arguing that she is the initial impulse of tragedy in any case
(III.1.59); Ovid resolves the debate by asking for indulgence from

---

[15] The text of the *Amores* is drawn from Showerman 1914; the translations are based on this
    edition.

Tragedy, and offering the (subversive) compromise of elegiac couplets: one hexameter, one pentameter.[16]

Possible parallels between the *Amores* and the opening of the *Confessio amantis* (*Ca*) are obvious: just as Richard commands a willing Gower-poet to produce a poem for the king's sake, which is then abandoned in Book I, so too is Ovid torn between the demands of tragedy and elegy – genres defined in one *accessus* as, respectively, the 'goddess of poetry about the deeds of nobles and kings', and the 'goddess of sorrow – and in love, miseries and adversities befall men'.[17] And just as Ovid registers the superior power of love over the sceptre of Tragedy, so too does Gower; both poets mark their transferred allegiance as Cupid hits them (*Amores* I.1.25–6; *Ca* I.143–7), and both poets adopt a different narrative persona, changing from the historical poet to the subject of love.[18] Gower's gloss to I.61 makes this explicit: 'Hic quasi in persona aliorum, quos amor alligat, fingens se auctor esse Amantem, varias eorum passiones ... scribere proponit.' And in both cases, this subjection to Cupid takes the form of a confession: Ovid confesses that he is unable to resist his love, despite his recognition of its impropriety:

> Non ego mendosos ausim defendere mores
> falsaque pro vitiis arma movere meis.
> confiteor – siquid prodest delicta fateri;
> in mea nunc demens crimina fassus eo.   (*Amores* II.4.1–4)[19]

I would not venture to defend my faulty morals or to take up the armour of lies to shield my failings. I confess – if owning my shortcomings is of any value; and now, having owned them, I madly rave in my sins. (p. 391, modified)

Ovid is not using the concept of confesion lightly here – the body of the *Amores*, like that of the *Confessio*, is itself a confession of the

---

16 This theme is also elaborated in *Amores* II.18 and III.12.13–18.
17 Huygens 1970, pp. 36–7, translation from Minnis and Scott 1988, p. 28 (with their 'misuses' changed here to 'miseries', translating *miseriae*).
18 For the range of Gower's *personae* in the *Confessio* (*amans*, poet, historical Gower), see Strohm 1982. The best discussions of the literary ancestry of Amans are Burrow 1983, pp. 5–11 and Zeeman 1991, both of whom argue that Gower is indebted to the *dit amoreux* of Machaut and Froissart. My discussion of Gower's debts to Ovid, and especially to the *Amores*, is complementary to these studies.
19 For the self-presentation of the *Amores* as a confession, see also *Amores* I.2.19–38; II.17.1–4; II.18.1–12; III.11a.1–8; III.11b.33–44.

intimate life of the lover's troubled and unsatisfying amatory relationship. Of course, there are significant differences between the
voice of Amans and that of the *Amores* narrator: Amans is relent-
lessly sincere and faithful, for example, whereas the lover of the
Amores knows 'the olde daunce'. But even if Gower's use of the confessional frame might owe its articulation to Christian traditions,
the idea of the lover's confession itself is Ovidian, drawn from the
Amores.

Both the *Amores* and the *Confessio*, then, establish the asymmetries
between politics and love. This is achieved essentially through the
represented experience of the narrators, but in both cases it
involves a change of discursive and generic allegiances. In Gower
these changes are particularly pronounced and awkward. In the
political discourse of the Prologue, we remember, the remedy for
political division is ethical reform, which lies within the power of
individuals. The beginning of Book I, however, is extremely
explicit about the impossibility of controlling desire (the speaker,
after all, is Desire himself, Amans, from whom we would hardly
expect a self-annihilation). Having said that he will 'change the
stile' of his writings, he says that he will

> speke of thing is noght so strange,
> Which every kinde hath upon honde,
> And wherupon the world mot stonde,
> And hath don sithen it began,
> And schal whil ther is any man.   (I.10–14)

This description suggests the procreative love of natural creatures,
rather than the love, or 'charite' (described in the Prologue) that
promotes civil peace, and by which every man should 'sette pes
with other / And loven as his oghne brother' (Prol. 1049–50). The
kind of love described by Amans here seems to provoke ferocity
rather than peace, if the Latin headlines (whose ambiguities point
in the same direction)[20] are to be believed:

---

[20] If we take *unanimes* to be a predicative adjective dependent on *feras*, then the lines suggest
that beasts are made to be of 'one mind'; the potentially positive suggestion of harmony
here is however ruled out by the context provided by the lines that follow, describing
love as provoking disruption. Either we should understand the lines to mean that beasts
are of one mind in their pursuit of disruptive love, or else we should take *feras* to be the
predicate of the second main clause: 'Created love provokes those in harmony to be
beasts.' See Echard and Fanger 1991, pp. 14–15 for a discussion of these lines, and the
fine article of Wetherbee 1991.

> Naturatus amor nature legibus orbem
> Subdit, et unanimes concitat esse feras.[21]

And this love, according to the narrator, is irresistible:

> For loves lawe is out of reule,
> That of tomoche or of tolite
> Welnygh is every man to wyte,
> And natheles ther is noman
> In al this world so wys, that can
> Of love tempre the mesure,
> Bot as it falth in aventure:
> For wit ne strengthe may noght helpe,
> And he which elles wolde him yelpe
> Is rathest throwen under fote,
> Ther can no wiht therof do bote.   (1.18–28)

'Shall I resist?' asks the narrator of the *Amores* after he has been struck by Cupid:

> Cedimus, an subitum luctando accendimus ignem?
> cedamus! leve fit, quod bene fertur, onus.   (*Amores* 1.2.9–10)

Shall I yield? or by resisting kindle still more the inward-stealing flame? Let me yield! Light grows the burden that is well borne. (p. 323, modified)

The philosophical positions of both narrators (of the *Amores* and of the *Confessio*) stand in direct conflict with the Prologue of the *Confessio*, which has it, as I have said, that Fortune is a personification of human instability itself:

> So that the man is overal
> His oghne cause of wel and wo.
> That we fortune clepe so
> Out of the man himself it groweth.   (Prol. 546–9)

The stance of the narrator in Book I, then, is a capitulation to 'the world as of his propre kynde', in which, in the specific case of love at any rate, men *can* be excused for submitting to an irresistible, natural force. These two prologues do not at all present themselves as any neat example of an extrinsic and an intrinsic

---

[21] Gower is invoking a Ciceronian context here, the opening of the *De inventione*, where Cicero describes a time before the establishment of political rule where men acted as beasts, controlled by blind appetite ('caeca ac temeraria dominatrix animi cupiditas') (*De inventione* I.2.ii).

prologue, of the kind we find in late medieval academic writing, where the intrinsic prologue neatly locates itself within, *and marks its subservience to*, the larger field of knowledge outlined in the external prologue. Instead, the two discursive blocks, politics (Prologue) and sexual love (Book I), stand in a philosophically hostile relationship. As with the opening of the *Amores*, the championing of irresistible sexual desire in Book I marks a discursive invasion and rout of the field of wisdom outlined in the *Confessio* Prologue.

The opening moves of the *Confessio*, then, are very like those of the *Amores*, even if Gower makes the disruptions between politics and sexual desire more pronounced and more philosophically explicit than Ovid. And, correlatively, the voice of Gower–Amans in Book I is closely squared with that of Ovid–*amans*. The connections between the *Amores* and the *Confessio* are, indeed, extensive: in both texts we have a lover who is divided against himself, humiliated by love though unable to stop loving;[22] solidarities between the lover and all with whom he consorts are dissolved in both texts;[23] and in both Ovid and Gower the lover must practise deception, not only against others, but more especially against themselves, and particularly in the matter of age: in the *Amores* (as in the *Confessio*), we are only gradually made to realize that the lover is impotent.[24]

If Gower is aligning Amans with the Ovidian voice of the *Amores*, then he would seem to be quite deliberately aligning Amans with

[22] It is in Book IV of the *Confessio* that Amans most fully confesses to his love as a debilitating mental obsession that he cannot escape; see *Confessio amantis* IV.557–709; 1122–223; 1648–770; 3458–501 (see also the powerful description of 'melancholy' at III.34–133). The narrator of the *Amores* in particular presents himself in exactly the same way, as divided against himself: see *Amores* 1.6.33–6 and II.4.1–6.

[23] Gower's Amans is entirely isolated through his obsessive love, distrustful of all those around him; see, for example, *Confessio amantis* II.235–77; 454–551; 1957–2076; 2328–428. Deceit and distrust are constant themes in the *Amores* – the lover must not only deceive his lady's husband (e.g. I.4), but also his lady (II.8). Equally, his lady is encouraged to deceive him and all her lovers (I.8), which she does (II.5). Even the pleasure of reconciliation provokes distrust – 'who taught my lady to kiss so well?' wonders the lover (II.5.55–62).

[24] In the *Confessio*, Amans's age is revealed in Book VIII. In the *Amores*, the lover is, apparently, young, but it emerges gradually that he is in some ways already old: I.15.1–6 give the impression that he is young; age of a kind is suggested at II.9a.19–24 and II.19.23, but in a sequence (III.7) which has many parallels with the *Confessio*, he confesses to a humiliating impotence: the lover says that he has imagined the pleasures he will have with his lady (lines 63–4), and that she could rejuvenate Nestor and Tithonus (lines 41–2); despite this, the sequence describes a humiliating impotence in the lover – 'Nec iuvenem nec me sensit amica virum' (III.7.20). For subtle accounts of Gower's strategy in not being clear about his age, see Burrow 1983 and Zeeman 1991.

the Ovidian erotic tradition. Attacks on Ovid's erotic verse are not hard to find in the later Middle Ages; for an example relatively close to Gower, suffice it to mention here the comments of John Ridevall, in his commentary (*c.* 1333) on the *De civitate Dei.* Ridevall is discussing Varro's comments on Roman poets, cited by Augustine in Book VI of the *De civitate Dei.* Ridevall's distinction is between philosophers who write for utility and poets who write simply to give pleasure. Ridevall wants the distinction to be finer; he says that many Roman poets, and in particular the satirists, did not write to promote sensual pleasure,

since many of them intended to rerephend the sin of the flesh, among other vices, as is evident in their satires. For those Roman poets whom they called satirists, were powerful and perceptive censors of sins and carnal pleasures, as we can see in the books of Juvenal, Persius and the poet Horace.

quia multi de eis intendebant reprehendere vitium carnis, una cum aliis vitiis, sicut patet in eorum satiriis. Illi enim poete romanorum, quos vocabant satiricos, fuerunt fortes et acuti reprehensores vitiorum et carnalium delectationum, sicut patet in libris Iuvenalis et Persii et poete Oratii.[25]

Having argued that poetry of this kind can offer cognitive and moral instruction, he finally concedes to Varro that many Roman poets did not in fact offer utility of this kind:

But this is not true of the songs of the poets, since many of them composed many works promoting sexual pleasures, as for example Ovid and many others, even if some poets (the satirists) composed their songs for the reprehension of such carnal sins.

Sed non sic fuit de carminibus poetarum, quia multi poete fecerunt multas poeses inducentes homines ad delectationes carnales, sicut poeta Ovidius et alii, licet aliqui, scilicet satirici, componebant sua carmina ad reprehendendum talia vitia carnalia.[26]

---

[25] Smalley 1960, Appendix 1, p. 319. For another English example of a powerful attack on Ovid, see Roger Bacon, in Brewer 1859, ch. 15, pp. 54–5, and in Massa 1953, V.3.7–8, p. 255. Some important witnesses to the tradition of Ovid as an immoral poet are listed by Hexter 1986, pp. 17–18. Any remark about Ovid's medieval reception should, however, bear in mind Hexter's statement that 'there was not one medieval Ovid, but several' (p. 11). This comment serves as a guiding principle for the present chapters. The vast topic of the medieval reception of Ovid awaits authoritative treatment; for a sketch of sorts, see Allen 1992, pp. 38–58, and pp. 111–17, and references. Hexter 1986 provides a model test case. See Pelen 1987 for closely focused discussions of how Ovid might be received.

[26] Smalley 1960, p. 319.

Gower, then, in the persona of Amans, would seem to have aligned himself with this tradition, the tradition radically opposed to the political satire of the Prologue both philosophically and generically.

GENIUS, *PRAECEPTOR AMORIS*

My reader might concede that the voice of Amans establishes a structural incongruence at the beginning of Book I, an incongruence which derives from the radical asymmetries between love and politics. But, he or she might object, that does not go far to assail the consensus outlined above, according to which the formal strategies of the poem are totally consistent with its moral pedagogy. For, my imagined reader might object, we expect the congruence between the Prologue and Book I to be achieved not by Amans, but rather by Genius, Amans's instructor. After all, a key aspect of the newer consensus is that Genius speaks for the tradition of the moralized Ovid – that moralizing enterprise which was applied, in different ways, to both the *Metamorphoses* and to the *Heroides*. J. A. W. Bennett, we remember, made the point that 'the creed of Genius ... is the poet's creed';[27] Alastair Minnis carried the argument further by identifying Genius's moralizations with the ways in which the *Heroides* were moralized;[28] and, more recently, Rita Copeland has developed Minnis's point by arguing that 'Genius serves the same function as the translator's moralizing commentary in the *Ovide moralisé*'; she also confirms Bennett's point about the identity of Genius and Gower as author: 'In ... accomodating the moral interests of Amans, Genius also functions as a projection of the "author", or as a voice of the *intentio auctoris* which monitors the purveying of meaning throughout the text, proposing to keep it in line with the *intentio* as announced in the two prologues. Genius's role is to act as guardian of Gower's argument, to keep Gower's reinvention of his *materia* on course.'[29] Copeland's argument here serves, indeed, as a neat summary of the stabilizing, constraining, harmonizing role assigned to Genius by these critics, and by almost all scholars who have studied Genius as a psychological personification.[30]

So, we might argue, even if Amans is an essentially Ovidian figure, actively opposed to the political interests of the Prologue, Genius

---

[27] Bennett 1966, p. 112.   [28] Minnis 1980.   [29] Copeland 1991, p. 205.
[30] Especially Economou 1970, and Chance Nitzsche 1975, pp. 125–30.

rights the balance, by representing 'another' medieval Ovid, that of the moralizers. This argument would be attractive, partly because it registers the fact that there *were* 'different' Ovids in the later medieval period. Ovid, who provides so much of the matter for his biography and critical reception in his own works, himself promotes the idea of different Ovids: this is certainly implicit in the shift from the erotic poetry to, say, the *Tristia* and *Epistulae ex Ponto* (in both of which Ovid presents himself as championing the solidarity of friendship and marriage), and it is explicit in the *Remedia amoris*. Having said that it is Ovid who has taught men to love (in the *Ars amatoria*), he goes on, in the *Remedia*, to say that it is 'the same' Ovid who will now cure them of love in this new work. Of course there are playful ambiguities here: does 'same' mean 'the same man teaching from a quite different perspective', or does it really mean (always a possibility in the *Remedia*) the 'very same Ovid, teaching, in fact, the very same thing'?:

> Naso legendus erat tum, cum didicistis amare:
> Idem nunc vobis Naso legendus erit
>
> (*Remedia amoris*, lines 71–2)[31]

You should have read Naso then when you learnt to love: you should read the same Naso now. (p. 183)

In any case, the very assertion that this is the 'same' Ovid clearly implies the possibility that there might be more than one. And any reading of the *Confessio* should take into account the full range of possible Ovids available to Gower, who, in the *Vox clamantis*, manifests a demonstrable, and intimate knowledge of the text of almost the full range of Ovid's works.[32]

---

[31]   The text of the *Remedia amoris* is drawn from Mozley 1929; the translations are based on this edition.

[32]   Twentieth-century readers are often unwilling to believe that medieval poets read classical poetry extensively and intelligently. That Gower was familiar with the entire Ovidian corpus is, luckily, empirically demonstrable, given the range and density of his borrowings from the entirety of Ovid's corpus in the *Vox clamantis*. These borrowings can be checked in the notes to Macaulay 1902, *The Latin Works*, and Stockton 1962, who reports that Ovid is the source of no fewer than 537 lines (a count which does not include phrasal borrowing), drawn from all Ovid's longer works (pp. 26–8). I have not been able to consult Frederick Crittenden Mish, 'The Influence of Ovid on John Gower's *Vox Clamantis*', unpublished Ph.D. thesis (University of Minnesota, 1973). The abstract of this thesis reports that Mish has found an extra 217 full line quotations, bringing the total to 754. Yeager 1990, pp. 45–60 (also Yeager 1989) considers these borrowings, suggesting that Gower was writing *cento*. The topic is capable of much wider treatment, given the range and intelligence of the borrowings. The *Tristia* recollections in the Prologue to the *Vox* are a particularly good example of Gower's confident, apposite deployment of Ovid.

But if there are in fact 'different' Ovids available to Gower, is it the Ovid of the *Ovide moralisé* in whom Genius's voice is subsumed? This is by no means an absurd suggestion – the very structure of Ovidian story followed by moralization provides *prima facie* evidence for it; and, indeed, it has been demonstrated textually that Gower did draw on such texts.[33] I do not want to dismiss this possibility entirely, but I will now argue, nonetheless, that Genius can also be convincingly related to 'other', less predictable Ovids, and in particular to the *praeceptor amoris* of the *Ars amatoria* and the *Remedia amoris*. These two texts, along with the *Amores*, are clearly companion pieces of sorts, whose relationship is (inevitably with Ovid) playfully complex: in each of the three cases it could be argued that the one text is a critique of the other two; it can just as easily be argued that all three promote exactly the same ideal of cynical sensual pleasure.[34] In any case, I want now to argue that, if Amans is indebted to the voice of the *Amores*, then Genius takes on the double role of *praeceptor amoris* who both promotes and, rather unconvincingly, dissuades from loving – Genius assumes, that is, the voice(s) of the Ovid of the *Ars amatoria* and the *Remedia amoris*. Gower builds the relationships of Ovid's *oeuvre* into the single structure of the *Confessio*. And Genius is, accordingly, a much less stable figure than the 'consensus' position would have us believe.

If Genius *were* representative of the exegetical voice of the Ovid commentary tradition, then why should Amans listen to him? Amans, after all, represents desire, and until the last book of the poem he shows no repentance for loving at all. On the contrary, what he wants from Genius is encouragement to love. He says as much on many occasions. In Book IV, for example, he dismisses the charge of negligence in love, but asks why it is that he is still unsuccessful in his pursuit:

> For thogh I be non of the wise,
> I am so trewly amerous,
> That I am evere curious

33 Mainzer 1972.
34 In arguing that Gower's meeting with Ovid is much more direct and much fuller than previous criticism has been prepared to allow, I am much indebted to the fine (largely) unpublished dissertation of McNally 1961 (a chapter, not about Ovid, was published, McNally 1964). He draws attention to Gower's use of the *Ars amatoria* and the *Remedia amoris* in the frame of the *Confessio*, esp. chs. 1–4. See also Hiscoe 1985 for an argument that Gower's playful strategy is very Ovidian. Hiscoe does not range beyond the *Metamorphoses*, however.

Of hem that conne best enforme
To knowe and witen al the forme,
What falleth unto loves craft.
Bot yit ne fond I noght the haft,
Which mihte unto that bladd acorde...
Yit so fer cowthe I nevere finde
Man that be resoun ne be kinde
Me cowthe teche such an art,
That he ne failede of a part.   (IV.920–6, 930–4)

Like other late fourteenth-century English poets, Gower is very sensitive, I think, to the psychology of reading and listening to literature, and especially to the place of desire in literary reception.[35] Amans, as desire, wants to be 'enformed' in 'loves craft': he continues, in the passage I have just cited, by saying how active his will is, 'to lerne al that he lerne may, / How that I mihte love winne' (IV.954–5). Passages of this kind draw on the lexis of pedagogy, but (like Ovid's erotic poems) do so to direct it only to teaching in the 'craft', or art of love. And later in Book IV Ovid is explicitly referred to as the teacher who might help him. Genius mentions the *Remedia amoris*, and suggests that Amans read that book, if 'that thou fiele / That love wringe thee to sore'; Amans's reply insists on the connection between desire and literary understanding; with regard to Ovid's books, he says this:

My fader, if thei mihte spede
Mi love, I wolde his bokes rede;
And if thei techen to restreigne
Mi love, it were an ydel peine
To lerne a thing which mai noght be.   (IV.2675–9)[36]

Amans, then, as desire, desires only the fulfilment of his very self; the logic of his listening to Genius for so long a time can only be that he sees, or rather hears in Genius what he wants to. *A priori*, we might therefore expect Genius to be the one who 'conne best enforme / To knowe and witen al the forme, /

35 This point is substantiated in chapter 8. For the connections between stylistic and psychological categories, as defined in thirteenth-century literary theory, see Simpson 1986a.
36 *Confessio amantis* VI.875–98 should also be mentioned in this connection, where Amans says how much (transitory) hope he derives from the reading of romances. See chapter 8 below.

What falleth unto loves craft' (IV.923–5), the *praeceptor amoris*
of the *Ars amatoria*. Does Genius fulfil this expectation?

At first sight Genius's appearance would seem to confirm precisely the opposition between political and amatory traditions
implied by the narrator's dismissal of satire in favour of treating
'kinde love'. Genius here is the priest of Venus, which role would
seem to promise an intellectual perspective even more limited than
the Genius of Jean de Meun's section of the *Roman de la Rose*, who
is the priest of Nature. Gower's Genius is called by Venus 'myn
oghne Clerk' (I.196), which itself evokes an Ovidian tradition by
recalling Chaucer's description of Ovid in the *House of Fame* as
'Venus clerk'.

Clerk he certainly is: he introduces his matter with a formal,
academic prologue (effectively the third, after the prologues of
'Gower' in the Prologue and of Amans in Book I). Genius specifies
author (Genius, priest of Venus); intention (to instruct Amans);
matter ('Venus bokes'); *modus agendi* (confession); order (first to treat
the vices, and then love); utility (Amans's improvement), and the
part of philosophy to which the work belongs (ethics). But whereas
Amans had indicated to his reader that he was going to leave aside
moral and political questions and treat of natural love, Genius,
instead, promises a reverse procedure. He repeats that he will treat
first the vices, but return finally to love as his concluding topic. It
belongs to the office of priest to treat of vice, he says,

> whos ordre that I bere,
> So that I wol nothing forbere,
> That I the vices on and on
> Ne schal thee schewen everychon;
> Wherof thou myht take evidence
> To reule with thi conscience.
> Bot of conclusion final
> Conclude I wol in special
> For love, whos servant I am,
> And why the cause is that I cam.   (I.243–52)

On a superficial reading, Genius would seem here (in contradiction
to his identification with Venus) to promise the kind of easy congruence between amatory and moral traditions which critics have
seen in the poem. But before we readily accept Genius as the
moral spokesman of the poem, we should question the possibility of
any such easy congruence between sexual desire and ethics. If

'love' is understood according to the description of Amans, as the power 'in which ther can noman him reule, / For loves lawe is out of reule', then Genius's promise to 'reule' Amans's conscience and *then* to treat of love is contradictory. What does Genius mean by 'love'? His definition will have to be broader than that of Amans, and will have to approach 'the lawe of charite, / Which is the pro-pre duete/ Belongende unto the presthode', as mentioned by the narrator in the Prologue (lines 257–9), if there is to be any possibil-ity of drawing the ethical discussion of vice into concordance with the 'matere of love'.

Whether or not Genius is capable of expounding the matter of love according to this broader definition is left uncertain in Genius's self-introduction. On the one hand, he promises to fulfil his duties as a priest in a way which suggests that his priestly func-tion is not merely metaphorical, as it is in, for example, Jean's *Roman de la Rose*. Jean's Nature (whom Genius unswervingly follows in the *Roman*) leaves to God all judgement of vice, whereas Gower's Genius, as I have just mentioned, promises to treat of other things, 'that touchen to the cause of vice / For that belongeth to thoffice / Of Prest' (I.241–3). On the other hand, this priestly function is felt to be *distinct* from his function as the servant of Venus. He dis-claims complete authority for himself as a moral instructor, pre-cisely on account of his obligation to Venus: having explained the vices, he says that he will demonstrate the properties of love,

> How that thei stonde be degrees
> After the disposicioun
> Of Venus, whos condicioun
> I moste folwe, as I am holde.
> For I with love am al withholde,
> So that the lasse I am to wyte,
> Thogh I ne conne bot a lyte
> Of othre thinges that ben wise:
> I am noght tawht in such a wise.   (I.258–66)

This description of his subservience to Venus might incline the reader to be wary of any moral advice offered by Genius; in the same way that Amans declares love to be an irresistible force in the opening of Book I, so too does Genius define his relationship to Venus as one of natural affinity and submission, which excuses any ignorance he might have in the field of moral instruction. He even

seems to disclaim knowledge of the kind of thing we find in the
Ovide moralisé, since he asserts, if not ignorance, then at least lack of
instruction in this moralizing, glossing tradition. He explains his
disclaimer to moral authority in this way:

> For it is noght my comun us
> To speke of vices and vertus,
> Bot al of love and of his lore,
> For Venus bokes of nomore
> Me techen nowther text ne glose.   (I.267–71)

It is at least possible, then, that Genius is speaking of ethics as a feint
for different interests, and that, like Amans's, Genius's voice is that of
an ironic persona. The strategy is more subtle than with Amans, who
declares his hand with touching sincerity; Genius, on the other hand,
comes with the accoutrements of priestly authority, but uses those
precisely to further interests which are opposed to that authority.

At this point, the argument could turn to the 'immediate' literary traditions behind Genius: one could point to Gower's reference
to Genius the priest in the *Vox clamantis*, where we see exactly the
kind of ironic exploitation of priestly and pedagogic authority I am
suggesting as a possibility in the *Confessio*:

> Quas Venus et Genius cellas modo rite gubernant,
> Carnis non claustri iura tenere docent:
> Conuentus custos Genius confessor et extat,
> Et quandoque locum presulis ipse tenet:
> Sub specie iuris in claustro visitat ipsas,
> Quas veniens thalamis, iure negante, regit.   (IV.14.595–600)[37]

Venus and Genius teach the cloister cells, which they now govern in their
fashion, to hold the law of the flesh, and not that of the cloister. Genius is
the convent's protector and confessor, and sometimes he holds the rank of
bishop. He visits the ladies in their cloister under the guise of righteous
authority, but when he comes to the bedchambers, he casts righteousness
aside, and wields his power over them. (p. 180, significantly modified)

And one could, of course, turn to Jean's *Roman de la Rose*, where the
priestly Genius promises individuals a beatification which might

---

[37] The text of the *Vox clamantis* is drawn from Macaulay 1902, *The Latin Works*. The translation is based on Stockton 1962, though he mistranslates this passage when he gives:
'Venus and Genius do not teach the cloister cells, which they now govern in their fashion, to keep the laws concerning the flesh' (p. 180).

preserve Nature forever (while the individuals who ensure Nature's preservation might themselves be damned – a snag Jean's Genius studiously avoids). He promises a return to the Golden Age in which technology is otiose, but the very means he promotes to achieve that return are themselves 'technological' (i.e. the 'ploughshare' of the penis).[38] At the same time, these examples of Genius as a morally questionable figure could be countered, as indeed they have been, by the example of Alan's *De planctu Naturae*, where Genius's procreative and ethical functions seem to be unified.

Literary tradition certainly allows for the kind of ironic instabilities I am suggesting as a possibility for Gower's Genius; but the argument about Genius's moral status could go either way, given the fascinating, seemingly contradictory range in the figure's literary history. Let us then go to Gower's text itself, and listen to Genius's pedagogy. The following examples are deliberately selective, and I do not for a moment pretend that they entirely characterize the position of Gower's Genius; but when we do listen to Genius's advice, we do hear, with remarkable frequency, the voice of Ovid's *praeceptor amoris*.

The narrator of the *Ars amatoria* (*Aa*) announces himself as a kind of royal tutor, both *praeceptor amoris* and *praeceptor Amoris*: 'Me Venus artificem tenero praefecit Amori' (1.7) (a challenging pedagogic project if ever there were one). He offers, accordingly, a *speculum principis*, but in love not politics, and he does so through his own experience: 'Usus opus movet hoc: vati parete perito; / Vera canam...' (*Aa*, 1.29–30). Gower's Genius, too, is, as we have observed, subject to Venus, and Amans pays him obeisance precisely because he is experienced in love: 'So as thou hast experience of love' (1.17). And it is this experience of love which prohibits Ovid's *praeceptor* from dealing with politics; on the contrary, he actively subverts any such instruction: his initial comparison between Chiron educating the prince Achilles and himself educating prince Cupid suggests how pedagogy in love occludes political instruction.

This neutralization of politics is everywhere apparent in the *Ars amatoria*: the very pedagogic project itself, which is modelled on the instruction of a prince, a warrior and an orator, is turned to

---

[38]   Jean de Meun, *Roman de la Rose*, lines 19439–20703.

entirely apolitical ends;[39] and the political implications of mythical stories are entirely ignored. Take for example the promotion of rhetoric in love from 1.437–86. The *praeceptor* begins by encouraging verbal promises to the lover rather than material gifts – it was entreaty, he says, which moved Achilles to give Hector back to Priam. 'Hoc opus, hic labor est', he says, citing *Aeneid* VI.129 – the words of the Cumean Sybil to Aeneas, warning him that descent to the underworld is easy, but much more difficult the return from the infernal regions to the heavens. This feat is achieved only by those who become the sons of the gods through being loved by Jupiter or through their ardent practice of virtue. For the Ovidian *praeceptor*, on the contrary, the *opus* and *labor* is for the lover to win the woman without material gifts. One presumably becomes, or approximates the 'son of a god' (Cupid) through such a feat. The *praeceptor* goes on to recommend skill in eloquence, which serves not only in the courts and the senate, but also to win a woman's love. This comparison between the public and private might suggest parallel, but separate realms of practice; as the *praeceptor* develops the argument, however, it is clear that they stand in a hostile relationship, the one (especially love) threatening to invade the other. If the woman is unmoved by entreaty, the lover should not despair; in blithe oblivion to the political naïveté of his advice, the *praeceptor* recommends perseverance:

> Penelopen ipsam, persta modo, tempore vinces:
> Capta vides sero Pergama, capta tamen.   (*Aa* I.477–8)[40]

Only persevere; you will overcome Penelope herself; late, as you see, did Pergamus fall, yet fall it did. (p. 45)

The small example of this section of the *Ars*, comic but not without its moments of startling narratorial arrogance and ignorance, is representative of the fabric of the work as a whole. Let us now turn to an example of Genius's moralizing in the *Confessio*; do we find the same instabilities?

In Book I Genius moralizes some stories in ways consistent with a long tradition of Neo-Platonic, ethical moralization of poetic

---

[39] See Solodow 1977 for a detailed account of the cultural ideals subverted in Ovid's amatory pedagogy.

[40] The text of the *Ars amatoria* is drawn from Mozley 1929; the translations are based on this edition.

fable;[41] the story of Medusa, for example (drawn from the *Metamorphoses*) is used to illustrate a moral point about not allowing the sight to dwell on illicit pleasure, and so becoming a slave to lust (1.436–44). But his moralization of other tales is more complex. In the story of Mundus and Paulina (the first tale exemplifying one of the Seven Deadly Sins), Genius's narration and moralization suggest that his conception of love is identical to the unphilosophical view of Amans, expressed in the opening of Book 1. He introduces the story by setting it historically in the reign of Tiberius; but whatever the time, all, he says, are subject to the a-historical law that reason is unable to withstand 'the lawe / Of thilke bore frele kinde, / Which makth the hertes yhen blinde' (1.772–4). Just as Tiberius's power is implicitly belittled by the description of love's power, so too is Mundus's; Genius introduces Duke Mundus through a description of his military power, and through the paradox that this was insufficient

> The strengthe of love to withstonde,
> That he ne was so broght to honde,
> That malgre wher he wol or no,
> This yonge wif he loveth so.   (1.787–90)

In itself, this does not indicate Genius's attitude towards such love; the moralization, however, does: whereas the priests, who assisted Mundus in his deception and rape of Paulina, are put to death, Mundus himself is merely exiled. Genius, without demur, reports that his behaviour was excused by the court because of his helplessness before love:

> For he with love was bestad,
> His dom was noght so harde lad;
> For Love put reson aweie
> And can noght se the rihte weie.   (1.1049–52)

The judgement here, the court's as much as Genius's, implies precisely the view of love expressed by Amans, as an irresistible force whose subjection of reason excuses moral failing. Interestingly, the figures who are judged in the tale are the priests, who are condemned, since

---

[41] For this tradition, see Buffière 1956.

whan men wolden vertu seke,
Men scholde it in the Prestes finde;
Here ordre is of so hyh a kinde,
That thei be Duistres of the weie:
Forthi, if eny man forsueie
Thurgh hem, thei be noght excusable.   (I.1024-9)

The species of pride being illustrated by Genius is hypocrisy; is it an over-reading to suggest that Genius might himself be guilty of a certain 'false semblance' here? After all, he is also a pagan priest, posing as a true guide of virtue;[42] and his position is noticeably different to the view of virtue expressed in the Prologue, according to which men *do* have power over themselves. A standard ploy of the ironist in medieval literature is to imply one's own probity by pointing to the falsehoods of others. Genius, it could be argued, is practising this strategy: he points to the fact that the pagan priests 'engined' Paulina (I.878) through 'fals ymaginacion' in such a way as to withdraw any focus on his own standing as an ethical teacher. If Genius is trying to dissuade Amans from loving, then the story of hypocrisy is otiose, since Amans rightly disclaims any hypocrisy; the effect of the story is rather to confirm Amans in his pursuit of love, since the Amans figure from within the tale, Mundus, is excused. Perhaps, it could be argued, Amans is being 'engined' by Genius himself.

And, like Ovid's *praeceptor*, who is blind to the political implications of his stories, so too is Genius here. He follows the story of

---

[42] If the unreliability of the pagan priests in the Paulina and Mundus story does have any bearing on Genius's own unreliability as a pagan priest, it may be relevant to mention other examples of pagan priests: in III.2555-7 we hear of Achastus, (like Genius) the priest of Venus, who absolved Peleus for the murder of his brother, 'Al were ther no repentance in that cas.' At V.1840, we are told about the self-deception of Thoas, who allows Antenor to steal the statue of Palladion:

> Bot Thoas at the same throwe,
> Whan Anthenor this Juel tok,
> Wynkende caste awei his lok
> For a deceipte and for a wyle:
> As he that scholde himself beguile,
> He hidde his yhen fro the sihte,
> And wende wel that he so mihte
> Excuse his false conscience.   (V.1840-7)

I do not, however, mean for a moment to suggest that virtue in this poem is the preserve of Christians; indeed, one of Gower's central interests is the way in which the impulse to Christian law is itself natural (e.g. the story of Constantine's conversion in II. 3187-496). I develop this point in chapter 8.

Mundus and Paulina with the hypocrisy of Aeneas and Antenor, who were 'engined' by the Greeks to betray their own city (I.1101). This is the first of many Troy stories in the *Confessio*, political stories which could have implications for Gower's London – the poem was commissioned, after all, 'under the toun of newe Troye' (first recension, Prol. 37); but Genius focuses only on the vice of hypocrisy, which, despite its success in this case, he rightly condemns. He ignores the causes of the war, for which he would, presumably, excuse Paris, just as he has excused Mundus for the uncontrollable passion which provokes his rape.[43] Skimming over these awkward implications, Genius rounds off his treatment of the sin of hypocrisy (in which, as I say, Amans is unquestionably innocent) in this way:

> 'For feigned semblant is so softe,
> Unethes love may be war.
> Forthi, my Sone, as I wel dar,
> I charge thee to fle that vice,
> That many a womman hath mad nice;
> Bot lok thou dele noght withal.'
> 'Iwiss, fader, nomor I schal.'   (I.1220–6)

This smooth, gratuitous and painless confession seems to me to ignore the ethical and political implications of the two previous stories; even if the implications are only touched on lightly, we should remember with regard to Genius (whose preaching is 'softe and faire' (I.232)) that 'feigned semblant is so softe, / Unethes love may be war'.

I have no wish to suggest that simply because Genius encourages Amans's love, he is morally dubious; why, someone might rightly ask, should encouragement of love be dubious at all; and, indeed, a fundamental point (*the* fundamental point) of the 'consensus' position is that a lover's sins are 'real' sins (and the same presumably holds for lovers' virtues). But there are inconsistencies: against the ethical discussion of the Prologue, Genius insists that love is uncon-

---

43 Genius, of course, knows the story of how the Trojan war began: he tells it at V.7195–590. But even here he seems to miss the political burden of the story; despite the fact that he sets Paris's abduction in a sharply defined political context, Genius himself sees the point of the story as being about sacrilege of holy places, since Paris abducted Helen from the temple of Venus. He implies that abduction from another place would have been blameless. See also Hiscoe 1985, p. 368.

trollable, and therefore concurs with the remission of Mundus; and, if he encourages love in Amans's case, then he is moving directly counter to his own advice in Book VIII, which is that Amans, who is a *senex amans*, should leave his love aside.

And the subtle encouragements of the Mundus and Paulina story become much less subtle in many later examples, where Genius, in close imitation of the Ovidian *praeceptor*, directly sustains Amans in his delusion. In several instances, he declares that the passion of love is irresistible.[44] And to the *senex amans*, Genius consistently holds out the possibility of *success* in love. In Book I, for example, after the story of Albinus and Rosemund, he warns against boasting, for him who 'thenkth to spede / Of love' (I.2654–5) (cf. *Aa* II.625–40); and in conclusion to the whole of Book I, he (gratuitously) encourages humility to Amans, so that, he says, 'the more of grace thou schalt gete' (I.3425) (cf. *Aa* II.143–60). The same encouragement is found in Book II, where Genius warns against detraction of rivals, simply because Amans will be more likely to be satisfied: 'Bot evere kep thi tunge stille, / Thou miht the more have of thi wille' (II.553–4) (cf. *Aa* II.535–46); again in the same book he advises that Amans set envy aside 'If thou wolt finde a siker weie / To love' (II.3153–4). In the third book Genius promotes patient eloquence, since fair speech has often brought success to the lover who would otherwise have 'failed mochel of his wille' (III.607) (cf. *Aa* I.459–68). Or again, in the same book, Genius warns Amans that if he desires to be 'in reste' (III.816), he must not follow the example of the crow who told tales about his master's wife's adultery (cf. *Aa* II. 553–60); Amans should 'drawe in be frendlihede' those whom he hates, 'so miht thou gete love algate / And sette thee, my Sone, in reste' (III.948–9) (cf. *Aa* I.579–86).

Again, in Book IV, Genius cites the example of Pygmaleon. He introduces the story against pusillanimity by saying that Fortune favours those who are bold in love:

> For after that a man poursuieth
> To love, so fortune suieth,
> Fulofte and yifth hire happi chance
> To him which makth continuance
> To preie love and to beseche.   (IV.365–9)

---

[44] See, for example, I.2620–5; II.2580–5; III.344–60; 390–1; VI.76–102; 306–18; 1235–60; 1261–92; VII.771–800.

These lines closely resemble advice in the *Ars amatoria*, where the
praeceptor is also promoting courage in speech:

> Conloquii iam tempus adest; fuge rustice longe
>   Hinc pudor; audentem Forsque Venusque iuvat.   (*Aa* 1.607–8)

Now is the time for talk with her; away with you, rustic shame! Chance
and Venus help the brave. (p. 55)

And after the success of Pygmaleon, who 'thurgh pure impression
/ Of his ymaginacion' falls in love with his statue, Genius rounds
off with encouragement to speak, since, 'if thou spare / To speke,
lost is al thi fare' (IV.439–40). In response to Amans's long account
of his debilitating mental obsession at this point, Genius, like
Ovid's *praeceptor*, simply continues to insist that he must pluck up
his courage and declare himself:

> Forthi pull up a besi herte,
> Mi Sone, and let nothing asterte
> Of love fro thi besinesse.   (IV.723–5)

Or again, at the end of Book IV, Genius encourages perseverance
in love. Amans cannot be said to have been a negligent lover at all,
but, says Genius, he should wait upon chance and the revolution of
the heavens:

> And therof, Sone, I wol thee rede,
> Abyd, and haste noght to faste;
> Thi dees ben every dai to caste,
> Thou nost what chance schal betyde.
> Betre is to wayte upon the tyde
> Than rowe ayein the stremes stronge:
> For thogh so be thee thenketh longe,
> Per cas the revolucion
> Of hevene and thi condicion
> Ne be noght yit of on acord.   (IV.1776–85)

Like the earlier advice to wait upon chance, this advice is strikingly
at odds with the ethical current of the Prologue; it is also strikingly
close to the advice of the *praeceptor amoris* of the *Ars amatoria*:

Si nec blanda satis, nec erit tibi comis amanti,
    Perfer et obdura: postmodo mitis erit.
Flectitur obsequio curvatus ab arbore ramus:
    Frangis, si vires experiere tuas.
Obsequio tranantur aquae: nec vincere possis
    Flumina, si contra, quam rapit unda, nates.   (*Aa* II.177–82)

Should she be neither kindly nor courteous to your wooing, persist and
steel your resolve; one day she will be kind. By compliance is the curved
bough bent away from the tree; you will break it if you try your strength.
By compliance are waters swum; nor can you conquer rivers, if you swim
against the current's flow. (p. 79)

In these examples, then, we can see that Genius offers practical
advice about how Amans should pursue his love, and that
he encourages Amans in the hope that he will be successful should
he only persevere.[45] Let me end this abbreviated review of instances
of Genius taking on the voice of a *praeceptor amoris* by pointing to
three further examples from Book V. Genius there dissuades Amans
from Jealousy, which, he says, enfeebles the lover 'thurgh feigned
enformacion / Of his ymaginacion' (V.593–4). The example he
offers against this 'feigned enformacion' is that of Mars and Venus,
trapped by the jealous husband Vulcan. The telling of the story
itself (V.635–97) is explicitly drawn from Ovid, and is apparently
abbreviated from *Ars amatoria* II.561–600. The advice of Genius is
identical to that of the narrator of the *Ars*: if earthly husbands find
themselves in Vulcan's position, they should, in Genius's words,

>   feigne, as thogh he wiste it noght:
>   For if he lete it overpasse,
>   The sclaundre schal be wel the lasse,
>   And he the more in ese stonde,   (V.710–13)

or, as Ovid's *praeceptor* (addressing husbands and lovers) teaches,
feigned ignorance is wise, but an even more subtle self-deception is
preferable:

---

45 The connections between Genius and Pandarus in this role are obvious. The triangle
    Ovid/Genius/Pandarus is one which deserves much fuller treatment. I make a small
    start in Simpson 1993, pp. 166–7. See also chapter 6, n. 11, and chapter 8, n. 37. Needless
    to say, there is a very large body of literature in Old French in which '*engin*' plays a criti-
    cal part in the construction of practical plans, often with amatory ends. For some
    twelfth-century examples, see Hanning 1977, pp. 105–38.

Sed melius nescisse fuit: sine furta tegantur,
  Ne fugiat ficto fassus ab ore pudor.
Quo magis, o iuvenes, deprendere parcite vestras:
  Peccent, peccantes verba dedisse putent.
Crescit amor prensis.   (*Aa* II.555–9)

But ignorance were better: allow deceptions to be hid, lest the shame of
confession fly from her dissembling countenance. Wherefore all the more,
O lovers, leave off detecting your mistresses: let them err, and erring
think they have deceived. Detection fans the flame of passion. (p. 105,
modified)

When we consider that Genius is advising an old lover, then all
these examples seem to me to be *themselves* instances of 'feigned
enformacion'. The gloss to Book IV.1452 (glossing Genius's words)
might accurately characterize much of Genius's advice: 'Non quia
sic se habet veritas, set opinio Amantum.'
  One might also observe, in this regard, Genius's advice to
Amans that he should give gifts to win love; he introduces the tale
of Babio and Croceus with some general observations on the effi-
cacy of gifts in matters of love:

> So was he wys that ferst yaf mede,
> For mede kepeth love in house;
> Bot wher the men ben coveitouse
> And sparen forto yive a part,
> Thei knowe noght Cupides art.   (v.4798–802)

Like the advice of Ami in Jean de Meun's *Roman de la Rose* (lines
8207–56), Genius's counsel is ultimately indebted to that of Ovid's
praeceptor in the *Ars amatoria* (II.251–72); the tale which follows concludes with indelicate admiration of the gift-giving lover's good
chance:

> And he that large was and fre
> And sette his herte to despende,
> This Croceus, the bowe bende,
> Which Venus tok him forto holde,
> And schotte als ofte as evere he wolde.   (v.4858–62)

Let us end with one particularly pathetic piece of encouraging
admonition from Genius to the *senex amans*, whose love is (we later
learn) irredeemably hopeless because of his age. Genius concludes

Book V by saying that because love is a matter of chance, things may yet turn to Amans's advantage:

> For ofte time, as it is sene,
> Whan Somer hath lost al his grene
> And is with Wynter wast and bare,
> That him is left nothing to spare,
> Al is recovered in a throwe;
> The colde wyndes overblowe,
> And stille be the scharpe schoures,
> And soudeinliche ayein his floures
> The Somer hapneth and is riche:
> And so per cas thi graces liche,
> Mi Sone, thogh thou be nou povere
> Of love, yit thou miht recovere.   (v.7823–34)

Genius, as I have mentioned, consistently suggests that love is an irresistible force; and very often he excuses participants in stories precisely for their helpless submission before the strength of love. In Book VI he elaborates on this theme:

> Who dar do thing which love ne dar?
> To love is every lawe unwar,
> Bot to the lawes of his heste
> The fissch, the foul, the man, the beste
> Of al the worldes kinde louteth.
> For love is he which nothing douteth:
> In mannes herte where he sit,
> He compteth noght toward his wit
> The wo nomore than the wele,
> No mor the hete than the chele,
> No mor the wete than the dreie,
> No mor to live than to deie,
> So that tofore ne behinde
> He seth nothing, bot as the blinde
> Without insyhte of his corage
> He doth merveilles in his rage.
> To what thing that he wole him drawe,
> Ther is no god, ther is no lawe,
> Of whom that he takth eny hiede...
> He stant so ferforth out of reule,
> Ther is no wit that mai him reule.   (vi.1262–80, 1283–4)

This is one of those curious moments in Middle English literature where a figure of authority undermines the basis of his or her teaching; here, towards the end of this long poem, Genius effectively tells us that the whole project of the poem (which has been, ostensibly, to teach the lover) is futile. Certainly such a jaundiced view of the project of teaching the lover is itself Ovidian: in both the *Ars amatoria* and especially in the *Amores*, Ovid the self-appointed expert confesses himself a failure in love.[46] Gower recognizes this undercurrent in Ovid's love poetry by representing him amongst the aged lovers, along with Aristotle, Virgil, Socrates and Plato (VIII.2705–25). Is Genius's speech about the impossibility of teaching lovers, then, a confession of the uselessness of his own moral teaching? Or is Genius rather revealing to us that his own teaching voice is in fact a *part of* the lover's self-deceiving discourse? Aristotle is described as falling in love through a lover's 'syllogism', which made him forget 'al his logique': this Ovidian subversion of pedagogic terms by those of amatory discourse may, after all, characterize the whole projection of Genius's voice. After all, as we have seen, Genius presents himself as *another* voice, a teaching voice; but when we notice the deep connections between the voices of Genius, Amans and the *Ars amatoria*, then we must ask ourselves whether or not Genius can speak for anything but desire.

In a recent study of Gower's use of Ovid, Bruce Harbert dismisses any structural use of Ovid's works by Gower: 'The mode of the narration is so different from Ovid's that Gower seems by this stage to regard Ovid's poetry as little more than raw material, to be manipulated and transformed without regard to its origin.'[47] It will be obvious from my argument in this chapter that this judgement looks to me like a pretty badly missed opportunity. Contrary to the usual view that Gower's use of Ovid is restricted to the tales (and then to *Metamorphoses* and *Heroides*), I have argued here that Ovid pervades the entire structure of the *Confessio*; certainly Gower draws on narratives from the *Heroides* and *Metamorphoses*, but these are set within a much larger and more coherent Ovidian structure: the lover's confession is heavily indebted to the *Amores*, just as the idea of Genius as an instructor in love is heavily indebted to the *Ars amatoria*. Gower works the dynamic relationships pertaining *between*

---

[46] See, for example, *Ars amatoria*, II.547–8; the whole of the *Amores*, with increasing pressure, bespeaks the failures of love. On the theme of the inevitable failure of the pedagogic project, see Fyler 1970.   [47] Harbert 1988, p. 96.

Ovid's works (here between the *Ars* and the *Amores*) into the *single* structure of his own work. The frame of the *Confessio* is at least as Ovidian as its inset narrative matter.

But given this, then we are left with a profound and Ovidian asymmetry between the political matter of the Prologue and the amatory current of much of Books I–VIII, both frame and tales. The pedagogic 'information' of Genius is subject, it seems, to the literary 'information' of the work itself, a literary 'information' which is by no means straightforward. As Ovid's Tragedy says to Ovid the poet, chastising him for his submission to Elegy, *materia premit ingenium*. Gower's Genius, as much as Amans and Ovid's narrator in the *Ars amatoria*, seems from this evidence to be subject to elegy, against the interests of 'tragedy' or satire. So far from keeping the meaning of the text 'in line with the *intentio* as announced in the two prologues',[48] Genius on the contrary deepens the disjunctions between the two prologues.

In the next chapter I propose to look at Book III, where we will see how close Genius is, indeed, to Amans; but we will also see, in the coherent structure of one book, how Genius is nevertheless capable of speaking beyond desire. He is capable, that is, of speaking for yet another Ovid, not so much the (unstable) voice of the *Remedia amoris*, as the voice of the *Tristia*. We shall also see how the dialogue between Amans and Genius reactivates the discourse of politics.[49]

---

[48] Copeland 1991, p. 205.
[49] If Gower is, as I suggest, implicitly building some relationships between the separate works of Ovid's *oeuvre* into the single structure of the *Confessio*, then his enterprise is in some ways parallel to that of the authors of many Ovid *accessus*. Many *accessus* authors attempted to construct a biography of Ovid from the evidence of his works. See Ghisalberti 1946

CHAPTER 6

Genius's psychological information in Book III

INTRODUCTION

I began discussion of the *Confessio amantis* in the last chapter by considering its outer form. As with Alan's poem, so too with Gower's: both present themselves as coherent formal structures which, on closer inspection, are in fact radically incoherent. In this chapter I would like to draw on one of the interpretative solutions which saved the *Anticlaudianus* from this radical incoherence. In discussion of Alan's poem, I reached a point (in chapter 3) where it was argued that the poem as a whole represents a psychological unity: Fronesis is the intelligence of the New Man, whose ethical perfection in Books VII–IX provokes, and is presupposed by, the effort of speculative perfection in Books I–VI. The inner form of the poem, I argued, is correlative with the form of the soul: the poem's own narrative trajectory is determined by the soul's fulfilment. As the soul reaches its perfection, so too does the poem come to an end. The form of the poem, that is, is a function of the form of the soul. And once the psychological unity of the poem becomes manifest, so too does the poem's deeper form emerge.

But for that solution to work, it was necessary to understand how the different participants of the *Anticlaudianus* can in fact be understood as faculties of the single human soul. Can the same be done for the *Confessio*? I think it can, and I should like in this chapter to show how Genius's 'information' is best understood psychologically: Genius represents the imagination, and Amans represents the will of the same soul. The 'information' of Genius is partly his 'informing' the will – i.e. bringing it to its own perfection, but it also involves Genius himself being informed, or perfected, through his interaction with desire. Any pedagogic 'information' given by Genius is subject to (and subject to the distortions of) his psychological status. I recall the point made by Boethius's Philosophia cited in chapter 1; with regard to those who doubt the possibility of certainty in science, she says:

And the cause of this errour is that of alle the thingis that every wight hath iknowe, thei wenen that tho thingis ben iknowe al only by the strengthe and by the nature of the thinges that ben iwyst or iknowe. And it is al the contrarye; for al that evere is iknowe, it is rather comprehendid and knowen, nat aftir his strengthe and his nature, but aftir the faculte (that is to seyn, the power and the nature) of hem that knowen. (Bo. V, p. 4, 132–41).[1]

Any 'information' we receive is invariably subject to the powers of the faculty by which we receive it.

In chapter 1, I showed how the word *informatio* has at least two senses which might be applied to our two poems, a philosophic, often specifically artistic, sense (of 'giving form') and a pedagogic sense (of 'teaching'). At this point I should like to introduce a further application of the word *informatio*, which is closely related to the two senses mentioned above. When scholastic writers discussed the operations of the soul, they often used the words *informatio* and *informare* to describe the action by which a faculty of the soul is impressed and perfected. Aquinas, for example, discusses the action of the intellect in this way:

Una enim actio intellectus est intelligentia indivisibilium sive incomplexorum, secundum quam concipit, quid est res, et haec operatio a quibusdam dicitur informatio intellectus.

For one action of the intellect is the perception of individual or simple ideas, according to which it understands what a thing is; and this action is called by some the information of the intellect.[2]

It is clear that this sense of the word is closely allied with both the philosophical and pedagogic senses: as the faculty of the soul is instructed, so too does it achieve its form, or ideal state.

But the psychological sense of the word is also closely allied with the specifically literary application of the word *informatio*: a poem will take its own shape and style according to what faculty of the soul is being instructed. Thus we also find the word *informare* in discussions of the ways in which different literary forms might affect and inform different parts of the soul. Thirteenth-century scholas-

[1] Text cited from Benson 1988, p. 463.
[2] Cited from Deferrari and Barry 1948, *informatio*, sense (1).

tic theorists in particular developed close and quite subtle connections between literary (especially formal) and psychological categories. In their discussion of a work according to the four Aristotelian causes (material, formal, efficient and final), scholastic theorists discussed the *causa formalis* of a given work (whether an academic treatise or a biblical text), by distinguishing between its *forma tractandi* and its *forma tractatus*. The second of these, the *forma tractatus*, describes the way in which a work is divided – what we might call its structure (the eight books of the *Confessio amantis*, for example). The *forma tractandi*, on the other hand, treats the *modus procedendi* of a work – what we might call its style. In theoretical discussions of the *causa formalis*, found in prologues to commentaries on the *Sentences* of Peter Lombard, or to *Summae Theologiae*, we might notice in particular the close connection writers establish between literary mode and psychological categories. Such a connection might not be surprising, after all, in a literary culture which is essentially instrumental: literary works are described as being written, that is, with a final cause or ultimate purpose, which is consistently defined in terms of the author's intention to affect an audience positively. Questions of style and structure are subordinated to this final cause, and are therefore defined with their psychological effect in mind.[3]

Theorists in this tradition distinguished between literary modes which appeal to the will, and those which appeal to the reason. Modes designed to move emotionally (e.g. prophecies, promises, admonitions, precepts, prayers and exhortations) appeal to the will, whereas analytical procedures, described as 'definitive', 'individuating' and 'argumentative' (*definitivus, divisivus, collectivus*), appeal to the reason. But we should especially observe that these formal, literary categories are defined not only as a way of affecting the soul, but more as a way of perfecting it, of bringing the soul to its proper form. In the *Summa theologiae* attributed to Alexander of Hales (d. 1245), for example, the author asks what modes are appropriate to Scripture. He defines these as *praeceptivus, exemplificativus, exhortativus, revelativus* and *orativus*, since these modes are appropriate to the emotion of piety – 'quia ii

---

3 For discussion of the four-cause *accessus*, and in particular the terms *forma tractatus* and *forma tractandi*, see Minnis 1981a, and 1984, pp. 118–59; and Sandkühler 1967, pp. 30–41. For the connection between these literary categories and the psychological categories to which they are designed to appeal, see Simpson 1986a.

modi competunt affectui pietatis'. Having related different modes to the respective sacred texts which they characterize, the author proceeds to elaborate on the relation between psychological and rhetorical categories in this way:

Note also that there should be one [rhetorical] mode of a body of knowledge whose aim is to 'inform' the will according to piety; there should be another mode for a body of knowledge whose function is to 'inform' the intellect alone to perceive the truth. That mode which is designed to 'inform' the *affectus* will be comprised of the above mentioned distinctions, since precepts, exempla, exhortations, revelations and prayers promote the emotions of piety.

Nota etiam quod alius modus debet esse scientiae quae habet informare affectum secundum pietatem; alius scientiae quae habet informare intellectum solum ad cognoscendam veritatem. Ille qui erit ad informationem affectus, erit per differentias quae dictae sunt, quia praecepta, exempla, exhortationes, revelationes, orationes introducunt pietatis affectiones.[4]

This psychological sense of the word 'information', although not listed separately in *MED*, is certainly used by Middle English writers. Thus in Chaucer's *Melibee* (a thinly veiled psychological personification allegory, where we might reasonably expect to find Latin psychological usage), the narrator concludes in this way:

Whanne Melibee hadde herd the grete skiles and resouns of Dame Prudence, and hire wise informaciouns and techynges, his herte gan enclyne to the wil of his wif, considerynge hir trewe entente, and conformed hym anon and assented fully to werken after hir conseil. (VII. Mel. 3058–64)

A passage like this reveals not only the psychological faculty (Prudence, a species of Reason), but also her *modus*, the 'skiles and resouns' she uses to inform the wilful Melibee, who now becomes a rational will, conforming himself to Prudence's information.

And Gower, too, uses this psychological sense frequently. Listen to Genius in his discussion of forgetfulness in love, which, he says, is a fault

> That noght mai in his herte impresse
> Of vertu which reson hath sett,
> So clene his wittes he foryet.
> For in the tellinge of his tale
> Nomore his herte thanne his male

---

[4] Alexander of Hales 1924, Bk I, tract. introd., q. 1, c. iv. art. 1, ad 2, vol.1, p. 8b.

Hath remembrance of thilke forme,
Wherof he scholde his wit enforme
As thanne, and yit ne wot he why.   (IV.542–9)

The 'forme' which should inform the wit, the *informatio rationis*, is
clearly designed to bring the soul to a kind of perfection – to
'impress' the heart with a given virtue. Not to be 'informed' is
therefore to be in self-ignorance – the forgetful person has no
remembrance of the form by which his or her reason should be
shaped.

This discussion of psychological 'information' of one faculty by
another has obvious implications for the psychological allegory of
both the *Anticlaudianus* and the *Confessio*, since both poems not only
inform the soul of their readers, but also represent the soul being
informed. When Alan's Fronesis perceives the divine form of the
soul, the action might be described as the *informatio intellectus*. The
whole poem, indeed, represents an 'information' of the soul. And
so too with Gower's poem, in which Genius is 'informing' the will,
or Amans. As I said in my last chapter, discussions of Genius have
tended to regard him as an ideal instructor figure, and those studies which have considered Genius as a specifically psychological
category have confirmed the general view. In this chapter I want to
argue that Genius is inherently an unstable psychological category,
with competing and opposing allegiances within the soul. Any
'information' he gives to Amans should, as we have already seen,
be regarded with care.

But when we look at Genius from a specifically psychological
perspective, we can see that he is not necessarily irrational. He *can*
give a rational information; he has access to territories outside the
jurisdiction of the will, and he can, accordingly, offer a genuine
remedium amoris. To see the process of Amans's reintegration in
action, however, it is necessary to look at the dynamic of a single
book, rather than observing select examples from across the whole
poem as we did in the last chapter.

I choose Book III as the site of my investigation, since it puts into
sharp focus Genius's shortcomings at moments of tension between
the natural and the ethical. In the following two sections I focus
simply on aspects of the poem's deliberate incongruences with
regard to Genius's information, or rather misinformation. In my
final section I turn to Gower's strategy in creating such an

unstable, ironic structure. I suggest that Genius, as Amans's own imaginative faculty, is as much a part of Amans's problem, as he is its solution; in the process of regeneration which the poem represents, Genius is psychologically 'informed' as much as Amans. I also suggest that Genius and Amans can both be reformed only through the movement from sexual ethics to politics.

MATERIA PREMIT INGENIUM

In Book V Genius points to the psychological effects of Jealousy. The experience of jealousy, he says,

> Makth the Jelous in fieble plit
> To lese of love his appetit
> Thurgh feigned enformacion
> Of his ymaginacion...   (V.591–4)

So Genius himself points to the possibility of a deceptive psychological 'information', an information according to which a man might be 'transformed' from his ideal state. Genius often points to those who deceive through false information,[5] but this example of 'feigned enformacion' through 'ymaginacion' might, I suggest, be revealing with regard to Genius's *own* information; for he is himself associated with the imagination, a faculty which is equally connected with the deceptions of sense perception and appetite as with the faculty of reason. I will develop this psychological point in the next section, but for the moment I should like simply to argue that Genius's information in Book III is, at certain revealing moments, a 'feigned enformacion', or at least a misinformation.

The sin treated in Book III is anger, the first branch of which is melancholy. Amans confesses to this 'vice', and beseeches Genius (who sits before him, he says, 'in loves stede'), to offer some example against melancholy (III.1312). The tale told by Genius suggests that he is indeed Love's spokesman, acting in Love's 'stede', since the perspective he takes on the story is almost completely determined by his acceptance of love as a natural, irresistible force. He narrates the Ovidian story of Canace and Machaire, in which Aeolus, their father, kills Canace after learning of her incestuous

---

[5] Examples where the word 'information' is used to designate unequivocally immoral instruction are as follows: II.559, II.2886, V.593, V.2879, VI.1927, VII.4098.

relationship with Machaire. Genius's introduction of the sexual love between brother and sister dwells on the overpowering force of love in youth, the *intolerabilem iuuentutis concupiscentiam*, as the Latin prose gloss puts it. He narrates that they grew up together,

> Whan kinde assaileth the corage
> With love and doth him forto bowe,
> That he no reson can allowe,
> Bot halt the lawes of nature.   (III.154–7)

Genius says that the two lovers were subject to the laws of Nature, who takes no account of 'lawe positif' (III.172–3). This reference to positive law might suggest that Genius is going to judge the story from that perspective. But he does not: in his narration he judges Aeolus harshly because he 'nothing couthe / How maistrefull love is in yowthe', and says that because of this lack of experience, 'he wolde noght his herte change / To be benigne and favorable to love' (III.211–16). The description of Canace's suicide has much of the moving, pathetic force of its Ovidian source (*Heroides* XI), and this emotional sympathy is sustained in the moralization. But surely Genius asks a great deal of Aeolus in suggesting that he should be 'benigne and favorable' to the incestuous love of his children. Genius condemns Aeolus for 'sodein Malencolie', and completely excuses the incestuous lovers in terms which recall those of Dante's Francesca in her claims for moral leniency in the matter of her technically incestuous love:

> For it sit every man to have
> Reward to love and to his miht,
> Ayein whos strengthe mai no wiht:
> And siththe an herte is so constreigned,
> The reddour oghte be restreigned
> To him that mai no bet aweie,
> Whan he mot to nature obeie.
> For it is seid thus overal,
> That nedes mot that nede schal
> Of that a lif doth after kinde,
> Wherof he mai no bote finde.   (III.344–54)[6]

---

[6] The lines from Dante read thus: 'Amor, ch'a nullo amato amar perdona / mi prese del costui piacer sí forte, / che, come vedi, ancor non m'abbandona' (Singleton 1970, *Inferno*, V.103–5). The argument that Gower knew at least *Inferno* V seems strong to me. See also his description of Venus's incestuous passion for her son in Book V:

The Ovidian story is moralized, then, wholly from within the tradition of love exemplified by Amans in the beginning of Book I, and wholly from within the frame of the law of Nature, rather than that of 'positif' law.[7]

As I said in the previous chapter, one of the positions which flows from the idea of Genius as an ideal moral instructor concerns the moralizations of Ovid. If Genius is an ideal figure, then his moralizations of Ovid, so the argument would have it, are entirely consistent with the tradition of the moralized Ovids and with the ethical current of the poem as a whole. I have dealt fairly extensively with this question in the last chapter, and will not repeat my arguments about Gower's use of the *Amores* and *Ars amatoria* here. But Alastair Minnis's argument was directed especially to Gower's use of the *Heroides*. Gower, Minnis argued, could be distinguished from Chaucer, whose use of the *Heroides* in the *Legends of Good Women* revealed a much more daring reading of Ovid than Gower, who remained firmly within the bounds of the moralized Ovid.[8]

The *Heroides*, from which the story of Canace and Machaire is drawn, pose a special problem for the moralist: they are not, like the *Metamorphoses*, fables, and are not therefore open to allegorical interpretation. The option open to the moralist was simply to present the different heroines of the work as exemplary of different kinds of love – a solution adopted by commentators in a long and

> And sche, which thoghte hire lustes fonde,
> Diverse loves tok in honde,
> Wel mo thanne I the tolde hiere:
> And for sche wolde hirselve skiere,
> Sche made comun that desport,
> And sette a lawe of such a port,
> That every womman mihte take
> What man hire liste...'   (V.1421–8)

The first example of a woman acting in this way is Semiramis, who loved her son (V.1432–3); compare Dante's description of Semiramis in *Inferno* V: 'A vizio di lussuria fu sí rotta, / che libito fe' licito in sua legge / per tòrre il biasmo in che era condotta.' (V.55–7). *Inferno* V would, after all, be the precise locus to which we would expect Gower to be drawn, being the circle of those 'che la ragion sommettono al talento' (V.39). Gower's knowledge of Dante needs to be investigated; Lynch 1988, pp. 190–8 offers a preliminary survey.

7   Points similar to my own about Genius's moralization of Canace and Machaire have been voiced by Hatton 1987, and Benson 1984 (see pp. 100–1 and notes for those critics who would excuse the lovers). See further Spearing 1993. For a view which makes Genius's moralization consistent with his later condemnation of incest in Book VIII, see Yeager 1990, pp. 254–7.   8   Minnis 1980.

coherent *accessus* tradition. Thus, for example, one standard form of the commentary reads in this way:

So in this work Ovid treats love according to all its species – that is, legitimate, or married love, stupid love (i.e. extramarital love), and illicit or incestuous love. He commends legitimate love through Penelope, censures stupid love through Phyllis, and condemns illicit love through both Phaedra and Canace. His intention is to reveal the effect of love in whatever its species.

In hoc ergo opere agit Ovidius de amore secundum amoris omnes species, que sunt legitimus amor, scilicet coniugium, stultus scilicet fornicatio, illicitus scilicet incestus. Legitimum commendat in Penelope, arguit in Phillide stultum, illicitum dampnat in Phedra et in Canace. Intentio sua est effectum amoris qualibet eius specie ostendere.[9]

Accessus of this kind in fact represent a fairly desperate defensive position, given the entirely unmoralistic quality of Ovid's moving narratives, of which Canace is a good example. Ovid himself has nothing to say about the moral effect of incestuous love, nor about the supposed effect of his poetry in the *Heroides*.[10] And the fact that Genius's moralization is so patently at variance with that of the moralizers suggests that Gower is aware of other, more subversive readings of the Ovidian narrative: whereas the moralizers often point particularly to Canace as the example of *amor illicitus*, Genius makes no moral condemnation of the incestuous love at all; he is instead concerned to criticize Aeolus for his anger and lack of sympathy for the young lovers.

Turning to further tales in the earlier part of Book III, we can see how Gower continues to reveal the inconsistency of Genius as a moral instructor in the particular (but vital) matter of human capacity rationally to control sexual desire. The next story Genius tells prompts the reader to make distinctions concerning 'kynde' love and natural law which are not made by Genius himself. Tiresias disturbed two snakes, coupling 'as nature hem taughte'. His subsequent transformation into a woman is described in this way:

---

[9] Cited by Edwards 1970, p. 36. See also Hexter 1986, pp. 154–63, and Minnis and Scott 1988, pp. 20–4.
[10] The *Ars amatoria* might also be mentioned in this regard, where the *praeceptor* uses examples of incest simply to demonstrate, and encourage, the heat of passion (*Aa* 1.283–330).

> And for he hath destourbed kinde
> And was so to nature unkinde,
> Unkindeliche he was transformed,
> That he which erst a man was formed
> Into a womman was forschape.   (III.373–7)

In a context where Gower is clearly using the word 'forme' and 'enforme' in their philosophical senses, we might expect Ovidian stories of *transformation* to pick up on the philosophical implications of metamorphosis, as indeed this passage suggests: Tiresias loses his natural 'form', or perfection, through being unnatural. The reader may well agree with Genius that Tiresias's disturbance of the snakes is an undue interference with the processes of nature, and therefore agree with the way in which Genius himself moralizes the story. But we are provoked to distinguish this case of disturbing nature from the case of Aeolus; with reference to the snakes, Genius begins his moralization in this way:

> Lo thus, my Sone, Ovide hath write,
> Wherof thou miht be reson wite,
> More is a man than such a beste.   (III.381–3)

This might gain the reader's assent, but it if did, then such an agreement would set us in conflict with Genius's own moralization of the preceding story, that of Canace and Machaire: Tiresias is certainly 'unkynde' in disturbing the animals, whereas Aeolus's case is quite different, since he is disturbing the incestuous love of human actors (however brutally), who are more than 'bestes'. Genius's further moralization of the Tiresias episode contains this same point, but simultaneously withdraws from it:

> So mihte it nevere ben honeste
> A man to wraththen him to sore
> Of that an other doth the lore
> Of kinde, in which is no malice,
> Bot only that it is a vice:
> And thogh a man be resonable,
> Yit after kinde he is menable
> To love, wher he wole or non.   (III.384–91)

Genius implicitly acknowledges here that following the law of nature *might* be a 'vice' (line 388), and this essential qualification gives us the intellectual purchase to distinguish the case of the coupling snakes from that of the incestuous Canace and Machaire. Incest is, however natural, clearly a 'vice', whether we think of 'vice' in Christian, personal and penitential terms, or as socially disruptive – an action which threatens the foundation of human culture (and Gower is as much if not more concerned with the second of these concepts of 'vice'). We might want to criticize Genius's lenient moralization of the Canace and Machaire episode, then, by the very distinction offered to us by Genius himself (i.e. that one should not disrupt nature 'bot only that it is a vice'). But Genius withdraws from the logic of this distinction, by placing 'kynde' above reason in the last three lines of the immediately preceding citation. Given the model of Ovidian 'transformation', one might ask whether or not Genius's 'information' of Amans itself constitutes a transformation of Amans's proper, specifically human 'forme' – it may be that Genius's instruction is a 'feigned enformacion', or at least a misinformation.

Genius's use of *Heroides* exempla is not unlike Pandarus's in Book I of *Troilus and Criseyde*, insofar as neither use the heroines as exempla of moral 'reprehencion'.[11] In Genius's moralizations of other Ovidian stories in Book III, we can see further parallels between Genius and Pandarus, insofar as both act 'in loves cause'; both are concerned with the practical aspects of success in love, and as such both represent the Ovidian tradition of the *Ars amatoria* rather than that of the moralized Ovids. Exemplifying Cheste, for example, Genius seems to set human reason above natural instinct in his story of the patience of Socrates. Doused by Xantippe, Socrates demurs that winter, 'as be weie of kinde', first makes the wind to blow, and then causes rain. Patience is set above natural instinct here, certainly, but what of the following, Ovidian stories? These ostensibly expound the same moral, but are in fact quite diferent in emphasis. In the story of Phebus and Cornide, for example, Genius

---

[11]   *Troilus and Criseyde*, 1.652–86; Pandarus disclaims any moral purpose in his use of the story: '...myn entencioun / Nis nat to yow of reprehencioun' (lines 683–4; Benson 1988, p. 482). Briefly discussed in Simpson 1993, pp. 166–7. Any comparison between Genius and Pandarus as *praeceptores amoris* should at least mention Genius's rush of worldly wise proverbs, III.1613–58.

  Although it is not from the *Heroides*, Genius's narration and moralization of Pyramus and Thisbe should also be noted here: near the beginning of his narration he comments on the irresistibility of love (III.1354–69), and in his moralization he simply counsels against 'folhaste'; he misses the more profound point made from within the tale itself: Thisbe complains, against Venus and Cupid, that blind love has destroyed the young lovers (III.1462–81).

follows the old dame in Chaucer's *Manciple's Tale*: the practical, worldly wise 'moral' has it that one should know when *not* to say the truth. Corvus is held up as an example of one who should not have spoken (about Cornide's illicit love). Despite the fact that this is ostensibly a tale about Cheste, a species of anger, it is Corvus who is held up as the moral anti-type ('a fals bridd', as Genius says (line 792)), when in fact Phoebus is the one subject to anger. Phoebus is apparently excused for loving Cornide in the tale's introduction:

> bot what schal befalle
> Of love ther is noman knoweth,
> Bot as fortune hire happes throweth.   (III.786–8)

But this 'excuse' applies equally to the young knight who 'upon a chaunce' had the 'aqueintance' of Cornide, 'and hadde of hire al that he wolde' (line 791). If sexual desire is the only criterion of justice, then Phoebus and the knight have equal claims on Cornide, as Cornide has equal rights to make love with both male figures. Genius ignores these complexities, and, as I say, focuses on the 'fals bridd', who, after all, only told the truth. Laar in the following Ovidian example is likewise punished for revealing Jupiter's illicit love (III.818–30). The idea of not disturbing 'kynde' takes quite different dimensions in these little stories, in short, from the sense drawn out of the stories of Tiresias or of Socrates. Here Genius is concerned especially to warn against the disturbance of human love affairs, regardless of their legality. In significant ways, then, in Book III as in other books of the *Confessio*, Genius represents many of the unmoralized Ovids of the later Middle Ages – not only the *praeceptor amoris* of the *Ars amatoria*, but also the subversive writer of the *Heroides*, whose allegiances are with suffering passion rather than rational and political control. In much of his 'information' in Book III, Genius answers to the kind of instructor described by Amans in Book IV:

> For thogh I be non of the wise,
> I am so trewly amerous,
> That I am evere curious
> Of hem that conne best enforme
> To knowe and witen al the forme,
> What falleth unto loves craft.   (IV.920–5)

And by the same token, much of Genius's exposition of matters concerning appropriate practice in love affairs might be described, as I suggested earlier, by the marginal gloss to his advice to Amans in Book IV: 'Non quia sic se habet veritas, set opinio Amantum' (gloss to IV.1450–60).

GENIUS, *DEUS NATURAE HUMANAE*

If Genius's moral authority is to be questioned in Book III, it is precisely on this fundamental point concerning the specifically human, rational power to control natural, and particularly sexual appetites. We have seen how his shufflings on this point are evident in his moralizations, and we can see the same ambivalence in his response to the psychomachia Amans describes. At line 1120 of Book III, Genius asks Amans whether or not he has been guilty of 'contek' and homicide. Amans replies that he certainly has not been guilty of these sins, and adds that they are in any case outside the matter of love with which Amans and Genius are ostensibly concerned. But even within the field of love, Amans continues, he does confess to an inner 'contek', between his reason and his will. The passage describing this psychomachia offers the psychological concomitant to the philosophical debate between right Reason and Kynde in the poem. Although Gower introduces it by way of an apparent digression, it is, in fact, central to the entire dialogue between Amans and Genius. Amans confesses to an internal battle between, as it were, two parties of courtiers, with reason, 'conseil' and 'witt' on the one side, against will and hope on the other:

> Witt and resoun conseilen ofte
> That I myn herte scholde softe,
> And that I scholde will remue
> And put him out of retenue,
> Or elles holde him under fote:
> For as thei sein, if that he mote
> His oghne rewle have upon honde,
> Ther schal no witt ben understonde...
> Thus with resoun and wit avised
> Is will and hope aldai despised.
> Reson seith that I scholde leve
> To love, wher ther is no leve
> To spede, and will seith therayein
> That such an herte is to vilein,
> Which dar noght love and til he spede.
>
> (III.1163–70, 1177–83)

Amans's position in this psychological 'contek' is identical with his unphilosophical position with regard to the force of 'kynde', as he expresses it in the opening of Book I. Just as he defined love as an irresistible force in Book I, so too here does he confess to complete psychological submission to the forces of will, despite what reason might advise:

> Bot yit I mai noght will forsake,
> That he nys Maister of my thoght,
> Or that I spede, or spede noght.   (III.1190–2)

If Genius were 'informing' Amans here with an eye to the perfection of his soul, or at least with an eye to conforming Amans's will to his reason, this is the moment we might expect him to align himself entirely with reason in the battle against will. In part he does align himself with reason, but he retains a distinct ambivalence. Just as Amans's position with regard to the irresistible power of love remains unchanged, so too does Genius's own judgement remain equivocal; he preserves this fence-sitting response, with one eye to the superiority of reason, and the other to his allegiances to Venus:

> Thou dost, my Sone, ayein the riht;
> Bot love is of so gret a miht,
> His lawe mai noman refuse,
> So miht thou thee the betre excuse.
> And natheles thou schalt be lerned
> That will scholde evere be governed
> Of reason more than of kinde.   (III.1193–9)

Why should Genius want to 'excuse' Amans for his helpless submission before the law of love? A selective account of the complex history of the concept 'genius', focusing especially on Alan of Lille's *De planctu Naturae*, will clarify differing allegiances of this single figure, and will equally elucidate Gower's subtle play with these differing, sometimes opposed allegiances. Jane Chance Nitzsche's learned and detailed study of the concept teaches us that in the late classical period the concept of genius as the 'begetting spirit of the paterfamilias ... has been metamorphosed into the generational and fatalistic force of the universal household';[12] in the same period an identification between the Platonic *daemon*, or rational soul, and

---

[12] Chance Nitzsche 1975, p. 41.

the individual genius of each individual was established.[13] When we turn to Alan's *De planctu* we can observe how he connects and elaborates both these fundamental principles of genius (i.e. the universal reproductive impulse and the principle of individual human, moral integrity). What is of particular interest to us in the present context of considering Genius's 'enformacioun' in the *Confessio* is that in each aspect of his function in Alan's work, Genius is associated with 'information', or, in one aspect, with human deformation.

Genius is introduced in person towards the end of the *De planctu*; Nature sends Hymeneus to summon him in order to excommunicate humans who have abandoned their human nature to become beasts. She addresses him in especially affectionate terms as *me alteram*, 'another me'. She appeals to Genius to enact the excommunication of humans because Genius is, according to a tradition originating in Horace, the *naturae deus humanae*:[14] the cosmic Genius operates in the same way as Nature, but his special province is the generation and individuation of humanity.[15] Nature's appeal to Genius to excommunicate sinful men suggests the second, later tradition of Genius, which associates him with the rational soul of individuals, and, therefore, with a moral function. But when we first see Genius, he is engaged in the process of human procreation, drawing the images of humans onto a parchment; with his right hand he draws images of natural perfection, with his left imperfect individuals. Beside him stand Veritas and Falsitas, who personify the artistic practice of Genius's right and left hands respectively. Veritas is said to have been born not by any 'promiscuous itch of Venus', but rather when the impression of divine Form made its image on formless matter, a union which is described as the 'genial' kiss of 'Nature and her son (i.e. Genius)'. Veritas herself clearly represents the perfection of that union of Nature and Genius in the generation of naturally perfect human beings:

…she was entirely the offspring of the generative kiss of Nature and her son, at the time when the eternal Idea greeted Hyle as she begged for the mirror of forms and imprinted a kiss on her through the delegated medium and intervention of Image.

---

[13]   Ibid., pp. 30–1.
[14]   Horace, *Epistles*, II.2.188; see Chance Nitzsche 1975, pp. 15–16; my discussion of Alan's concept of Genius is indebted to Chance Nitzsche, ch. 5.
[15]   This point has been made by Brumble 1970.

...ex solo Nature natique geniali osculo fuerat deriuata, cum Ylem formarum speculum mendicantem eternalis salutauit Ydea, eam Iconie
interpretis interuentu uicario osculata.[16]

In Alan's usage, *ydea* designates the essential, divine form in the
mind of God, while *iconia* designates forms intermediate between
the divine Idea and sensible images.[17] Alan presents Genius in his
first appearance, then, in his cosmic, generative, function, as a procreative artist, impressing the divine form to inform examples of
perfect human nature. Equally, we should note, he is responsible
for generating the deformed images of human perversion.
Falsehood 'deforms' what Truth 'informs': 'quicquid illa [Veritas]
conformiter informabat, ista [Falsitas] informiter deformabat'.[18]

Genius's further, and final function in the *De planctu* is a priestly
one,[19] where he must don priestly garments in order to pronounce
the moral anathema against those humans who are vitiated by sin.
But clearly for Alan these two aspects of Genius, the procreative
and the moral, are closely associated.[20] Even before Genius takes
on his priestly role, he greets Nature by saying how thoroughly he
agrees with her edict, and how he longs for this concord between
himself and Nature, despite the fact that his mind has been
deformed by the vitiated behaviour of humans:

For, although my mind, straitened by man's deformed vices, travelling
down to the hell of gloom, knows not the paradise of joy, yet the seedlings
of delightful joy are sending me their fragrance because I see that you
join in my sighs of longing for due punishment.

Quamuis enim mens mea, hominum uiciis angustiata deformibus, in
infernum tristicie peregrinans, leticie nesciat paradisum, tamen in hoc
amenantis gaudii odorat primordia, quod te mecum uideo ad debite uin-
dicte suspirare suspiria.[21]

---

[16] Häring 1978, XVIII.94–7, p. 877. The translation is from Sheridan 1980, XVIII, prose 9,
pp. 217–18.

[17] See Chance Nitzsche 1975, pp. 94–5; Alan's distinction between divine ideas, which
should alone properly be called 'forms' and 'outer forms', which should properly be
called 'images', derives from Boethius, *De trinitate*, Bk II. I develop this distinction in
chapter 8.   [18] Häring 1978, XVIII.111–2, p. 877.

[19] As part of his priestly function, it should be noted that Alan's Genius acts in the manner
of a philosopher–poet, just as Gower's Genius does. See Chance Nitzsche 1975, pp.
107–4, and chapter 8 below.

[20] For the close connection of Alan's Nature with an ethical consciousness, see chapter 4, n.
15 and Raynaud de Lage 1951, ch. 4.

[21] Häring 1978, XVIII.126–129, p. 878; Sheridan 1980, XVIII, prose 9, p. 219.

Genius's longing, then, is clearly a moral longing; his function is not simply human procreation, but a desire for human, moral perfection is inherent to the conception of the figure. And it is this moral longing which induces Genius to take on his specifically priestly function. But what is especially interesting in this moment, immediately preceding his priestly role, is the fact that Genius accounts himself an imperfect figure, whose own judgement has been narrowed by the deformed vices of men, as he wanders in the hell of misery ('hominum uiciis angustiata deformibus, in infernum tristicie peregrinans'). It is his meeting with Nature which restores him to his original dignity, and which allows him to take on his priestly role of moral judgement with confidence.

So Genius, in Alan's *De planctu*, is not simply the solution to the problem of human deformity, but he is also a part of the problem itself. It is under his aegis that Falsity deforms the human types which Truth 'informs'. Genius is a natural capacity, but one which can tend towards the highest rational practice (which includes human sexuality), or to a deformed concupiscence. This doubleness of Genius is highlighted by other twelfth-century accounts of the concept. We can see it, for example, in the *Aeneid* commentary of (?)Bernard Silvestris, in his interpretation of the legend of Eurydice and Orpheus (including the Virgilian account of Eurydice being chased by Aristaeus and being bitten by a snake in her flight). Bernard sees the story as a myth of wisdom and eloquence seeking to recuperate the natural concupiscence of *genius*. After he reads Orpheus as wisdom and eloquence, he interprets Eurydice in this way:

Eurydice, or natural concupiscence, is wife unto Orpheus – that is, she is joined to him naturally. For nobody exists without their natural desire. On account of this we find in poems a certain genius, the god of human nature, who is born and dies with a man.

Huic [i.e. to Orpheus] Euridice, id est naturalis concupiscentia, coniunx est, id est naturaliter iuncta. Nemo enim sine sua naturali concupiscentia est. Unde in poematibus legitur genium quendam, naturalem deum humane nature, esse qui nascitur cum homine et moritur.[22]

---

[22] Jones and Jones 1977, p. 54. Dido is also interpreted as a misguided *ingenium* and reason; as she looks down from Aeneas in their underworld meeting, she is interpreted thus: 'Dido occulos in terram figit dum luxuriosus ingenium et rationem suam ad celestia non erigit' (p. 96).

He goes on to say that Eurydice is the 'appetite for the good', and
that Aristaeus's pursuit of her represents a divine virtue that wishes
to unite itself to good desire. Eurydice's flight from virtue and subsequent snake bite represent the soul's immersion in the temporal
goods of the world. Orpheus descends to the underworld of
worldly life in order that he might extract his desire from worldly
things:

> Moved on account of his wife, Orpheus descends to the infernal regions
> (that is, to temporal life by way of his understanding), in order that he
> should detach his desire from worldly things, having observed their
> fragility.

> Uxore sua permotus Orpheus ad inferos descendit, id est ad temporalia
> per cognitionem, ut visa eorum fragilitate concupiscentiam inde
> extrahat.[23]

So when Alan's Genius says to Nature that his mind, 'wandering in
the hell of misery', has been 'ignorant of the paradise of bliss' until
his meeting with Nature ('in infernum tristicie peregrinans, leticie
nesciat paradisum'), Alan is invoking, I think, this tradition of
genius as natural concupiscence with a potential for worldly
appetites, as for divinely sanctioned virtue.

So in the *De planctu* Genius's generative role is closely associated
with his moral awareness, but his moral awareness is not simply
active upon his human products: as human desire, he can himself
be deformed by fleshly desires. Nature does not simply evoke
Genius as her moral executor, but the very act of this evocation, so
Alan's mythic allegory would have it, itself enables Genius to act
morally, now that he perceives the rationality of Nature.

Genius himself requires an 'information', and this information
is the premise of his informing humans truly, by bringing them
to their natural perfection. Given this, we can perhaps understand
why Gower's Genius also has sympathies with Amans's obsessive
and irrational love. We might want to say that Genius in Gower's
poem, as in the *De planctu*, is himself part of the moral problem,
given the width of his sympathies, which extend from the irrational
to the rational. With regard to the matter of irresistible
sensual concupiscence, Genius, I suggest, is himself in need
of psychological 'enformacioun' as much as Amans is. And if

---

[23] Jones and Jones 1977, p. 55.

this is true, then we should ask how successfully can Genius fulfil his other (and, indeed, his major) roles in Gower's poem – his role as priest and as literary artist, as one who not only 'informs' Amans, but who also 'informs' tales for Amans's moral edification.

A PHILOSOPHICAL GENIUS

We have seen, then, why Genius's psychological information of Amans might not be unswervingly rational. How does this affect his pedagogic information? Towards the end of Book III Genius instructs Amans concerning homicide, in both personal and political contexts. Here, perhaps surprisingly, his pedagogic 'information' is rationally conducted and makes subtle distinctions between the realm of ethics and that of politics. Given what we have seen of Genius in Book III up to this point, how is this possible?

In his account of the battle of wit and will, Amans portrays them as mutually exclusive, warring possibilities. He mentions no faculty which might mediate between them, and which might, therefore, resolve this psychomachia. In this final section I want to suggest how the solution is literally staring Amans in the face, since the mediating faculty is in fact standing before Amans, in the person of Genius himself. Genius, as Amans's own genius, gradually moves Amans towards a reintegrated, rational self. But because Genius is, as I have argued, part of Amans's very problem, and not simply its solution, I shall also suggest that Genius's 'information' in Book III (and implicitly, across the whole poem) is not only his information of Amans, but also of himself. Like the *Anticlaudianus*, the *Confessio* is a fable of the soul, in which the soul's natural powers interact constructively. By way of returning to Book III, I should like to offer some small account of genius as it was conceived within a psychological frame.

In his *Metalogicon*, John of Salisbury gives an account of 'art', by which he means the rational organization of bodies of knowledge. We develop arts through the interaction of our natural faculties, or *ingenium*, and our reason. As part of his exposition of what he calls *ingenium*, he recounts the teaching of Bernard of Chartres on the topic. He says that, according to Bernard's teaching, there are three kinds of *ingenium*:

The first flies, the second creeps, the third takes the intermediate course of walking. The flying one flits about, easily learning, but just as quickly forgetting, for it lacks stability. The creeping one is mired down to earth, and cannot rise, wherefore it can make no progress. But the one that goes to neither extreme (and walks), because it can settle, and because it is capable of elevating itself, does not despair of progress, and is admirably suited for the act of philosophizing.

Aliud enim aduolans, aliud infimum, aliud mediocre est. Aduolans quidem eadem facilitate, qua percipit, recedit a perceptis, nec in aliqua sede inuenit requiem. Infimum autem sublimari non potest, ideoque profectum nescit; at mediocre, et quia habet in quo sedeat, et quia sublimari potest, nec de profectu desperat, et philosophantis exercitio accommodissimum est.[24]

John is giving us access here to a refined account of the psychological faculty of the imagination, or *phantasia*. When twelfth-century writers (in both 'scientific' and spiritual traditions) discussed psychological powers, they either drew on the Boethian classification of sense, imagination, reason and intelligence,[25] or else, if they were following medical traditions of placing psychological powers within particular cavities of the brain, they used the classification imagination (or phantasy), reason and memory.[26] In their discussion of imagination, writers (especially in the 'scientific' tradition) often used the word *ingenium*. In his commentary on the *Aeneid*, for example, (?)Bernard Silvestris consistently defines the parts of the brain as 'the *ingenium*, or power of finding; the reason, or the power of discerning between things found (by the *ingenium*), and the memory, or power of conserving'.[27] Writers in both traditions distinguish different possibilities for the imagination, saying that it can be either 'bestial' or 'rational'. When we are subject to

---

[24]   Webb 1929, Bk I.11, p. 29. The translation is based on McGarry 1955. I have altered McGarry's translation of this particular passage.

[25]   See chapter 3 above, nn. 22–32, especially Michaud-Quantin 1949. The Boethian classification is found in *De consolatione Philosophiae*, Bk V, prose 4.

[26]   My accounts of the psychological placing of *ingenium* are indebted to the following: Gregory 1955, pp. 167–74; Wetherbee 1976; Minnis 1981b; and White 1986. See further chapter 8, nn. 34–5. Even though Minnis and White are not concerned to make the connection between *ingenium* and *imaginatio*, dealing as they are with Langland, their expositions are extremely useful, given the identity of the two psychological powers. My argument about the psychological status and placing of Genius has been anticipated by Lynch 1988, pp. 182–5.

[27]   Jones and Jones 1977, p. 47; see their index for fifteen examples of *ingenium* so defined in this commentary. See also Gregory 1955, p. 171, n. 2, which gives examples to support his comment: 'frequente lo scambio tra *fantasia* e *ingenium*'.

the bestial imagination, 'we vaguely run through in our minds those things which we have recently seen or done, hither and thither, without any profit or deliberation' (John of Salisbury's *aduolans*).[28] Likewise, as we have seen, it can be fixed on sensual pleasure, where it becomes a kind of 'skin' to the reason, clouding and overshadowing rational activity (John's *infimum*).[29] It can, however, be a profound source of rational knowledge and human integration, by participating with the reason in offering reflection, through images, on the past and future.[30] Thus Alan of Lille, for example, again in the *De planctu*, defines the imagination (which he calls *uirtus ingenialis*) twice, both times declaring the rational power and importance of the faculty. In the first instance, Nature says that she gave psychological powers to the soul, beginning with the *ingenium*:

I allotted to the spirit the native faculty and power of hunting down subtle matters in the chase for knowledge and of retaining them when it apprehends them.

Cui ingenialis uirtutis destinaui potentiam, que rerum uenatrix subtilium in noticie indagine easdem intellectas concluderet.[31]

This last faculty clearly corresponds with John's *ingenium mediocre*, 'admirably suited for the act of philosophizing'.

---

[28] 'Bestialis itaque imaginatio est, quando per ea quae paulo ante vidimus, vel fecimus, sine ulla utilitate, absque omni deliberatione huc illucque vaga mente discurrimus', Richard of St Victor, *Benjamin minor*, PL 196, cols. 1–64, ch. 16, col. 11.

[29] Hugh of St Victor, in his *De unione corporis et spiritus*, PL 177, cols. 285–94, says that when the imagination surpasses the reason, 'obnubilat eam, et obumbrat, et involvit, et contegit' (col. 288). He elaborates this image of covering by saying that when the imagination serves the reason, it is like a garment, which can be easily taken off; when the imagination is fixed in earthly pleasure, it is like a skin: 'si vero etiam delectatione illi adhaeserit, quasi pellis ei fit ipsa imaginatio ita ut non sine dolore exui possit' (col. 287).

[30] The imagination alone is, of course, a passive faculty, simply storing images. But, as Wetherbee, Minnis and White (see n. 26 above) all make clear, the imagination can take on deliberative functions, using images to reflect on past and future, and surveying the rational order of nature. For this last function, see especially White 1986, who cites Richard of St Victor's *Benjamin major*, where Richard describes the second grade of contemplation, in which those things in nature which we admire through imagination alone are subject to rational investigation to reveal their rational order: 'Haec itaque contemplatio in imaginatione, sed secundum rationem consistit, quia circa ea quae in imaginatione versantur ratiocinando procedit' (*Benjamin major*, PL 196, col. 70). The fact that the imagination can reflect rationally on the past through sense images explains why Genius's chosen method should be poetic *exempla* from the past. See further chapter 8 below.

[31] Häring 1978, VI.34–6, p. 825; Sheridan 1980, VI, prose 3, p. 118. See also Häring 1978, VI.92–6, p. 828.

Although John of Salisbury reports Bernard as saying that
these are *different* 'geniuses', we may understand this as the artificial
analysis of the teacher; creative poets like Alan or Gower realize
these different tendencies (or at least some of them) within the
one figure, and produce accordingly unstable, dynamic structures.[32] While Gower's Genius is clearly not *aduolans*, I think it
is the case that Gower exploits his *infimum* and *mediocre* aspects.
Let us now turn back to the *Confessio* to observe how Gower's
Genius moves, within the bounds of Book III, from being partially
blinded by the will's desires, to being 'philosophantis exercitio
accommodissimum'.

The first story that Genius tells by way of exemplifying the
possibility of reason to control the will is that of Diogenes
and Alexander. This is the first of many Alexander stories in
the poem, stories which culminate in the compendium of
philosophical knowledge in Book VII, presented as the instruction
given to Alexander as his preparation for kingship. In the tale
of Diogenes and Alexander in Book III, the philosopher explains
his courageous but dangerous conundrum that Alexander is, as
he says, 'mi mannes man'. Diogenes unfolds the conundrum
by arguing that ever since he understood reason he has restrained
'the will which of my bodi moeveth, / Whos werkes that the
god reproeveth' (III.1273–4). Subject to his own will, Alexander
is, according to the logic of the conundrum, the servant
of Diogenes's servant. This little story is designed to contribute
to the larger question being treated by Genius, concerning
homicide in love. When Genius returns to this point, then at least
as far as the extreme case of homicide is concerned, he
is quite unambiguous about the necessity of restraining will by
reason; just as Alexander has been 'enformed' by Diogenes
(III.1313), so too should Amans be by the example of restraining the
will:

---

[32] Gower seems to me to exploit different senses within the one figure in much the same
way that Langland does. Apart from 'Genius', there are different senses of, for example,
'Venus', 'love', 'pes' and 'nature'. For Venus, see Yeager 1990, pp. 180–7, though I think
Yeager flattens Gower's complexity in saying that Gower keeps different senses of Venus
(as well as of Cupid and Genius) 'strictly apart' (p. 186). My own view is that he reveals
the complex inter-relations and strains between different senses of the terms. For the
subtlety with which Gower distinguishes between 'Nature' and 'kynde', see Yeager 1991.

> For love is of a wonder kinde,
> And hath hise wittes ofte blinde,
> That thei fro mannes reson falle;
> Bot when that it is so befalle
> That will schal the corage lede,
> In loves cause it is to drede. (III.1323–8)

The example of the philosopher and the king, then, constrains the discussion of the power of will in love, since it points unequivocally to the power of, and necessity of reason to control will. The same is true for the rest of Book III, since it moves steadily from this point towards political and civil stories, which are moralized in such a way as to stress the power of reason over natural desire. The very terms used by Genius to discuss questions of love become unsettled from their normal referents in this political context. Genius, in advising patience in love, for example, says this:

> Who may to love make a werre,
> That he ne hath himself the werre?
> Love axeth pes and evere schal,
> And who that fihteth most withal
> Schal lest conquere of his emprise. (III.1645–9)

These terms could easily be applied back to Alexander in the Diogenes story, who, according to Diogenes, could never take a day of rest from his labour of conquering the transitory goods of the world, 'wher', Diogenes says to Alexander, 'thou no reson hast to winne' (III.1289). The terms describing proper action in love tend to spill over, in the context of these more political stories, into political application.

The stories Genius now chooses contribute to this widening of perspective from questions of love to political questions. He signals the shift himself; just before the story of Athemas and Demephon (a purely political tale), Genius instructs Amans that rashness is to be avoided:

> Noght only upon loves chance,
> Bot upon every governance
> Which falleth unto mannes dede. (III.1739–41)

And the story itself focuses on the 'pes' brought about through Nestor's rational control of the young warriors' 'folhastif'. But the 'pes' here is of a political, not an amatory kind; the tale ends thus, with Athemas and Demephon's subjects suing for peace:

> And forto seche pes and grith
> Thei sende and preide anon forthwith,
> So that the kinges ben appesed,
> And every mannes herte is esed.   (III.1847–50)

But however political this moral may be, Genius applies it back to the problematic of love, advising Amans not to let any 'will' distemper his 'wit' (III.1858–9). His next story, that of Orestes (also essentially political in nature) provides a more powerful constraint on the discussion of love. In this tale, the structure of events forces the reader to recognize the inadequacy of the 'lawe of kynde' alone, in either politics or love. The speech of Orestes to Clytemnestra focuses the limitations of the law of 'kynde'; is one 'unkynde' act justly dealt with by another?:

> O cruel beste unkinde,
> How mihtest thou thin herte finde,
> For eny lust of loves drawhte,
> That thou acordest to the slawhte
> Of him which was thin oghne lord?...
> Unkyndely for thou hast wroght,
> Unkindeliche it schal be boght,
> The Sone schal the Moder sle.   (III.2055–9, 2065–7)

Whereas the 'unkynde' transformation of Tiresias for his 'unkinde' act of disturbing natural law is readily understandable (given that the snakes contravene no other law), here an appeal to arbitration by a higher law than that of nature is necessary, to judge the unnatural, but potentially just matricide of Orestes.[33]

---

[33] When I describe the matricide of Clytemnestra as 'potentially just' I refer to the way the story is presented from within Gower's text. Gower's presentation of both the vengeance and the deliberations of the Athenian parliament are significantly different from the presentation of the same scene in his source, Benoit de Sainte-Maure's *Roman de Troie*. At the point of vengeance, Orestes's speech in the *Confessio* about one unkindness being repaid by another (lines 2055–69) is not found in the source (cf. lines 28365–9). The parliament scene in Benoit is altogether different: Menesteus peremptorily and threateningly puts an end to the deliberations (lines 28498–517). The *Confessio* scene looks identical between lines 2147–53, but Gower adds a sequence in which he reports that Menesteus argued the case thoroughly ('alleide / Ful many an other skile'), and that the parliament is persuaded by this reasoning ('Whan thei upon the reson musen') (lines 2155–71). The especial point against Clytemnestra is that she murdered her own 'lord', a point made by the gods (line 2003), by Orestes (line 2059) and by Menesteus (line 2162). In Gower's England this was a formally treasonous crime, for which see Strohm 1992, pp. 121–44. Orestes calls Clytemnestra's action 'treson' at line 2061.

I think this is a critical moment in the argument of Book III. This book began, as we saw, with the tale of Canace and Machaire, where Genius's moralization seemed to follow the dictates of natural law, a law which is sympathetic to incest, but obviously hostile to the murder of one's own children. Genius saw no reason to consider the claims of positive against natural law in that case, whereas in the tale of Orestes the story brings its own pressure to weigh up competing legal claims. It is, interestingly, not Genius who registers the doubt about how to judge the story; such doubt is registered from within the tale itself, in a passage which recalls Chaucer's House of Fame, or more of Rumour, where there is no fixed authority:

> Tho fame with hire swifte wynges
> Aboute flyh and bar tidinges,
> And made it cowth in alle londes
> How that Horestes with hise hondes
> Climestre his oghne Moder slowh.
> Som sein he dede wel ynowh,
> And som men sein he dede amis,
> Diverse opinion ther is.   (III.2107–14)

Finally, from within the tale itself, the parliament at Athens judges that Orestes is fit to rule, on the basis of two kinds of law: Menesteus argues that Orestes killed his mother out of no cruelty, but because the gods ordered him to do so; besides this defence on the basis of divine law, he also argues from positive law that Clytemnestra deserved 'wreche' not only because she was guilty of adultery, but also because she murdered 'hire oghne lord' (III.2158–62), where in Menesteus's usage 'lord' has political as well as marital senses.

So the tale of Orestes brings to light inadequacies within the terms of natural law alone: there are certain cases where natural law cannot decide the issue, since both parties are guilty of being 'unkynde'. Here recourse to bodies of law (divine, and especially positive, or human law) which surround and constrain natural law is necessary. The implication of such a moment for Amans is that personal ethics cannot be grounded on natural law alone; instead, the formation of a personal ethics demands a placing of the self within the human constraints which govern relationships in society more broadly. An ethics, that is, demands a politics.[34]

From this moment, it is, interestingly, Amans who requests (for the first time in the poem) information about matters essentially unrelated to love. Earlier he had refused teaching in any subject except that of his emotional state; after the story of Daphne and Apollo, for example, in which Daphne is transformed into a tree, Amans amusingly, but obsessively replies that regardless of what Fortune brings, he will serve his lady:

> Mi fader, grant merci of this:
> Bot while I se mi ladi is
> No tre, but halt hire oghne forme,
> Ther mai me noman so enforme,
> To whether part fortune wende,
> That I unto mi lyves ende
> Ne wol hire serven everemo.   (III.1729–35).

After the tale of Orestes, by contrast, Amans actively solicits Genius for further information – the will begins to desire information on a rational model. Genius himself relates the story of Orestes back to questions of love, by saying that whoever thinks to further his love with murder will shame both himself and his love (III.2198–200). Amans, however, has been impressed and disturbed by the tale of Orestes:

> Mi fader, of this aventure
> Which ye have told, I you assure
> Min herte is sory forto hiere,
> Bot only for I wolde lere
> What is to done, and what to leve.
> And over this now be your leve,
> That ye me wolden telle I preie,
> If ther be liefull eny weie
> Withoute Senne a man to sle.   (III.2201–9)

The civil questions that have been more insistently raised by stories such as that of Alexander and Diogenes, Athemas and Demophon, and of Orestes, now come explicitly to the surface, and the poem patently breaks the bounds set by the narrator in

---

[34] For the inter-relation of ethics and politics, which is at the heart of Gower's poem, see chapter 7.

Book I (i.e. to leave aside questions of politics, and to remain within questions of love (I.1–92)). The current of the poem now returns to the civil questions raised by the Prologue, and Genius speaks from a position of a divine and positive law which might constrain a simple version of natural law.[35] He argues that it is legal to kill (in legal cases where a person is convicted of treason, murder or robbery, and in self-defence of both country and self in time of war (III.2210–40)). But these cases of legal killing are, in Genius's eyes, defensible as a means of achieving a genuine peace;[36] he goes on, again in response to Amans's questioning, to attack murder in the pursuit of unjust wars. In this political discourse, the terms 'love' and 'peace' are transformed to apply to civil and religious ideas; in condemning war, for example, Genius's exposition runs thus:

> Whan goddes Sone also was bore,
> He sende hise anglis doun therfore,
> Whom the Schepherdes herden singe,
> Pes to the men of welwillinge
> In erthe be among ous here.   (III.2255–9)

He also cites the law of Nature and positive law ('bothe kinde and lawe write' (line 2330)) against unjust wars of aggrandizement. In contrast to the 'love and pes' commanded by Christ (III.2288), Genius poses the examples of vicious kings, who 'alle put resoun aweie', and who suppress their wit with their will (III.2333–7). Once again, Genius turns to Alexander (Alexander and the Pirate and the Death of Alexander (III.2363–480)) to exemplify his argument about the irrational covetousness of kings,

> whan reson is put aside
> And will governeth the corage.   (III.2428–9)[37]

---

[35] For the relations between different kinds of law in the poem, see Collins 1981, Olsson 1982 and White 1989. All stress the point that Gower presents and emphasizes (at least) *two*, competing versions of natural law, one animal, the other rational.

[36] Langland's treatment of Pees in *Piers Plowman*, B.IV is very close to that of Gower here.

[37] Whereas Genius had seemed to retreat from the political implications of Chaucer's *Manciple's Tale* (as the Manciple himself does) in his tale of Phebus and Cornide, here, in the tale of Alexander and the Pirate, he holds to the rhetorical and ethical importance of calling a spade a spade (the Manciple also refers to the Alexander and the Pirate story (*Canterbury Tales*, IX.223–34)).

So again the terms used in an earlier discussion of love are used here in a political context – 'will', 'reson' and 'pes' (e.g. III.2428–80). But it is not simply that the conceptual terms used to define amatory love are also applicable to civil and political questions; in carrying over such terms, the instabilities of Genius's treatment of love are steadied. By insisting that the will can be controlled by reason in civil concerns, and by recognizing the need for a natural law to be constrained by divine and positive law, Genius implicitly recognizes the shortcomings of the priest of Venus, or of Venus's purely sensual aspect anyway. And Genius's wider, more stable perspective here is promoted by Amans himself: it is Amans who asks the questions about the legality of killing; about the legality of war; and about the legality of crusades. Genius informs Amans, but Amans encourages Genius: the poem represents an optimistic fable of the soul, in which the will (Amans) gradually moves spontaneously towards reason through the mediation of Genius as the increasingly rational imagination.[38] The stories told by Genius are not only *about* the control of the will by reason, but they effect that very control in their listener Amans – they act as an *informatio voluntatis*, bringing the soul towards its perfection.

Equally, as the will moves towards conformity with reason, so too does the focus of the poem shift from the ethical to the political. Amans's situation cannot be fully understood within the context of natural law alone, since, as we have seen in the case of Orestes (and in that of Canace and Machaire), natural law is incapable of deciding certain cases. Genius needs to invoke principles of law, both divine and positive, which constrain, *though by no means efface*, the powerful source of natural law. As Amans, representing the will, moves towards conformity with his reason, so too do the stories become increasingly political. This is as true of Book III, in its movement towards questions of homicide, as it is in the disposition of discourses in the poem as a whole, with its movement

---

[38] With regard to the poem as a fable of the (one) soul, this is a convenient moment to register a criticism of Olsson's very fine book (Olsson 1992). Olsson does perceive the slipperiness of Genius, but he can give no account of the dynamics of the poem, because he regards Genius and Amans as separate people (he refers, for example, to 'Genius's own unstable *ingenium*' (p. 145)). For Gower's optimism, see Chance Nitzsche 1975, pp. 128–30, a view radically opposed to that of White 1988, who argues that the *Confessio* is 'permeated with a sense of failure', and that the poem is characterized by a 'rueful pessimism' (p. 615).

towards the *speculum principis* in Book VII.[39] Within this process, the reader, too, is 'informed': the reader recognizes that Amans's promise in Book I to treat only of love, and to abdicate responsibility for political wisdom, is a strategic ploy on Gower's behalf. Gower's ironic procedure is to promise not to deal with the larger question of political stability, but then to move towards precisely that area of consideration through the stories of love. He does this not simply as a way of leading to graver matter through more entertaining matter (though this is also true), but more importantly in order that the reader will also perceive the fundamental inter-relationship between questions of sexual and political control – neither is able to be treated without reference to the other. As with Alan's *Anticlaudianus*, the reader is 'informed' by perceiving the essential 'form', or organizing idea, behind the work's apparent heterogeneities.

Consideration of the matter of love has entirely converged with the political matter of the Prologue by the end of Book III. This is evident in, for example, Genius's discussion of the legality of crusades, where the discourse he uses is indistinguishable from the genre practised by Gower in the Prologue. In response to Amans's question, Genius attacks the Church's covetous promotion of homicide in crusades; he says that the sin is 'now so general', that it is to be found even in the Church,

> So is it all noght worth a Stree,
> The charite wherof we prechen,
> For we do nothing as we techen:
> And thus the blinde conscience
> Of pes hath lost thilke evidence
> Which Crist upon this Erthe tawhte.   (III.2538–43)

Earlier in Book I Genius promised that he would 'enforme' Amans's shrift in such a way as to 'remene' discussion of sin to the 'matiere of love' (I.272–80). This promise holds true for Book III at least; but it is holds true only as long as we understand the promise

---

[39] My point about the disposition of discourses in the poem, moving from amatory to political within individual books as it does within the structure of the poem as a whole, coincides with Peck 1978: 'in the *Confessio*, where welfare of community comprises Gower's central concern, those sins having greatest political implications ... are dealt with last as if in climax' (p. 59).

in a different sense from that in which it was offered: Genius does indeed lead discussion of sins to love, but it is the 'lawe of charite' rather than the blind, irresistible love described by Amans in Book I (lines 1–60). We understand, in fact, that discussion of the vices and virtues could not lead to love in Amans's limited sense of the word, since discussion of the political questions raised in Book III forces us to qualify the 'lawe of kynde', and to appeal to adjacent, constraining laws, both divine and positive.

It is true, then, for Book III at least, that Genius does 'ultimately' serve 'not the God of Love, but the God of medieval Christianity',[40] as Alastair Minnis has argued. But a great deal hangs on that 'ultimately': the congruence between natural, positive and divine law is not by any means felt immediately in the book; on the contrary, Genius's treatment of many of the earlier stories suggests blind spots in his perception on the matter of rational control of natural, sexual love. Ultimately there *is* a congruence between different kinds of law felt from within Book III, but this is achieved by a long and subtle shifting of intellectual perspective across the whole of the book, from the discussion of love to that of politics. The same is true for the structure of the poem as a whole, with its movement towards the political mirror for princes in Book VII, which opens up the way for the resolution of the key problem of incest in Book VIII (the key problem insofar as it highlights the conflict between natural and positive law).

In conclusion we can say that Genius is the path to Amans's reintegration and 'information' in its ideal sense. But the mode of reintegration is by no means transparent and direct: Genius is, after all, Amans's genius – his natural generative and imaginative power, whose sympathies extend in one direction into the senses and in the other into the reason. The means to recovery, through the regenerative powers of Genius, are themselves a part of the problem. But because Genius is not locked into the realm of sensual desire, he can participate with Amans in a process of informing Amans as the will into conformity with the reason. And in this

---

[40] It should be mentioned, however, that Gower's ethics in the *Confessio* are not specifically Christian; I think that for Gower, as for Alan in the *Anticlaudianus*, the foundations for an ethical system are classical and secular. This point is substantiated in the following chapter.

book concerning anger, Genius does, ultimately, meet his own ethical and literary standard:

> Mi Sone, that thou miht enforme
> Thi pacience upon the forme
> Of olde essamples, as thei felle,
> Now understond what I schal telle.   (III.1753–6)

Gower represents the naturally regenerative powers of the soul inter-acting with each other, bringing the will back into its proper mediation with, or conformity with, the reason. And as this happens, so too does the poem move into areas of positive law – Amans's ethical recovery is impossible without appeal to laws beyond the natural; an ethics both implies and requires a politics. Genius's 'information', then, designates not only the actual matter he brings to the attention of Amans; it also designates his literary informing of tales, his pedagogic informing of Amans, and, not least, the process by which he is himself informed, to become 'ingenium mediocre, philosophantis exercitio accommodissimum'.

CHAPTER 7

The primacy of politics in the Confessio amantis

INTRODUCTION

In Book VII of *Confessio amantis* Genius recounts the parts of philosophy to Amans, the second element of which is Rhetoric. Words
are the most powerful amongst earthly things, and they should,
accordingly, be truthful:

> For if the wordes semen goode
> And ben wel spoke at mannes Ere,
> Whan that ther is no trouthe there,
> Thei don fulofte gret deceipte;
> For whan the word to the conceipte
> Descordeth in so double a wise,
> Such Rethorique is to despise
> In every place, and forto drede. (VII.1550–7)

But if plain, unequivocal speech is recommended to a king here,
it is clear that Gower's larger sense of persuasive discourse cannot
be summarized so simply. For in the model of the poem which
I have suggested in the last two chapters, we can see how verbal
strategy must be characterized by a good deal of 'double speche'
(VII.1733). The whole poem, I have been arguing, is generated
out of fundamental incongruences and indirections, which are
particularly pronounced in the figure of Genius. Once we understand the psychological status of Genius, we realize that his claim
to authority over Amans cannot be accepted without qualification:
he is, after all, *Amans's* genius, the very imaginative faculty which
feeds the concupiscent will, with which he is so closely associated.
But, we have observed, his potential allegiances are also wider,
through his connection with the reason. Rather than it being the
case that Genius cures Amans of his problem, it is more that
Amans and Genius share a problem; through the interaction of
these two faculties, Amans can move towards being more of a

rational will, and, at the same time, move towards the psychic reintegration which reconstitutes John Gower. In exactly the same way as we resolved the formal incongruences of the *Anticlaudianus*, so too can we see how the perception of the psychological structure of *Confessio* provides its dynamic, and offers a potential resolution of its formal dividedness.

If my model is persuasive, then it invokes one further Ovid we have not so far mentioned. In chapter 5 I argued that Amans is derived from the aged, self-divided, obsessive lover of Ovid's *Amores*, and that Genius speaks from the position of the *praeceptor amoris* of the *Ars amatoria*. In that chapter I suggested that, by a selective reading at any rate, these two voices confirm and encourage each other, much in the same way that the *Amores* and the *Ars amatoria* can be seen as complementary companion pieces. This argument needs to be revised once we look at the structure of a single book as we did in the last chapter. There we see how Genius represents more than the apolitical, amoral voice of the *praeceptor amoris*, since within the movement of a single book (and in the movement of the poem as a whole) Genius moves insistently towards political narratives and towards specifically political perceptions. It is rather as if Gower introduces into Genius's voice a critique of the narrative voice of the *Ars amatoria*. If this is so, then Gower is introducing another Ovid, that of the *Remedia amoris*.

Or is he? The *Remedia amoris* would be the obvious text for comparison with the *Confessio amantis* – both texts, after all, present themselves as therapeutic for suffering lovers. And the therapeutic strategies are, it could be argued, very similar, for in both cases we could see the teachers using homeopathic techniques for restorative effect. Ovid's *praeceptor*, for example, calls the men suffering in love to him in this way:

> Ad mea, decepti iuvenes, praecepta venite,
> Quos suus ex omni parte fefellit amor.
> Discite sanari, per quem didicistis amare:
> Una manus vobis vulnus opemque feret. (*Ra* 41–4)[1]

---

[1] The text of the *Remedia amoris* is taken from Mozley 1929; translations are based on this edition. McNally 1961 has suggested that the *Confessio* is a *remedium amoris*; despite the fact that McNally does see the *Confessio* as infused with Ovidian strategies and content, he does not see Genius as an unstable, Ovidian instructor (e.g. pp. 123, 135). For accounts of the subtle relationship (crafted by Ovid himself) between the *Ars amatoria* and the *Remedia amoris*, see Durling 1965, pp. 26–43, and Allen 1992, pp. 15–37.

Come, attend to my precepts, deceived youths, you whom your own love
has utterly betrayed. Learn to be cured from him through whom you
learned to love. One hand alike will wound and heal.

Touch Ovid, and possible ironies suggest themselves: perhaps
decepti refers to the way in which the men have been beguiled by
women, or, possibly, by their teacher. This last suggestion is given
extra force in the idea that it is the one hand which both wounds
and cures. Possible ironies, but, at this early stage of the work,
unsustainable: the passage which these lines introduce continues by
asserting that if only the figures of myth had listened to the narrator's counsels, then the personal and political catastrophes of myth
would have been circumvented:

> Crede Parim nobis, Helenen Menelaus habebit,
>   Nec manibus Danais Pergama victa cadent.
> Impia si nostros legisset Scylla libellos,
>   Haesisset capiti purpura, Nise, tuo.   (*Ra* 65-8)

Entrust Paris to me: Menelaus will keep Helen, nor will vanquished
Pergamum fall by Danaan hands. Had impious Scylla read my verse, the
purple had stayed on your head, O Nisus.

And if the voice of the *Remedia* is particularly kind towards love,
then this, too, is presented as part of the therapeutic strategy. The
upset and impatient lover detests words of advice (*Ra* 123-4); the
narrator will, accordingly, broach his task more skilfully:

> Quin etiam accendas vitia inritesque vetando,
>   Temporibus si non adgrediare suis.   (*Ra* 133-4)

No, you would inflame the malady, and by forbidding irritate it, should
you not attack it at the right time.

All this is extremely suggestive for Gower's strategies in the
Confessio. For Genius is introduced (in the Latin verses at I.202) as
one who might provide a medicine for the wound of love;[2] he
speaks through experience of love (I.217-18), and, as we have seen,
he speaks 'softe and faire' (I.232), with considerable sympathy for
Amans as lover, to the extent of frequently encouraging him. And,

---

[2] Lines translated by Echard and Fanger 1991, p. 19: 'Confession made to Genius, I will
seek / A salve, for sores that Venus wrought on me. / Limbs harmed by sword to sound-
ness may be nursed; / It's rare that wounds of love will find a cure.'

like Ovid in the *Remedia*, it could be argued that Gower has Genius use mythical stories of love with the ultimate aim of circumventing the repeated catastrophes of those narratives.

But does Ovid really hold to the ambitious project announced at the opening of the *Remedia*? The narrator of the *Remedia* appeases Love in his invocation by saying that he addresses only unhappy lovers; as for those who are happy, may they continue, he says, to deceive jealous husbands. The god of Love himself accedes to Ovid's request, and gives his imprimatur to the work. And well he might: for the narratorial voice of the *Remedia* is, ultimately, wholly within the frame of the *Amores* and *Ars amatoria*. Despite the fact that the work is proposed as a cure for love, the remedy is only superficial: the overall current of advice by the *Remedia*'s *praeceptor* is to forget one love by replacing it with another. The lover should, he teaches, make love to someone else to help him forget his main love (*Ra* 400–6); or he should have two mistresses (*Ra* 441–88). If he follows the advice of the *Remedia*, his 'ship will soon be full of lovers' (*Ra* 488). Like Pandarus, the only cure for love the narrator of the *Remedia* can conceive of is to repeat the malady: 'Successore novo vincitur omnis amor' (*Ra* 462). (Chaucer, after all, is himself commenting on the relation between the *Ars amatoria* and the *Remedia*: Pandarus's advice to Troilus in Books I–III of *Troilus and Criseyde* represents the voice of the *Ars*, while in Book IV he takes up the stance of the *Remedia*; but, as with Ovid, the teacher can offer no real cure for the lover's wound, except to prescribe more of the 'same').

Overall, then, the narrative voice of the *Remedia* offers only strategies of self-deception, strategies which equally characterize the advice of *Ars amatoria*. What is missing from the narrative position of the *Remedia* is any real cure for the isolated, deceiving and self-deceived position of the lover as depicted in the *Amores* and the *Ars*. From my argument in the last chapter, it will be clear that I think Genius does move well beyond the position of the *praeceptor* of all these works: if Gower is implicitly writing a critique of the narrative position of the *Ars* and the *Amores*, he is equally replying to the limited narrative position of the most obvious Ovidian model for the *Confessio*, the *Remedia amoris*. Gower is clearly indebted to the ironic strategies of the *Remedia* (pretending to cure amatory obsession while encouraging it), but that is only part of Gower's larger design, whereas the narrator of the *Remedia* never moves beyond it.

But if Genius does move beyond the limited perspective of the Ovidian narrators, what is the end point to which the trajectory of the poem moves? Criticism has proposed at least three answers to this question: critics working in the frame first established by Lewis argue that the end point of Gower's poem is his promotion of 'honeste love'; the virtues of the good lover are those of the good Christian, and to promote lovers' virtues is to promote Christian virtues. The ultimate focus of the poem for these critics is the praise of marriage, of legitimate love.[3] Another, closely related set of critics argue or imply that the end point of Amans's instruction is religious and transcendent, in which Amans must move from sexual love to love of God, much in the manner proposed by the epilogue to *Troilus and Criseyde*.[4] And, finally, a third group argue that Gower's most 'significant role' is as a political thinker.[5]

In this chapter, I want to reject the second of these proposals (that Gower is promoting a religious and personal transcendence from worldly life), by arguing a compromise position between the first and third of the positions outlined immediately above – i.e. (with the qualification that I do not think Gower's ethics are specifically Christian) I want to suggest that Gower's praise of marriage is only possible in the move from obsessive and isolating amatory love to politics. Developing the argument of an excellent article by Elizabeth Porter, I will show how Gower moves consciously within the scope of the practical sciences in the 'Aristotelian' scheme (ethics, economics and politics).[6] The praise of marriage itself is part of what Gower would call an 'economic' discourse. The poem,

---

3   Especially Lewis 1936; Bennett 1966; Economou 1970.
4   This is the accent of the studies by Lynch 1988 (e.g. p. 198) and by Olsson 1992 (e.g. p. 242).
5   Thus Peck 1978. This is also true of the precursors to Peck's study: Coffman 1945, and Fisher 1964, pp. 185–203.
6   Porter 1983. The inter-relations of ethics and politics is also at the heart of the argument of Minnis 1980. Both Yeager 1990, pp. 196–216, and ch. 5, and Peck 1978, *passim*, make the point about the inter-relations of ethics and politics, which they see to be essential to the poem's coherence. Neither, in my view, put sufficient accent on the strains between the realm of the ethical and the political, strains which the poem dramatizes through the figure of Genius. Peck states the case for the inter-relations of ethics and politics lucidly: 'What is unique about Gower's social commentary is its insistent correlation of social criticism with a benevolent psychology of personal ethics. He seems always mindful of man as a double entity, both social and individual. When exploring man's individual psyche he turns to metaphors of state; when criticizing the state he conceives of a common body' (p. xxi). But the argument of the book focuses simply on the theme of 'common profit', without examining how this theme emerges in response to Genius's treatment of ethics.

like the *Anticlaudianus*, is pointed towards politics, even if (as I will show) Gower gives a primacy to political discourse which it does not have in Alan's poem. And, as with the *Anticlaudianus*, the *Confessio* makes its 'scientific' trajectory by way of the soul's integration. The 'information' offered by the poem is not so much information in the sciences of ethics, economics and politics themselves (though it clearly does this, too), rather an understanding of the inter-relations *between* different sciences, and an understanding of the points at which the soul resists or desires the passage from one science to another. And the soul to which Gower directs the poem is finally that of the reader: as with Alan, Gower's ideal philosopher–king is the reader of his poem.

'KNOW THYSELF' IN THE *CONFESSIO AMANTIS*

In chapter 4 I argued that the effect of the *Anticlaudianus* was to produce self-knowledge in its readers. Medieval commentators defined this as the 'utility' of the work, and the argument has considerable force: the poem not only represents the integration of the soul, but it also asks its reader to activate that same integration in the experience of reading. We experience the poem's primary level through our senses and imagination; we try to make sense of its order through our reason, and we pose a satisfying order through intellectual perception of the poem's informing idea, or archetype. The real meaning of the poem is to be located not so much in its represented action as in the experience it provokes in its reader.

I think the same is true of the *Confessio*: we ourselves, as readers, are drawn into the dynamic of the work, given that Gower provides no stable authority-figure from within it. And that dynamic is essentially psychological: Genius, as the imaginative faculty, activates our own desire and reason; we recognize the divisions between desire and reason, and we are provoked to search for points where they might be reconciled. In so doing, we ourselves move beyond a purely affective and imaginative response to the text, and move towards an integrated reading, which accommodates reason, imagination and desire. In this reading experience, we converge with Amans and Genius: beginning as the subjects of the text through their subjection to Cupid and Venus, Amans and Genius become the subjects of, or rather co-partners with, reason.

A concept of self-knowledge is, then, implicit in the structure of the whole poem.[7] At certain points in the *Confessio* Gower explicitly refers to texts which encourage self-understanding; in the brief story of the Roman triumph in Book VII, for example, Genius relates how the emperor rides in triumph with the fool beside him, who reminds him that, for all his power and glory, he should not forget himself: 'Let no justice gon aside, / Bot know thiself, what so befalle' (VII.2388–9) (the Latin gloss cites the Delphic Oracle, '*nosce teipsum*'). And in the story of Ulysses and Telegonus in Book VI, Ulysses wakes out of his sleep, anxious about the foreboding dream he has just experienced; unable to fathom it, Genius comments: 'Men sein, a man hath knowleching / Save of himself of alle thing' (VI.1567–8), and the Latin gloss cites the maxim attributed to Saint Bernard: 'Plures plura sciunt et seipsos nesciunt.'

This last citation, drawn from monastic texts which were used in English writing contemporary with Gower, is usually deployed by way of attacking the human sciences.[8] In that monastic tradition of self-knowledge, knowledge of the sciences is felt to be inimical, or at best obstructive, to knowledge of the soul. These monastic texts play at length on the topos of the man who knows the structure of the heavens and of the natural world, but who is ignorant of himself. And the literary texts which incorporate this particular version of the *nosce teipsum* tradition (and I am thinking particularly of *Piers Plowman*) represent knowledge of the sciences and of the self as being in a strained, often conflictual relationship.[9] But is this the version of 'self-knowledge' drawn upon by Gower in the *Confessio*? He might cite the pseudo-Bernadine maxim in a single episode,

---

7   It should also be mentioned at this point that Ovid, too, promotes a concept of self-knowledge through his *praeceptor* in the *Ars amatoria*: Apollo appears to the *praeceptor* and invites the teacher to lead his pupils to the temple of Apollo at Delphi, where they will read the famous dictum that everyone should know themselves (*Ars amatoria*, II.493–510). But the presentation of the dictum by the *praeceptor*, who so often encourages a deliberate self-deception, represents a drastic narrowing of the force of the Apollonian maxim. Gower, I have been arguing, plays at length (great length, indeed) with the ways in which self-analysis can at the same time be self-deception. He sees a great value in that, in fact (desire, after all, cannot and should not be simply crushed). But he is not prepared, however, to let the self-analysis rest there.

8   Probably the best known of these pseudo-Bernadine texts is the *Meditationes piisimae de cognitione humanae conditionis*, PL 184, cols. 485–508. For discussion of a group of closely related texts around the *Meditationes*, see Bultot 1964. The tradition of self-knowledge within which they are working is discussed by Courcelle 1974 (see chapter 4, n. 49 above, for references). Langland cites the *Meditationes* at a critical moment, *Piers Plowman* B.XI.3.

9   For Langland's indebtedness to this group of texts, see Wittig 1972, and Simpson 1986b.

but, across the poem as a whole, does he see knowledge of the human sciences as obstructive to knowledge of the self? Or does he see 'scientific' knowledge rather as *essential* to self-understanding? Is Gower following pessimistic or (like Alan) optimistic traditions of human knowledge?

The humanist tradition whereby knowledge of the sciences is essential to knowledge of the self is, clearly, the tradition represented in a particularly pronounced form by the *Anticlaudianus*: there the soul can know its own origins only by the moral and political information of Books VII–IX, and then by traversing, and understanding the structure of the cosmos in Books IV–VI. In my view, Gower is working broadly within the same tradition, according to which knowledge of the human sciences is integral to knowledge of the self; the soul can achieve an integration of its different faculties only through specifically 'scientific' information.[10] And, furthermore, Gower is working within largely the same hierarchy of sciences as Alan (the 'Aristotelian' scheme, outlined in chapter 2), although he gives primacy to politics whereas Alan sees theology as the highest science. Let us now turn to the *Confessio* to see how self-knowledge necessarily involves knowledge of the sciences, and how the structure of Gower's poem is informed by a hierarchy of sciences.

The *speculum principis* of Book VII is the obvious point of the *Confessio* to demonstrate the ways in which knowledge of the sciences is integral to self-knowledge. For here the poem most consistently and explicitly breaks the bounds of a lover's confession, and introduces matter of an encyclopaedic kind, structured around a *divisio philosophiae*. But we should first observe how Book VI prepares the way for Book VII.

The initial transition may seem a little abrupt. By way of exemplifying the misuse of sorcery, the final story told by Genius in Book VI has been that of Nectabanus and Alexander; in one of those interesting moments where Amans asks for matter outside his immediate amatory interests ('beside that me stant of love'), Amans asks Genius about princely instruction:

---

[10] Bennett 1979 points out that Gower adopts the more pessimistic view of human knowledge in the *Vox clamantis* and the *Mirour de l'omme*. See *Vox clamantis* II.9; VII.8.671–716; and *Mirour de l'omme*, lines 1612–20. I agree that those two works tend to take the monastic, pessimistic view of the human sciences; the *Confessio* is exceptional to Gower's *oeuvre*, in this as in so many other ways.

> Hou Alisandre was betawht
> To Aristotle, and so wel tawht
> Of al that to a king belongeth,
> Wherof min herte sore longeth
> To wite what it wolde mene.
> For be reson I wolde wene
> That if I herde of thinges strange,
> Yit for a time it scholde change
> Mi peine, and lisse me somdiel.   (VI.2411–19)

All the moments of 'scientific' information in the *Confessio* are in fact provoked by Amans, rather than being forced upon him in any way. I observed this in the last chapter (the discussion of homicide), and we can see it again here in a particularly acute form: Amans's 'herte sore longeth' to know about the instruction of Alexander by Aristotle, and he longs to know it 'be resoun'. In the last chapter, not only did we observe that Amans participates in the process of his instruction, but also that Genius is informed as much as Amans. The ending of Book VI suggests the same point, since Genius also *longs* to consider this 'scientific' matter. He initially responds by saying that he is unable to provide such information, subject as he is to Venus:

> Bot touchende of so hih aprise,
> Which is noght unto Venus knowe,
> I mai it noght miselve knowe,
> Which of hir court am al forthdrawe
> And can nothing bot of hir lawe.   (VI.2424–8)

But we understand, by now, that Genius is only 'forthdrawe' by Venus as long as he is participating with Amans as irrational desire. His potential sympathies are wider, and, the moment he is prompted to go beyond his role as *praeceptor amoris*, he can respond immediately. How else could we account for the fact that Genius clearly *is* capable of expounding the pedagogic matter to which Amans refers? He longs to know this matter, too:

> Bot natheles to knowe more
> Als wel as thou me longeth sore;
> And for it helpeth to comune,
> Al ben thei noght to me comune,
> The scoles of Philosophie,

Yit thenke I forto specefie,
In boke as it is comprehended,
Wherof thou mihtest ben amended.   (VI.2429–36)

The encyclopaedic matter of Book VII, then, is produced out of
the joint desire of Amans and Genius, and it is Amans who first
provokes that rational desire. When we look further back into Book
VI, I think we can see why it might be necessary for both Amans
and Genius to move beyond the bounds of Amans's instruction as a
lover. For in that book Amans articulates very precisely the psychological dead-end to which an imagination wholly linked to concupiscent desire leads.

Very often in Book VI Genius insists on the impossibility of
resisting love. He opens his discussion of love-drunkenness (a
species of gluttony) by saying that it is irresistible:

> Bot love is of so gret a main,
> That where he takth an herte on honde,
> Ther mai nothing his miht withstonde.   (VI.90–2)

And in Amans's specific case, he makes the same point (VI.317–18),
backing it up with the story of Bacchus in the desert, whose prayer
to Jupiter for drink was successful (VI.391–466). Bacchus, one
would have thought, is a particularly ill-chosen example to cure
drunkenness of any kind, and the strange contradictions of the
choice emerge as Genius pursues the analogy. Like the Ovidian
praeceptor amoris, he positively encourages Amans to keep praying
his lady for love; eventually Amans's thirst (which, presumably, is
causing his 'drunkenness') will be quenched, and so his drunkenness be cured by drinking from the 'tun' of love controlled by
Cupid (a reference to Genius's previous story):

> Forthi to speke thou ne lete,
> And axe and prei erli and late
> Thi thurst to quenche, and thenk algate,
> The boteler which berth the keie
> Is blind, as thou hast herd me seie;
> And if it mihte so betyde,
> That he upon the blinde side
> Per cas the swete tonne arauhte,
> Than schalt thou have a lusti drauhte
> And waxe of lovedrunke sobre   (VI.450–9)

This very Ovidian *remedium amoris* reveals its contradictions, and reveals that Genius is as much participating in Amans's 'disease' as curing it. Amans himself clearly wants more of this medicine: he says that he cannot possibly be cured of love-drunkenness, but he desires Genius to go on all the same to the question of 'delicacy' in love (VI.600–10).

Amans's delicacy of 'thoght' in particular reveals how Amans and Genius, as long as they are participating in the same psychological movement, cannot progress. When he is away from his lady, Amans recounts, he thinks of her in 'thoght'. Sight and hearing bring in this third 'delicacy', which has taken the central place in Amans's heart:

> and nameliche on nyhtes,
> Whan that me lacketh alle sihtes,
> And that myn heringe is aweie,
> Thanne is he redy in the weie
> Mi reresouper forto make,
> Of which myn hertes fode I take.
> The lusti cokes name is hote
> Thoght, which hath evere hise pottes hote
> Of love buillende on the fyr
> With fantasie and with desir,
> Of whiche er this fulofte he fedde
> Min herte, whanne I was abedde   (VI.907–18)

'Thoght' in Middle English often designates an obsessive, anxious and debilitating mental state which characterizes the melancholy spirit.[11] Clearly it involves reflection on images, as this passage indicates: the mention of images being produced when the object of attention is no longer before the senses is the standard way of describing the imagination. In Book IV, indeed, this very experience of mentally running back over the lady's body in her absence is described as 'pure ymaginacioun' (IV.1143). But the imagination is wholly irrational in this state, subject to desire and productive only of unreal 'fantasies'.

Of course Genius does more than provide 'fantasies' for Amans; but, as we have seen, Amans does himself represent desire, and Genius often encourages that desire, no matter how hopeless it is. So

---

[11] *MED* s.v. 5. The opening of Hoccleve's *Regement of Princes* (lines 1–112) offers a particularly powerful and extended example of 'thought' being used in this way.

in Book VI we can see Genius's role as *praeceptor amoris* from a psychological perspective, as an example of fantasy and memory co-operating with desire in a cul-de-sac of obsessive and debilitating mental activity. Amans is not unlike Pygmaleon in Book IV, who falls in love with his statue (Amans's lady is, after all, particularly stony) 'thurgh pure impression / Of his ymaginacion' (IV.389–90). Even when Genius stands outside his subjection to Amans, in his conclusion of the 'delicacy' sequence, he nevertheless maintains his characteristic fence-sitting position about the possibility of ever really escaping the domination of will in the experience of love. He begins his summary by saying how in love 'delicacy' and drunkenness are to be feared, precisely because they give power over reason to will:

> For thanne hou so that evere it falle,
> Wit can no reson understonde,
> Bot let the governance stonde
> To Will, which thanne wext so wylde,
> That he can noght himselve schylde
> Fro no peril...   (VI.1240–5)

The moment he makes this point, however, he collapses back into a statement which suggests no escape from the tyrannical domination of will:

> Bot whan that love assoteth sore,
> It passeth alle mennes lore;
> What lust it is that he ordeigneth,
> Ther is no mannes miht restreigneth,
> And of the godd takth he non hiede.   (VI.1251–5)

'It passeth mennes lore': this might seem like an unpromising position from which to enter into a summary of philosophy. And the two stories that follow (and end Book VI) seem to suggest the same thing; Genius proceeds to declare the powers of love (VI.1261–92), under which no instruction can help:

> Ther is no god, ther is no lawe,
> Of whom that he takth eny hiede;
> Bot as Baiard the blinde stede,
> Til he falle in the dich amidde,
> He goth ther noman wole him bidde;
> He stant so ferforth out of reule,
> Ther is no wit that mai him reule.   (VI.1278–84)

Coming from Genius (himself a 'god' supplying 'lawe'),[12] this is
depressing news for Amans, and for us. How do the stories that follow prompt Amans to ask for Aristotle's instruction of Alexander?

Like the narrator of the *Ars amatoria* and the *Remedia amoris*,
Genius argues against the use of sorcery in love;[13] but the examples
he chooses have immediate political implications, since they both
concern kings whose sons, conceived through magic powers, murdered them. Both the story of Ulysses and Telegonus and that of
Nectabanus and Alexander stress the philosophical expertise of the
kings: Ulysses is a 'worthi knyght and king / And clerk knowende
of every thing' (VI.1397–8), while Nectabanus (ex-king of Egypt) is a
'clerk' equally expert in science (e.g. VI.1881–8). Nectabanus acts
very much like the pagan priests in the tale of Mundus and
Paulina, promising 'enformacion' through an 'avision' to Olimpias,
but, like those pagan priests (and, one might add, not wholly unlike
Genius, 'Venus clerk'), he uses his science in subjection to Venus,
in order to deceive Olimpias. Alexander, the child born of this
deceptive union, finally murders his tutor by pushing him off a
tower during an astronomy lesson. As with Ulysses, so with
Nectabanus: both are described as ignorant of themselves despite
their knowledge of sciences. Alexander shoves his tutor to his
death:

> Ly doun there apart:
> Wherof nou serveth al thin art?
> Thou knewe alle othre mennes chance
> And of thiself hast ignorance:
> That thou hast seid amonges alle
> Of thi persone, is noght befalle.   (VI.2311–16)

The irony is, of course, that Alexander is both right and wrong:
Nectabanus has just predicted that he would die by the hand of his
own son; Alexander pushes him off the tower to prove him wrong.
The murder in fact demonstrates Nectabanus's scientific skill (to
his cost), but Alexander's essential point remains valid, that
Nectabanus was ignorant of himself.[14]

---

[12] I think there is an implicit Ovidian reference here: at *Amores* II.9B.25–6, the lover says
that even if a god told him to stop loving, he would not obey.

[13] The *praeceptor* of the *Ars amatoria* warns against sorcery at II.99–107; the same advice is
given in *Remedia amoris* at lines 249–90.

[14] This passage is discussed by Bennett 1979.

Both these stories, then, point to a self-ignorance in the learned, and the political consequences of that ignorance: in the case of Ulysses, a king is murdered, and in the case of Nectabanus, a prince is the murderer. Although the stories are offered to Amans purely as examples of not using sorcery in love, they have immediate political implications, and lead into what is effectively the companion piece to these last two stories of Book VI, the *speculum principis* of Book VII: if Nectabanus was the anti-type of Alexander's tutor, then Aristotle is the positive pedagogic model. As we have seen, Amans *longs* to hear this *speculum principis*, just as Genius does; this suggests in itself that the soul, naturally desiring self-knowledge, responds to these stories of self-ignorance by desiring the 'scientific' knowledge which will bring the soul to knowledge of itself. Almost despite themselves, the different powers of the soul tend towards integration.

GENIUS'S DIVISION OF PHILOSOPHY

But how can knowledge of the sciences, presented explicitly as the parts of philosophy, provide the self-knowledge which Ulysses and Nectabanus were lacking? The precise point of their fall was that they *were* knowledgeable in the sciences, but ignorant of themselves.

Genius begins with a *divisio philosophiae*, derived immediately from Brunetto Latini's *Livres dou Tresor*, and ultimately from the 'Aristotelian' division transmitted especially through Boethius.[15] The division is basically the same as that within which the *Anticlaudianus* is working: the theoretical and the practical sciences, where the theoretical sciences comprise physics, mathematics and theology, while the practical sciences follow in the order ethics, economics and politics. Following Boethius, Brunetto (and Gower after him) adds a third division, concerned with the verbal arts.[16]

---

[15] For the *Li Livres dou Tresor*, see Carmody 1948. Gower's division of philosophy diverges from Brunetto in one respect: Brunetto makes a triple division of philosophy, into Theory, Practice and Logic. Under Logic he treats words, but only dialectic. He places rhetoric as a part of politics (Carmody 1948, I.1–5, pp. 6–22). For the history of the 'Aristotelian' scheme, see chapter 2, n. 34 above. Fox 1931 presents Gower's knowledge of the sciences in a schematic way, as if Gower is writing a mini-encylopaedia. The argument of this chapter suggests that Gower's omissions and emphases within his presentation of the sciences are strategic.

[16] For Boethius's addition of Logic as a third branch of philosophy, see the second edition of his commentary on the *Isagoge*, in Schepss and Brandt 1906, pp. 138–43.

Genius divides philosophy in this way, but his exposition of the
parts of philosophy is highly selective: in his theoretical division, he
focuses briefly on theology, but more especially on physics and
astronomy (a subdivision of mathematics); what interests Genius in
the theoretical sciences is the creation of the cosmos and the human
soul by God; the complexion of physical bodies; and the astrological
influences of the heavens on those bodies (VII.633–1506). His account
of rhetoric is very brief (VII.1507–640), and by far the largest exposition is devoted to the practical sciences (VII.1711–5438). But even
here, he has large gaps: there is no account of ethics (governance of
self), or of economics (governance of a household); this whole section
is instead devoted to a fivefold subdivision of politics, into Truth,
Liberality, Justice, Pity and Chastity, the last of which receives the
largest treatment (VII.4215–5439). In this selectiveness Gower is quite
unlike his principal sources: the *De regimine principum* of Giles of Rome
treats only the practical sciences (as one would expect) and is divided
up into ethics, economics and politics;[17] Brunetto Latini's *Tresor* provides the ground for Gower's tripartite division, but Latini himself
gives extensive treatment to each part of philosophy.[18] The reasons
for Gower's selectiveness, and particularly for his omission of ethics
and economics, will become clear as we pursue our larger question
about how this treatment of science provides the self-knowledge that
Amans requires.

In his account of astrological influences (a part of his exposition
of the theoretical sciences) Genius points to the power of Venus,
which controls lovers, 'of whiche', Genius says to Amans, 'I trowe
thou be on' (VI.776). Whoever falls under the influence of this
planet shall 'desir joie and merthe'; he shall (like Genius) speak
'softe and faire' (VII.786), and seek the pleasure of love wherever he
can find it, to the point of a certain moral blindness:

> He is so forforth Amourous,
> He not what thing is vicious
> Touchende love, for that lawe
> Ther mai no maner man withdrawe,
> The which venerien is bore
> Be weie of kinde...   (VII.791–6)

---

[17]   For the text, see Giles of Rome 1607. There is an English translation of this text attributed to John Trevisa, in Oxford, Bodleian Library, Digby 233.
[18]   See Carmody 1948.

The influence of each star is described by Genius, but Venus is obviously the planet which most nearly touches Amans; the fact that Genius gives most weight to chastity in his account of the practical sciences equally suggests how this *divisio philosophiae* is pointed at Amans. But whereas the planetary influence is presented as irresistible in a purely astrological discourse (VII.633–1506), Genius's account of chastity, under a political discourse, affirms the necessity and possibility of constraining (though by no means effacing) sexual desire (VII. 4215–5397).

The stories devoted to the first four points of 'Policy' are, on the whole, very brief. The longest story in this book, the joint narratives of Aruns and the Gabines and Aruns and Lucretia (closely translated from Ovid, *Fasti*, II.685–852),[19] falls in the section dealing with chastity. This double story is equally balanced between politics and ethics: the first part deals with the treacherous deception and murder of the Gabines by Aruns and his father King Tarquin, while the second presents the rape of Lucrece by Aruns. Genius's introduction makes no real distinction between the political and physical lust of Tarquin and his son:

> So that withinne a fewe yeres
> With tresoun and with tirannie
> Thei wonne of londe a gret partie,
> And token hiede of no justice,
> Which due was to here office
> Upon the reule of governance;
> Bot al that evere was plesance
> Unto the fleisshes lust thei toke.   (VII.4600–7)

The treacherous invasion of the Gabines is followed by the equally treacherous invasion of Lucretia. After witnessing Lucretia's fidelity, Aruns desires her in his imagination, the description of which is strikingly close to Amans's own delicacy of 'thoght' to which he confessed in Book VI (lines 899–938); Aruns goes to bed,

> noght forto reste,
> Bot forto thenke upon the beste
> And the faireste forth withal,

---

[19] For a close comparison, see McNally 1961, pp. 161–90. Mainzer 1972, p. 223 explains that the name 'Aruns' for Tarquin's son (not found in Ovid's account), is found in the glosses to this story in *Fasti* manuscripts.

> That evere he syh or evere schal,
> So as him thoghte in his corage,
> Where he pourtreieth hire ymage.   (VII.4871–6)

The description of Amans's unrestrained will, which produced the
'thoght' of his lady in Book VI, may have seemed harmless enough
there. But here, in the political discourse of Book VII, the tyranny
of the will is seen not from the point of view of the subject lover,
but rather from the woman subject to violence and tyranny.
Genius describes the lusting Aruns as 'this tirannysshe knyght', and
makes the obvious point that he was determined to fulfil his lust
'althogh it were ayein hire wille' (VII.4889–94).

All previous stories which have involved rape have cushioned us
from the reality of rape. They have either stressed how helpless the
rapists were to resist pursuing their lust (Mundus in Book I, and
Nectabanus in Book VI), or else, despite (or because of) the story's
power, they have provided a comic contrast with the idea of the
pathetic, obedient Amans ever doing such a thing (Tereus in Book
V). Here, however, in the political discourse of Book VII, Genius
stresses the fact that men do have the power *not* to submit to their
imagination, especially when the woman's desire remains uncon-
sidered. He introduces the discussion of chastity by saying that
Aristotle instructed Alexander to 'guide and reule' his body:

> For in the womman is no guile
> Of that a man himself bewhapeth;
> Whan he his oghne wit bejapeth,
> I can the wommen wel excuse:
> Bot what man wole upon hem muse
> After the fool impression
> Of his ymaginacioun,
> Withinne himself the fyr he bloweth,
> Wherof the womman nothing knoweth,
> So mai sche nothing be to wyte.
> For if a man himself excite
> To drenche, and wole it noght forbere,
> The water schal no blame bere.   (VII.4266–78)

And not only does Genius insist here that a man can rule the
'fool impression / Of his ymaginacioun', but that very point connects Amans himself with Aruns: both are subject to the tyranny
of will, which pulls the imagination into subjection. There can

be no escape from the realm of the political, since the soul is a political arena.

The discourse of politics, then, places constraints not only on the amatory discussion outside Book VII, but also on the astrological discourse within Book VII, which had suggested that humans cannot control their planetary influence. The story centred on Lucrece reveals that it is against a king's interests to give way to 'fool ymaginacioun' (the Tarquins are expelled from Rome); and from the wider perspective of political discourse Genius also feels pity (defined as itself a political virtue) for the victims of male desire, something he often fails to do in the purely amatory stories. And if the political stories constrain the amatory, it is equally true that the 'amatory' stories constrain the political: Lucrece's rape equally reveals the violent concupiscence of territorial invasion.[20]

But how, my reader might ask, does all this provide a self-knowledge for Amans? For, he or she might object, Amans remains unmoved and uninstructed at the end of Book VII; he politely dismisses Genius's information:

> Do wey, mi fader, I you preie:
> Of that ye have unto me told
> I thonke you a thousendfold.
> The tales sounen in myn Ere,
> Bot yit myn herte is elleswhere,
> I mai miselve noght restreigne,
> That I nam evere in loves peine. (VII.5408–14)

The psychological process of the poem seems to be at a dead stop.

But is it? Genius himself undergoes a sea-change in Book VII, from which he never retreats.[21] He does not by any means promote virginity here,[22] but he does insist on the possibility of a 'constitutional' compromise between the demands of the body and those of reason:

---

[20] The comparison between territorial and sexual concupiscence is also implicit in the Diogenes and Alexander and the Death of Alexander stories (*Confessio amantis* III.1201–330, 2438–80).

[21] It is true that Genius seems to retreat in Book VIII.2203–9, when he promises to take Amans's supplication to Venus. But the retreat is strategic, made in the knowledge that Amans will make the critical moves himself.

[22] In Book V, however, Genius does praise virginity, which I find very puzzling (V.6359–451). Gower seems to have felt uncomfortable with this passage, too, since he cut most of it after the first recension.

> For god the lawes hath assissed
> Als wel to reson as to kinde,
> Bot he the bestes wolde binde
> Only to lawes of nature,
> Bot to the mannes creature
> God yaf him reson forth withal,
> Wherof that he nature schal
> Upon the causes modefie,
> That he schal do no lecherie,
> And yit he schal his lustes have.   (VII.5372–81)

This is characteristic of the position of Genius from this point on to the end of the poem, and it is a very significantly different position from the one he has promoted throughout the poem up to this point – where, as I have frequently shown, he often points to the necessity of restraining will by reason, but equally often immediately goes on to say that desire is irresistible and will have its way.

So up to Book VII, as I have argued in the previous two chapters, Genius is Amans's genius, or imagination; and he is, accordingly, often a 'fool ymaginacioun'. But in Book VII, through his political instruction, Genius seems to me to mark his *balanced* allegiances to reason and the body unequivocally. Genius is the point of mediation between the will and the reason, and even if the will remains held in his obsessive desire, it will no longer have the help of a concupiscent imagination (the one story told by Genius in Book VIII is that of Apollonius of Tyre, in praise of marriage).

Once we recognize that Genius is Amans's imagination, then we also recognize that the soul of which Amans is a part *has* undergone a very significant shift towards integration in Book VII. The Latin head verses to Book VII themselves point to who is being instructed in this book – they affirm that 'doctrine' overcomes nature, and that knowledge will provide what the prompting of a 'teachable genius' did not give ('Naturam superat doctrina, viro quod et ortus / Ingenii docilis non dedit, ipsa dabit').[23] But if knowledge does provide what a 'genius' cannot, it is precisely by informing a receptive *ingenium docile* that this comes about. Genius, then, is the pupil as much as the teacher in Book VII, and his changed position with regard to controlling the will is itself demon-

---

[23] My translation differs slightly from Echard and Fanger 1991, p. 73 (they give 'native wit, as yet untaught'). My translation is closer to the syntax of the original; both point in the same direction – i.e. that Genius will himself be taught by philosophical instruction.

stration that the mind *can* resist the tyranny of the will. And, indeed, when we think that Genius's scientific discourse was prompted in the first place by Amans's longing, then we understand how the will itself remains unsatisfied with its conflictual isolation from reason. These psychological perceptions are not matters of explicit affirmation from within the poem; they are instead implicit in the poem's structure, which is much subtler than any statement could be.

The psychological process of the *Confessio* has not stopped at all by the end of Book VII; Amans is a good deal closer to recognizing himself. In a wonderful irony, which is itself Ovidian, the person who will finally be won over in the *Confessio* is not the lady, but Amans himself.

POLITICS AS THE 'CONSERVE AND KEPERE' OF THE SCIENCES

Politics and the matter of love are, then, inextricably related discourses, each leading into the other. Elizabeth Porter has given a very lucid account of the theoretical background to this inter-relation. She argues that the macrocosmic-microcosmic theory which Gower could have read in the *Secreta secretorum* informs a more specific idea that Gower found in both that work and another of his main sources for Book VII, the *De regimine principum* (*c.* 1285) of Giles of Rome (d. 1316) – i.e. that ethical control of the individual is both productive of, and modelled on, the ideal political order of the state. This theoretical connection makes sense of the shift from the political discourse of the Prologue to the amatory concerns of the body of the work, just as it accounts for the shift back to political concerns in Book VII. Referring to the idea of ethical self-governance, Porter says:

This is the idea which links Gower's interpretation of the dream of Nebuchadnezzar to the education of Alexander *in sui regimen* (suggesting self-governance and perhaps also the governance of others) and in turn to the education of Amans. Genius' confession of the lover will be an education in the grounds of personal kingship... Since the teaching of Aristotle, as Gower found it in the *Secreta Secretorum* and in *De Regimine Principum*, made concord in the body politic dependent upon ethical self-governance within the individual, the remedies that Genius proposes will not only resolve the lover's personal dilemma but bring peace to the political community. Personal peace of mind and public peace, both within the body politic and between nations, depend on the same ethical process.[24]

I am in essential agreement with Porter here, though of course it could be mentioned that Gower would have known the theory of macro-microcosm from more sophisticated sources than the *Secreta secretorum*.[25] Neither do I need to argue here that Porter's apparently unproblematic understanding of the ways in which Genius provides resolution of disturbance in both Amans and the body politic requires fairly massive qualification, of the kind I have made in the previous two chapters. But her fundamental point, which she develops with great lucidity, squares exactly with my own sense of the way in which the homology of ethics and politics works in the *Confessio*: the theory of macrocosm and microcosm is founded on, and itself provokes, reflection on the inter-relation of apparently diverse discourses; and in the *Confessio* the discourses which are of particular interest to Gower are ethics, economics (in the Aristotelian sense) and politics. We need not look far in, say, the *De regimine principum* to find explicit statements which elucidate the analogies between ethics and politics. In defining the utility of the work, Giles says that although the book is directed to a king (Philip the Fair), it is nevertheless useful for anyone to read it, since they gain control over themselves:

for just as a king cannot be said to control his kingdom (nor a lord his city), should there be those in that kingdom or city who reject the authority of the king or lord, so too any individual man cannot be said to be in control of himself, if his sensual appetite pulls away from his reason, and if his rational activity is not itself consonant with the essence of reason.

sicut ergo rex non dicitur habere regnum, nec dux dicitur habere ciuitatem, si in regno vel ciuiate sunt aliqui, qui non obediant regi, vel duci: sic homo aliquis singularis dicitur non habere seipsum, si appetitus dissentiat rationi, et si rationale per participationem non obediat rationali per essentiam.[26]

---

[24] Porter 1983, p. 144. This inter-relation between ethics and politics is, as I mentioned above, also central to the argument of Minnis 1980.
[25] Gower elaborates the macro-microcosm analogy in each of his three major works, *Confessio amantis*, Prologue, 945–66; *Vox clamantis*, VII.8.637–716; *Mirour de l'omme*, lines 26869–940. He cites Gregory, *Moralia*, VI.16 (PL 75, col. 740). But this passage is brief and philosophically unsophisticated. Gower would have had access to much more extended and elaborate versions of the idea, in, for example, Calcidius's commentary on the *Timaeus*, or in Alan of Lille's *De planctu Naturae*, VI, 41–120 (Häring 1978, pp. 826–8). For Gower's knowledge of the *Secreta secretorum*, see Porter 1983 and Manzalaoui 1981.
[26] Giles of Rome 1607, p. 9.

And, as Genius encourages a rational pursuit of love in Book VIII, he also makes the same point explicitly:

> Thus love is blinde, and can noght knowe
> Wher that he goth, til he be falle:
> Forthi, bot if it so befalle
> With good conseil that he be lad,
> Him oghte forto ben adrad.
> For conseil passeth alle thing
> To him which thenkth to ben a king;
> And every man for his partie
> A kingdom hath to justefie,
> That is to sein his oghne dom.   (VIII.2104–13)

So Porter's argument that Genius's ethical instruction of Amans is at the same time a *speculum principis* is very persuasive. Like Alan in the *Anticlaudianus*, Gower directs the burden of his poem to the instruction of a king, whose philosophical instruction must be in ethics as much as politics. I will take up the historical implications of this point in chapter 9, where I consider the *Confessio* as implicitly addressed to English kings. In the last section of this chapter I would like to develop Porter's argument by elucidating the ways in which the poem's structure is determined by the hierarchy of sciences by which Gower's king is to be philosophically informed.

The *Anticlaudianus*, as I argued in chapter 2, is a poem whose structure is modelled on a division of philosophy, and whose dynamic is determined, in part, by the hierarchy of sciences within that division. The structure of the poem is modelled on the Aristotelian division of sciences, with Books VII–IX being directed towards the practical sciences, culminating in politics, whereas Books I–VI are shaped around the theoretical sciences, represented in Book I by Reason's three mirrors. The dynamic of the poem is produced not only by the psychological movement of the soul in its search for integration and self-knowledge through knowledge of its origins; that movement is itself correlative with the hierarchy of the sciences, according to which theology, the study of pure form through the intellect, is at the apex. The poem is, as I argued in chapter 4, pointed towards politics, but it reveals how an understanding of politics is inseparable from an understanding of the justice which informs both the cosmos and the soul. And that, for Alan, can only be understood, ultimately, through theology.

Gower, following Brunetto Latini, also presents a version of the Aristotelian scheme of sciences in Book VII. In this chapter and the last we have seen how the movement of the *Confessio*, like that of the *Anticlaudianus*, is produced out of a psychological process, whereby the soul's different faculties move towards integration. And it will also be obvious that I think the movement of the *Confessio* is informed both by a division of philosophy, and by the hierarchy within that division. But, it might be objected, Gower leaves out of account any discussion of economics and ethics in his *divisio philosophiae* of Book VII, and, moreover, his treatment of the theoretical sciences is very selective, concentrating only on those parts of theology and physics that affect the creation of the soul and the composition of the human body. Let me answer these objections in turn; when we do so, we recognize that Gower is indeed working within the Aristotelian division of science, but that his way of hierarchizing it is very different from that of Alan of Lille, and, it might be added, from that of the theologian Giles of Rome. Gower's position is much closer to the lay citizen and scholar, Brunetto Latini.[27]

Why does Genius omit any account of ethics and economics from his description of philosophy in Book VII, despite his clear articulation of the three parts of the 'Aristotelian' practical sciences in Book VII.1649–98? I think the answer is not that Gower has been structurally incoherent, as has been claimed;[28] on the contrary, there is a profound logic to this omission: once we understand the structure of sciences within which Gower is working, we realize that the whole poem outside Book VII is a discussion of ethics and economics, a discussion which leads inevitably to the explicit political discourse of Book VII. I have argued in the last chapter how the current of stories in Book III at least (but I think the same is true of each book) tends towards political questions – ethical consideration of Amans's amatory concerns cannot be conducted without recourse to politics. Genius does not theorize this relationship until Books VII and VIII, but it is always implicit; once we realize the connection explicitly in Book VII, then we are invited to reconsider

---

[27] For details of Brunetto Latini's life, see Singleton 1968.
[28] See, for example, Macaulay 1900–1, vol. I, p. xix. For more modern examples of Macaulay's view, see those cited by Yeager 1990, p. 199, n. 81.

and revise our sense of the entire structure of the *Confessio* (the kind of reading always invited by *involucra*), seeing it at every point as a discussion of politics through ethics and economics. Very many of the stories which were offered to Amans 'in loves cause', and which were heard by Amans for what information they had to offer in that 'cause' can, from the perspective of Book VII, be seen as contributing to a political discourse. One need only think of the stories of Mundus and Paulina, the Trojan Horse, Florent, Capaneus, the Trump of Death, Albinus and Rosemund, Nebuchadnezzar, and the Three Questions in Book I, for example, to see narratives with direct political implications. Or, we might add, all the stories related to Troy (and there are very many of them) have obvious political implications for Gower's London, 'Troynovant'.[29] On a first reading there is a comic discrepancy between the tragic power of some of these stories and the elegaic, winning and apparently harmless figure of Amans, who seems a nugatory target for such *exempla*. From the perspective of Book VII, where we understand the political corollary of desire's tyranny in Amans, the gap between the stories and their target begins to close.

And many of the stories, as well as the frame itself, have evident 'economic' implications, too. In keeping with traditions in which he is working, Gower defines 'Iconomique' as that science

> Which techeth thilke honestete
> Thurgh which a king in his degre
> His wif and child schal reule and guie,
> So forth with al the companie
> Which in his houshold schal abyde. (VII.1671–5)

The importance of the *familia* in late medieval English political and social life is gradually becoming more apparent.[30] In Gower's poem, as Porter has pointed out, the praise of marriage in Books VII and VIII is itself part of an 'economic' discourse: in his discussion of economics Giles of Rome's principal concern is with

---

[29] These stories form a leitmotif throughout the whole *Confessio*. They are particularly relevant for Gower, given both the parallelism between Troy and London, and the ways in which ethics and politics are inevitably interwoven when considering the genesis and aftermath of the Trojan War. See *Confessio amantis*, I.1077–209; II.2451–8; III.973–1083; III.1757–856; IV.147–233; IV.731–886; IV.1693–705; IV.1815–900; IV.1900–34; IV 2135–82; V.2961–3201; V.6434–75; V.7195–695; V.7596–602; VI.1391–788; VII.1557–63; Trojan references in VIII.2460–665.

[30] See, for example, the excellent article by Starkey 1981.

marriage.[31] He defines the household, in fact, as the primary unit of society: after specifying the kinds of community possible (household, town, city, realm), he goes on to say that all these communities *praesupponunt communitatem domesticam*.[32] But Gower's interest in economics is evident not only in his explicit promotion of marriage, but also in more subtle ways. He can describe economic disturbance in literal terms: in his own household, he is, he says, so ready to lose his temper that 'ther nys servant in myn hous ... / That ech of hem ne stant in doute' (III.88–90); or in the king's court, the vice of Supplantatioun has his heart set

> upon these grete Offices
> Of dignitees and benefices:
> Thus goth he with his sleyhte aboute
> To hindre and schowve an other oute.   (II.2337–40)

But given the homology between the body politic and the physical body, we can see the way in which 'economic' language is used to describe the most intimate details of the inner life. Thus the *psychomachia* to which I referred in the last chapter is, we might notice now, essentially the representation of a divided household: in the one 'partie' stands 'conseil', 'wit' and 'resoun' all 'in compaignie'; against them stand Hope and Will:

> Witt and resoun conseilen ofte
> That I myn herte scholde softe,
> And that I scholde will remue
> And put him out of retenue,
> Or elles holde him under fote.   (III.1163–7)

As with Book I of the *Anticlaudianus*, the inner workings of the soul are pictured in courtly terms here, as operating along the model of a courtly household.[33] The dialogue between Genius and Amans, seeking as it does to mediate between the opposed parties of will

---

[31]   Giles of Rome 1607, II.11–24, pp .214–86.   [32]   Ibid., II.1.7, p. 238.

[33]   In the economy of the present argument, I cannot elaborate this point here; but just as Alan draws on the lexis of politics to describe relations in the universe, so too does he model relations within the self (i.e. the inter-action between Nature, Reason, Fronesis and Concord in Books I and II) on a courtly pattern. See chapter 9 for a fuller discussion.

and reason, is, metaphorically at least, an 'economic' discussion, contributing to concord within the *familia* of the soul.[34]

The real 'frame' of the *Confessio*, then, is not the confession of Amans, but rather the *divisio philosophiae* of Book VII: the confession of the lover, and his instruction by Genius, are themselves part of an ethical and economic narrative no less than the stories themselves; and that ethical and economic narrative insistently leads towards, and cannot be resolved without recourse to, politics, the practical science which is treated explicitly in Book VII. Unlike the treatises from which he is working, Gower does not neatly subdivide the practical sciences and treat them consecutively: the whole point of his poetic structure is that these sciences cannot be treated separately. And, furthermore, his poetic structure reveals the moments at which the soul resists (and desires) movement between these sciences, in a complex and subtle psychology of learning of which the treatises are quite incapable.

So the *Confessio*, like the *Anticlaudianus*, is informed by a given structure of philosophy. But we observed that the hierarchy of sciences within that division also provides the dynamic of Alan's poem: the fact that the soul remains in a state of disturbance 'after' the political triumph of Book IX implies that until the soul has exercised its deepest power to perceive the truths of the highest science (theology), it can enjoy no rest. The narrative of the poem is energized as long as the soul remains ignorant of the highest science in Alan's hierarchy. Is the same true of Gower? What hierarchy is generating the movement of Gower's poem?

Genius describes the theoretical sciences as

> the conserve
> And kepere of the remnant,
> As that which is most sufficant
> And chief of the Philosophie. (VII.54–7)

But does the structure and movement of the poem really sustain this statement? As we have already observed, the actual account of the theoretical sciences in Book VII is very selective; it focuses only on those aspects of creation and procreation which directly affect

---

[34] There are many other examples in the *Confessio* of moral, psychological and physical relations being described in the terms of the household. See I.1328 (and gloss to I.1343); II.438; II.1895; IV.27; IV.3267; V.2229–37 (partly referring to the king's literal household); V.2859–62; V.4383–8; VII.463–89; VIII.2122–5; VIII.2345–9. See chapter 9, pp. 274–84.

humanity: the creation of the elements; the complexions of man and the human soul; the divisions of the earth; and, among the mathematical sciences (i.e. the Quadrivium), he presents only astronomy. And the account of astronomy is itself angled very directly towards the human body, since it is really an astrological account of the powers of each planet and each constellation. There is no account of God outside his initial act of physical creation, just as there is no account of the structure of the universe for its own sake – it is pointed wholly to man.

The selectivity of Gower's account suggests to me that the theoretical sciences are by no means a 'sufficant' part of philosophy. On the contrary, they offer a double, potentially contradictory, aspect of the human soul which requires a psychology, an ethics and a politics to be resolved. For in his presentation of the theoretical sciences Genius on the one hand describes the body as the natural product of elements combining to produce four complexions, subject to the influence of the heavens. But, on the other hand, he declares the soul to be in opposition to the body. He summarizes his discussion of the body, and leads into the soul in this way:

> And thus nature his pourveance
> Hath made for man to liven hiere;
> Bot god, which hath the Soule diere,
> Hath formed it in other wise.
> That can noman pleinli devise;
> Bot as the clerkes ous enforme,
> That lich to god it hath a forme,
> Thurgh which figure and which liknesse
> The Soule hath many an hyh noblesse
> Appropred to his oghne kinde.
> Bot ofte hir wittes be mad blinde
> Al onliche of this ilke point,
> That hir abydinge is conjoint
> Forth with the bodi forto duelle:
> That on desireth toward helle,
> That other upward to the hevene.   (VII.490–505)

The account of the theoretical sciences itself takes us no further than this passage into how the union of soul and body might be mediated. It is only with the account of the practical science of politics, which focuses the ethical and economic themes of the poem as a whole, that we can understand how a mediation between body and soul might be possible.

But even here, that resolution does not suggest that the reconstituted John Gower of Book VIII turns away from the world (despite the very last few lines of the poem, abbreviated in the second recension). The focus is, rather, on marriage as the basis of the body politic. The all but final leave-taking in Book VIII marks these proportions of interest between the divine and earthly very firmly. The poem returns to the political discourse of the Prologue; Gower begins by invoking God:

> He whiche withinne daies sevene
> This large world forth with the hevene
> Of his eternal providence
> Hath mad, and thilke intelligence
> In mannys soule resonable
> Hath schape to be perdurable,
> Wherof the man of his feture
> Above alle erthli creature
> Aftir the soule is immortal...   (VIII.2971–9)

But the burden of the invocation is not to pray for personal immortality. Instead Gower prays to God

> That he this lond in siker weie
> Wol sette uppon good governance
> For if men takyn remembrance
> What is to live in unite,
> Ther ys no staat in his degree
> That noghte to desire pes,
> With outen which, it is no les,
> To seche and loke in to the laste,
> Ther may no worldes joye laste.   (VIII.2986–94)

This is the final emphasis which brings the whole poem together, rather than any wish for personal salvation or for transcendent vision. Alan's poem is structured from an amalgam of Neo-Platonic cosmology and Stoic ethics and politics; Gower, in my view, like his contemporary Chaucer in, say, the *Parlement of Foules*, has no independent interest in Neo-Platonic cosmology. They are interested in the theoretical sciences only insofar as they have bearing on the practical sciences, and especially politics. The vision of 'constitutional' compromise between body and soul equally provokes a vision of constitutional harmony in the body politic.

Gower's poem, then, is not only modelled on a division of sciences, but its movement is in part determined by a hierarchy within that division: for Gower the 'science' which is really 'the conserve / And kepere of the remnant' is politics. In this I think his primary influence is Brunetto Latini rather than Giles of Rome. For Giles, a professional theologian, theology remains the highest science, despite his evident commitment to a coherent Aristotelian politics, which involves ethics and economics as subsidiary sciences. Early in the *De regimine* he says that of three lives (the voluptuous, the political and the contemplative), a king should live the last two of these, citing theologians to the effect that the speculative, contemplative life is the highest.[35] And of the two *'felicitates'*, the political and the contemplative, he says that a king should place his happiness in both, but with especial emphasis on the contemplative.[36] And again, when he comes to describe the sciences in which children should be taught, he names the Liberal Arts, but says that there are sciences of greater nobility than these, particularly theology, which is 'per inspirationem divinam longe et incomparabiliter nobilior et dignior omnibus aliis'.[37]

This is the kind of hierarchy we should expect from a professional theologian. When we look to a roughly contemporary figure, the Florentine notary Brunetto Latini (1220–94), we can see a more convincing source for Gower's understanding of the hierarchy of the sciences. The certain and direct influence of Brunetto's *Livres dou Tresor* on Book VII of the *Confessio* was first noticed by Macaulay.[38] Many passages are translated from the *Tresor*, including, as I have already mentioned, the actual *divisio philosophiae* used by Gower. But let us look more especially to Brunetto's remarkable defence of politics as a science. The opening of the *Tresor*, as we might expect, divides the sciences; in keeping with the economic metaphor (taking 'economic' in the modern sense) of his title, Brunetto describes the theoretical sciences as money (*deniers*); the second book, which treats of ethics, he describes as precious stones; but the third part, which contains rhetoric and politics, is 'pure gold': 'Car si comme li ors sormonte toutes manieres de metal, autresi est la sience de bien parler et de

---

[35] Giles of Rome 1607, I.I.4, p. 13.   [36] Ibid., I.I.12, pp. 38–9.
[37] Ibid., II.2.8, p. 308.   [38] Macaulay 1900–1, vol. 2, p. 522.

governer gens plus noble de nul art du monde.'[39] Brunetto then
moves to a particular discussion of the three parts of philosophy,
where his division squares almost exactly with Gower's: philosophy is
divided up into the theoretical, the practical and the logical sciences.
He acknowledges that theology is the most noble of the theoretical
sciences, but his place of honour is reserved again for politics; after
defining the first two of the practical sciences, he goes on:

> La tierce est politique; et sans faille c'est la plus haute science et dou plus
> noble mestier ki soit entre les homes, car ele nos ensegne governer ...
> selonc raison et selonc justice.[40]

At critical points throughout the *Tresor*, Brunetto makes clear the
connections between sciences, and the fact that they point to politics
as the highest science. Thus, following Aristotle, he begins and ends
his translation of the *Nichomachean Ethics* (a part of Brunetto's treatment of ethics) with a discussion of the governance of cities, just as he
elides rhetoric and politics as part of the same book. Whenever he
discusses politics, he points to its disciplinary power and superiority.
Take, for example, an introductory chapter in the discussion of ethics:

> Donques li ars ki ensegne la cité governer est principale et soveraine et
> dame de tous ars, pour ce que desous lui sont contenues maintes honor-
> ables art, si come est retorique, et la science de fere ost et de governer sa
> maisnie. Et encore est ele noble, pour ce k'ele met en ordre et adrece
> toutes ars ki sous li sont, et li sien compliment; et sa fin si est fin et com-
> pliment des autres.[41]

Like the powers of the soul, the disciplines themselves are arranged
in a hierarchy, according to which one science is felt to 'contain' all
the others, in a process of what scholastic thinkers called scientific
'subalternation'.[42] The remarkable difference between Brunetto's
account of this hierarchy and subalternation and that of scholastic
theologians is the genuinely Aristotelian superiority Brunetto gives
to politics.[43] From the argument of this chapter, it seems to me

---

[39] Carmody 1948, I.1.4.27–9, p. 17.   [40] Ibid., I.4.5.24–7, p. 21.
[41] Ibid., II.3.1.1–6, p. 176.   [42] For these terms, see Chenu 1969, pp. 71–5, 80–4.
[43] Aristotle's *Nichomachean Ethics* begins with a discussion of the hierarchy of sciences, the
point of which is to ascertain the science to which ethics is directed: ' ... we must try, in
outline at least, to determine what it (the science of ethics) is, and of which of the sciences or capacities it is the object. It would seem to belong to the most authoritative art
and that which is most truly the master art. And politics appears to be of this nature',
I.2, 1094a1–1094b1 (Barnes 1984, p. 1729). See Wieland 1982 for the late medieval reception of Aristotle's *Ethics*, and Dunbabin 1982 for the late medieval reception of Aristotle's
Politics.

clear that Gower follows the secular, Aristotelian scheme of his source, equally transmitted in the vernacular.

The *speculum principis* of Book VII is, therefore, intimately connected with the implicit themes of the *Confessio* as a whole. The *praeceptor amoris* of the *Ars amatoria*, we remember, presents himself as offering a kind of *speculum principis* to Cupid, offering his services as *praeceptor Amoris*. Seen from the perspective of Book VII, we can see that Genius has been able to achieve what the inevitably unsuccessful Ovidian *praeceptor* has not. He has been able, that is, to reactivate the political, that discourse which is constantly evoked only to be neutralized in Ovid's erotic poems. He has been able to transform the *speculum principis* of Cupid into a *speculum* which promotes personal and political solidarities above the egocentric and isolating tyranny of Cupid (tyranny always isolates). He has been able to retrieve from the margins of Ovid's irony the authorial Ovid who is (in my view) aware of the neutralization of politics in his narratives, and who asks us to recognize that (an invitation which Augustus, later, apparently failed to accept). It is no accident, I think, that the main narrative of Book VII, that of Aruns and Lucretia, should be translated so closely from Ovid – neither the Ovid of the *Amores* or the *Ars amatoria*, nor the Ovid of the *Remedia*; the text is *Fasti*, Book II, a text which, like the *Tristia* and *Ex Ponto* (all known to Gower) praises the solidarities of marriage and friendship. With this story Gower nearly completes his total absorption of the entire Ovidian corpus and its complex internal relations.

Gower, then, like Alan in the *Anticlaudianus*, creates a poem whose outer form is incoherent; through understanding the psychological dynamic, or 'information' behind these works, we recognize at the same time that both are working through a hierarchy of sciences. But Gower's psychological range is 'narrower' than Alan's: whereas Alan's poem does not come to rest until the 'highest' faculty of the soul, the intellect, has been informed, Gower's poem moves within the relations between will, imagination and reason. Accordingly, the hierarchy of sciences within which Gower works is correspondingly more limited: in Alan's poem, politics is a subsidiary but pivotal science, understanding of which requires an understanding of the cosmos through the 'highest' science, theology. Gower, on the contrary, seems to me to give priority to politics; the uncertainties of both ethics and the theoretical sciences find their resolution in the highest of the practical sciences, politics. Both poems, nevertheless, are designed to imagine, and to provoke, the 'information' of the philosopher–king. But, as with the *Anticlaudianus*, the real focus of the *Confessio* is not the action represented by the poem (the information of Amans), so much as the reader, who is informed by understanding that represented action. Each reader 'a kingdom hath to justefie' (VIII.2112).

In chapter 9 I want to elucidate the nature of the actual political statement implicit in both these poems: Alan seems to me to be working within an intensely intellectualist, elitist tradition of humanism; the politics of the vernacular *Confessio*, on the other hand, might be described as liberal humanist. Gower, like Alan, has a humanist faith in the power of reason and the human sciences; and, like Alan, his world-view emerges, in humanist fashion, from his sense of the structure of human being. But unlike Alan, Gower gives much more consideration to the demands of the body. Gower's politics are worked out as a 'constitutional' compromise between sensual desire and reason; Alan's absolutist politics tend to marginalize the power and force of the body.

I shall, as I say, elucidate these differences in chapter 9; but before I do that, the opportunity to understand the respective positions of both these poets with regard to poetry itself should not be lost. The next chapter is, accordingly, devoted to the poetics of the intellect and the imagination for Alan and Gower respectively.

CHAPTER 8

Poetics

THE PLACE OF POETRY AMONG THE SCIENCES

The preceding six chapters have illuminated the parallelisms between the *Anticlaudianus* and the *Confessio amantis*: both poems are fables of the soul, in which the impetus of the soul to reach its own perfection, or form, determines the narrative form taken by both poems – in both works the form of the soul determines the form of the narrative. Alan and Gower are writing in humanist traditions of self-information, in which knowledge of the self requires 'scientific' information, by which the soul can place itself in the cosmos and in society; accordingly, both poems work within disciplinary structures, in which politics plays a prominent role. Alan the Neo-Platonist, certainly, is working within a 'broader' spectrum of disciplines, which seeks to realize and harmonize the inter-relations between the practical and the theoretical sciences, whereas Gower is writing within a genuinely Aristotelian hierarchy, with politics being the science to which ethics and economics tend.

What place can there be for the 'science' of poetry in poems that give such high profile to 'scientific' knowledge, and whose very structure is determined, in part, by hierarchies of the sciences? In the relatively rare instances where poetry is given a place within hierarchies of knowledge from the twelfth to the fourteenth centuries, that place tends to be fairly humble.[1] In poems that are so

---

[1] The place of poetry in schemes of the sciences between and including the twelfth and the fourteenth centuries is, of course, a huge topic, the materials for which are only recently coming into definition. The kinds of evidence are various and sometimes overlapping (e.g. *divisiones philosophiae*; personal accounts of education; *accessus* to commentaries; commentaries themselves; ideal schemes of education; polemical or satirical pieces; medieval library catalogues). One is, however, justified in saying that the norm amongst this vari-

sensitive to hierarchies of knowledge, we might therefore expect poetry to fare badly. I want to argue in this chapter that this is far from being the case – on the contrary, both poems make, in their different ways, very high claims for poetic knowledge. And they make these claims in the presence of poetry's most persuasive disciplinary competitors for cognitive power.

In his account of Bernard of Chartres's teaching of poetry, John of Salisbury relates that Bernard showed in what way 'the section of his proposed reading related to other disciplines' ('sui proposite lectionis articulus respiciebat ad alias disciplinas').[2] This comment reveals a fundamental attitude of almost the entire spectrum of twelfth-century theoretical statements about secular poetry – i.e. that poetry 'looks to' other disciplines, and, implicitly, serves them in an ancillary function. The ubiquity of this conception of poetry (as providing a service for other, superior disciplines) makes it difficult to find coherent, powerful theoretical defences of poetry's philosophical strength in the twelfth century. Defences of poetry as a primary training ground for stylistic practice, or as a source of

ety is a fairly humble place for poetry. In twelfth-century *divisiones scientiae*, for example, we can see poetry either placed in a lowly position (e.g. Hugh of St Victor, in Buttimer 1939, II.29 (p. 45), and III.1 (p. 48), where poetry is included as part of grammar); or placed outside the scheme of wisdom altogether (thus, for example, the schemes presented by the *Ysagoge in theologiam* (Landgraf 1934, p. 72); the *Ordo artium* (Gompf 1966); the commentaries on Martianus Capella and the *Aeneid* attributed to Bernard Silvestris (respectively Westra 1986, VI.1–51, pp. 130–1; and Jones and Jones 1977, VI, p. 32); and Ralph of Longchamps (Sulowski 1972, 28, p. 39). In each of these cases poetry is presented as an instructor in morals.

With the introduction of the Aristotelian corpus, poetry is included in schemes of the sciences as the last part of logic, after rhetoric (under the impression that Aristotle's *Rhetoric* and *Poetics* were the seventh and eighth parts of the *Organon*). These texts give poetry the place of lowest cognitive power among the logical sciences, and, like twelfth-century accounts of poetry's function, tend to see poetry as the locus of ethical instruction. This might confirm poetry's relatively lowly scientific status, and scholastic theologians, indeed, often qualify their account of the Bible's use of a poetic mode by distinguishing biblical poetry from the low cognitive status of human poetry (for examples of this, see Simpson 1989, nn. 17–27). It should be mentioned, however, that some thirteenth-century scholars, influenced by an Aristotelian concept of politics as the highest science, see the importance of poetry precisely for its power to move its recipients to moral action. For a conspectus of views in this Aristotelian tradition, see Dahan 1980, and for a concise summary of the reception of these texts in the West, see Minnis and Scott 1988, pp. 277–88. For praise of poetry in this tradition, see the *quaestio* translated by Minnis and Scott 1988, pp. 307–13, and, especially the vigorous defence of poetry's place in moral philosophy by Roger Bacon in Massa 1953, V.2–33, pp. 250–5 and Massa 1955.

For general treatments of the place of poetry in schemes of knowledge see also Hardison 1974, pp. 3–38, and McKeon 1946.   [2]   Webb 1929, I.24, 854d, p. 55.

moral instruction, are not difficult to find[3] (though even these defences are not without their detractors[4]), but neither of these defences suggest that poetry's field of influence should range beyond the pedagogic nursery.

The view of poetry's subsidiary relation to other disciplines, and the implications of that view, are succinctly expressed by Hugh of St Victor in his *Didascalicon* (written in the late 1120s). Hugh distinguishes between what he calls the arts (academic disciplines proper, which have 'a certain and determinate philosophical subject matter'), and appendages to the arts, those kinds of writing which (again using the metaphor of 'looking across') 'merely look to philosophy' (*tantum ad philosophiam spectant*). In this broadly defined 'genre' he includes 'all the songs of the poets' (by which Hugh seems to mean all classical poetry),

as well as the writings of those fellows whom we are now accustomed to call philosophers, who tend to extend a short matter with long verbal circumlocutions, and to obscure a simple sense with intricate discourses; likewise lumping diverse things together, from many colours and forms, as it were, they make a single picture.

illorum etiam scripta quos nunc philosophos appellare solemus, qui et brevem materiam longis verborum ambagibus extendere consueverunt, et facilem sensum perplexis sermonibus obscurare. vel etiam diversa simul compilantes, quasi de multis coloribus et formis, unam picturam facere.[5]

The arts, according to Hugh, are autonomous and systematic. 'Literature', on the contrary, is not only wholly dependent on the philosophical solidity of the arts, but also unsystematic in its presentation of philosophical matter. Hugh accordingly advises his

---

3   See Delhaye 1958 and Allen 1982 for the ubiquitous concept of poetry serving ethics. Often the benefits of poetry for stylistic and ethical models are stressed together. Thus, for example (?)Bernard Silvestris, to choose from any number of examples; he is discussing the value of reading the *Aeneid* as poetry: 'Itaque est lectoris gemina utilitas: una scribendi peritia que habetur ex imitatione, altera vero recte agendi prudentia que capitur exemplorum exhortatione' (Jones and Jones 1977, Prologue, p. 2, lines 19–21).

4   Criticism of the place of classical poetry in the curriculum was given its most forceful expression by Augustine (see Marrou 1938, p. 407), and finds occasional voice throughout the medieval period; in the twelfth century, the detractors are sometimes unsurprising, insofar as they object to the reading of all pagan writing (e.g. Gauthier of St Victor (Glorieux 1952, pp. 273–4)); but criticism can also come from the most unexpected quarters: Abelard, defending integumental readings of pagan philosophers in his *Theologia christiana*, pauses to provide a vigorous attack on the reading of pagan poets in the teaching of grammar. The passage reads like a catalogue of authorities against poetry (Buytaert 1969, II.122–29, pp. 187–93).

5   Buttimer 1939, III.4, p. 54. The translation is indebted to Taylor 1961, p. 88.

readers to ignore poetry except for pleasure, since no serious philosophical wisdom will be found there.[6]

Hugh dismisses the formal shaping of poetry as a source of
poetry's philosophical wisdom. He certainly registers the formal
complexity of the works he is considering, and the wholeness of the
finished artefact – he says that artist-philosophers seek to construct
a 'single picture'.[7] But this aesthetic wholeness does nothing, in
Hugh's view, to strengthen the philosophical fragility of literature –
its unsystematic, confused quality, and its philosophically dependent status. On the contrary: according to Hugh, the verbal shaping of a whole picture serves simply to obscure what limited philosophical value the work may have had in the first place.

But if both classical poetry and (if we are to feel the full force of
Hugh's '*nunc*') contemporary poetry are to be dismissed from the
pedagogic programme of the canons of St Victor, it is clear that in
some contemporary educational institutions, and in particular in
cathedral schools, the 'picture' of poetry was awarded a higher
philosophical status. Rather than simply 'looking across' to other
disciplines, John of Salisbury suggests how literary works might
themselves be worthy of being *looked at* for their own image, or picture of philosophy. I began by referring to John's description of
Bernard of Chartres's teaching method as one whereby Bernard
would specify what parts of philosophy a given work 'looks to'; this
is, as I said, the characteristic view of poetry's philosophical status
in the twelfth century – i.e. as philosophically dependent. But in
the same passage, we can see that John's own sense of how literary
works 'contain' philosophy is more complex. In what could have
served as an apt description of Alan's *Anticlaudianus* before its composition, John describes how the combination of a poet's knowledge and rhetorical skill, along with the matter of a story, all
combine to produce an 'image':

---

6 Buttimer 1939, III.4, pp. 54–5.
7 The phrase 'artist-philosophers' here implies an interpretation of Hugh's reference to the
   writers 'quos nunc philosophos appellare solemus'. It is of course uncertain as to whether
   or not Hugh is referring here to contemporary writers, but it seems plausible to me:
   Hugh is certainly referring to philosophical writing which draws on poetic procedures
   (the remark is made in the context of a discussion of unequivocally 'literary' texts). The
   nunc makes the argument for a contemporary reference stronger (though not of course
   watertight); and, as Wetherbee has pointed out, Hugh's critique of integumental thinking
   (if that is what this passage amounts to) would be correlative with his critique of
   'Chartrian' cosmology (Wetherbee 1972, pp. 49–66).

For when the *auctores*, by way of *diacrisis* (which we may call *illustratio* or *picturatio*) took up the unformed matter either of a history or a verisimilar story, or of a fable, or any other narrative whatever, they refined it with such plenitude of learning, and with such grace of composition and taste, that the completed work seemed to be in some way an image of all the arts.

Illi [the *auctores*] enim per diacrisim, quam nos illustrationem siue picturationem possumus appellare, cum rudem materiam historie aut argumenti aut fabule aliamve quamlibet suscepissent, eam tanta disciplinarum copia et tanta compositionis et condimenti gratia excolebant, ut opus consummatum omnium artium quodammodo uideretur imago.[8]

This passage uses cosmological, Timaean language to describe poetic making: the 'rude material' of the narrative is shaped and adorned by the poet's knowledge and rhetorical skill, to produce an image, or picture (the continuation of this passage elaborates the visual metaphors) of all the arts. And this Timaean language – a language of formation, embellishment and wholeness – implies that the meaning of a work of literature is to be located in its wholeness; like the universe created, shaped and embellished by God, the *opus consummatum* of the poet finds its meaning through the inter-relation of its different parts. Philosophy is not felt, in this account, to be scattered *sparsim et confuse* in the poetic work, as it is in Hugh's dismissal of the 'picture' of poetry. Neither is the pictorial idea seen to be merely a superficial formal pattern, imposed upon, and distorting, the underlying philosophical content of a poem. Instead the philosophical content is, implicitly, very closely aligned with the *picturatio* or *imago* of the finished work. The poem's formal information and its philosophical information (in the modern sense) are correlative.

Scholars looking for a sophisticated twelfth-century poetic theory have focused on the words *integumentum* and *involucrum*, as concepts which allow for the formal qualities of a narrative to bear philosophic meaning in themselves.[9] In this chapter I want to contribute to the effort of these studies by delineating the poetic implicit (and occasionally explicit) within our two texts, rather than adducing

---

[8]   Webb 1929, I.24, 854b, p. 54.
[9]   The main studies here are Jeauneau 1957; Stock 1972, pp. 49–54; Wetherbee 1972, pp. 36–48; Dronke 1974a, pp. 13–32; (more superficially) Brinkmann 1971; and Westra 1986, pp. 23–33.

poetic theory in abstract form. I will look initially to the poetic theory implicit and explicit in the *Anticlaudianus*, and in particular focus on the visual metaphors of poetic making used by both Hugh of St Victor and John of Salisbury (e.g. *pictura, imago*), since these terms, as we shall see, are near the heart of Alan's poetic. The conclusion of this discussion will corroborate the undercurrent of my argument in chapters 3 and 4 – i.e. that the meaning of Alan's poem is inextricably bound up with its formal shaping, and that this formal, poetic shaping provides philosophical meanings of a primary kind, unavailable to the academic tract, with its discursive stabilities. In the second half of the chapter I turn to the poetics of the *Confessio amantis*, where we also find a powerful implicit defence of poetry's high place in the hierarchy of the sciences. And, like Alan, Gower centres this defence in the role of images; indeed, given Gower's Aristotelian habits of mind, his defence of images and the imagination is much more emphatic than that of the Neo-Platonist Alan. Alan's is a poetic of the intellect, in which images give way to ideas; the poetic of Gower, on the other hand, is centred in the imagination, in which ideas can never be wholly extracted from the images which produce them.

UT PICTURA POESIS

The 'argument' of the *Timaeus* is built around, and is itself designed to provoke, analogies between different discourses. The fundamental analogy is that between the structure of the universe as macrocosm and that of man as microcosm. From this basic comparison, at once structural and ontological, analogies between many other discourses become possible. The set of comparisons which most concerns us now is that between divine, natural and human making. In his commentary on the *Timaeus*, Calcidius remarks that there are three kinds of 'work' (*opus*) – of God, of Nature and of the human artificer. Calcidius himself does not discuss human making in his development of this point,[10] but his twelfth-century readers certainly did. Although they do not discuss *poets* as makers, twelfth-century thinkers associated with Chartres do bring the analogy between divine and human making into very sharp focus. In his gloss (written 1144–9) on the *Timaeus*, for example, William of

---

[10] Waszink 1962, ch. 23, lines 10–12, p. 73.

Conches defines God's wisdom as the formal cause of the world, since God formed the world according to the pattern of his wisdom. William immediately goes on to make a comparison with a human maker:

As, indeed, an artisan, if he wishes to make something, first disposes it in his mind; afterwards, having sought the material, he works according to his mental pattern. So too the creator, before he should create anything, first had it in his mind, and then fulfilled it in act. It is this which is called by Plato the world archetype: 'world' because it contains everything which is in the world; 'archetype' because it is the principle form (or model).

Ut enim faber, volens aliquid fabricare, prius illud in mente disponit, postea, quesita materia, iuxta mentem suam operatur, sic Creator, antequam aliquid crearet, in mente illud habuit, deinde opere illud adimplevit. Hec eadem a Platone dicitur archetipus mundus: mundus quia omnia continet que in mundo sunt, archetipus id est principalis forma.[11]

We also find this comparison between different makers in both the literary and discursive works of Alan of Lille.[12] Unlike his 'Chartrian' forebears, however, Alan consistently uses words associated with painting (and other visual arts) to describe the act by which the inner, mental, form produces a material product.[13] Take, for example, the way in which Alan addresses God in his prayer for inspiration in Book V of the *Anticlaudianus*. After describing God as 'enclosing all things by numbers', Alan goes on to win God's favour by describing to God God's own formation of the world:

Qui rerum species et mundi sensilis umbram
Ducis ab exemplo mundi mentalis, eumdem
Exterius pingens terrestris ymagine forme.   (v.288–90)

---

[11] Jeauneau 1965, 27d, ch. 32, p. 99.
[12] See, for example, *Expositio Prosae de angelis*, in d'Alverny 1965, pp. 194–217 (at pp. 199–200); the comparison between Nature and God as makers is essential to both the *De planctu Naturae* and the *Anticlaudianus*. See also Jean de Meun, *Roman de la Rose*, lines 16005–148 (though here the comparison is between Nature and the human artificer; God is omitted. It is significant that immediately after this account of how human makers imitate Nature, Jean himself seems to deny that by refusing to describe her (lines 16165–248)). Dante also makes the comparison (central to his art as a whole), *Inferno* XI.97–105. See also Chaucer, *Physician's Tale*, lines 9–28.
[13] Two earlier studies have noted the frequency with which Alan uses the lexis of painting: Huizinga 1932, pp. 59–65; and de Bruyne 1946, vol. 2, 296–8. De Bruyne goes no further than to remark on the lexis of painting; Huizinga's excellent study is, like mine, concerned with the philosophical sense of *pictura* in Alan's works; my study is more comprehensive and differently directed.

who bring the species of things and the shadow of the sensible world from the exemplar of the conceptual world, painting it on the exterior in the image of an earthly form. (p. 147, modified)

Or again, a few lines later, God is described as the formal cause of the world, *dum pingis eam* (V.295). And if God creates the world by painting his inner idea with the image of external form, so too does he create the soul of man by a kind of painting. Fronesis explains her mission to ask for a newly created soul by saying that only God, not Nature, is capable of creating a soul:

> In superis nil iuris habens animamque creare
> Nescia, quam sola pictoris dextra superni
> Format. (V.217–19)

Having no rights in the heavenly realm, and ignorant of how to create a soul, which only the right hand of the heavenly painter forms. (p. 144, modified).

Like the 'divine painter', Nature, too, operates by painting her works. In Book I she declares the inability of her art to produce a soul; she defines her art as especially one of painting:

> Ergo cum nostra genituram regula talem
> Nesciat et tantam stupeat pictura figuram
> Occasumque manus talem patiatur ad ortum... (I.388–90)[14]

Since, then, our rule knows no such birth, and our power to paint is staggered at so great a model, and our hand suffers failure at the very beginning of such a work... (pp. 60–1, modified)

In the *De planctu* the concept of Nature as painter is given greater force. After the description of the pictures on Nature's dress, we see Nature herself in the act of painting:

In latericiis uero tabulis arundinei stili ministerio uirgo uarias rerum picturaliter suscitabat imagines. Pictura tamen, subiacenti materie familiariter non coherens, uelociter euanescendo moriens, nulla imaginum post se relinquebat uestigia. (IV.3–6, p. 821)

With the aid of a reed-pen, the maiden called up various images of things by drawing on clay tablets. The picture, however, did not cling closely to the underlying material but, quickly fading and dying, left no trace of the images behind. (p. 108, modified)

---

[14] I emend Bossuat's reading *nostram* to *nostra* in I.388.

The works of God and Nature, then, are seen as related by Alan, and both are described as acts of painting. What about the works of humans? Speech itself is represented by Alan as the act of painting an inner idea: when Fronesis speaks, she is said to 'paint her mind' (*mentem ... pingit*, 1.324), or to 'paint her thoughts in speech' (*tali pingit concepta loquela*, V.177).[15] But whereas the earlier reception of the *Timaeus* had not focused specifically on the art of poetry as an example of human making, Alan does. And, as with God and Nature, the human act of making poetry is presented as painterly. Comparison between poetry and painting is very frequent in both Alan's literary works, but especially so in the *Anticlaudianus*.

We might approach this set of examples of human making, and in particular of poetic making, by looking to the description of Rhetoric, in Book III. Rhetoric is said to be especially beautiful through her knowledge of painting:

> Cui magis arridet species et gracia forme,
> Quod comites multa pictoris preuenit arte,
> Totam pictoris artem sub pectore claudens. (III.148–50)

On whom beauty and grace of form smile, since she outstrips her peers in many of the painter's skills and enfolds in her bosom the complete art of the painter. (pp. 96–7).

And the emphasis of her skill as a painter is put, as we might expect, on the brilliance of her surface colour, a brilliance described by Alan in a passage which is itself exuberantly colourful rhetorically. Rhetoric's dress,

> picturata colore
> Multiplici, gaudet uarios inducta colores.
> Hic pictoris ope splendet pictura coloris
> Retorici, sic picturam pictura colorat. (III.166–9)

painted in a variety of tints, rejoices that it is overlaid with various colours. Here with the painter's aid gleams a picture of Rhetoric's colour, and thus a picture adds colour to a picture. (p. 98, modified)

---

[15] Nature's act of speaking in the *De planctu* is, we might notice, produced on a Timaean model: 'Que ... mentales intellectus materialis uocis michi depinxit imagine, et quasi archetipa uerba idealiter preconcepta uocaliter produxit in actum' (VI.11–13, Häring 1978, p. 825). See also *Anticlaudianus*, III.340–58 for a description of the way in which a human idea is carried across into material form.

Here Alan's witty point is really that there are *three*, not two pictures: for just as the picture embroidered on Rhetoric's dress is a colourful picture of the pictures of rhetoric, so too, obviously enough, is Alan's own rhetoric a further (highly coloured) picture of the first two.

This description of rhetoric as a painter raises the most obvious level at which the tradition of *pictura ut poesis* might apply to Alan's own concept of poetry: just as the painter uses colours, so too does the poet adorn his work with the colours of rhetoric. But in the context of all the other uses of the word *pictor* or *pingere* we have observed, we can see that the connection between the colour of poetry and painting is, for Alan, only the most superficial of connections between the two arts.[16] If the connection stays at the level of rhetorical schemes alone, of verbal embellishment, or 'colours', then it remains, literally, superficial. For in all the other examples we have observed, the idea of painting is adduced to evoke not the idea of colour, but rather that of form, and especially the way in which the outer form of the painting is modelled on the form, or idea, within the mind of the painter. Three of the words most often associated with the lexis of painting in Alan's works are *forma, figura* and *imago*. Alan is using each of these words in a philosophical sense, where each can designate both the outer shape of an artefact, or, in the case of *forma* and *figura*, the inner, mental form upon which the artefact is modelled.

The notion of painting is for Alan an active one, designating the action of drawing an inner exemplar out into material shape: God, we remember, 'draws' the material world 'from the exemplar of

---

[16] As the argument of this chapter evokes Horace, it should be mentioned here that the topos *ut pictura poesis* of *De arte poetica* (line 361) was not understood by late twelfth-century writers of poetic treatises to be restricted to the superficial level of verbal colouring by rhetorical schemes. See Geoffrey of Vinsauf, *Documentum de arte versificandi*:

Superficies enim verborum ornata, nisi sana et commendabili nobilitetur sententia, similis est picturae vili quae placet longius stanti, sed displicet propius intuenti. Sic et ornatus verborum sine ornatu sententiarum audienti placet, diligenti intuenti displicet. Superficies autem verborum ornata cum ornatu sententiae similis est egregiae picturae, quae quidem, quando propius inspicitur, tanto commendabilior invenitur. Unde dicit Horatius: 'Ut pictura poesis.' (Faral 1924, III.2, pp. 284–5)

See also Geoffrey's *Poetria Nova*, lines 737–55, in Faral 1924, p. 220. These texts are clearly drawing not only the connection of painting and poetry from Horace, but also elaborating the close-up/long-distance comparison made by Horace in the *De arte poetica* (lines 361–5). Horace does not, however, himself dispraise the poem which pleases only from a distance; for the Horatian idea, see Trimpi 1978.

the world in the divine mind, painting it on the exterior with the image of an earthly form' (V.289–90). The act of painting is formative rather than merely colourative: it resides in the action of maintaining an inner form through the process of shaping a material image. And if the making of a poem involves formative 'painting' of this kind, then this has, by the same token, implications for the way in which we read a 'painted' poem: reading a painting, in Alan's view, involves appreciating not merely its colourful surface, but also penetrating its inner sense, or form.

I want to elaborate this philosophical conception of poetry as painting in a moment, because we can see in it a powerful defence of poetry as a form of knowledge. By way of ending this set of examples about poetic makers as painters, however, let me adduce a few of the many points in the *Anticlaudianus* at which Alan makes a connection between poetry and painting. Classical rhetorical treatises recommended the practice of bringing action before the eyes of listeners, using technical terms like *demonstratio, enargeia, illustratio* and *evidentia* to describe the techniques by which an orator might do this. What they generally mean is simply to speak in such a way as to make the audience believe that they are present at the scene being described, by bringing the events 'before the eyes' of an audience.[17] The treatises do not mention a more specific case of *illustratio*, that of describing an actual artefact in poetry, or what we would call *ecphrasis*. Like many other late medieval poets (and, of course, like classical poets), Alan includes description of such visual artefacts in the *Anticlaudianus*.[18] When we look to these descriptions we can see how, even at a first glance, they provide models of visual art by which we might understand the making of poetry.

[17] See *Rhetorica ad Herennium*: 'Demonstratio est cum ita verbis res exprimitur ut geri negotium et res ante oculos esse videatur' (Caplan 1954, IV.55.68, p. 404); Quintillian, *Institutio oratoria*: 'Insequitur enargeia, quae a Cicerone illustratio et evidentia nominatur, quae non tam dicere videtur quam ostendere; et adfectus non aliter, quam si rebus ipsis intersimus, sequentur' (Butler 1920, VI.2.32, vol. 2, pp. 434–6) (though the term *illustratio* does not appear in Latin before Quintillian).

[18] Take, for example, Chrétien de Troyes, *Erec et Enide*, lines 6651–728 (descriptions of faldstools and the embroidered cloak); Dante, *Purgatorio*, X.28–102; XII.16–69 (bas-reliefs of humility and pride respectively); Guillaume de Lorris, *Roman de la Rose*, lines 139–462 (paintings on the outer side of the walls enclosing the garden of Love); Chaucer, *Knight's Tale*, lines 1914–2088 (descriptions of the temples of Venus, Mars and Diana respectively, which contain both paintings and sculptures); *House of Fame*, lines 140–475 should be mentioned here, where writing and painting are deliberately confused in the abbreviation (and distortion) of Virgil's *Aeneid*; *Parlement of Foules*, lines 284–94 (lovers painted on the walls of Venus's temple).

In Nature's palace, we find two murals, one depicting ideal natural models, the other images of natural deformity. A brief look at the words used to describe these and other pictures in the poem reveals how the lexes of writing and painting are inextricably intertwined: *picture gracia scribit* (I.119); Virgil is depicted 'colouring' (I.142); Walter of Châtillon is said to fail as he tries to 'paint' (I.169) (both these last being paintings of poets 'painting'); what Nature gives is shown by the fable of the painting, 'inscriptum calamis picture fabula monstrat' (I.186). Or on the dresses of the Arts are embroidered further pictures; these images are described as *scriptura* (II.509); reading them is like reading a book ('velud in libro legitur'); in another, although the picture is silent, it 'speaks through writing' ('pictura loquens scripto', III.299); 'the letter' of a further picture proclaims the original masters of Geometry: 'Illic artifices pictoris littera clamat' (III.522); and, finally, one 'reads' the images on the dress of the *puella poli* ('Hic legitur…', V.147).

FORMA, IMAGO

For Alan, then, the arts of writing and painting are equivalents. And, as we have already seen, the comparison between poetry and painting does not reside essentially in the surface colouring processes common to each. The principal connection is, rather, formal – it is to do with the way in which a visual image carries a mental form across into matter. When we read a painting, we are implicitly being asked to read back into this process of translation – looking at visual images involves a dynamic relationship between three elements: the image itself, the mind of the viewer, and the mind of the maker implied in the image. The image pleases the senses, but once we apprehend it mentally, it activates a sense of its maker's presence in our mind. We can see this dynamic relationship between image, mind and maker in the description of the images embroidered on Grammar's dress:

> Hec artis series seriatim picta propinat
> Delicias oculis et menti fercula donat,
> Nam pictor predoctus eam descripserat, immo
> Plus pictore potens, picturaque clamitat illum.   (II.472–5)

This painted series of pictures serially sets pleasures before the eyes and offers feasts to the mind; for an extremely learned painter had painted it, or rather one more powerful than any painter, and the painting declares him. (p. 89, modified)

The image appeals both to the senses and to the mind of its recipient; and this experience itself produces a sharp sense of the *pictor predoctus* behind the image.

Pictor predoctus: this could easily be a covert reference to Alan himself, a *predoctus* philosopher in the vanguard of various disciplines in the late twelfth century, including the newly defined discipline of theology.[19] But once we recall Alan's kind of theology, we might initially be surprised to find him praising the power of images. For one of the key texts behind Alan's theology is, as I argued in chapter 2, the *De trinitate* of Boethius. And in Book II of that work Boethius defines the methods of the speculative disciplines, physics, mathematics and theology. For Boethius (and for Alan) theology is not that wide-ranging discipline it was to become in the thirteenth century, but rather an intensely philosophical study of pure form. In it, says Boethius, we should proceed 'intellectually', by which he means *without* recourse to images. Alan cites the relevant text many times in his works of speculative theology:

in Theology we shall be bound to use intellectual concepts, and we should not be diverted to play with imaginations, but rather apprehend that form which is pure form and no image.

in divinis intellectualiter versari oportebit neque diduci ad imaginationes, sed potius ipsam inspicere formam quae vere forma neque imago est.[20]

The key distinction here is between 'form' and 'image', where 'form' designates the pure idea, and 'image' its realization in matter. But given that the material product takes its outer form from the pure form, this distinction opens the way for a certain fuzziness in the use of the word 'form'. Boethius recognizes this at the end of Book II, and is very firm about the proper distinctions between 'form' and 'image'. He says that the forms which are in matter and produce bodies derive from those forms which are outside matter;

---

[19] For the emergence of theology as an academic discipline in the twelfth century, see chapter 2, n. 38.

[20] Stewart, Rand and Tester 1973, II.17–20, p. 8. For references in Alan's works of speculative theology to this text, see, for example, *Liber in distinctionibus dictionum theologicalium*, PL 210, cols. 685–1012 (col. 796); and Glorieux 1953, II.144, p. 282.

so, he says, we should not use the word 'form' for material bodies at all:

> We misname the entities that reside in bodies when we call them forms, since they are mere images; for they only resemble those forms which are not incorporate in matter.

> Nam ceteras quae in corporibus sunt abutimur formas uocantes, dum imagines sint. Adsimulantur enim formis his quae non sunt in materia constitutae.[21]

Boethius's rejection of images might seem like an unpromising basis for the theological poet Alan to praise the art of painting above all, and for a defence of poetry via its connections with the visual arts. But unlike Boethius in the *De trinitate*, Alan is passionately concerned with the ways in which the mind can pass from material images back into the pure forms which produced them. And the single path of this passage back into pure form is that of metaphor. In his work of speculative theology known as the *Quoniam homines*, we remember, he says that words have no literal purchase on the nature of God, who is pure form; only, he says, can metaphor hope to designate the immateriality of pure form:

> With regard to God literal designation has no place, because God is 'godness' itself ... only metaphorical, not literal reference has any purchase in divine matters.

> In Deo vero non habet locum denominatio quia Deus est ipsa deitas ... Transnominatio locum habet in divinis, sed non denominatio.[22]

Alan's Neo-Platonic defence of metaphor here is essential for his literary works: it is precisely this notion of metaphor which justifies the role of poetry in treating the pure ideas of God; by the same token, it is the notion of metaphor which equally justifies Alan's readers in looking back into his literary works for Alan's own 'pure idea' as a literary artist. But in the context of our discussion of pictures, we can now define Alan's concept of the pictorial image as essentially 'metaphor', a translation from pure form into image. And turning back to earlier examples of making, we can see how the idea of metaphor, or 'carrying across', is implicit in the description of painting; we can also read the words 'image' and 'form' with a sharper idea of

---

[21] Stewart, Rand and Tester 1973, II.53–6, p. 12.   [22] Glorieux 1953, Ii.9b, p. 143.

their philosophical sense. God is addressed as a maker of the world:

> Ducis ab exemplo mundi mentalis, eumdem
> Exterius pingens terrestris ymagine forme.					(V.289–90)[23]

Alan plays with the double sense of 'form' here, though reserving the word 'image' for its role as defined by Boethius. But the especial point we might now notice here is the verb *ducis*: the art of painting involves a leading, or carrying across; it is essentially metaphorical.

Painting, then, is code in Alan's usage for metaphor. The image of painting is not static, but has the movement implied in the spatial metaphor behind the word 'metaphor' itself. And the space in which the image as metaphor works is between the reader, the image itself and the mind of its creator. As for fifteenth-century Italian Neo-Platonists, so too for Alan it is the function of metaphor which justifies (even necessitates) the lies of poetic or visual fiction.[24] We can see the root of this in the way in which God himself is said to think metaphorically. About the picture embroidered on the dress of the *puella poli* in Book V, we read this:

> Hic archana Dei, divine mentis abyssum
> Subtilis describit acus formaque figurat
> Informem, locat immensum monstratque latentem.
> Incirconscriptum describit, visibus offert
> Invisum, quod lingua nequit pictura fatetur.					(V.114–18)

Here a fine needle has traced the secrets of God and the depths of the divine mind; a form informs the formless, localizes the boundless and reveals the hidden; it describes the uncircumscribed, and brings the invisible into view. What the tongue cannot tell the picture does. (p. 141, modified)

This set of paradoxes suggests how, through metaphor (or *pictura*), painting can do more than words. This is a representation of an artefact, but its procedures are themselves modelled on God's own

---

[23]	This formulation is, of course, indebted to Boethius, *De consolatione Philosophiae*, III, metre 9, 6–8, where Boethius, however, does not use the word *pingens*: 'tu cuncta superno / Ducis ab exemplo, pulchrum pulcherrimus ipse / Mundum mente gerens similique in imagine formans' (Stewart, Rand and Tester 1973, p. 272).

[24]	For the later Neo-Platonic defence of poetry, see, for example, Pico della Mirandola, *De hominis dignitate* (Garin 1942, p. 162), and Gombrich 1972.

way of thinking; for, a few lines further on, we see how the picture reveals that God contains the names of all things, and

> Cuncta tamen, mediante tropo, dictante figura
> Concipit et uoces puras sine rebus adoptat.   (v.126–7)

However he conceives everything by means of a trope and by way of a figure, and assumes the unadulterated name without the object. (p. 141)

God himself, then, thinks poetically, by unravelling literal names into their pure form by means of metaphor.[25]

And if the pictures of theological discourse work in this way, we can also see how, on this model, human artefacts might also be pictured as a kind of miracle, bringing a sharper sense of reality to their recipients through a fictive, metaphorical play. The murals in Nature's palace are described in ways which might apply to the human making of Alan's own poetry:

> Hic hominum mores picture gracia scribit:
> Sic operi proprio pictura fideliter heret,
> Ut res picta minus a uero deuiet esse.
> O noua picture miracula! Transit ad esse
> Quod nichil esse potest picturaque simia ueri,
> Arte noua ludens, in res umbracula rerum
> Vertit et in uerum mendacia singula mutat.   (I.119–25)[26]

Here the beauty of the picture inscribes the characters of men. The painting faithfully fastens its attention on its special project, so that the representation may the less depart from reality. Oh new wonders of painting! What can have no real existence comes into being, and painting, aping reality and diverting itself with a new art, turns the shadows of things into things and changes every lie into truth. (p. 49, modified)

In keeping with his Boethian background, Alan recognizes the falsity of images here: the picture produces something which could not really exist; it is the 'ape of reality'; its materials are mere 'shadows' and 'lies'. But this very description of the lies of poetry suggests its truth value: despite the accent on the surface falsity of the fictive picture's image, it is said to act 'faithfully'; not to deviate from the truth; to turn lies into reality. These paradoxes of lies

---

[25] This passage has been discussed by Dronke 1986, p. 12.

[26] The idea of words being renewed in theological discourse is central to Alan's theology. See, for example, *Quoniam homines*: 'Cum enim termini a naturalibus ad theologica transferuntur, novas significationes admirantur et antiquas exposcere videntur' (Glorieux 1953, Prologue, p. 119).

being truthful are possible through the playful, even miraculous, *movement* of the picture, where the verbs *transit, vertit* and *mutat* all designate the movement of metaphor between the pure idea in the mind of the artist and the image itself.

This is a remarkable defence of poetic fiction, which declares at once the truth of lying fiction and the playful originality of such a poetry (*arte nova ludens*). Alan describes his poem as itself new: 'Scribendi nouitate uetus iuuenescere carta / Gaudet' (Prol., lines 4–5), just as he often refers to the newness of paintings: 'O noua picture miracula' (I.122); 'Illic arte noua pictor nouus' (III.33). The simplest sense in which painting renews is through recollection, or *re*presentation: thus the embroidery on the dress of Fides is said to renovate the models of faith: 'Hic renouat ueteres uiuens pictura magistros' (VI.35). But there is a more profound sense in which the recuperation of ideal form renovates. Thus words themselves are painted as wanting to return to their old senses in the empyrean, where they are renewed through metaphor: the embroidery on the dress of the *puella poli* shows

> Quomodo Nature subiectus sermo stupescit,
> Dum temptat diuina loqui, uiresque loquendi
> Perdit et ad ueterem cupit ille recurrere sensum.　　(V.119–21)

How language, subject as it is to Nature, is dumbfounded when it tries to express things divine, loses its power of communicating and tries to take refuge in its old meaning. (p. 141, modified)

Humans and things are renewed through contact with the divine form on which they are modelled. (It is in this sense, too, that we should understand the formation of the 'New Man' in the poem, just as we should understand the newness of Alan's own poem by perceiving its inner form, or idea.) Like God who thinks through the trope of metaphor, so too does the human maker. But the truth and newness of these images only appears if we mentally enter into the movement implied by metaphor, the movement between the image on the one hand and the idea of the picture's maker on the other.

And, before we leave this defence of fiction, we should observe how Alan distinguishes poetry from, and prizes it above, other forms of deceptive discourse. Immediately following the passage cited immediately above, Alan goes on to praise the powers of poetry above those of sophistic logic:

Sic logice uires artis subtiliter huius
Argumenta premunt logiceque sophismata uincunt:
Hec probat, ista facit; hec disputat, impetrat illa
Omne quod esse potest: sic utraque uera uideri
Falsa cupit, sed ad hoc pictura fidelius instat.   (1.126–30)

Thus this art's power subtly checks logic's arguments and triumphs over the sophisms of logic. Logic gives proof, painting enacts; logic argues, painting brings to pass everything that can exist. Thus, both wish the false to appear true, but painting pursues this end more faithfully. (p. 49, modified)

Poetry and sophistic logic are comparable because both deal in lies, and both seek to pass lies off as truth. But, the argument of the passage implies, the picture lies (paradoxically) 'more faithfully' because it *enacts*, by 'doing' and 'accomplishing' (*facit, impetrat*), while sophistic logic remains in the realm of words alone. Painting, and therefore poetry, do more than merely designate the truth through their 'lies' – they somehow enact that truth. It is only with this defence of fiction in mind that we can see how what might seem a dismissive description of Virgil, among the portraits painted on the walls of Nature's palace, is in fact high praise:

Virgilii musa mendacia multa colorat
Et facie veri contexit pallia falsi.   (1.142–3)[27]

Thus Virgil's muse colours many lies and weaves cloaks of falsehood with the appearance of truth. (p. 50, modified)

Likewise in the description of logic's rules in Book III we can see how painting might measure up with different kinds of logic. Logic itself is presented as a ferociously aggressive discipline armed with a sword, cutting back the false, and disallowing what is false to hide under the shade of truth ('recidit/ Falsa, negans falsum ueri latitare sub umbra', III.37); beside this logician is placed the pseudo-, sophistic logician, who tries to sell the false as truth ('temptat pro uero uendere falsum', III.41). In this opposition between different kinds of logic Alan's might seem like a straightforward presentation of how truth is arrived at; but the logicians are themselves presented in a painting, made by a 'new painter'

---

[27] I emend Bossuat's reading *falso* to *falsi* in 1.143.

who mimics the truth: 'Illic arte noua pictor nouus, histrio ueri, /
Monstrat elenchorum pugnam', III.33–4). The ideas used to
describe the sophistic logician negatively (lying, wishing to present
falsehood as truth) are presented as positive and powerful virtues
when applied to the painter, that *histrio ueri*, and, by implication, to
the poet. The same revaluation of the apparently negative language of semiotic deceptiveness can be seen in the description of
the pictures embroidered on Concord's dress, where the (normally
negative) language of sophistic logic is used positively:

> Hec pictura suis loquitur misteria signis;
> Non res ipsa magis, non lingua fidelius unquam
> Talia depingit talique sophismate uisum
> Decipiens oculis, rerum concludit in umbra.   (II.200–3)

Here the picture declares mysteries with its signs; the thing itself does not
give a fuller, nor does the tongue ever paint a more faithful representation
of such things; the painting encloses them in the shadows of things,
deceiving our sight with such a fallacy. (p. 74)

IUNCTURA

My discussion of Alan's concept of poetic making has constantly
implied the presence of a reader, whose own intellect is activated
by responding to poetry's invitation to see the coherent, inner sense
behind the poetic surface, a sense which can only be located in the
mind of a poetic maker. As I argued in chapter 4, indeed, I think
the reader comes to self-knowledge in this poem not through
observing its outer, referential action, but rather through the experience of understanding the poem, exercising the imagination, the
reason and finally the intellect. Because the poem is itself an ana-
logue of God's creation, it invites its reader to 'theological' experience (which for Alan means the experience of pure forms).

In saying, however, that the reader is invited to perceive the
pure form 'behind' the poetic surface, my spatial metaphor of
'behind' could lead to misunderstandings. I seem to be suggesting
that we should read the images of Alan's poetry by moving to the
idea behind individual images. I want to hold on to the concept of
movement backwards from the image into the mind of a maker,
but it would be a mistake to think of moving back simply from *individual* images to the sense behind them. Instead, we only arrive at a

satisfying idea behind the surface of the poem by moving back
from the *whole* poem.

Because the meaning of the cosmos, according to the *Timaeus*, is
inherently bound up with its wholeness, the inter-relation of all its
parts, the kind of thinking invited by the dialogue is ecological and
structuralist rather than focused on any individual aspect of the
universe in isolation.[28] My own interpretation of the *Anticlaudianus*
is sensitive to its Timaean background in this, as in other respects.
My reading, I do not need to rehearse, involves the structure of the
whole poem through a kind of backwards reading – we arrive at
the end only to discover that we are being sent back to the beginning. And in so doing we are not only following through the logic
of the soul's 'information', but also, at the same time, we are perceiving the intimate connections and homologies between different
scientific discourses: a politics grounded in nature naturally gives
rise to a cosmology which is ultimately supra-natural. In this section, I would like briefly to suggest one further, essential aspect of
the picture/poetry comparison, which gives theoretical focus for
Alan's evident passion for the philosophical possibilities of aesthetic
wholeness. Poems are necessarily sequential, whereas we see pictures all at once. Narrative is predisposed to suit the historical
imagination, whereas pictorial art more readily serves ecological,
systemic, a-historical habits of mind.

---

[28]   This cardinal distinction is best expressed by Wetherbee 1969. He distinguishes the rationalist (Chartrian) view of Nature from the symbolist (Victorine) view thus: 'It is the difference between seeing in nature as a whole the copy of a higher world – analogous to,
and so metaphorically accessible in terms of, the world of nature – and seeing the natural world as a cluster of individual natures, any one of which is fully comprehensible
only as it is seen to embody the divine' (Wetherbee 1969, p. 96).
      It should be mentioned here that Alan's structuralist conception of meaning in the *De
plinctu* and the *Anticlaudianus* is quite different from (Victorine) principles of understanding the natural world expressed by Alan's own lyric (so often cited as typical of the late
medieval view of nature):

> Omnis mundi creatura,
> Quasi liber, et pictura
> Nobis est et speculum,
> Nostrae vitae, nostrae mortis,
> Nostri status, nostrae sortis
> Fidele signaculum
> Nostrum statum pingit rosa,
> Nostri status decens glosa,
> Nostrae vitae lectio...

PL 210, col. 579. See d'Alverny 1965, pp. 39–40 for the attribution to Alan.

When we look to Alan's own explicit defence of poetry in the *De planctu*, we see the same language of 'picture', and the same concentration on the wholeness of the poetic picture. The narrator of the *De planctu* asks Nature about homosexuality as it is represented in classical poetry. This reference to poetry elicits Nature's anger, which she vents in a dismissal of poetry as, interestingly, a false, shadowy, painting: 'should you', she says to the narrator, pay any credence to 'umbratilibus poetarum figmentis, que artis poetice depinxit industria?' (VIII.125–6, p. 837). Nature's angry dismissal of poetry is pitched in terms of its deceptive falsity – poets, she says, prostitute 'naked falsity', or else they cover falsity with the mantle of hypocritical probability. These dismissals of poetry seem to be unpromising for any defence of fiction, but suddenly, without apparently changing tack, Nature does acknowledge that some poets hide an inner truth; she asks whether or not the narrator is aware that

in superficiali littere cortice falsum resonat lira poetica, interius uero auditoribus secretum intelligentie altioris eloquitur, ut exteriori falsitatis abiecto putamine dulciorem nucleum ueritatis secrete intus lector inuen- niat. (VIII.133–6, p. 837)

the poetic lyre gives a false note on the outer bark of the composition but within tells the listeners a secret of deeper significance so that when the outer shell of falsehood has been discarded, the reader finds the sweeter kernel of truth hidden within. (p. 140)

This is a very succinct statement of the three-way dynamic I have described above, involving image, reader and maker: by throwing aside the false poetic exterior, the intelligence of the reader is satisfied by discovering the sweeter nucleus of truth within. But this sweeter, inner truth is discovered only through approaching the outer image, or picture, of the poem as a *whole*. For Nature goes on, in the way I read this rather choppy passage, to elaborate the kind of fiction she admires:

Poete tamen aliquando hystoriales euentus ioculationibus fabulosis quadam eleganti sutura confederant, ut ex diuersorum conpetenti iunc- tura ipsius narrationis elegantior pictura resultet. (VIII.137–9, p. 837)

However, at times poets combine accounts of historical events and enter- taining fables by a kind of elegant stitch-work, so that, from a fit construc- tion of diverse elements in their narrative, a more elegant picture may emerge. (p. 140, modified)

For Alan it is, as it is in Chrétien's use of the word *conjointure*, precisely the 'construction' of a whole artefact, its *iunctura*, that should provoke the reader to construct the idea behind the poem.[29] Alan always stresses not the radical disjunctions between image and idea, but rather the way in which the image 'faithfully', or 'familiarly' adheres to its idea; but the image, as we can see from this discussion, is the picture of the whole poem.[30]

The description of the finished chariot in Book IV provides a model from within the poem of an artefact whose wholeness implies the presence of a shaping hand. And the word *iunctura* is also used to designate the unifying action. Concord's finishing touches are described in this way:

> Apponensque manum supremam, fine beato
> Concludens operam, sparsas Concordia partes
> Ordine, lege, loco confederat, unit, adequat.
> Ergo iunctura, clavis gumfisque ligate
> Partes effigiant currum qui luce decoris
> Preradians, facie propria demonstrat in ipso
> Divinam sudasse manum superumque Mineruam.   (IV.76–82)

Concord, applying the finishing touch, brings the work to a happy end, unites the scattered parts in order, binds them by law and fits them in place. With their articulations, nails and connections to unite them, they make a chariot which, as it gleams forth with the light

---

[29] For Chrétien's use of the word *conjointure*, see *Erec et Enide*, line 14. For discussion of this word as meaning 'the arrangement of different elements found in the poet's *matière*', see Kelly 1970. Kelly agrees with, but extends, the definition given to *conjointure* by Robertson 1951.

[30] Unlike the practice of much allegoresis in the later medieval period, Alan insists on an intimate connection between outer (artificial) and inner (natural) form. Take, for example, the description of Nature's boots and their decoration:

Calcei uero, ex alutea pelle traducentes materiam, ita familiariter pedum sequebantur ideas, ut in ipsis pedibus nati ipsisque mirabiliter uiderentur inscripti. In quibus vix a uera degenerantes essentia sub picture ingenio flores amenabantur umbratiles. (II.288–92, Häring 1978, p. 819)

Here there are two examples of the outer form sticking close to the inner – both the boots (to the feet, significantly described as *ydeas*) and the flowers (to the true form of flowers). In the prose immediately following, we hear of how Nature's pictures fade quickly, because they do not 'cohere familiarly' to the material: 'pictura tamen, subiacenti materie familiariter non coherens' (IV.4–5, Häring 1978, p. 821). The model of a perfect picture for Alan is one whose outer form coheres closely to its inner form, and therefore to the material it shapes. For the (same) idea of the picture doing its work *fideliter*, see *Anticlaudianus* I.120, 130; II.201.

of beauty, shows by its very appearance that a divine hand and Minerva from the gods above have toiled over it. (p. 120)

If we do not move beyond the surface, and beyond the *whole* surface, then we are left with 'fragments' only, as Alan says about the 'grammarians' (by which term he means what we would call 'literary critics') who are not embroidered on Grammar's dress.[31] These are the readers who

> sola cortice gaudent,
> Quos non dimittit intus pinguedo medulle:
> Si foris exposcunt framenta, putamine solo
> Contenti, nequeunt nuclei libare saporem.   (II.510–13)

who rejoice in mere husks, whom the richness of the marrow within does not set apart: if they seek fragments from the outside, content with mere shells, they cannot taste the flavour of the nut. (p. 90)

IMAGES AND THE 'FOL YMAGINACION'

The *Anticlaudianus*, then, makes a coherent case for the place and power of poetry in the hierarchy of the sciences. The explicit defence of pictures as poetry provides a model for reading the 'picture' of the poem as a whole, insofar as we are invited to move from the external surface of the picture (the whole picture) to the idea behind it that makes sense of the surface image/s. The highest science in Alan's poem is theology, which necessarily draws on metaphor; because Alan is himself shaping a theological artefact, he necessarily relies on poetry as the one art which is capable of revelatory metaphor. The structure of the whole poem stands as a metaphor for divine making, a metaphor which, like the universe, draws us into the pure idea behind it.

Alan's defence of poetry as metaphor is, of course, centrally related to the difficulty of naming the divine. But if the poetic mode is accounted for in terms of its subject matter, this should not obscure the fact that it is also determined by reference to its audience: Alan not only represents the information of the soul, but he

---

[31] Alan's concept of wholeness in poetry is often expressed in terms of cloth-making; a good poem will, as we have seen, be 'sewn' (*De planctu Naturae* VIII.138, Häring 1978, p. 837). Poems which are bad in Alan's view are described as 'patchwork' affairs: Joseph of Exeter is mocked as popularizing 'pannoso ... carmine' (I.165).

wishes to enact that information in his readers. There is no locus of authority from within the action of the *Anticlaudianus* that makes coherent sense of its narrative structure. Only in the reader can the structural incoherences of the work be resolved; and this can happen only when the reader exercises the intellect, having first passed from the images of action to rational appraisal of the sense of those images. The reader, as I argued in chapter 4, effectively becomes the poem's central figure as the soul is renewed by recovering a sense of its highest point and origin. Alan's is a reader-oriented poetic, which addresses itself to the full cognitive range of the soul, and especially to the intellect. Just as he is concerned to reveal the dynamic of the full range of the sciences, so too must Alan necessarily reveal (not merely represent) the full range of the soul.

What implications do these reflections have for the poetic of the *Confessio amantis*? I argued in the last chapter that a range of sciences more limited than the range we find in the *Anticlaudianus* informs the structure of the *Confessio*: whereas Alan is concerned to connect the practical and the theoretical sciences, Gower works almost wholly within the practical sciences of ethics, economics and politics. And if the disciplinary range of the *Anticlaudianus* has immediate consequences for the psychological range represented in and enacted by the poem, then we should not be surprised to find that Gower centres his poem much further 'down' the hierarchy of the soul. Alan wants us to move towards an intellectual, quasi-divine perception, in which we are asked not to permit our reason to sleep in 'filthy images'. Gower, on the contrary, never asks us to move beyond the reason; and even when we do reflect rationally, as I shall argue, we never forget the role of the imagination and of images as mid-way between the senses and the reason. The presiding spirit of Alan's poem is Fronesis, the intellect; the genius of the *Confessio amantis* is Genius himself. Alan's is a poetic of the intellect, Gower's of the imagination. The remainder of this chapter will try to define the poetics of the *Confessio* from this psychological perspective.

Alan not only represents the movement of the soul, but also activates different powers of the soul in his reader. Gower equally represents the powers of the soul interacting, and, like Alan, he does so in such a way as to activate the powers of the reader's own soul. Amans (as the concupiscent will) draws on the imagination (i.e. Genius); and as we have seen, Genius does not by any means provide straightforward rational advice: how could he, evoked as he is in the first place by a concupiscent will? As I have argued in chapter 6 especially, the reader is implicitly asked to supply a rational (and a political) voice which the text itself as often as not evades, and with which it only gradually converges.

Like Alan, then, Gower's is a reader-oriented aesthetic, where the reader must participate in the construction of meaning through the activation of higher powers of the soul than those represented from within the poem. But if Gower's procedure can be paralleled to Alan's in this respect, we should notice an essential difference: Gower represents Amans as *himself* a reader, and, implicitly, a reader against whom the reader of the *Confessio* might measure him or herself. Once we understand that Genius is *Amans's* genius, or imagination, then what else is being represented in the dialogue of the *Confessio* than an extended recollection of texts from the past? What else is the *Confessio amantis* than, at one level, an extended and extremely subtle account of the psychology of reading?

Let us consider Amans as 'reader'. In Book IV he declines Genius's suggestion that he read Ovid's *Remedia amoris*:

> My fader, if thei mihte spede
> Mi love, I wolde his bokes rede;
> And if thei techen to restreigne
> Mi love, it were an ydel peine
> To lerne a thing which mai noght be.   (IV.2675–9)

If Amans had bothered to read the *Remedia*, he would have found the advice that the lover should not read the 'tender poets' – those-who talk of love (*Ra*, line 757); but Amans himself reads and listens only to love poetry. This is as true of his profession of reading only Ovid's straightforwardly amatory works, as it is of his confession in Book VI that he reads romances which relate situations similar to his own. After he has confessed his 'delicacy' of sight, he goes on to describe how his ear is fed with reading:

> And ek in other wise also
> Fulofte time it falleth so,
> Min Ere with a good pitance
> Is fedd of redinge of romance
> Of Ydoine and of Amadas,

That whilom weren in mi cas,
And eke of othre many a score,
That loveden longe er I was bore.
For whan I of here loves rede,
Min Ere with the tale I fede;
And with the lust of here histoire
Somtime I drawe into memoire
Hou sorwe mai noght evere laste;
And so comth hope in ate laste.   (VI.875–88)

This is an extremely rich account of a particular kind of reading: it is provoked by desire ('lust'), and is designed to satisfy desire. Such reading involves a collapse of 'otherness', both personal and historical, into a complete identity with the reader: heroes from the past are identified by Amans with himself. The experience of reading provides hope through this identification, but this is only temporary – Amans goes on to say that his hope 'endureth but a throwe' (VI.890); nevertheless, Amans commits the story to memory, presumably in order that a further process of delusive relief might be replayed in the future. Different parts of the soul are enlisted in this emotional process: the sense of hearing (hearing a text is here closely allied with reading it) produces images for the imagination, which acts as a kind of memory. And the entire process is generated and governed, clearly, by the will, or desire itself.[32]

This account of Amans's reading is set within an ostensibly therapeutic structure, which might distract our attention from its potentially self-referential aspects: when we step back from the passage, we might reflect that it is a peculiarly close description of what is going on across the whole of the *Confessio amantis*. Certainly, the *Confessio* is not a representation of direct reading being transmitted to the memory; but it does portray texts which have been remembered being recalled from the treasury of the imagination, in the service of a readerly desire. Genius is responding to Amans's need; every story he tells is, accordingly, an example of the imagination recalling texts in the service of desire. Some of the linking passages reveal this dynamic in particularly clear form. Take, for example, the link between the stories of Achilles and Deidamia on

---

[32] The idea of Amans (or will) as reader evokes a large, and as yet largely unexplored field of medieval poetics; Simpson 1986a provides a preliminary account of poetic theory designed to move the will, but leaves untouched the question of how the will itself is represented as a reader in late fourteenth-century English poetry.

the one hand and of Jason and Medea on the other, in Book V. Amans thanks Genius for the Achilles story as an example of false-witness, but provokes him to call up another story; Genius readily responds. The courteous psychological interaction between desire and imagination produces a movement from an abstract concept to a story recalled from the memory. The dialogue reads thus:

> 'Bot for ye seiden otherwise,
> Hou thilke vice of Covoitise
> Hath yit Perjurie of his acord,
> If that you list of som record
> To telle an other tale also
> In loves cause of time ago,
> What thing it is to be forswore,
> I wolde preie you therfore,
> Wherof I mihte ensample take.'
> 'Mi goode Sone, and for thi sake
> Touchende of this I schal fulfille
> Thin axinge at thin oghne wille,
> And the matiere I schal declare,
> Hou the wommen deceived are,
> Whan thei so tendre herte bere.'   (V.3223–37)

Or in Book III, for example, Genius abstracts a 'moral' from the tale of Canace and Machaire, which prompts the recollection of a further tale from Ovid (the story of Tiresias and the snakes):

> What nature hath set in hir lawe
> Ther mai no mannes miht withdrawe,
> And who that worcheth therayein,
> Fulofte time it hath be sein,
> Ther hath befalle gret vengance,
> Wherof I finde a remembrance.
> Ovide after the time tho
> Tolde an esample and seide so,
> How that whilom Tiresias...   (III.355–63)

Genius, then, here as in every other instance of his telling a story to Amans, is participating in the same process of reading as that described by Amans above: as the imagination, he is recalling a previously read text in the service of Amans as desire. Of course this is ostensibly part of a therapeutic process, but, as I argued in chapter 6, this particular story does nothing to change Amans; on the contrary, it is reproduced from the treasury of the imagination precisely by way of confirming the impossibility of change: no one,

Genius is saying, can, or even should, try to disturb the course of nature. Like the romances of 'Ydoine and Amadas', this story (and many others) feeds Amans's inner ear – here Genius, as he promises Amans, 'schal fulfulle / Thin axinge at thin oghne wille' (v.3233–4). In the psychological economy of the *Confessio*, indeed, the story of Tiresias must be one of the stories Amans has read in the past, and which he has stored in the imagination for future solace.

So this (representative) example of a story being recalled from the imagination suggests an identity between the supposedly therapeutic reflection on texts offered by Genius, with the self-deluding practice of reading confessed to by Amans in Book vi. The *reproduction* of reading experience in both Amans's recollection and Genius's retelling is, then, rooted in the same psychological need. And Amans's *response* to the supposed therapy of Genius is also like his response to the romance stories he reads in order to give him a delusive solace. We observed how Amans, when reading romances, tends to collapse all sense of 'otherness', whether historical or personal, into personal identification. Repeatedly in the *Confessio* Amans tells Genius that he is only interested in his own case – he will only read, or listen to, stories which touch directly on his situation. In his 'real life' Amans cannot be said to have any real imaginative interest in the life of others – he tells Genius that he is not inquisitive

> To knowe an other mannes lif:
> Wher that he love or love noght,
> That toucheth nothing to my thoght,
> Bot al it passeth thurgh myn Ere
> Riht as a thing that nevere were,
> And is foryete and leid beside. (ii.1988–93)

If another man should ask him for advice in love, Amans says that he keeps it secret; but this can hardly be described as an act of fidelity, since Amans says that he simply cannot remember what has been said to him:

> His tales with myn Ere I herde,
> Bot to myn herte cam it noght
> Ne sank no deppere in my thoght. (ii.2068–70)

But if Gower is so sensitive to the psychology of listening and remembrance (or forgetting), then how can we account for

Amans's attentiveness to Genius's remembrance of old stories? Only by recognizing that Amans's response as a 'reader' is premised on a narrowing of 'imaginative' engagement simply to matter of love, which implicitly involves himself. Let us observe, for example, the way in which Amans responds to those stories he dismisses as irrelevant. After Genius has recounted the (essentially political) education of Alexander in Book VII, Amans dismisses the entire sequence in this way:

> The tales sounen in myn Ere,
> Bot yit myn herte is elleswhere,
> I mai miselve noght restreigne,
> That I nam evere in loves peine:
> Such lore couthe I nevere gete,
> Which myghte make me foryete
> O point, bot if so were I slepte,
> That I my tydes ay ne kepte
> To thenke of love and of his lawe. (VII.5411–19)

Tales of a non-amatory kind are immediately forgotten, since the only thing Amans can remember is his own love. This is the evident motive for the attentiveness of Amans's inner ear to the wealth of love stories produced by his own imagination.

The discussion so far points to a poetic (if that is not too narrow a word to describe a theory of poetic production and response) rooted in desire, but reliant principally on the imagination: Amans, as the concupiscent will, desires stories from the past that answer directly to his own position as lover; Amans's own imagination, in the figure of Genius, supplies these stories. Gower is working within a coherent and traditional psychology of the sensitive soul (or inward wits) here, whereby the three powers of imagination, cogitation (estimation in animals), and memory interact to provide rational information.[33] The imagination receives images gathered from all the senses by the 'common sense', and serves as a repository, or 'thesaurus' of sensible forms; these are then passed on to the estimative faculty in animals (cogitative or rational in humans), which perceives the 'intention' of the sensible image (which essentially involves the recognition as to whether the sensation is to be

---

[33] The best overall account of the 'inward wits' is Harvey 1975. See also Minnis 1981b for a lucid account of this psychology, aimed at elucidating the role of Imaginatif in *Piers Plowman*. For an account of the image in Aristotle's psychology, see Eden 1986, pp. 75–9, and pp. 141–7 for the scholastic reception of this psychology.

desired or feared); this rational abstraction is then passed on to the memory, which stores the information.[34]

But if this is the traditional scheme, how do we explain the fact that the process is, apparently, blocked at the point of the imagination? The essential point here is, I think, that the process of reflection is controlled by Amans (the concupiscent will), who prohibits a rational appraisal of the force of Genius's stories. As long as Amans governs Genius, his reading remains superficial and merely imaginative. Whereas animals have no choice but to obey the dictates of their estimative faculty, humans are more complex creatures. Before the human can obey the dictates of the reason, the will must also accede to them; images which the animal might readily and instinctively flee cannot move the human unless the will agrees.[35]

Amans's own reading, then, represents a limited use of the imagination, whereby the treasury of images stored in the imagination remains, as it were, unprocessed, blocked by the force of an irrational desire. The opposition between will and wit is everywhere apparent in the *Confessio* – one need only think of the internal 'political' battle described by Amans in Book III, where Will and

---

[34] My account of this psychology is drawn especially from Aquinas, *Summa theologiae*, Ia.78.4, resp.:

> Sic ergo ad receptionem formarum sensibilium ordinatur sensus proprius et communis... Ad harum autem formarum retentionem et conservationem ordinatur phantasia, sive imaginatio quae idem sunt; est enim phantasia sive imaginatio quasi thesaurus quidam formarum per sensum acceptarum. Ad apprehendendum autem intentiones quae per sensum non accipiuntur, ordinatur vis aestimativa. Ad conservandum autem eas vis memorativa, quae est thesaurus quidem hujusmodi intentionum. Cuius signum est, quod principium memorandi fit in animalibus ex aliqua hujusmodi intentione; puta quod est nocivum vel conveniens. (Gilby 1964, vol. II, pp. 138–140)

After saying that the imagination works in the same way in animals as in humans, he goes on to distinguish the treatment of these sensible images in the human and the animal soul:

> nam alia animalia percipiunt hujusmodi intentiones solum naturali quodam instinctu, homo autem etiam per quandam collationem. Et ideo quae in aliis animalibus dicitur aestimativa naturalis in homine dicitur cogitativa, quae per collationem quandam hujusmodi intentiones adinvenit. Unde etiam dicitur ratio particularis, cui medici assignant determinatum organum, scilicet mediam partem capitis. (Gilby 1964, vol. II, p. 140)

[35] I cite Aquinas again for a convenient statement of this position (*Summa theologiae* Ia.81.3, resp.):

> In aliis enim animalibus statim ad appetitum concupiscibilis et irascibilis sequitur motus, sicut ovis timens lupum statim fugit, quia non est in eis aliquis superior appetitus qui repugnet. Sed homo non statim movetur secundum appetitum irascibilis et concupiscibilis, sed expectatur imperium voluntatis, quod est appetitus superior. (Gilby 1964, vol. II, p. 212)

Wit are portrayed as two counsellors in outright and strident opposition (III.1148–92). Here Wit accuses Will of threatening the 'state' of the heart by promoting the interests of 'wihssinge and ... fantasie', a psychological description in the same tradition as Spenser's melancholy Phantastes in *The Faerie Queene*, whose chamber is filled with 'idle thoughts and fantasies ... And all that fained is' (II.IX.51).[36] And however much the imagination is a kind of thesaurus, a treasure house of memory (thus Genius's ability to remember so many stories from the past), purely imaginative 'thinking' involves a kind of *forgetting*. As long as the images do not go through to the reason (and thence to memory), their full force is ignored; Genius's own description of forgetfulness in Book IV makes exactly this point; he says that the forgetful man

> noght mai in his herte impresse
> Of vertu which reson hath sett,
> So clene his wittes he foryet.
> For in the tellinge of his tale
> Nomore his herte thanne his male
> Hath remembrance of thilke forme,
> Wherof he scholde his wit enforme
> As thanne, and yet ne wot he why.   (IV.542–9)

This is a description of telling rather than responding to tales, but once we understand that Genius is Amans's own imagination, then we equally realize that Amans is in some sense telling the tales: Gower is representing a process of purely imaginative, desire-rooted reflection on and rereading of texts. And very often in this process the rational form of the tale, and, therefore, its rational psychological information, is ignored: the 'heart', or reason, has no remembrance of the story.

If Gower is developing a poetics rooted in the imagination, the discussion so far implies that the imagination is a feeble base for a powerful poetics: if Amans reads wholly through his imagination, then the psychological 'information' of the tales remains superficial. And indeed, when Gower does use the word 'ymaginacioun', he refers to it, more often than not, dismissively. In Book VII, for example, Genius warns Amans that the man of melancholy complexion is

---

[36] Citations from Spenser are from Roche 1978.

> Full of ymaginacion
> Of dredes and of wrathful thoghtes,
> He fret himselven al to noghtes. (VII.410–12)

And later in the same book he criticizes the man who beguiles himself by deceiving his own 'wit' by musing on a woman (who knows nothing of his desire) 'After the fool impression / Of his ymaginacioun' (VII.4271–2). And many of the vices are associated with the 'feigned enformacion' of the imagination: this is true, for example, of the 'fantasie' of jealousy (V.590–4); of pusillanimity, where imagined dangers neutralize courage (IV.313–39); and of

> thilke vice of Pride,
> Which torneth wisdom to wenynge
> And Sothfastnesse into lesynge
> Thurgh fol ymaginacion. (I.2266–9)[37]

The psychological impression is made by Genius as a kind of literary artist, since he 'impresses' Amans through the recollection and representation of tales. Amans asks Genius in Book I if he would 'in eny forme / Of this matiere a tale enforme' (I.1973–4); or Genius elicits Amans's attention by saying that he might 'enforme / Thi pacience upon the forme / Of olde essamples' (III.1753–5), where the literary form of the story is elided with the psychological form or impression it is designed to make.[38] But the examples of a

---

37 Further examples of the negative functions of the imagination are as follows: I.958 (the 'fals ymaginacion' provoked by Mundus's hypocrisy); II.2845 (the 'fals ymaginacioun' of Pope Boniface in his stratagem of supplantation); IV.1143 (Amans's 'pure ymaginacioun' of 'besi thoght' when he remembers how attractive his lady is). The first two of these examples suggest senses of 'imagination' very close to Old French (and Middle English) *engin*, meaning 'deceitfulness, trickery; evil intention or design; a trick, a snare' (*MED*, sense 1 (b)). Gower also uses the word in these senses elsewhere (II.1956; IV.2637; V.2156; V.7239); and as verbs (I.878; I.1101; II.2116; V.4571). The psychological and practical senses are combined, it might be noticed, in Pandarus's remark to Troilus: 'And were it wist that I, thorugh myn engyn, / Hadde in my nece yput this fantasie...' (*Troilus and Criseyde*, III.274–5). The practical, busy aspect of the imagination also has, of course, its positive aspects; it is no accident that it should be Genius who encourages labour by praising the inventors of the arts (V.2363–2700), those who exercised 'excellentis prudentie ingenium' (gloss to V.2365).

38 The only other scholar to have suggested that Genius himself is a kind of artist-philosopher is Chance Nitzsche 1975, pp. 125–30: 'Genius, the ideal of human nature and agent of this remarriage of body and soul, is an Orphic poet or scribe rewriting Amans ... This poet–philosopher weds wisdom to eloquence – as the priest reconciles soul to body' (p. 129). It will be obvious that, while I agree (as I do at length in the following section), I think the point needs fairly massive qualification, which takes account of Genius's unstable nature.

'feigned' psychological information cited above would imply that the poetic information of Genius as a shaper of tales will be open to question.

By way of ending this discussion of Genius's dangers as a literary 'enformer' of tales, let us focus briefly on the tale of Pygmaleon – itself, after all, a story about artistic shaping and the power of images. Pygmaleon fashions the image of a woman, 'an ymage of entaile / Lich to a womman in semblance' (IV.378–9). His response to his own creation is powerfully imaginative:

> For with a goodly lok sche smyleth,
> So that thurgh pure impression
> Of his ymaginacion
> With al the herte of his corage
> His love upon this faire ymage
> He sette.   (IV.388–93)

Of course, in this case, the statue comes to life – 'the colde ymage he fieleth warm' (IV.422). This story has obvious connections with Amans's own position – his lady is thoroughly stone-like towards him; in Book V, indeed, Amans tells how in church he prays for 'som miracle ... Mi ladi herte forto chaunge'; like Pygmaleon, he sees her as an image worthy of devotion:

> So that al mi devocion
> And al mi contemplacion
> With al min herte and mi corage
> Is only set on hire ymage.   (V.7125–8)

But if Amans's lady will not change, then how does Genius moralize this story of the transformative powers of imagination and desire? Instead of distinguishing Amans from Pygmaleon's case, Genius encourages, as we have seen elsewhere in Amans's 'reading', an identification: like Pygmaleon, Amans should pluck up his courage and speak – 'worde mai worche above kinde' (IV.438).

The imagination, we remember, presents images to the estimative part of the soul which judges images worthy of either desire or fear, to which we respond with the concupiscent or the irascible passion respectively. In humans the reason and the rational will judge the true 'intention' of that desire or fear. Genius certainly aims to shake Amans out of imaginative cowardice with the story of Pygmaleon – the pusillanimous fear everything through imagining dangers,

> And of ymaginacioun
> He makth his excusacioun
> And feigneth cause of pure drede. (IV.329–31)

Genius wants Amans to avoid the dangers of what the psychological theorists would call his irascible passion, but he does so by encouraging his concupiscent passion instead. In neither case, it seems to me, does Genius ask Amans to moderate the powers (and dangers) of the imagination, through the judgement of reason: Amans is being encouraged to move from an irascible to a courageously desirous attention to images; in neither case is he moving beyond the (limited) powers of the imagination. Chaucer's Miller makes the point I am making:

> Lo, which a greet thyng is affeccioun!
> Men may dyen of ymaginacioun,
> So depe may impressioun be take.[39]

IMAGINATIVE READING AND REINTEGRATION

I have been arguing, then, that Amans and Genius together represent the model of a (desire-centred) reader. And, as we have seen, the imagination is the psychological locus of this kind of reading. Given the insistently egocentric nature of Amans's imaginative reflection on texts, we might expect that the imagination will play no part in the abstract realm of politics to which the poem (as I argued in the last two chapters) tends. This is not the case.

When Spenser's Guyon passes from the chamber of Phantastes to that of Reason, he sees the walls painted with pictures

> Of Magistrates, of courts, of tribunals,
> Of commen wealthes, of states, of pollicy,
> Of lawes, of iudgements, and of decretals.
>
> (*Faerie Queene*, II.IX.53)

---

[39] Chaucer, *Miller's Tale*, lines 3611–13, in Benson 1988, p. 73. It is worth observing that people really could 'die of imagination' in Chaucer's England: the Statute of Treasons of 1352 states that a man who 'fait compasser ou ymaginer la mort nostre Seigneur le Roi' will be guilty of treason (*Statutes of the Realm*, 11 vols. (London, 1810), vol. 1, 25 Ed.III, Statute 5.c.2, p. 319). For an example of men found guilty of this charge, see *Select Cases in the Court of King's Bench under Richard II, Henry IV and Henry V*, edited by G. O. Sayles, Seldon Society, 88 (London, 1971), p. 102. I am grateful to Professor Paul Strohm for this reference.

In Book VII Genius, at the prompting of Amans, himself turns his attention to the realm of politics, and in so doing he brings to the surface the political pressure which so often makes itself felt in the amatory stories. And, as I have argued, Amans is transformed, in Book VIII, from being a concupiscent will to being a rationally informed will. What kind of reading by Amans does this new direction of Genius imply? I should like to end this chapter by arguing that the imagination is, however potentially misleading a faculty, an essential part of this movement towards the rational in Amans; and, moreover, that the 'political' reading of amatory stories that Gower invites us to make inevitably requires imaginative sympathy and engagement. For Gower the imagination is the cardinal faculty of human psychological integration; it is, equally, the presiding faculty of Gower's poetic. Amans's own version of imaginative reading, obsessively egocentric as it is, is not the model of reading that we as readers of the *Confessio* are ourselves invited to follow; we can, nevertheless, only make sense of the whole structure of the *Confessio* through imaginative engagement and imaginative reflection.

The *Confessio amantis* as a whole reveals that there is no escape from politics. The opening of Book I ostensibly dismisses the realm of the political as being too unmanageable, and promises instead to focus on love, which 'is not so strange' (I.10). As Amans unfolds his inner state, however, it becomes obvious that he has abandoned the realm of politics proper only to find himself under the tyranny of Cupid. The political metaphor of 'tyranny' is partly a matter of homology: in the 'state' of the heart desire dominates reason, but the relations between the tyranny of the blind boy-prince Cupid and political tyranny can also be related by causality: in the story of the prince Aruns in Book VII political and sexual tyranny are registered as feeding each other. At the heart of these two, self-sustaining tyrannies, lies the imagination: Aruns deceives the Gabines by an imagined, premeditated fraud, and so too does he deceive Lucrece *ymaginata fraude*, as the Latin gloss puts it (VII.4763). We are presented with the psychological processes of Aruns's imagination, in terms strikingly similar to Amans's own 'delicate' thoughts (as presented in Book VI.899–938, where they are described as *impressiones ymaginativas* in the gloss); Aruns is 'wo besein / With thoghtes', and goes to bed

> forto thenke upon the beste
> And the faireste forth withal,
> That evere he syh or evere schal,
> So as him thoghte in his corage,
> Where he portreieth hire ymage.   (VII.4872–6)

Under the impulse of this sensual imagination, Aruns exercises his '*engin*' to plan the rape.

But if the imagination is central to tyranny of whatever kind, it is also, we should observe, equally central to acts of mercy. And such acts are, in the *Confessio amantis*, often associated with acts of imaginative remembrance. In Book II, for example, the (still pagan) Emperor Constantine spares the children whose blood is to be used to cure him of leprosy. He hears the cries of mothers and children, looks out at them, and, 'abreide / Out of his slep'; he then delivers a powerful, philosophical speech in which he recognizes his fundamental, natural equality with the children he is about to kill to save his own life (II.3243–73). He also 'tok a remembrance' of the (pagan) god's 'lawe of kinde' that one should only treat others as one would be treated oneself. Constantine stands 'with himself ... in debate', weighing up the pity he feels for the children and their mothers with his own desire for life; out of a responsive imagination of the pain he is about to inflict, he places the interests of others above himself, for which (the Christian) God rewards him with conversion and cure. This story reveals Gower's humanist trust in the natural powers of mankind – Christian revelation does not invade the realm of pagan virtue, but is instead provoked by, and itself confirms, that virtue.[40] For our present purposes, however, we should especially observe that this turning point in Christian history is provoked by the imagination: it is Constantine's compassionate response to hearing and seeing the near victims of his power that provokes rational 'remembrance' of his place in the cosmos generally, and persuades him to renounce his own interests. The senses, imagination, reason and memory

---

[40] There are many examples of pagan virtue in the *Confessio*, especially in Book VII; one other story that insists on the naturalness of pity, and that explicitly places pagan virtue above revealed religion is the story of the pagan and the Jew (VII.3207–329* (in the first recension only)).

all conspire to provoke selfless pity.[41] The essence of the ethical act lies in the simultaneous recognition of identity and difference: through imagination we recognize identity, through the reason, difference. Whereas Amans (and, say, Aruns) can only recognize identity through imaginative appropriation, Constantine passes beyond imaginative identification with the suffering children to a recognition that they might suffer on his account. But the force of this recognition depends intimately on the act of imaginative sympathy. Without this, reason fails to understand the fullness of experience.

It is no accident that this central story of Christian history should be told by Genius. Genius is, after all, a natural faculty, uninformed by grace. As the imagination, he is placed between the body and the rational soul; a reason informed by the imagination is not purely abstract, but draws its fundamental impulses from the whole body. For Gower pity is a natural impulse, felt in the psyche with especial force by the imagination. Genius's telling of this story reveals the psychological continuities between paganism and Christianity – the natural act of human compassion, registered in what may be called the moral imagination, provokes the divine pity of God (rather than *vice versa*).

We have seen how the imagination can sustain psychological tyranny, particularly in matters of sexual love. But the imagination, as a natural faculty, is also open to other forms of human relationship – it is Genius, after all, who articulates the five points of policy in Book VII, which are all in themselves 'natural' – truth (or fidelity), liberality, justice, pity and chastity. In chapters 6 and 7 we saw how the variousness of Genius's (natural) attachments pre-

---

[41] Pity is associated with remembrance throughout the *Confessio*: in Book VII kings are encouraged to be merciful in this way:

> And ek toward hise enemis
> Fulofte he may deserve pris,
> To take of Pite remembrance,
> Wher that he myhte do vengance:
> For whanne a king hath the victoire,
> And thanne he drawe into memoire
> To do pite in stede of wreche,
> He mai noght faile of thilke speche
> Wherof arist the worldes fame,
> To give a Prince a worthi name.   (VII.3205–14)

Here the king is encouraged to remember pity itself; in other examples, it is clear that pity is produced through remembrance; this is true of, for example, the story of Telaphus and Teucer (III.2639–717).

cludes any static obedience to the sensual will. In the many instances where Genius, or the imagination, recognizes a natural affinity which is not sexual, he is perfectly capable of submitting it to rational appraisal. Out of this unstable structure emerges the overall tendency in the poem towards a sexuality constrained by, rather than constraining, the political. For Gower, the soul is naturally regenerative, and naturally given towards political 'self-placing' through the interaction of desire, imagination, reason and memory.

This 'self-placing' through the inter-action of the commonwealth of the soul is, for Gower, as much a matter of reading as it is of living. I suggested in the previous section that Amans's own habits of reading the stories *in* the *Confessio* were subject to the tyranny of the will, which enlists the imagination; the reader alive to the ironies *of* the *Confessio* will distance him or herself from the Amans/Genius model of reading, by submitting stories like, say, Pygmaleon, to rational appraisal. But the two kinds of reading I am proposing (Amans's and ours) do converge in Book VIII. The magnificent denouement of the *Confessio* provokes a revisionist reading in Amans of the whole experience of his dialogue with Genius. The point of view itself changes, as the dialogue becomes something remembered in the past; Genius, now an unwilling partner in Amans's obsession, advises Amans to be ruled by reason rather than will:

> Tho was betwen mi Prest and me
> Debat and gret perplexete:
> Mi resoun understod him wel,
> And knew it was soth everydel
> That he hath seid, bot noght forthi
> Mi will hath nothing set therby.
> For techinge of so wis a port
> Is unto love of no desport. (VIII.2189–96)

Amans suggests a double reading, in which the self is divided around two points of authority, the reason and the will, where both are operative. Amans can only become integrated ('John Gower') through allowing the authority of reason, but this itself can happen only through a fully imaginative remembrance, in which he remembers his own difference from the Amans he has imagined himself to be throughout the dialogue: 'Remembre wel hou thou art old', he is advised by Venus (VIII.2441).

This process of integration, however, happens not only through remembrance of oneself; it is also intimately bound up, in Gower's poem, with remembrance and 'rereading' of texts. Dante's faint at the end of *Inferno* V registers the clash of two forces: an intense emotional engagement with Francesca along with the love-literature that has nourished her on the one hand, and on the other a rational recognition of the terrible consequences of Francesca's (and Dante's own) literary culture. Amans, as John Gower, also faints in a deathly swoon in Book VIII, in such a way as to provoke a rational reflection on the whole literary culture which has inspired both Amans and Genius throughout the *Confessio*. He sees a parlement of lovers, the abbreviated description of which serves both to recall and to distance many of the very same stories with which Amans had entered into imaginative engagement earlier:

> The pleignte of Progne and Philomene
> Ther herde I what it wolde mene,
> How Tereus of his untrouthe
> Undede hem bothe, and that was routhe;
> And nexte to hem I sih Canace,
> Which for Machaire hir fader grace
> Hath lost, and deide in woful plit.
> And as I sih in my spirit,
> Me thoghte amonges othre thus
> The doghter of king Priamus,
> Polixena, whom Pirrus slowh,
> Was there and made sorwe ynowh,
> As sche which deide gulteles
> For love, and yit was loveles. (VIII.2583–96)

This vision is itself an experience of reflective reading, but one where the abbreviation implies distance; these stories are being drawn not merely from the treasury of the imagination, but from the memory, in which they have been placed after a rational appraisal of the destructive violence of love. Amans continues to read (and to read the same stories, by and large), but the texts are now informing the 'wit'. By the same token, the 'wit' is only fully informed by images which have been imaginatively experienced earlier.

Amans moves towards this rational reading through remembrance and imagination: he draws his 'olde dayes passed' into remembrance, and makes a 'likness of miselve' with the pattern of the seasonal year, with its conflicts and inevitable passage. From this 'imaginative' recollection, he passes painlessly to reconciliation with reason:

> And thus thekende thoghtes fele,
> I was out of mi swoune affraied,
> Wherof I sih my wittes straied,
> And gan to clepe hem hom ayein.
> And whan Resoun it herde sein
> That loves rage was aweie,
> He cam to me the rihte weie,
> And hath remued the sotie
> Of thilke unwise fantasie,
> Wherof that I was wont to pleigne.   (VIII.2858–67)

The end of the poem, then, reveals the way in which the imagination plays an intrinsic part in the process of psychic reintegration, and in particular in the movement towards rational sovereignty. Amans's mode of reading converges with and confirms our own, as we, too, are provoked to reflect back across the whole of the dialogue.[42]

---

[42] This chapter tries to elucidate a poetics from within the actual practice of Alan and Gower. I should remark, nevertheless, that my account of Gower's 'imaginative poetics' squares pretty exactly with a strain of Aristotelian derived thinking about the role of poetry, both in terms of the psychological function of poetry, and of its disciplinary place between ethics and politics.

Writers who placed Aristotle's *Poetics* within the field of logic defined the kind of thinking provoked by poetry as an 'imaginative syllogism'; in describing this psychological process, writers recognize its power and its dangers, just as Gower does. Take, for example, the discussion in Gundissalinus's *De divisione philosophiae* (1150) (see Minnis and Scott 1988, p. 280 for the context of this work):

Proprium est poetice sermonibus suis facere ymaginari aliquid pulchrum vel fedum, quod non est, ita, ut auditor credat et aliquando abhorreat uel appetat; quamuis enim certi sumus, quod non est ita in ueritate, tamen eriguntur animi nostri ad abhorrendum uel appetendum quod ymaginatur nobis. Ymaginacio enim quandoque plus operatur in homine quam scientia uel cogitacio: sepe etenim sciencia vel cogitacio hominis contraria est eius ymaginacioni et tunc operatur homo secundum quod ymaginatur, non secundum quod scit uel cogitat, sicut hoc quod dicitur: mel videtur esse stercus hominis. (Baur 1903, p. 74).

A passage like this admits of poetry's power to move or disgust, without suggesting that these effects are necessarily in conformity with a rational approach to the same matter. But when writers in this Aristotelian tradition come to define poetry's disciplinary function as a part of moral philosophy, then they recognize (under Aristotle's influence) that moral philosophy does not admit of certainty or demonstration, but instead treats individual actions. For this reason the literary procedure in ethical and political science must, as Giles of Rome says in his *De regimine principum*, be *grossus et figuralis* (Giles of Rome 1607, p. 2) ('the processe in moral matter mote be boistous and by liknes of figuris', from the translation of this work into Middle English attributed to Gower's

But if the imagination does play an intrinsic part in this psychic reintegration, we should observe that the sovereignty of reason is profoundly modified by the action of the imagination. In Book III the will and the reason are represented as being in outright, irreconcilable opposition: Wit and Reason counsel Amans that he should put Will 'out of retenue, / Or elles holde him under fote' (III.1165–6). The actual process whereby reason does regain the sovereignty of the soul is in fact much more graceful than this model of supplantation would suggest. Genius repeatedly suggests at the end of the poem that Amans should set his heart under 'that lawe, / The which of reson is governed / And noght of will' (VIII.2134–6), which advice Amans (or rather John Gower) eventually, and movingly, accepts. But the process is only achievable through sympathetic recognition of the proper place of sensual desire. And the impulse towards that reintegration has been, and can only be generated out of imaginative understanding both of the power and the dangers of desire.[43]

So the revisionist reading provoked by the end of the poem is not simply a matter of 'politicizing' narratives whose political implications seem to have been wilfully ignored at first reading (the story of Paris and Helen in Book V, for example, or, indeed, all the Trojan stories). The revisionist reading also involves an imaginative sym-

---

contemporary John Trevisa (Oxford, Bodleian Library, Digby 233, fo. 2rb). The anonymous *quaestio* on the art of poetry edited by Dahan 1980, pp. 214–19 (translated by Minnis and Scott 1988, pp. 307–13) provides an excellent example of the way in which the Aristotelian tradition conceived of poetry as mediating between ethics and politics:

Because all things which relate to the life of the community have to be watched over by judges and rulers ... therefore rhetorical persuasion is said most of all to have its place in the sphere of judicial acts. But in his own private domain any person is his own judge and master... So, poetic composition relates to acts which are private and more on the voluntary side. So, because a man is most praised for voluntary acts if these are honourable, and reviled if they are dishonourable, the major part of poetic discourse is concerned with praise and blame... But because ... it is required for the common good that no one should mismanage what is his own ... therefore rhetorical persuasion in some way descends to the bestowal of praise and vituperation, while poetic composition sometimes rises to the level of judicial acts. (Minnis and Scott 1988, pp. 309–10).

43 See Runacres 1983 for persuasive arguments that Gower's narratives, by working through individual actions, contribute substantively to the moralizations. He also evokes the Aristotelian concern for particulars in moral argument here (pp. 114–20). The classical background to this interest in narrative particulars, in both legal and literary practice, is explicated by both Trimpi 1983, ch. 10, and Eden 1986.

pathy with the place of sexual desire itself. In the psychomachia of
Book III the will replies to the reason that

> where an herte sit
> Al hol governed upon wit,
> He hath this lyves lust forlore.   (III.1185–7)

And many stories sustain the point made very early in Book I that
humans can suffer equally from *too little* love as from too much
(I.19): the first tale Genius tells (of Diana and Acteon) suggests the
violence of repressed sexuality, as does, for example, the story of
Iphis and Araxarathen; many other narratives point to the violence
of love suppressed from the outside (e.g. Piramus and Thisbe), or
of unrequited love (e.g. Acis and Galathea; Hercules and Deianira;
Demephon and Phyllis).[44] Despite the explicit affirmations at the
end of the poem, the *Confessio* is not a poem which champions the
absolute sovereignty of reason; on the contrary, it champions
human integration (or male integration at least), and this can only
be achieved through the harmonization of the whole body; the
pivot of this harmonization is the imagination itself. Genius is the
inventor of sciences (IV.2362–671), and he also has a central role in
sexual desire. But it is through his role as maker of poetry that science and desire are harmonized.

The poem presents psychic integration in the figure of
John Gower at its end, but, as I have just indicated, the full
force of this final reintegration is only perceptible by a reflective,
revisionist reading. The reading inspired by the poem itself offers
a model, as no formal academic tract could, of the soul's own
integrated operations. The exercise of the imagination tends
ultimately to rational appraisal of the common profit, but, equally,
rational appraisal of the common profit points back, via a sympathetic imagination, to the private, passionate sources of the
political. In the soul, the imagination mediates between the senses
(and therefore the body) and the reason; in our reading of texts,
the imagination mediates between the body of the text and its
moralization; in both instances is the movement reciprocal.
Without this reciprocal movement, the reason stands uninformed,
ignorant of the particularities of experience, the particularities
of narrative.

---

[44] See Minnis 1991, p. 62 for a forceful presentation of the point about possibly having too
little love.

CHAPTER 9

Conclusion: varieties of humanist politics

INTRODUCTION

The readings of the *Anticlaudianus* and the *Confessio amantis* offered
in this book are mutually illuminating, insofar as both poems
reveal certain parallels of conception. Both are what may be
described as 'person-shaped' poems: in both, a process of teaching,
or pedagogic information, leads to a state of human integration;
and the literary form of both works – their literary information – is
correlative with the form of the soul whose integration is imagined.
In both, that is, the poem's own shape is determined ultimately by
the end of informing the reader/s for whom each poem is
designed. Psychological and literary information go hand in hand.

This correlation between literary form and the form of the soul
pertains, I think, to many other works written between the twelfth
and fourteenth centuries (and well beyond). But, as we have seen,
Alan and Gower are usefully compared not only because they
make this connection between literary and psychological information, but also because they both accept that psychological information is a matter of philosophical as much as moral understanding. Both are working in what I have called humanist
traditions, in which the fullness and integration of the soul can
only be achieved by perceiving, and experiencing, the subtle inter-
relations of the sciences. Self-knowledge in both poems requires a
knowledge of psychology, ethics, politics and cosmology. Both are
working within the Aristotelian hierarchy of the sciences, and both
poems provide a profound commentary of sorts on this *divisio
philosophiae* by revealing the homologies between the sciences, and
by highlighting the points at which the soul moves from, or resists
the move from, one science to another. The poems not only make
the connection between literary and psychological information, but
the teaching processes represented in and activated by the poems
provoke philosophical reflections – philosophical information in

272

the modern sense. The interaction of literary and psychological information produces philosophical information.

In this final chapter I would like to investigate one aspect of the philosophical information offered by these poems. In chapters 4 and 7 especially I have argued that politics is a cardinal science for both poets – in the *Confessio*, indeed, I think it is the science in which Gower is primarily interested. In this chapter I would like to develop the arguments of those chapters by defining the respective political positions of both poets. When we do this, we can observe fundamental and exemplary differences between the two works. The two poets have a sophisticated and subtle understanding of the place of politics in the constellation of the sciences, but the respective positions of both about the nature of kingship are sharply different. Both might be humanists, and both, in their own different ways, might imagine that characteristically humanist figure of the learned courtier or king, whose power lies in his knowledge. But once these similarities have been taken into account, it remains true that these two works represent two opposed poles of humanist thought (and notably humanist political thought) across this period.

These differences can be listed. Alan's philosophical and literary allegiances lie with Plato and Virgil respectively, Gower's with Aristotle and Ovid. Alan writes for a very small elite, while Gower addresses his work to a much wider audience. Alan's political thought is grounded in his intensely intellectualist conception of theology, while for Gower the secular science of politics is the focus of interest. Correspondingly, the primary psychological faculty for Alan is the intellect, capable of perceiving pure form, whereas the psychological space of the *Confessio* is bounded by the will and the reason, but centred in the imagination, mediating between reason and will. Correlative with the psychology of these poems, their politics might be described as absolutist (Alan) and constitutionalist (Gower). Alan's chosen language is Latin (an extremely mannered Latin at that), while Gower's vernacular is limpid and readily accessible. Alan imagines the glorious triumph of absolutist power located in a young king sweeping all before him in military triumph, whereas Gower represents a constitutionalism, whose agreements are arrived at through dialogue and through the wisdom of an aged man in an aged world. Alan's optimism in the possibility of a Golden Age is unchecked, whereas the Golden Age lies in the irretrievable past for a more sceptical (though still optimistic) Gower.

This skeletal list could be extended. Much of the substance of the claims made in it appears in preceding chapters. In conclusion, I shall assimilate many points made separately about either Alan's or Gower's poem into an argument whose aim is not only to develop and synthesize points implicit in earlier discussions, but also to set these two poems into sharply contrastive relief. The points of difference will, I hope, provide a kind of sketch map for the history of literary humanism in the period between the twelfth and the fifteenth centuries in England and France.

PSYCHOLOGY AND POLITICS

Historians of political thought habitually look for political ideas in works that declare themselves as being about politics – works with titles such as *Policraticus, De regimine principum, Monarchia* and so on.[1] A reasonable enough procedure in itself, this tends to impoverish the real depth of political thought in a given period by ignoring the discursive relations between politics and other realms of experience and knowledge. It is for this reason that we might profitably look to poetry for a sophisticated conception of politics, since in great poetry the boundaries between different discourses are certain to be more fluid. Like all really interesting political thinkers, both Alan and Gower did not think of politics in a vacuum; instead, their conception of political power and practice is intimately shaped by their understanding of other disciplines, notably psychology, ethics and cosmology. These other disciplines, or discourses, shape political thought either

---

[1] The histories of political thought that I have found most useful have been Wilks 1963; Ullmann 1974; Skinner 1978; and Burns 1988. Running throughout these is a conflict between what Ullmann calls 'descending' and 'ascending' theories of political legitimacy, associated with Augustine and Aristotle respectively (Ullmann 1974, pp. 19–31). In this chapter I am not concerned to make detailed parallels between the political positions of the poems treated in this book and political theories contemporary with them. In general, however (as will become clear in this final chapter), it might be said that the political positions of Alan and Gower correspond with descending and ascending theories respectively. For Alan the political power of the king derives ultimately from God and is located wholly in the person of the monarch. For Gower the king's power derives from his people, and his exercise of power must be checked by constitutional consensus. Gower's position squares closely with Aristotelian-inspired theorists (Wilks 1963, pp. 84–117, 123–44, 200–27). Alan's is certainly a descending theory, but it is not dependent on Augustine, and neither is it hierocratic nor sacramental: the king achieves his power through his knowledge, much of it secular knowledge.

by analogy, or by causality, or both. Let us turn back to our two poems and begin by considering their psychology. In what way does the psychology of these poems relate to their political position? In what ways can the very different political conceptions of either poem be accounted for by differences of psychology?

Both the *Anticlaudianus* and the *Confessio* are, as has been argued consistently throughout this book, psychological allegories, fables of the soul representing the information of a single psyche. Different actors (e.g. Ratio and Fronesis in Alan's poem, Amans and Genius in the *Confessio*) are faculties of the one soul; the poem's actions are, in the manner of psychological allegory, anatomized accounts of the soul's workings. Any psychological allegory must imagine the relations between different parts of the soul, and must model those relations on social relations of one kind or another. The *Confessio* and the *Anticlaudianus* are of course no exceptions here. The model of relations they imagine is, however, ultimately very different.

Alan represents the soul in epic terms. In the *Illiad* of the *Anticlaudianus* (Books VII–IX) the soul is imagined as a young king, endowed with gifts and training by courtly, moral and rational powers (Books VII–VIII.146), before an epic battle against the vices. In my reading of the poem, the royal soul's victory in this battle is a prelude to the *Odyssey* of the poem, the soul's journey to God (Books I–VI). The psychological preparations for this journey are also pictured in courtly, essentially political terms. At every point of the poem the primary action is psychological, but the contours of this psychological action are consistently described in the language of political order.

The very making of the New Man's body is itself described in political terms: the elements themselves, habitually inclined to internal strife, are here given to fraternal peace:

> Ergo materiam colere uis ignea donat
> Que, quamuis soleat totam turbare quietem
> Corporis et bellum plus quam ciuile mouere,
> Hic pacata iacet, nullos motura tumultus.
> Materiam purus traducit ab aere sanguis,
> Nec iam luxuriat proprio torrente superbus,
> Sed pacem seruat reliquis humoribus humor
> Sanguineus nullasque mouet cum fratribus iras.   (VII.20–7)

The element of fire supplies material to be treated and fire here lies still and will cause no upheavals, though it customarily disturbs the whole repose of a body and stirs up a greater than civil war. Pure blood draws its components from air and no longer runs riot with pride of special race, but this humour, blood, maintains peace with the others, and vents no rage against its fellows. (p. 173)

And after the fashioning of the body, the joining of body and soul (effected by Concord) is also described in terms of the peaceful, if slightly unwilling, submission of one political power to another:

> Sic diuersa tenent pacem, sic dissona litem
> Deponunt propriam nec iam caro bella minatur,
> Spiritui cedens sed non sine murmure multo.   (VII. 63–5)

Thus contraries live in peace, discordants lay aside the contention natural to them and flesh no longer threatens war, as it yields to the spirit, though not without many a murmur. (p. 175)

Of course the language of political and military conflict used in this way is partly a matter of metaphorical felicity: the analogy of social conflict is a very vivid and rather revealing way of imagining the internal balance of the body and its relations with the soul. But the narrative refuses to allow this language to remain simply a matter of analogy. The psychological, moral action depicted in Books VII–IX is the psychological and moral history of a king, and as such the politics of his soul have immediate *causal* effects on the politics of his kingdom. We can see the language of political order oscillating between a metaphorical and a literal referent in the speech of Allecto, for example. She rouses her troops in the manner of the demagogue preparing to assume tyrannical power. Of course the realm over which she is seeking control is the soul of the New Man; but it is also, unavoidably, the literal realm over which the New Man is king:

> incestus aberit, regnante pudore?
> Languescet facinus mundum pietate regente?
> Cedet auaricia, si munera fundat ubique
> Hostis auaricie? fraudis censura silebit,
> Regna tenente fide? feret ira silencia pacis?
> Ius nostrum pax subripiet, quod tempore tanto
> Deffendens nobis prescriptio uendicat, usus
> Confert et iusto titulo collata tuetur?
> Sed pudeat nos iura sequi, quas uiuere iuste
> Non decet, aut precibus uti. Pro legibus ergo

Sumende uires, uis pro uirtute feratur.
Nos pro iure decet assumere robur et armis
Res dictare nouas et sanguine scribere leges.   (VIII.185-97)

Will incest be gone, with modesty in power? Will crime languish and a sense of duty rule the world? Will avarice concede victory if the enemy of avarice should pour out her gifts everywhere? Will the official voice of fraud be silenced, while honesty holds sway in the land? Will resentment submit to a silence imposed by peace? Will peace quietly dislodge our regime to which protective prescription of such long standing establishes our claim, which actual possession bestows on us and guards what is bestowed by a just title? But shame on us if we join the train of justice, we whom it ill befits to live a life of justice or to turn to supplication. Instead of law, then, we must choose force; let violence instead of virtue be our standard. It is fitting that we should adopt might instead of right, dictate armed revolution and write laws in blood. (p. 196)

Allecto's political mentors are Sulla, Nero, Rufinus and Cataline (VIII.208-10). The force of these historical figures is not simply metaphorical, as Allecto seeks to tyrannize over the soul of the New Man. For, as we saw in chapter 2, the gifts given by the Virtues in Book VII are essentially virtues of political practice. By attacking the realm of the New Man's soul, Allecto equally threatens to vitiate the political realm over which he rules. By the same token, the New Man's victory in Book IX produces not merely concord in himself, but equally allows the political virtues of Book VII to flourish in the literal realm:

Regnat Amor, nusquam Discordia, Fedus ubique.
Nam regnum mundi legum moderatur habenis
Ille beatus homo, quem non lasciuia frangit,
Non superat fastus, facinus non inquinat...   (IX.386-9)

Love rules, nowhere is there Disagreement but Agreement everywhere. For that blessed man guides the earthly kingdom with the reins of law, that man whom licentiousness does not impair, pride does not overcome, crime does not sully. (pp. 215-16)

Physiology, ethics and politics are, then, intimately connected discourses in the *Anticlaudianus*. And they point towards an absolutist formulation of political power. As we can see in the final episode of Book IX, the natural and the political realms are intimately tied to the person of the king himself: the king is imagined as the very epicentre of health in the natural and political realms. The person of the king embraces his entire kingdom, and extends even to the regenerative powers of nature.

The young king achieves his power by total suppression of oppositional forces. If, as I have argued, the king's self is an analogy for his kingdom, then the 'body' has no part to play in the governance of the kingdom. The desires of the body are entirely suppressed – Venus, for example, is attacked and killed by the New Man's deft flight (IX.228–70), which is virtually the last we hear in the poem of the powers of the body. Nothing could provide a sharper contrast with the *Confessio*, whose narrative pays such extended attention, both comic and serious, to the tyrannical power of Venus and Cupid over the king's body.

From this point on (in my reading) the action of the *Anticlaudianus* moves wholly within the rational and intellectual sphere of the soul, now that the body lies conquered. As we move to the palace of Nature in Book I, we see that the soul, too, is pictured in political (or 'economic') terms, as a courtly household: the forces of the soul (both rational faculties and Virtues) assemble at Nature's command, and they conduct themselves in the manner of courtly counsellors, advising one ruler (Nature) as to how she should approach a higher power (God). They gather as a *curia* (I.426), where they are swayed by the rhetorically persuasive speeches of first Fronesis (I.326–424), then Reason (II.77–157) and finally Concord (II.213–309). As I argued in chapter 4, the psychological calm effected by Concord equally produces harmony both in the political order and in nature. But that psychological harmony depends on entrusting the fate of Nature's kingdom to one faculty of the soul, its highest power the intellect (named by Alan as Fronesis). Just as the soul gains mastery over the body, so too does Fronesis come to contain the force of the soul. The means to supremacy are different: the soul gains mastery over the body by military suppression, whereas all the virtues actively long for Fronesis to represent them, swayed as they are by Concord's rhetorical persuasion. But in both narrative blocks, the action depends on one part of the whole person (the soul in Books VII–IX, the intellect in Books I–VI) taking control. For Alan the self achieves integration through submission to the highest, most incorporeal faculty of the soul, whose power resides in its arcane knowledge. And if concord of the soul is effected in this way, then the operations of concord in the political realm would imply that the realm finds its integration through submission to its highest, most incorporeal member, the king, whose own power derives from his arcane knowledge. The transcendent intellect stands as figure for the transcendent power of a king.

Like Alan, Gower also imagines the internal relations of body and soul in terms of a courtly household. The physiological constitution of the body is a little *familia*, where the principal organs

> alle unto the herte ben
> Servantz, and ech in his office
> Entendeth to don him service,
> As he which is chief lord above. (VII.466–9)

And this household itself ideally serves a higher lord, the soul. Genius explains that soul and body only stand 'in evene'

> Bot if the fleissh be overcome
> And that the Soule have holi nome
> The governance, and that is selde,
> Whil that the fleissh him mai bewelde. (VII.507–10)

The central action, even the single principal action, of the *Confessio* deals with disruption in the state of the whole person: one part of the soul, the will, desires to please the body, while supremacy over the body is desired by reason. The sins, who flourish under these circumstances of constitutional disorder, are often themselves described in the language of courtly service and intrigue, as *secreciores* and *ministri* (gloss to I.1343), having 'a proper office' in the 'household and ... compaignie' (II.428–9) of more powerful sins.[2] And within the 'household' of the soul, two parties of courtiers form around wit and will, standing in outright opposition:

> Witt and resoun conseilen ofte
> That I myn herte scholde softe,
> And that I scholde will remue
> And put him out of retenue,
> Or elles holde him under fote. (III.1163–7)

The topos underlying all these applications of 'economic' and political imagery to the internal operations of the self is the notion of the self as a kingdom, over which every individual is ruler.

---

[2] For other examples of moral relations being described in the language of the household, see chapter 7, n. 34.

Genius, as we saw in chapter 7, deploys this topos explicitly in his final attempts to persuade Amans to accept the 'conseil' of reason:

> For conseil passeth alle thing
> To him which thenkth to ben a king;
> And every man for his partie
> A kingdom hath to justefie,
> That is to sein his oghne dom.   (VIII.2109–13)

Like Alan, then, Gower imagines the inner self in political terms; and, as with Alan, Gower's use of this topos does not stop at analogy: as we have seen in chapter 7 especially, the 'political' state of the self has immediate causal consequences for the actual state. Just as Allecto seeks to gain control over the literal state by tyrannizing over the state of the New Man's soul, so too does the tyranny of the boy-prince Cupid over Amans have actual political implications for the governance of Gower's England. In both chapters 6 and 7 we saw how the ethical dialogue between Genius and Amans very often overspills its stated boundary (the matter of love), and flows instead into political discussion and political narratives. The topos of the soul as state is not, in the *Confessio*, simply a matter of metaphorical convenience to describe the dislocations and power struggles within Amans; on the contrary, the rule of will in Amans's soul has immediate political implications for the conduct of government. The tyranny of will in either love or politics is disastrous.

But if Alan and Gower share this perception about the relations of both analogy *and* causality between the soul and the state, we should also observe a critical difference between them. Alan's New Man is the king: as I argued above, he incorporates the life of the *polis* and of nature; all power and knowledge is centred in him, and from the integrity of his person emanate concord in the state and in nature. But is Amans the king? There are certainly powerful arguments to suggest that he is a figure for the monarch. As I suggested in chapter 7, for example, the often comically wide gap between the pathetic Amans and the 'tragic', royal figures of the narratives tends to diminish in stories of the Tarquin kind (VII.4593–5130), in which the disastrous results, both personal and political, of will's tyrannical domination of the imagination are revealed. On the other hand, Amans, moving irresistibly towards self-integration, names himself unequivocally as 'John Gower' at VIII.2321. What sense can we make of this oscillation between

Amans as figure for the king, and Amans as an aspect of John Gower?

Alan is writing panegyric, of however sophisticated a kind. He has nothing to fear from a king. The simplest explanation for the oscillation between Amans as figure for the king and Amans as John Gower is political wariness: the *Confessio* is deeply critical of monarchical claims to absolute rule, as I shall argue in a moment. Gower, it could be suggested, chooses a cunning model of the king in choosing Amans, since he can readily escape from any charge of criticizing the king by claiming that Amans is a pathetically nugatory, comic figure, and is in any case John Gower, not the king at all. But I think this argument stops short of appreciating the subtlety of Gower's political position in the *Confessio*: for Gower the king's self is inextricably bound up with the selves of his subjects. As with Hoccleve's Aristotelian *Regiment of Princes*, the person of the subject insists on its own place in Gower's mirror for princes.

This is evident in the psychological frame of the story as much as in individual narratives. Often in the poem it is suggested to Amans that he suppress his will: Reason, for example (as reported by Amans in Book III), wants to put will 'out of retenue', or else 'hold him under fote' (III.1166–7); or at the end of the poem Genius recommends to Amans that he should govern his 'herte under that lawe, / The which of reson is governed / And noght of wille' (VIII.2134–6). And sure enough, Amans does finally achieve a rational self-governance and integration, when he can name himself as John Gower. But the psychological process by which he arrives at this self-governance can in no way be described as a suppression of will. Reason (who hardly appears as a psychological personification) achieves no military triumph over the forces of Venus, as does the New Man in Book IX of the *Anticlaudianus*. Instead, as I have often shown in this book, the opposition between will and reason is managed by dialogue. And in this dialogue Amans is never forced to accept the authority of reason: at every point, even in the extraordinarily subtle closing moments of the poem, Genius apparently follows Amans's desire. The poem as a whole reveals an optimistic confidence in the soul's impulse towards integration, since Amans, through the naturally regenerative powers of the whole soul, finally comes round to a rational acceptance of his position. He becomes what the scholastics would call a *voluntas* – a rational will, and so John Gower can name himself again. The *res publica* of the soul can only be ruled by consensus and mediation, not by diktat and suppression. And so any account of the healthy rule of reason necessarily involves a long mediation with reason's subject, the will, who becomes by far the dominant presence of the poem. If reason in the body is a figure for the good king in the *polis* (and will the image of the tyrannical king), then Gower's reason can only rule by recognizing the powers and rights of the body, just as his king can rule only by recognizing the energies and rightful scope of the whole body politic.[3]

And if this constitutionalism is implicit in the subtle psychology of the poem, it is occasionally explicit in the political narratives themselves. The reformation of kings in the *Confessio* often takes the form of proud kings recognizing that they are subject to the same laws as their subjects. This is true of the proud kings in Book I, Nebuchadnezzar (I.2785–3042), and the king in the tale of the Three Questions (I.3067–402). It also applies to the rather less proud Emperor Constantine (II.3187–496), and to Darius in the exemplum of truth in Book VII (VII.1783–984). This last tale in particular succinctly encapsulates the forces which might constrain a king. The first counsellor, asked which is stronger, wine, women or a king, answers that nothing can constrain the power of a king:

> The pouer of a king stant so,
> That he the lawes overpasseth;
> What he wol make lasse, he lasseth,
> What he wol make more, he moreth;
> And as the gentil faucon soreth,
> He fleth, that noman him reclameth;
> Bot he al one alle othre tameth,
> And stant himself of lawe fre.　　　　　　(VII.1838–45)

---

[3] By far the most subtle account of Gower's political position as expressed in the formal properties of the *Confessio amantis* is Strohm 1979. The basic distinction of this article is between Chaucer's commitment to a 'poetic of horizontal juxtaposition' and Gower's presentation of 'vertical structures which reassert hierarchical principles' (p. 36). This argument is underwritten by an understanding of the 'central role of Genius in maintaining the hierarchical form of the poem' (p. 29). It will be obvious from the argument of chapters 5–7 that my understanding of the poem's politics is less rigidly hierarchical than Strohm's arguments would suggest, since in my view Genius is a much more unstable figure. It remains true, nevertheless, that Gower *does* affirm possibilities of personal and political integration which we do not find in the overall shape of the (admittedly unfinished) *Canterbury Tales*. I nearly agree with Strohm's formulation: he says that by admitting the forces of disorder, 'Gower moves beyond a single opposition between outdated theories of hierarchy and the reality of selfish desires, to an imagined resolution where such desires are once again controlled within a restored hierarchical frame' (p. 36).

The next two counsellors successively have it that the king can be constrained, but only by the internal forces of, respectively, inebriation and sexual passion. The third answer, concerning the irresistible power of sexual passion, is revealing for the whole of the *Confessio*, since, like the poem, it sets psychological and political forces in play together. This counsellor, Zorobabel, first replies that the power of women is greatest, since a king must succumb to it, whether or not he wants to. To prove his point, he tells two tales (the only example of tales within tales in the *Confessio*), the first about an obsessive sexual love, the second about the power of love in marriage. The tyrant Cyrus, he recounts, was himself tyrannized by his love for his concubine; Zorobabel ends the Cyrus story in a Genius-like way, concluding that the 'jolif peine' of Cupid's arrow 'al the world hath under fote' (VII.1908–11). He then gives an abbreviated but moving version of the story of Alceste, whose truthful love for Admetus preserved him from death by Alceste taking his illness upon herself. This narrative opens out new possibilities: whereas Cyrus's concubine merely replaces one tyranny with another, Alceste's selfless love and fidelity transcend the laws of nature. Truth, as instantiated in a woman, is itself revealed to be more powerful and liberating than any of the three possibilities which had seemed to govern the story (a king, wine or women). And so Zorobabel concludes that truth is the most powerful force, liberating the tale itself from its apparent confines. The king, 'for trouthe, which to mannes nede / Is most behoveliche overal' (VII.1974–5), awards the prize to Zorobabel, and so conforms himself to the rule (that the prize will go to the best answer) established at the beginning of the competition. The king demonstrates Zorobabel's affirmation of truth, and at the same time negates the absolutist claims made by the first counsellor, that the king 'stant himself of lawe fre' (VII.1845).

This apparently simple tale might serve as a model of the whole *Confessio, in parvo*: the political question raised initially seems to be set aside for amatory questions, which at first simply confirm the ubiquity of tyranny in both politics and love. But, like the *Confessio* itself, the narrative then moves to married love, from whose liberating model it can return to, and transform, the political questions of royal power that it had seemed to abandon. And the model of royal power it adopts is a constitutional model, in which a king willingly accepts his responsibilities under the law. Under such constraints the king can no longer consider himself in isolation: his own health is inextricably bound up with that of his subjects.[4]

Alan's political position, then, might be fairly described as absolutist – the integrity of nature, the state and of the self depends on the larger body wholly indentifying its interests with a higher power. The body politic must identify with the king, and the king's own body must identify with the king's soul, the parts of which must themselves commit their interests to their highest faculty, the intellect. And the position should also be described as humanist: the king's power derives not from any special sacramental relationship with God, but rather from his knowledge; he approaches God not through prayer but by intellectual ascent through Nature and the stars.[5]

Gower's political position can also be described as humanist, insofar as his conception of political concord involves the king's rational governance of himself, a governance which requires philosophical information. But the means to that governance of self, and, therefore, the means of governing society, can in no way be described as absolutist. At every point Gower's politics should be described as consensual and constitutionalist. If the different parts of the body politic must recognize the king as their head, so too must the king recognize, and allow for the energies and jurisdiction of his subjects.

PLATO VS ARISTOTLE, VIRGIL VS OVID

For both poets, many allegiances are implicit in, and many consequences flow from their 'political' imagination of the psyche.

---

[4] Peck 1978, pp. 143–4 makes a point similar to mine about the king/wine/women example imitating the structure of the entire *Confessio*. My suggestion that this *exemplum* has political force is sustained by the fact that Gower seems to have used it for polemical ends in the *Mirror de l'omme* (lines 22765–800), where the very different telling of the story seems directed as a criticism of Edward III's relations with Alice Perrers. See Stillwell 1948. Gower's telling in the *Confessio* is rather different from its source in the apocryphal 1 Esdras, 3–4.42 (often known as 3 Esdras), where the king is implicitly criticized in relation to Truth. But Truth in the apocryphal book is identified with God, and is therefore a power inherently beyond the king's; in Gower's version truth is a virtue, within reach of the king (indeed, actively practised by him in his reward).

[5] It is true that Nature's petition to God is often described as a 'prayer' (e.g. II.81–9). But in the poem's narrative the 'prayer' is constituted by the noetic journey of Fronesis; her perception of the causes of things qualifies her to petition God, and guarantees the success of her petition.

Implicit in both positions are allegiances to Plato and Aristotle respectively. Very early on in the *Anticlaudianus* Alan declares his admiration for Plato above Aristotle, both painted on the walls of Nature's palace among the models of human achievement. Although the only work of Plato known directly by Alan was the Calcidian *Timaeus*, Plato is for him the all-round philosopher, while Aristotle is primarily a logician:[6]

> Illic arma parat logico logiceque palestram
> Pingit Aristoteles, sed eo diuinius ipsa
> Sompniat archana rerum celique profunda
> Mente Plato, sensumque Dei perquirere temptat. (1.131–4)

There Aristotle prepares arms for the logician and presents his school of logic, but Plato's profound mind has a more inspired vision of the secrets of heaven and earth and he tries to search the mind of God. (p. 49)

For Gower on the other hand, Aristotle is quite obviously 'il maestro di color che sanno' in the *Confessio*, sometimes indicated by no more than the word *philosophus* (gloss to VI.663), but named often in Book VII as the *praeceptor principis par excellence*, in his role as Alexander's tutor. Of course this Aristotle is indebted to post-classical traditions, notably that of the *Secreta secretorum*.[7] But, as I have argued at length in chapters 4 and 7, Alan and Gower represent genuinely classical versions of Plato and Aristotle respectively: both poets place politics in a discursive constellation true to their philosophic mentors. And the world Alan represents, as indeed the *Anticlaudianus* itself, is grounded in a 'supercelestial form', which animates but transcends the phenomena it produces. In the *Confessio*, on the other hand, the soul, in keeping with Aristotle, finds its highest form in the body.

The primary literary allegiances of both poems also contribute to their political positions. Alan borrows from many classical and late classical authors.[8] But even if his debt to Virgil is not as profound as Gower's is to Ovid, it is nevertheless true that Virgil's poetry and its twelfth-century reception stands closely behind the *Anticlaudianus*. On the literal level, Alan's choice of epic for his

---

[6] Compare III.110–28, where Alan expresses a certain distaste for the difficulty of Aristotle's works on logic.   [7] See Manzalaoui 1981.

[8] See Bossuat 1955, pp. 34–42 for a superficial survey. A systematic treatment of Alan's literary borrowings is required.

psychological allegory is unsurprising, given the intimacy of connection between psychological and political supremacy. The *Aeneid*'s own plot (journey in Books I–VI, followed by the conquering of the new territory of empire in Books VII–XII) provides a schema for the *Anticlaudianus*. At certain pivotal moments, indeed, the progress of the New Man clearly evokes the actions of the hero Aeneas. The last line of the *Aeneid*, for example, describing the departure of the dead Turnus's shade, is echoed at the critical moment of the New Man's military victory over Allecto's troop:

> Vitaque cum gemitu fugit indignata sub umbras.
>
> (*Aeneid* XII.952)[9]

...and life, with a moan, passed indignant to the shades below.

> Non creditur illi
> Quod uidet, et Stigias fugit indignata sub umbras.   (IX. 382–3)

The cohort does not believe what is before their eyes, and flee indignant to the Stiygian shades below. (p. 215)

But the engagement with the *Aeneid* does not stop at the literal level of imitating epic plot in the verse form of epic poetry. As I argued in chapter 3, Alan is deeply indebted to twelfth-century psychologizing interpretations of the *Aeneid*, as an epic story with two orders, whose natural order describes the moral and philosophical growth of the individual. As in these interpretations of the *Aeneid*, so too in Alan's poem does the hero achieve the most profound philosophical understanding in Book VI of either work, in journeys to the otherworld.[10] Fronesis's entrance to the locus of wisdom in Alan's poem recalls the entrance of Aeneas to the Elysian Fields:

> Ascendit loca leticie, loca plena fauoris,
> Celesti loca grata Deo, loca grata Tonanti.   (V.376–7)

---

9   Citations and translations from the *Aeneid* are from Fairclough 1934. The text has been checked against *P. Vergili Maronis opera*, edited by R. A. B. Mynors (Oxford, 1969).

10   (?)Bernard Silvestris explains his more detailed treatment of *Aeneid* VI thus:

> Quoniam in hoc sexto volumine descensus Enee ad inferos enarratur ... et quia profundius philosophicam veritatem in hoc volumine declarat Virgilius, ideo non tantum summam, verum etiam verba exponendo in eo diutius immoremur. (Jones and Jones 1977, p. 28)

She [Fronesis] made her way up to the realms of happiness, realms abounding in good will, realms dear to God in heaven and to the Thunderer. (p. 150)

> His demum exactis, perfecto munere divae,
> devenere locos laetos et amoena virecta
> Fortunatorum Nemorum sedesque beatas.   (*Aeneid* VI.637–9)

This at length performed and the task of the goddess fulfilled they came to a land of joy, the green pleasances and happy seat of the Blissful Groves.

Both the *Eclogues* and the *Georgics* also exercise a powerful influence on Alan's poem. The conception of the Golden Age dawning with the maturity of the perfect ruler is closely indebted to the fourth Eclogue,[11] just as the entire journey through the atmosphere and the heavens in Book IV is indebted to the ideal enunciated in the *Georgics*, 'felix qui potuit rerum cognoscere causas' (II.490).[12] Alan draws heavily on what explicit philosophy he can draw from Virgil's works in his 'psychologizing' of epic, without abandoning the literal idea of imperial conquest proclaimed by the *Aeneid*.

Indeed, as with Gower's absorption of Ovid's *oeuvre* into the structure of the *Confessio*, so too with Alan's response to Virgil's three great works: the epic action of the *Aeneid* (both journey and military encounter) is framed by the Golden Age of Eclogue 4, and the entire poem is underwritten by the philosophical knowledge of both the natural world (expressed by the *Georgics*) and of the divine

---

[11] Claudian's influence should not be ignored here: Allecto's speech in the *In Rufinum* evokes the possibility of a Golden Age, in the face of which Allecto decides to let the entirely evil man Rufinus loose on the world (I.51–65).

[12] Nature is said to have a knowledge of the causes of things in Book I: 'Scrutatur rerum causas et semina mundi' (I.190). The knowledge of Nature's secrets desired by the narrator of the *Georgics* (II.475–82) serves as a good description of the knowledge achieved by Fronesis in Book IV of the *Anticlaudianus*:

> Me vero primum dulces ante omnia musae,
> quarum sacra fero ingenti percussus amore,
> accipiant caelique vias et sidera monstrent,
> defectus solis varios lunaeque labores;
> unde tremor terris, qua vi maria alta tumescant
> obicibus ruptis rursusque in se ipsa residant,
> quid tantum Oceano properent se tingere soles
> hiberni, vel quae tardis mora noctibus obstet.

For an excellent discussion of this passage in the context of both Lucretius and the *Aeneid*, see Hardie 1986, pp. 33–51.

world (expressed in Book VI of the *Aeneid*). The shifts of mode announced by Virgil between different works are incorporated into Alan's *one* work. Thus Virgil promises to sing of Caesar after the *Georgics* (III.1–39), a promise which is recalled at the very end of the work:

> Haec super arvorum cultu pecorumque canebam
> et super arboribus, Caesar dum magnus ad altum
> fulminat Euphraten bello victorque volentis
> per populos dat iura viamque adfectat Olympo.
>
> (*Georgics* IV.559–62)

Thus I sang of the care of fields, of cattle and of trees, while great Caesar thundered in war by deep Euphrates and gave a victor's laws unto willing nations, and essayed the path to heaven.

During the period of Caesar's triumphs, Virgil admits (*Georgics* IV.563–6) to a certain shame for having playfully composed the *Eclogues* in pastoral peace ('studiis ... ignobilis oti, / carmina qui lusi pastorum'). So too does the opening of the *Anticlaudianus* mark the poem's mode as playful and bucolic: he says that the muse sports with a slender reed ('in tenui lasciuit harundine musa' (Prol. 1.6), an evident recollection of *Eclogue* VI.8, where Virgil disclaims epic, and promises to sing in pastoral mode: 'agrestem tenui meditabor harundine Musam'. As Fronesis (like Caesar) is about to enter the empyrean, however, Alan signals a generic change. The natural and cosmological matters of the previous books will now give way to prophecy (of the kind found in *Aeneid* VI.756–886):

> Hactenus insonuit tenui mea Musa susurro,
> Hactenus in fragili lusit mea pagina uersu,
> Phebea resonante cheli; sed parua resignans,
> Maiorem nunc tendo liram totumque poetam
> Deponens, usurpo michi noua uerba prophete.   (v.265–9)

Thus far my Muse has sung in gentle whisper; thus far my page has sported in fragile verse to the accompaniment of Phoebus' lyre of tortoise-shell. But abandoning things petty, I now pluck a mightier chord and laying aside entirely the role of poet, I appropriate a new speaking part, that of prophet. (p. 146)

Alan writes epic which embraces pastoral, Gower elegy. Gower's (more profound) engagement with Ovid has been analysed at length in chapters 5–7; the essence of that argument is that Gower writes the dialogue between Ovid's many works into the one poem of the *Confessio*. He is especially indebted to the *Ars amatoria*, the *Amores* and the *Remedia amoris* for the frame of his work, where the *Ars* provides the source for Genuis as *praeceptor amoris*, offering a *speculum principis* to Cupid; the *Amores* serves as the model for the confessions of a hopelessly self-divided, obsessive, ageing and basically unsuccessful lover; and the *Remedia* is a model for a work which pretends to cure a lover's obsession, while quietly encouraging that very obsession. In each of these works we find mythological stories put to the service of a lover's fantasies, and in each we find the political implications of these stories flamboyantly, often comically neutralized by the lover's obsessive and self-interested concerns. In addition to this store of mythological stories, Gower of course also draws on the *Heroides* and the *Metamorphoses* for the material of his *exempla*. But Gower's poem is, ultimately, a genuine *remedium*, and in the move towards his praise of marriage and political 'truthe' he moves to the position of Ovid's later works (e.g. the *Fasti*), but especially the post-exile works, the *Tristia* and *Ex ponto*, both of which praise marriage and friendship. Ultimately Gower models himself upon the harper Arion, a poet-figure capable of bringing concord among the most ferocious of natural and human conflicts (Prol. 1053–88). It is fitting that Gower's knowledge of Arion is derived from Ovid's *Fasti* (II.79–118).

It seems to me that Gower's deep commitment to Ovid is entirely consonant with his constitutionalist politics. Ovid is the poet who recognizes what power and reason ignore. He brings to the surface the private, passionate realm that imperialism represses. He is the poet who recognizes the terrible power of sexual desire to neutralize political responsibilities, but who equally recognizes the folly of political power which takes no account of human passion. All this serves equally well as a description of Gower as it does of Ovid.

READERSHIP

So philosophical and literary allegiances are written into both Alan's and Gower's political imagination of the self. Consequences for the readership of both poems also flow from their representation of the self. Alan's New Man, as I argued in chapter 4, is the poem's reader, who can intuit the poem's 'supercelestial form'. At this stage it is necessary to say who Alan wanted that reader to be. He is certainly of noble birth. The last of the virtues who endow the New Man in Books VII and VIII is Nobility. Like later humanists, Alan felt profoundly diffident about admitting nobility of birth as an essential qualification of human nobility.[13] But he does, nevertheless, preserve this traditional element of panegyric, in however muted a form. Nobilitas is pictured in both Books I and VII as the last and least beautiful of the virtues; in order to endow the New Man she is obliged to gain permission from her mother Fortune, who argues that she has nothing to offer the ideal work of Nature, since her gifts depend completely on chance, whereas the work of Nature is entirely planned (VIII.77–105). Lest her failure to offer gifts be attributed to spite, Fortune agrees to give nobility of birth. So, in one of the few genuinely comic moments of the *Anticlaudianus*, she awkwardly stumbles into Nature's court, where she is received with discreet, if slightly astonished courtesy (VIII.109–27). Her gift is, nevertheless, accepted:

> Confertur tamen ad laudem titulumque fauoris
> Nobilitas augusta, genus presigne, parentes
> Ingenui, libertas libera, nobilis ortus.   (VIII.128–30)

However, as an honour and token of favour, he has conferred on him impressive nobility, illustrious lineage, free-born parents, unrestricted liberty, noble birth. (p. 193)

Alan further qualifies the hero's nobility of birth in Book V, where, among the moral qualifications for entering Paradise, it is specified that *nobilitas generis* is of no value, only *virtus animi*, 'facta nobilitas, non nata sed insita menti' (V.62–7). But however much Alan's philosophical predispositions move him to underplay nobility of birth, it remains one of the New Man's gifts, and it sharply reduces the readership who might identify with the New Man.

That Alan's readership should be small would have come as no disappointment to him. On the contrary, here as in his works of

---

[13] For the position of humanists in the fifteenth and sixteenth centuries on nobility of blood versus nobility of soul, see Skinner 1987, pp. 135–40.

speculative theology,[14] he warns readers off the work, claiming that it is designed for a very small elite:

Let those not dare to show disdain for this work who are still wailing in the cradles of the nurses and are being suckled at the breasts of the lower arts. Let those not try to detract from this work who are just giving promise of a service in the higher arts. Let those not presume to undo this work who are beating the doors of heaven with their philosophic heads. (p. 40)

Hoc igitur opus fastidire non audeant qui adhuc nutricum uagientes in cunis, inferioris discipline lactantur uberibus. Huic operi derogare non temptent qui altioris scientiae militiam spondent. Huic operi abrogare non presumant qui celum philosophie uertice pulsant. (Prose Prologue, p. 56)

If, as I argued in chapter 4, the ideal reader for Alan's poem is the New Man, then the restrictions on that reader are becoming difficult to fulfil: not only must he be a man, but he must also be of noble birth and expert in the entire cursus of philosophical and theological study (surely a rare combination).

At this point we can only allow for a certain exaggeration on Alan's part, the hyperbole characteristic of panegyric. As both Wilks and Marshall have convincingly argued, the New Man in Alan's poem should be seen as a figure for the young king of France, Philip II. These two articles (which appeared in 1977 and 1979 respectively, without reference one to the other) agree in all essentials as to the historical and political context of Alan's poem. The argument (taken from Wilks) runs like this: in 1179 Philip Augustus was fourteen years old; although his father Louis VII did not die until 1180, Philip was effectively the sole ruler in France from his coronation, which took place in 1179. The negative types in the poem (published in final form, according to Wilks, in 1180, though having possibly appeared in an earlier

---

[14] See above, chapter 2, n. 46. The topos of intellectual elitism is of course deeply embedded in the Neo-Platonic tradition. Examples with which Alan would have been familiar are Boethius, *De trinitate* (a work addressed to an audience of one, Boethius's father-in-law), Prologue; and Macrobius's Commentary on the *Somnium Scipionis*, where *narratio fabulosa* is defended on the grounds that Nature disapproves of a frank and open exposition of her secrets (1.2.17). See chapter 4 above, n. 62.

form¹⁵) represent the most powerful rivals of Capetian power, the Plantagenets under Henry II. Following Hutchings,¹⁶ both Wilks and Marshall accept that the negative *exempla* painted on the walls of Nature's palace (Nero, Midas, Ajax, Paris and Davus, described at 1.171–83) designate respectively Henry II and his four sons Henry, Richard, Geoffrey and John. This argument gains strength, Marshall argues, from the mocking reference to Walter of Châtillon and Joseph of Exeter, both also painted among Nature's 'mistakes' (1.165–70), since both poets were associated with the house of Plantagenet.¹⁷ Wilks also argues that Allecto is 'a thinly veiled allusion to Henry II, who claims to rule the kingdom of France by legal title, prescriptive right and possession'.¹⁸

It will be obvious from my discussions in chapters 2–4 that I think the *Anticlaudianus* is more than a *roman à clef*, designed to satisfy the personal pride and military ambitions of the young king Philip Augustus. While many works of the period designed for the instruction of princes promote the idea of the philosopher–king,¹⁹ none do so with the philosophical and literary sophistication of the *Anticlaudianus*, a sophistication which recommends the work to our attention as literary and intellectual historians. That having been said, it is equally fair to describe the poem as a particularly philosophical example of panegyric, designed initially for the ears and eyes of a very small courtly elite.

Alan's humanist knowedge, then, seems designed to appeal to, and cultivate a small readership. What of Gower? We have seen in chapter 7 that the range of sciences traversed by the *Confessio* is more restricted than the range represented in Alan's poem; correlatively, the psychological range exercised by the *Confessio* is less extensive than the psychological territory of the *Anticlaudianus*: Alan's epic demands an intellectual engagement, whereas Gower's

¹⁵ Wilks's date of 1180 (Wilks 1977, p. 145, n. 39) is determined by his understanding of the poem's political context, and in particular of the Franco-Flemish alliance, which began to turn sour from summer 1180. The fact that Walter of Châtillon's *Alexandreis* did not appear until 1181 would seem to confirm the slightly later date of 1181–3. Both Jung 1971, p. 73 and Wilks 1977, p. 145, n. 39 argue persuasively, however, that the *Anticlaudianus* as we have it is a revised version of a text which had circulated earlier.
¹⁶ Hutchings 1924.   ¹⁷ Marshall 1979, pp. 78–9.   ¹⁸ Wilks 1977, p. 151.
¹⁹ For the ideal of the learned ruler as expressed by writers between the twelfth and fifteenth centuries, see Born 1928; Berges 1938, pp. 50–1, 66–70, 190–2; Bezzola 1967, pp. 1–80; Jaeger 1985, pp. 213–26; Orme 1984, pp. 143–63.

poem is centred in the imagination. These disciplinary and psychological characteristics of both poems suggest that the audience for the *Confessio*, in theory at least, is much wider than that of the *Anticlaudianus*.[20] Many other aspects of the poem confirm this. Let me briefly develop the idea that Gower's poem is ideally designed to inform every one of the king's literate male subjects, as much as the king himself.

It is true that the three recensions of the *Confessio* are directed to rulers. The first recension, which appeared in 1390, is effectively dedicated to Richard II:

> I thenke make
> A bok for king Richardes sake,
> To whom belongeth my ligeance
> With al myn hertes obeissance
> In al that evere a liege man
> Unto his king may doon or can.
> (Prologue, first recension, 23–8)

This recension did, however, end with a dedication to Henry of Lancaster (later Henry IV); by the time of the third recension (1392–3), Gower has entirely replaced Richard with Henry as the person to whom the poem is directed. The passage above, and its continuation, has been cancelled and replaced. The gloss to Prologue 23 in the recension of 1393 tells us that Gower sends the book *specialiter* to Henry. This change of dedication was clearly envisaged as early as 1391, since the second recension (between 21 June 1390 and the same date 1391) cancels the fulsome praise of Richard in the epilogue of the first recension, and replaces it with a mordant account of division in England and royal responsibilities (VIII.2971–3105).[21] It would seem, then, that Gower began

[20] Though see chapter 1, n. 32.
[21] I am describing the view first proposed by Macaulay 1900–1, vol. 1, pp. xxi–xxvi; see also Fisher 1964, pp. 116–27. I largely accept this view despite three articles by Nicholson, all of which challenge it from a different perspective. Nicholson 1984b convincingly argues that the three revisions of the first recension are not authorial. The force of this conclusion is applied to the three recensions themselves in Nicholson 1987, where it is argued that many aspects of the revision of the second and third recensions are 'merely the accidental product of several different layers of textual history', in none of which Gower's hand can be discerned with certainty (p. 138). Nicholson 1984a argues what he sees as a corollary of this position, that Gower's 'political concerns had little to do with the rededication; that his relationship with both men at the time of the presentation was literary rather than political in nature' (pp. 160–1). While these articles, especially those of 1984b and 1987, contribute substantially to our understanding of how these recensions were

writing the *Confessio* when Richard was a very young king (he was
only twenty years old in 1387, by which time Gower must surely
have already begun the *Confessio*).²² By the time of the second
recension, Gower seems utterly disenchanted with Richard, and,
long before Richard's deposition (1399), Gower has publicly cancelled his dedication to, and praise of Richard.

In the *Anticlaudianus*, there is simply not room for disenchant-
ment with the young king. The change of dedication in the
Confessio, on the contrary, does nothing at all to alter the force of
Gower's poetic structure. This is because, as I have already argued
in this chapter, the image of the ruler in the *Confessio* is indissolubly
both the ruler and his subject. The *Confessio* is not directed solely to
the king; on the contrary, its constitutionalist political complexion
produces an address to the whole commonwealth. The politics of
the *Confessio* emerge from the universal problematic of sexual love,
'which every kinde hath upon honde' (I.11). None of Gower's readers can claim to be outside that commonwealth.

And none can claim to have been excluded from access to power
through knowledge as outlined by the poem. Governance in the
Confessio certainly requires philosophical information, but access to
that information is not restricted to an aristocratic caste. In his

produced, I cannot agree with the central conclusions of the article of Nicholson 1984a.
The deletions of praise of Richard in the second recension's epilogue (VIII.2971–3105) are
not replaced by anodyne moralizing, as Nicholson suggests (pp. 164–5); praise of Richard
is replaced by an account of political division and by a direct account of a king's responsibilities. The revised epilogue, then, is still about Richard, but the address has changed
from one of praise to one of implied criticism. The change is directly comparable to the
changes to *Vox clamantis*, VI.545–80, and 1159–200: in both these passages (found in two
manuscripts, derived apparently from a first version of the *Vox*) excuses for Richard are
replaced in a later version by revisions which place the blame squarely on Richard
(Stockton 1962, p. 13). I also find Nicholson's account of Gower's quite precise dating of
the recensions unconvincing ('Gower was obviously not trying to give an exact account
of his revisions here, and consequently the dates that he provided need to be taken
rather loosely' (p. 172)); in fact the dates given are much more precise than what we normally find in poetry of this period. Why should we take them 'loosely'?

This argument about the political implications of the dedications has no bearing on
my essential point (argued below), which is that Gower's final, and certain disillusion-
ment with Richard is in a sense predicted by Gower's representation of Alexander, the
king whose first class education produced a rotten apple. See Strohm 1979 for an argument that Gower's 'unaligned' status allowed him a freedom to criticize not open to
many poets contemporary with him.

For the distribution of manuscripts between these three recensions, see Macaulay
1900–1, vol. 1, pp. cxxxviii–clxvii, and Fisher 1964, pp. 303–9.
²² Fisher 1964, pp. 235–50 argues convincingly that both the *Confessio* and Chaucer's *Legend
of Good Women* were begun in the years 1385–6.

formulation of true nobility, for example, it is significant that Genius connects nobility with the active pursuit of knowledge. In Book IV Amans asks that critical question for the humanist: 'What gentilesce is forto seie?' (IV.2201). Unlike Alan, who, in however embarrassed a way, restricts access to power to the nobly born, Genius (and I take this to be Gower's view) unhesitatingly produces the *nobilitas animi* argument we find in Jean de Meun, Dante and Chaucer:[23]

> For after the condicion
> Of resonable entencion,
> The which out of the Soule groweth
> And the vertu fro vice knoweth,
> Wherof a man the vice eschuieth,
> Withoute Slowthe and vertu suieth,
> That is a verrai gentil man,
> And nothing elles which he can,
> Ne which he hath, ne which he mai.   (IV.2269-77)

Genius proceeds to enumerate the founders of sciences as part of the same argument (IV.2363-671) – these are the people who achieved knowledge through using the *ingenium* with which they were naturally endowed (gloss to IV.2366). The way remains open for Amans (and each of the poem's male readers) to achieve his own nobility of spirit by acquiring knowledge through his own *ingenium*, which is, after all, a natural faculty.

The style of Gower's verse, it should be added in this context, lacks, according to Gower's own just estimation at VIII.3110-25, what the style of Alan's poetry has in such abundance, 'curiosite' (VIII.3114). Alan is perfectly aware of the necessity of a lucid style for an untutored audience,[24] but a more mannered style than that of the *Anticlaudianus* is difficult to imagine; Gower's style in the

---

[23] The principal *loci* are as follows: Jean de Meun, *Roman de la Rose*, lines 18607-718; Dante, *Convivio*, IV.3, 10-15; Chaucer, *Wife of Bath's Tale*, lines 1109-76. For further discussion of the topos in Middle English literature, see Simpson 1985, Minnis 1986 and Olsson 1989 (a powerful discussion of gentilesse in the *Confessio*).

[24] See, for example, his discussion of the style appropriate to preaching in the *Summa de arte praedicatoria*:

Quia, si mimis esset picturata, videretur nimio studio excogitata, et potius elaborata ad favorem hominum, quam ad utilitatem proximorum, et ita minus moveret animos auditorum ... In sententiis vero debet habere praedicatio pondus, ut virtute sententiarum animos auditorum emolliat, excitet mentem, pariat contritionem, compluat doctrinis, tonet minis, blandiatur promissis, et ita tota tendat ad utilitatem proximorum. (*PL* 210, cols. 112-13)

Confessio, on the contrary, holds a 'middel weie' (Prol. 17), 'nec in ima ruens, nec in ardua turgens', as Alan's own description of the middle style has it (III.245). And, needless to say, Gower's choice of the vernacular for his poem (he could have written in Latin, just as, presumably, Alan could have written in the vernacular) is essential for the purposes of addressing a larger audience than would have been able to read, for example, his *Vox clamantis*.

PROPHECY

And, finally, one further consequence flows from the different conceptions of the self in the *Anticlaudianus* and the *Confessio*. Alan has unbounded confidence in the young king's power, given that he sees the world wholly from the point of view of its ruler. Gower, whose understanding of a king necessarily evokes an understanding of the king's subjects, is, even in the first recension of the *Confessio*, considerably more sceptical about the chances of success for the young king.

In keeping with its absolutist formulation of power, I have been suggesting that the *Anticlaudianus* is designed ideally for an audience of one, very young king. Every level of the poem's conception proclaims its confidence in youth and renovation. Old age features, astonishingly, among the vices, just as Iuventus appears in Books I and VII as a virtue. As I argued in the previous chapter, Alan describes his poem as itself rejuvenated by novelty: 'Scribendi nouitate uetus iuuenescere carta / Gaudet' (Verse Prologue, 4–5).[25] The simplest sense in which art renews is, we saw, through recollection, and thereby renovation, but there is a more profound sense in which the recuperation of ideal form renovates. Thus words themselves are painted as wanting to return to their old senses in the empyrean, where they are renewed through their theological, metaphorical senses. The embroidery on the dress of the *puella poli* shows how words are renewed in theological usage (V.119–21). Words (and humans), that is, take on *novas significationes* when they come into contact with their divine form.[26] This theological and

---

[25] See chapter 8 above, p. 246.
[26] See chapter 2 above, nn. 51–3. The phrase *novas significationes* is taken from a tiny person-ification allegory in the *Quoniam homines*: 'Cum enim termini a naturalibus ad theologica transferuntur, novas significationes admirantur et antiquas exposcere videntur' (Glorieux 1953, Prologue, p. 119).

poetic concept sits well with the youth for whom the poem is designed, the New Man who is himself renewed and empowered by his perception of ideal human form.

Gower's poem presents a remarkable contrast to this emphasis on youth and unbounded optimism in the *Anticlaudianus*. For Gower, human and (in his eyes) therefore political integration is possible. And this comes about through the natural inter-action of the soul's powers. To that extent, Gower's poem can be described as optimistic. But the poem puts a brake on any unchecked optimism, since Gower might be said to prophesy the failure of his own pedagogic project. Both Gower and Alan can be described as prophets of sorts. Alan, as we have seen, proclaims in a remarkable passage (V.265-77) that he will lay down the lyre of the poet, and will henceforth adopt *noua uerba prophete* (V.69). But Gower, although not laying claim formally to a prophetic voice as he does in the *Vox clamantis*,[27] does also effectively prophesy about the young king for whom he writes. But whereas Alan's is a prophecy of brilliant success, Gower foresees failure. As I mentioned a moment ago, the model royal tutor in the *Confessio* is Aristotle. But what of his pupil? Does Aristotle have any more success in his *speculum principis* for Alexander than Ovid's *praeceptor amoris* has in teaching anything to the young prince Cupid? Long before we read Alexander's cursus of study in Book VII, we have seen the emperor in action, especially in the story of Diogenes, where the old philosopher courageously dismisses the young tyrant as being subject to his will (III.1270-92). Diogenes is said to have 'enformed' Alexander (III.1313), but the fact that Alexander needs information implies that Aristotle had failed. The later references to Alexander in Book III equally imply that Diogenes had no more success than Aristotle: Alexander implicitly concedes to the pirate that he, the emperor, is no different from the pirate in the nature of his activity (III.2363-417); Genius concludes this sorry episode by pointing to the tyrannical Alexander's wretched death, and saying that

[27] Cf. *Vox clamantis*, Prologue to Book I, lines 7-16. For a discussion of Gower as prophet, see Minnis 1984, pp. 168-77.

> reson mihte him non governe,
> Bot of his will he was so sterne,
> That al the world he overran
> And what him list he tok and wan.   (III.2443–6)

Gower's changes of dedication to the *Confessio* have, in a sense, been prohesied by the poem itself, in its scepticism about controlling human concupiscence.

This scepticism might seem to be the scepticism characteristic of the old towards the young; Gower was, after all, a man past middle age who had been suffering from illness (by his own account) for a long time before the composition of the poem (Prologue, first recension, 79–80). But while Gower is conscious of the difficulties of an old man writing to the young,[28] the poem's scepticism extends equally to the follies of age. One of the great surprises of the *Confessio* is that Amans turns out to be an old man.[29] We first learn about his age in a very passing comment by Venus (VIII.2368), but this quickly develops into a moving crescendo, in which the fact of the lover's old age bears down upon him: Venus, 'halvynge of scorn', advises him frankly to 'make a beau retret' (VIII.2398–439); the shock of her advice produces a vision in Amans (now effectively Gower), in which he sees the companies of lovers, both young and old, from a position of detached sympathy. The lovers who feel most pity for his condition are the aged, among whom stand Virgil, Socrates, Plato, Ovid and, not least, the royal tutor Aristotle (VIII.2705–19). Once their imprecations have persuaded Cupid to withdraw his arrow, Venus anoints the poet with a cooling remedy, and offers him a mirror in which he examines his aged face dispassionately.

Just as no class of people is excluded from wisdom in the *Confessio*, so too is no class exempt from folly; age and philosophical knowledge provide no sure protection. For Alan the Golden Age lies in the possible future, and he is its prophet. The events of Gower's poem occur in an old world, still capable of immense folly, which has long since passed out of the Golden Age (Prol. 670–89). Whereas Ovid's *praeceptor amoris* in the *Remedia* confidently promises that the disasters of myth could have been circumvented if only

---

[28] *Vox clamantis*, Prologue to Book II, lines 31–42.   [29] See Burrow 1983.

lovers had followed his advice (55–68), Gower (like Ovid himself) knows better: the past, properly remembered, is our only salvation, but it can equally foreshadow our downfall. While the imagination is the source of all our solidarities, both personal and political, and of all our knowledge, it can equally threaten our destruction.

Works cited

Alexander of Hales (1924). *Summa theologiae* (Quaracchi).

Allen, Judson Boyce (1982). *The Ethical Poetic of the Late Middle Ages: a Decorum of Convenient Distinction* (Toronto and London).

Allen, Peter L. (1992). *The Art of Love: Amatory Fiction from Ovid to the 'Romance of the Rose'* (Philadelphia).

D'Alverny, M.-T. (1946). 'Sagesse et ses sept filles', in *Mélanges Félix Grat*, 2 vols. (Paris), 1: 245–78.

(1964). 'Alan de Lille et la Theologia', in *L'homme devant Dieu: Mélanges Henri de Lubac*, 3 vols. *Théologie* 56–8 (Paris), 2: 111–28.

(1968). 'Maitre Alain – "*Nova et Vetera*"', in *Entretiens sur la renaissance du XIIe siècle*, edited by Maurice de Gandillac and Edouard Jeauneau (= *Decades du centre culturel international de Cerisy-la-Sale*, n.s. 9) (Paris), 117–45.

D'Alverny, M.-T., ed. (1965). *Alain de Lille. Textes inédits*, Etudes de philosophie médiévale, 52 (Paris).

Baker, Denise N. (1976). 'The Priesthood of Genius: a Study of the Medieval Tradition', *Speculum* 51: 277–91. Reprinted in Nicholson, ed. 1991, 143–57.

Barnes, Jonathan, ed. (1984). *The Complete Works of Aristotle. The Revised Oxford Translation*, Bollingen series, 71.2 (Princeton).

Baron, Hans (1988). 'The Memory of Cicero's Roman Civic Spirit in the Medieval Centuries and in the Florentine Renaissance', in Hans Baron, *In Search of Florentine Civic Humanism*, 2 vols. (Princeton), 1: 94–133.

Baswell, Christopher (1995). *Virgil in Medieval England: Figuring the 'Aeneid' from the Twelfth Century to Chaucer* (Cambridge).

Baumgartner, M. (1896). *Die Philosophie des Alanus de Insulis in Zusammenhänge mit den Anschauungen des 12. Jahrhunderts*, BGPTM, 2.4.

Baur, Ludwig (1903). 'Die philosophische Einteilungsliteratur bis zum Ende der Scholastik', in *Dominicus Gundissalinus, De divisione philosophiae*, BGPTM, 4.2–3: 316–97.

Bayart, P., ed. (1930). *Ludus super Anticlaudianum, by Adam de la Bassée* (Lille).

Bennett, J. A. W. (1966). 'Gower's "Honeste Love"', in *Patterns of Love and Courtesy: Essays in Memory of C. S. Lewis*, edited by John Lawlor (London), 107–21. Reprinted in Nicholson, ed. 1991, 49–61.

(1979). '*Nosce te ipsum*: some Medieval Interpretations', in *J. R. R. Tolkien: Scholar and Storyteller*, edited by Mary Salu and Robert T. Farrell (Ithaca and London), 138–58.

Benson, C. David. (1984). 'Incest and Moral Poetry in Gower's *Confessio Amantis*', *Chaucer Review* 19: 100–9.

Benson, Larry D., gen. ed. (1988). *The Riverside Chaucer*, 3rd edn (Oxford).

Berges, Wilhelm (1938). *Die Fürstenspiegel des höhen und späten Mittelalters*, Schriften des Reichsinstituts für ältere deutsche Geschichtskunde, 2 (Leipzig).

Bezzola, Reto R. (1967). *Les Origines et la formation de la littérature courtoise en occident (500–1200)*, 3 parts in 5 vols. (1958–67), *La societé courtoise: littérature de cour et littérature courtoise*, 3.1.

Born, L. K. (1928). 'The Perfect Prince', *Speculum* 3: 470–504.

Bossard, E. (1885). *Alani de Insulis 'Anticlaudianus' cum divina Dantis Alighieri 'Comoedia' collatus* (place of publication not given).

Bossuat, R., ed. (1955). *Alain de Lille, Anticlaudianus*, Textes philosophique du moyen âge, 1 (Paris).

Brewer, J. S., ed. (1859). *Rogeri Bacon, opera quaedam hactenus inedita*, Chronicles and Memorials, 15 (London).

Brinkmann, Hennig (1964). 'Wege der epischen Dichtung im Mittelalter', *Archiv für das Studium der neueren Sprachen und Literaturen* 200: 401–35.

(1971). 'Verhüllung ("Integumentum") als literarische Darstellungsform im Mittelalter', in *Der Begriff der Repraesentatio im Mittelalter*, edited by Albert Zimmermann, Miscellanea Mediaevalia, 8, 314–39.

Brumble, H. David (1970). 'The Role of Genius in the *De planctu Naturae* of Alanus de Insulis', *Classica et mediaevalia* 31: 306–23.

De Bruyne, Edgar (1946). *Etudes d'esthétique médiévale*. 3 parts, Rijksuniv. te Gent. Werken uitg. door de Fac. van de Wijsbegeerte en Letteren, 97–9 (Bruges).

Buffière, Félix (1956). *Les Mythes d'Homère et la pensée grecque* (Paris).

Bultot, R. (1964). 'Les *Meditationes* Pseudo-Bernadines sur la connaissance de la condition humaine. Problèmes d'histoire littéraire', *Sacris erudiri* 15: 256–92.

Burns, J. H., ed. (1988). *The Cambridge History of Medieval Political Thought, c.350 – c.1450* (Cambridge).

Burrow, J. A. (1982). *Medieval Writers and Their Work: Middle English Literature and its Background 1100–1500* (Oxford).

(1983). 'The Portrayal of Amans in *Confessio Amantis*', in *GCARR*, 5–24.

(1993). *Thinking in Poetry: Three Medieval Examples*, The William Matthews Lectures, 1993, delivered at Birkbeck College, London (London).

Butler, H. E., trans. (1920). *The Institutio Oratoria of Quintillian*, 4 vols. (Cambridge, Mass. and London).

Buttimer, Charles H., ed. (1939). *Hugonis de Sancto Victore Didascalicon de studio legendi*, Studies in Medieval and Renaissance Latin, 10 (Washington).

Buytaert, E. M. (1969). *Petri Abaelardi opera theologica*, 3 vols., vol. 2: *Theologia christiana, Theologia scholarium*, CCCM, 12 (Turnholt).

Caplan, Harry, trans. (1954). *Rhetorica ad Herennium* (London and Cambridge, Mass.).

Carmody, Francis J. (1948). *Li livres dou tresor de Brunetto Latini*, University of California Publications in Modern Philology, 22 (Berkeley and Los Angeles).

Chance, Jane (1983). 'The Artist as Epic Hero in Alan of Lille's *Anticlaudianus*', *Mittellateinisches Jahrbuch* 18: 238–47.

Chance Nitzsche, Jane (1975). *The Genius Figure in Antiquity and the Middle Ages* (New York and London).

Chatillon, J. (1980). 'La méthode théologique d'Alain de Lille', in *Alain de Lille, Gautier de Châtillon, Jakemart Giélée et leur temps*, edited by H. Roussel and F. Suard, Actes du colloque de Lille, 1978 (Lille), 47–60.

Chenu, M.-D. (1935). 'Un essai de méthode théologique au xiie siècle', *Revue des sciences philosophiques et théologiques* 24: 258–67.

(1969). *La théologie comme science au xiiie siècle*, Bibliothèque thomiste, 33 (Paris).

Ciotti, A. (1960). 'Alano e Dante', *Convivium* n.s. 28: 257–88.

Coffman, George R. (1945). 'John Gower in his Most Significant Role', in *Elizabethan and Other Essays in Honour of George F. Reynolds*, University of Colorado Studies, series B, Studies in the Humanities, 2.4: 52–61. Reprinted in Nicholson, ed. 1991, 40–8.

Collins, Marie (1981). 'Love, Nature and Law in the Poetry of Gower and Chaucer', in *Court and Poet, Selected Proceedings of the Third Congress of the International Courtly Literature Society*, edited by Glynn Burgess (Liverpool), 113–28.

Copeland, Rita (1991). *Rhetoric, Hermeneutics, and Translation in the Middle Ages: Academic Traditions and Vernacular Texts*, Cambridge Studies in Medieval Literature, 11 (Cambridge).

Cornet, D. (1945). 'Commentaires de l'*Anticlaudianus* d'Alain de Lille', unpublished dissertation, Ecole des Chartes (Paris).

Cornford, Francis M., trans. (1937). *Plato's Cosmology: the 'Timaeus' of Plato* (London).

Courcelle, Pierre (1974). *Connais toi-même de Socrate à Saint Bernard*, 2 vols. (Paris), 1.

Creighton, Andrew J., ed. (1944). *Anticlaudien. A Thirteenth Century French Adaption of the 'Anticlaudianus' of Alain de Lille, by Ellebaut*, Studies in Romance Languages and Literatures, 27 (Washington).

Croce, Benedetto (1921). *La Poesia di Dante*, Scritti di storia letteraria e politica, 17 (Bari).

Curtius, E. R. (1950). 'Dante und Alanus ab Insulis', *RF* 62: 28–31.

Dahan, G. (1980). 'Notes et textes sur la poétique au moyen âge', *AHDLMA* 47: 171–239.

Deferrari, Roy J., and Inviolata M. Barry (1948). *A Lexicon of St Thomas Aquinas* (Washington).

Delhaye, Philippe (1949). 'Une adaption du *De officiis* au xiie siècle: le *Moralium dogma philosophorum*', *Recherches de théologie ancienne et médiévale* 16: 227–58.

———(1958). '"Grammatica" et "Ethica" au xiie siècle', *Analecta Mediaevalia Namurcensia*, hors série, 2 (Louvain).

———(1963). 'La vertu et les vices dans les œuvres d'Alain de Lille', *Cahiers de civilisation médiévale* 6: 13–25.

Donovan, M. J. (1957). 'The *Anticlaudian* and Three Passages in the *Franklin's Tale*', *Journal of English and Germanic Philology* 56: 52–9.

Dronke, Peter (1966). 'Boethius, Alanus and Dante', *RF* 78: 119–25. Reprinted in Dronke 1984, 431–8.

———(1969). 'New Approaches to the School of Chartres', *Anuario Estudios Medievales* 6: 117–40.

———(1974a). *Fabula. Explorations into the Uses of Myth in Medieval Platonism*, Mittellateinische Studien und Texte, 9 (Leiden).

———(1974b). 'Chaucer and the Medieval Latin Poets', Part A, in *Geoffrey Chaucer*, edited by Derek Brewer (London), 154–72.

———(1984). *The Medieval Poet and His World*, Edizioni di storia e letteratura, 164 (Rome).

———(1986). *Dante and Medieval Latin Traditions* (Cambridge).

———(1988). 'Thierry of Chartres', in *HTCWP*, 358–85.

Dronke, Peter, ed. (1978). *Bernard Silvestris, 'Cosmographia'*, Textus minores, 53 (Leiden).

Duhem, Pierre (1914). *Le système du monde: histoire des doctrines cosmologiques de Platon à Copernic*, second edn, 5 vols. (Paris).

Dunbabin, Jean (1982). 'The Reception and Interpretation of Aristotle's *Politics*', in *The Cambridge History of Later Medieval Philosophy, 1100–1600*, edited by Norman Kretzmann, Anthony Kenny and Jan Pinborg (Cambridge), 723–37.

Durling, Robert M. (1965) *The Figure of the Poet in Renaissance Epic* (Cambridge, Mass.).

Dutton, Paul Edward (1983). '*Illustre Civitatis et Populi Exemplum*: Plato's *Timaeus* and the Transmission From Calcidius to the End of the Twelfth Century of a Tripartite Scheme of Society', *Mediaeval Studies* 45: 79–119.

Echard, Sian, and Claire Fanger, trans. (1991). *The Latin Verses in the 'Confessio Amantis', An Annotated Translation*, Medieval Texts and Studies, 7 (East Lansing and Woodbridge, Suffolk).

Economou, George D. (1970). 'The Character Genius in Alan de Lille, Jean de Meun, and John Gower', *Chaucer Review* 4: 203–10. Reprinted in Nicholson, ed. 1991, 109–16.

Eden, Kathy (1986). *Poetic and Legal Fiction in the Aristotelian Tradition* (Princeton).

Edwards, M. C. (1970). 'A Study of Six Characters in Chaucer's *Legend of Good Women*, with reference to Medieval Scholia on Ovid's *Heroides*', unpublished B.Litt. thesis (University of Oxford).

Enright, D. J., and Ernst DeChickera, eds. (1962). *English Critical Texts, Sixteenth to Twentieth Century* (London).

Evans, G. R. (1980). *Old Arts and New Theology. The Beginnings of Theology as an Academic Discipline* (Oxford).

　　(1983). *Alan of Lille: the Frontiers of Theology in the Later Twelfth Century* (Cambridge).

Fairclough, H. Rushton., trans. (1934). *Virgil*, revised edn, 2 vols. (Cambridge, Mass. and London).

Faral, Edmond, ed. (1924). *Les arts poétiques du XIIe et du XIIIe siècles*, Bibliothèque de l'école des hautes études, 238 (Paris).

Festugière, André J. (1944–54). *La révélation de Hermès Trismégiste*, 4 vols.; *Le dieu cosmique*, vol. 2 (1949); *Les doctrines de l'âme*, vol. 3 (1953) (Paris).

Fisher, John H. (1964). *John Gower: Moral Philosopher and Friend of Chaucer* (New York).

Fox, George C. (1931). *The Mediaeval Sciences in the Works of John Gower*, Princeton Studies in English, 6 (Princeton) (reprinted New York, 1966).

Fyler, John M. (1970). '*Omnia Vincit Amor*: Incongruity and the Limitations of Structure in Ovid's Elegaic Poetry', *The Classical Journal* 66: 196–203.

Gagner, Sten Anders (1960). *Studien zur Ideengeschichte der Gesetzgebung*, Acta Univ. Upsaliensis, Studia iuridica Upsaliensia, 1 (Stockholm).

Garin, Eugenio (1942). *Giovanni Pico della Mirandola, 'De hominis dignitate', 'Heptaplus', 'De ente et uno', e scritti varii*, Edizioni nazionali dei classici del pensiero italiano, 1 (Florence).

Georgi, Annette (1969). *Das lateinische und deutsche Preisgedicht des Mittelalters in der Nachfolge des genus demonstrativum*, Philologische Studien und Quellen, 48 (Berlin).

Gersh, Stephen (1986). *Middle Platonism and Neo-Platonism, The Latin Tradition*, 2 vols. (Notre Dame, Indiana).

De Ghellinck, J. (1948). *Le Mouvement théologique du xiie siècle*, Museum lessianum, section historique, 10 (Bruges, Brussels, Paris).

Ghisalberti, Fausto (1946). 'Mediaeval Biographies of Ovid', *Journal of the Warburg and Courtauld Institutes* 9: 10–59.

Gibson, Margaret T. (1969). 'The Study of the *Timaeus* in the Eleventh and Twelfth Centuries', *Pensamiento* 25: 183–94.

Gibson, Margaret T., and Nigel F. Palmer (1987). 'Manuscripts of Alan of Lille, *Anticlaudianus* in the British Isles', *Studi medievali*, series 3, 28: 905–1001.

Gilby, T., gen. ed. (1964). *St. Thomas Aquinas. Summa Theologiae*, 61 vols. (London).

Giles of Rome (1607). *Aegidii Columnae Romani. De regimine principum, Libri III* (Rome).

Glorieux, P., ed. (1952). 'Gautier de St Victor, *Contra quatuor labyrinthos Franciae*', *AHDLMA* 27: 187–335.

(1953). 'La Somme *Quoniam homines* d'Alain de Lille', *AHDLMA* 20: 113–369.

Gombrich, E. H. (1972). '*Icones Symbolicae*', in his *Symbolic Images, Studies in the Art of the Renaissance* (London), 123–95.

Gompf, Ludwig (1966). 'Der Leipziger *Ordo artium*', *Mittellateinische Jahrbuch* 3: 94–128.

Grabmann, Martin (1909). *Die Geschichte der scholastischen Methode*, 2 vols. (2nd vol. 1911) (Freiburg im Breisgau).

Graff, Gerald (1970). *Poetic Statement and Critical Dogma*, second edn (Evanston).

Green, R. H. (1967). 'Alan of Lille's *Anticlaudianus*: *Ascensus Mentis in Deum*', *Annuale Mediaevale* 8: 3–16.

Greenfield, Concetta C. (1981). *Humanist and Scholastic Poetics, 1250–1500* (Lewisburg and London).

Gregory, Tullio (1955). *Anima Mundi: La filosofia di Guglielmo di Conches e la scuola di Chartres*, Pubblicazioni dell'istituto di filosofia dell'università di Roma, 3 (Florence).

(1958). *Platonismo medievale: studi e ricerche*, Istituto storico italiano per il medio evo. Studi storici, 26–7 (Rome).

Hanning, Robert W. (1977). *The Individual in Twelfth-Century Romance* (New Haven and London).

Harbert, Bruce (1988). 'Lessons from the Great Clerk: Ovid and John Gower', in *Ovid Renewed: Ovidian Influences on Literature and Art from the Middle Ages to the Twentieth Century*, edited by Charles Martindale (Cambridge), 83–97.

Hardie, Philip R. (1986). *Virgil's 'Aeneid': Cosmos and Imperium* (Oxford).

Hardison, O. B., ed. (1974). *Medieval Literary Criticism: Translations and Interpretations* (New York).

Häring, N. M. (1965). *Life and Works of Clarembald of Arras. A Twelfth Century Master of the School of Chartres*, Studies and Texts, 10 (Toronto).

Häring, N. M., ed. (1966). *The Commentaries of Boethius by Gilbert of Poitiers*, Studies and Texts, 13 (Toronto).

(1971). *Commentaries on Boethius by Thierry of Chartres and his School*, Studies and Texts, 20 (Toronto). (*Glosa super Boethii librum de trinitate*, 257–300.)

(1978). *De planctu Naturae*, *Studi medievali*, series 3, 19: 797–897.

(1981). '*Regulae caelestis iuris*', *AHDLMA* 48: 97–226.

Harvey, E. Ruth (1975). *The Inward Wits. Psychological Theory in the Middle Ages and the Renaissance*, Warburg Institute Surveys, 6 (London).

Hathaway, Baxter (1962). *The Age of Criticism, the Late Renaissance in Italy* (Ithaca, N.Y.)

Hatton, Thomas J. (1987). 'John Gower's Use of Ovid in Book III of the *Confessio Amantis*', *Mediaevalia* 13: 257–74.

Hexter, Ralph J. (1986). *Ovid and Medieval Schooling. Studies in Medieval School Commentaries on Ovid's 'Ars amatoria', 'Epistulae ex Ponto', and 'Epistulae heroidum'*, Münchener Beiträge zur Mediavistik und Renaissance-Forschung, 38 (Munich).

Hiscoe, David W. (1985). 'The Ovidian Comic Strategy of Gower's *Confessio Amantis*', *Philological Quarterly* 64: 367–85.

Holmberg, John, ed. (1929). *Gulielmus de Conchis. Das Moralium dogma philosophorum* (Paris, Uppsala and Leipzig).

Huber, C. (1988). *Die Aufnahme und Verarbeitung des Alanus ab Insulis in mittelhochdeutschen Dichtungen*, Münchener Texte und Untersuchungen, 89 (Munich).

Huizinga, J. (1932). *Uber die Verknüpfung des Poetischen mit dem Theologischen bei Alanus de Insulis*, Mededeelingen der Koninklijke Akademie van Wetenschappen, Afdeeling Letterkunde, 74, B, 6 (Amsterdam).

Hunt, Tony. (1972). 'Tradition and Originality in the Prologues of Chrestien de Troyes', *Forum for Modern Language Studies* 8: 320–37.

Hutchings, C. M. (1924). 'L'*Anticlaudianus* d'Alain de Lille: étude de chronologie', *Romania* 50: 1–13.

Huygens, R. B. C., ed. (1970). *Accessus ad auctores, Bernard d'Utrecht, Conrad d'Hirsau, dialogus super auctores* (Leiden).

Jaeger, Stephen C. (1985). *The Origins of Courtliness. Civilizing Trends and the Formation of Courtly Ideals 939–1210* (Philadelphia).

Jauss, Hans Robert (1960). 'Form und Auffassung der Allegorie in der Tradition der *Psychomachia*', in *Medium aevum vivum: Festschrift für Walter Bulst*, edited by H. R. Jauss and Dieter Schaller (Heidelberg), 179–206.

  (1968). 'Allegorische Dichtung in epischer Form', in *La Littérature didactique, allégorique et satirique, Grundrisse der romanischen Literaturen des Mittelalters*, edited by H. R. Jauss and E. Kohler (Heidelberg), 6.1: 215–24.

Jeauneau, Edouard (1954). 'Le *Prologus in Eptateuchon* de Thierry de Chartres', *Mediaeval Studies* 16: 171–5.

  (1957). 'L'usage de la notion d'integumentum à travers les gloses de Guillaume de Conches', *AHDLMA* 34: 35–100.

  (1960). 'Macrobe, source du platonisme chartrain', *Studi medievali*, series 3, 1: 3–24.

  (1964). 'Notes sur l'école de Chartres', *Studi medievali*, series 3, 5: 821–65.

  (1973). *'Lectio Philosophorum': recherches sur l'école de Chartres* (Amsterdam).

Jeauneau, Edouard, ed. (1965). *Gulielmus de Conchis. Glosae super Platonem*, Textes philosophiques du moyen âge, 13 (Paris).

Jolivet, Jean (1966). 'Quelques cas de "platonisme grammatical" du viie au xiie siècle', in *Mélanges René Crozet*, edited by Pierre Gallais and Y.-J. Riou, 2 vols. (Poitiers), 1: 93–9.

  (1980). 'Remarques sur les *Regulae Theologicae* d'Alain de Lille', in *Alain de Lille, Gautier de Châtillon, Jakemart Giélée et leur temps*, edited by H. Roussel and F. Suard, Actes du colloques de Lille, 1978 (Lille), 83–111.

Jones, J. W., and E. F. Jones, eds. (1977). *The Commentary on the First Six Books of the Aeneid of Vergil Commonly Attributed to Bernardus Silvestris* (Lincoln, Nebr. and London).

Jourdain, C. (1862). 'Des commentaires inédits de Guillaume de Conches et de Nicolas Triveth sur la *Consolation de la Philosophie* de Boèce', in *Notices et extraits des manuscrits de la Bibliothèque Impériale*, 20.2 (Paris), 40–82.

Jung, Marc-René (1971). *Etudes sur le poème allégorique en France au moyen âge*, Romanica Helvetica, 82 (Bern).

Kaske, R. E. (1988). *Medieval Christian Literary Imagery: a Guide to Interpretation*, Toronto Medieval Bibliographies, 11 (Toronto, Buffalo and London).

Kelly, Douglas (1970). 'The Source and Meaning of "*Conjointure*" in Chrétien's *Erec*', *Viator* 1: 179–200.

Klibansky, Raymond (1939). *The Continuity of the Platonic Tradition During the Middle Ages* (London) (reprinted Kraus International Publications, 1982).

Kristeller, Paul Oskar (1979). *Renaissance Thought and its Sources* (New York).

(1988). 'Humanism', in *The Cambridge History of Renaissance Philosophy*, gen. ed. Charles B. Schmitt (Cambridge), 113–37.

Landgraf, Arthur, ed. (1934). *Ysagoge in theologiam*, in *Ecrits théologiques de l'école d'Abélard, Textes Inédits*, Spicilegium sacrum lovaniense, études et documents, 14 (Louvain).

Lenaz, Luciano, ed. and trans. (1975). *Martiani Capellae 'De Nuptiis Philologiae et Mercurii' Liber Secundus* (Padua).

Leonardi, Claudio (1959). 'I codici di Marziano Capella', *Aevum* 33: 443–89; continued in *Aevum* 34 (1960), 1–99; 411–524.

Lewis, C. S. (1936). *The Allegory of Love. A Study in Medieval Tradition* (Oxford, reprinted 1972).

Lottin, Odon (1949). *Problèmes de Morale: Psychologie et Morale aux xiie et xiiie siècles*, 6 vols. (Louvain and Gembloux, 1942–60), 3.

Lottin, Odon, ed. (1960). *De virtutibus et vitiis et de donis spiritus sancti*, in *Psychologie et morale aux xiie et xiiie siècles*, 6 vols. (Louvain and Gembloux, 1942–60), 6: 45–92.

Luttrell, Claude (1974). *The Creation of the First Arthurian Romance: a Quest* (London).

Lynch, Kathryn L. (1988). *The High Medieval Dream Vision: Poetry, Philosophy and Literary Form* (Stanford).

Macaulay, G. C., ed. (1900–1). *The English Works of John Gower*, 2 vols., EETS, e.s. 81–2 (London).

(1899–1902). *The Latin Works*, in *The Complete Works of John Gower*, 4 vols. (Oxford).

McGarry, Daniel D., trans. (1955). *The Metalogicon of John of Salisbury* (Berkeley and Los Angeles).

McKeon, R. (1946). 'Poetry and Philosophy in the Twelfth Century: the Renaissance of Rhetoric', *Modern Philology* 43: 217–34.

McNally, John Joseph (1961). 'Gower, Ovid and the "Religion" of Courtly Love: the Shaping of the *Confessio amantis*', unpublished Ph.D. dissertation (University of Chicago).

(1964). 'The Penitential and Courtly Traditions in Gower's *Confessio Amantis*', in *Studies in Medieval Culture*, edited by John R. Sommerfeldt, Western Michigan Univ. Faculty Contributions. Series 7.2 (Kalamazoo), 74–94.

Mainzer, C. (1972). 'John Gower's Use of the "Mediaeval Ovid" in the *Confessio Amantis*', *Medium Aevum* 41: 215–29.

Manitius, Maximilian (1931). *Geschichte der lateinischen Literatur des Mittelalters*, 3 vols., Mullers Handbuch der klassichen Altertums-Wissenschaft, 9.2 (Munich), 3.

Manzalaoui, M. A. (1981). '"Noght in the Registre of Venus": Gower's English Mirror for Princes', in *Mediaeval Studies for J. A. W. Bennett, aetatis suae LXX*, edited by P. L. Heyworth (Oxford), 159–83.

Marenbon, John (1988a). 'Gilbert of Poitiers', in *HTCWP*, 328–52.

(1988b). 'A Note on the Porretani', in *HTCWP*, 353–7.

Mariétan, J. (1901). *Le problème de la classification des sciences d'Aristote à saint Thomas* (St Maurice and Paris).

Marrou, H.-I. (1938). *Saint Augustin et la fin de la culture antique*, Bibliothèques des écoles francaises d'Athènes et de Rome, 45 (Paris).

(1958). *Histoire de l'éducation dans l'antiquité*, fourth edn (Paris).

Marshall, Linda E. (1979). 'The Identity of the "New Man" in the *Anticlaudianus* of Alan of Lille', *Viator* 10: 77–94.

Massa, Eugenio, ed. (1953). *Rogeri Baconi moralis philosophia* (Zurich).

(1955). *Ruggero Bacone; etica e poetica nella storia dell' 'Opus maius'*, Uomini e dottrine, 3 (Rome).

Meier, Christel (1977). 'Zum Problem der allegorischen Interpretation mittelalterlicher Dichtung', *Beiträge zur Geschichte der deutschen Sprache und Literatur* 99: 250–96.

(1980). 'Die Rezeption des *Anticlaudianus* Alans von Lille in Textkommentierung und Illustration', in *Text und Bild: Aspekte des Zusammenwirkens zweier Künste in Mittelalter und früher Neuzeit*, edited by C. Meier (Wiesbaden), 408–549.

Micha, Alexandre, ed. (1957). *Les Romans de Chrétien de Troyes*, vol. 2, *Cligés*, Classiques français du moyen âge, 84 (Paris).

Michaud-Quantin, P. (1949). 'La classification des puissances de l'âme au xiie siècle', *Revue du moyen âge latin* 5: 15–34.

Michaud-Quantin, P., ed. (1956). *Godefroy de Saint-Victor, Fons Philosophiae*, Analecta mediaevalia namurcensia, 8 (Namur, Louvain and Lille).

Miller, Paul (1983). 'John Gower, Satiric Poet', in *GCARR*, 78–105.

Miller, Walter, trans. (1913). *Cicero, De officiis* (Cambridge, Mass. and London).

Minnis, A. J. (1980). 'John Gower, *Sapiens* in Ethics and Politics', *Medium Aevum* 49: 207–29. Reprinted in Nicholson, ed. 1991, 158–80.

(1981a). 'The Influence of Academic Prologues on the Prologues and Literary Attitudes of Late-Medieval English Writers', *Mediaeval Studies* 43: 342–83.

(1981b). 'Langland's Ymaginatif and Late-Medieval Theories of Imagination', *Comparative Criticism* 3: 71–103.

(1982). *Chaucer and Pagan Antiquity*, Chaucer Studies, 8 (Cambridge).

(1983). '"Moral Gower" and Medieval Literary Theory', in *GCARR*, 50–78.

(1984). *Medieval Theory of Authorship, Scholastic Literary Attitudes in the Later Middle Ages* (London).

(1986). 'From Medieval to Renaissance? Chaucer's Position on Past Gentility', *Proceedings of the British Academy* 72: 205–46.

(1991). '*De Vulgari Auctoritate*: Chaucer, Gower and the Men of Great Authority', in *Chaucer and Gower: Difference, Mutuality, Exchange*, edited by R. F. Yeager, English Literary Studies, 51 (Victoria, B.C.), 36–74.

Minnis, A. J. and A. B. Scott, eds. (1988). *Medieval Literary Theory and Criticism, c.1100 – c.1375: the Commentary Tradition* (Oxford).

Mozley, J. H., trans. (1929). *'The Art of Love' and Other Poems*, second edn, revised by G. P. Goold (1979) (Cambridge, Mass. and London).

Muscatine, Charles (1953). 'The Emergence of Psychological Allegory in Old French Romance', *Publications of the Modern Language Association* 68: 1160–82.

Nicholson, Peter. (1984a). 'The Dedications of Gower's *Confessio Amantis*', *Mediaevalia* 10: 159–80.

(1984b). 'Gower's Revisions in the *Confessio Amantis*', *Chaucer Review* 19: 123–43.

(1987). 'Poet and Scribe in the Manuscripts of Gower's *Confessio Amantis*', in *Manuscripts and Texts, Editorial Problems in Later Middle English Literature*, edited by Derek Pearsall (Cambridge), 130–42.

Nicholson, Peter, ed. (1991). *Gower's 'Confessio amantis', A Critical Anthology*, Publications of the John Gower Society, 3 (Cambridge).

Nims, Margaret F., trans. (1967). *'Poetria Nova' of Geoffrey of Vinsauf* (Toronto).

Nock, A. D., and André J. Festugière, eds. and trans. (1960). *Corpus hermeticum*, second edn, 4 vols., vol. 2 (Paris).

Norton-Smith, John (1966). *John Lydgate. Poems* (Oxford).

Ochsenbein, Peter (1969). 'Das *Compendium Anticlaudiani*. Eine neu entdeckte Vorlage Heinrichs von Neustadt', *Zeitschrift für deutsches Altertum* 98: 81–109.

(1975). *Studien zum 'Anticlaudianus' des Alanus ab Insulis*, Europäische Hochschulschriften. Band 1: Deutsche Literatur und Germanistik, vol. 114 (Bern and Frankfurt).

Olsson, Kurt (1982). 'Natural Law and John Gower's *Confessio Amantis*', *Medievalia et Humanistica*, n.s. 11: 229–61. Reprinted in Nicholson, ed. 1991, 181–213.

(1989). 'Aspects of *Gentilesse* in John Gower's *Confessio Amantis*, Books III–V', in *John Gower: Recent Readings. Papers Presented at the Meetings of the John Gower Society 1983–88*, edited by R. F. Yeager, Studies in Medieval Culture, 26 (Kalamazoo), 225–73.

(1992). *John Gower and the Structures of Conversion: a Reading of the 'Confessio amantis'*, Publications of the John Gower Society, 4 (Cambridge).

Orme, Nicholas (1984). *From Childhood to Chivalry: the Education of English Kings and Aristocracy, 1066–1530* (London).

Osgood, Charles G. (1956). *Boccaccio on Poetry*, second edn (Indianapolis).

Paetow, Louis J., ed. and trans. (1914). *The Battle of the Seven Arts. A French Poem by Henri d'Andeli*, Memoirs of the University of California, 4.1, History, 1.1 (Berkeley).

Parent, J. M. (1938). *La doctrine de la création dans l'école de Chartres*, Publications de l'institut d'études médiévales d'Ottawa, 8 (Ottawa).

Peck, Russell A. (1978). *Kingship and Common Profit in Gower's 'Confessio Amantis'* (Carbondale, Illinois and London).

Pelen, Marc M. (1987). *Latin Poetic Irony in the Roman de la Rose*, Vinaver Studies in French, 4 (Liverpool).

Pickles, J. D. and J. L. Dawson (1987). *A Concordance to John Gower's 'Confessio amantis'*, Publications of the John Gower Society, 1 (Cambridge).

Piehler, Paul (1971). *The Visionary Landscape: a Study in Medieval Allegory* (London).

Porter, Elizabeth (1983). 'Gower's Ethical Microcosm and Political Macrocosm', in *GCARR*, 135–62.

Quadlbauer, Franz (1982). 'Zur Theorie der Komposition in der mittelalterlichen Rhetorik und Poetik', in *Rhetoric Revalued*, Medieval and Renaissance Texts and Studies, 19, edited by Brian Vickers (Binghampton, New York), 115–31.

Raynaud de Lage, G. (1951). *Alain de Lille: poète du xiie siècle*, Université de Montreal, publications de l'institut médiévale, 12 (Montreal and Paris).

Robertson, D. W. (1951). 'Some Medieval Literary Terminology, with Special Reference to Chrétien de Troyes', *Studies in Philology* 48: 669–92.

Roche, Thomas P. (1978). *The Faerie Queene* (Harmondsworth).

Roques, R. (1954). *L'univers dionysien; structure hiérarchique du monde selon le pseudo-Denys*, *Théologie* 29 (Paris).

Runacres, Charles (1983). 'Art and Ethics in the "Exempla" of *Confessio Amantis*', in *GCARR*, 106–34.

Sandkühler, B. (1967). *Die frühen Dantekommentare und ihr Verhältnis zur mittelalterlichen Kommentartradition*, Münchener Romanistische Arbeiten, 19 (Munich).

Schepss, G. and S. Brandt, eds. (1906). *Boethius, In isagogen Porphyrii commenta*, Corpus scriptorum ecclesiasticorum latinorum, 48 (Leipzig).

Schueler, Donald G. (1972). 'Gower's Characterization of Genius in the *Confessio Amantis*', *Modern Language Quarterly* 33: 240–56.

Sheridan, James J., trans. (1973). *Alan of Lille, Anticlaudianus, or the Good and Perfect Man* (Toronto).

(1980). *Alan of Lille. The Plaint of Nature*, Medieval Sources in Translation, 26 (Toronto).

Showerman, Grant, trans. (1914). *Ovid, Heroides and Amores*, second edn, revised by G. P. Goold (1977) (Cambridge, Mass. and London).

Simone, F. (1949). 'La "reductio artium ad Sacram Scripturam" quale espressione dell'umanesimo medievale fino al secolo xii', *Convivium* 6: 887–927.

Simpson, James (1985). 'Spiritual and Earthly Nobility in *Piers Plowman*', *Neuphilologische Mitteilungen* 86: 467–81.

(1986a). 'From Reason to Affective Knowledge: Modes of Thought and Poetic Form in *Piers Plowman*', *Medium Aevum* 55: 1–23.

(1986b). 'The Role of *Scientia* in *Piers Plowman*', in *Medieval English Religious and Ethical Literature, Essays in Honour of G. H. Russell*, edited by Gregory Kratzmann and James Simpson (Cambridge), 49–65.

(1988). 'Ironic Incongruence in the Prologue and Book I of Gower's *Confessio Amantis*', *Neophilologus* 72: 617–32.

(1989). 'Poetry as Knowledge: Dante's *Paradiso* XIII', *Forum for Modern Language Studies* 25: 329–43.

(1993). 'Genius's "Enformacioun" in Book III of the *Confessio Amantis*', *Mediaevalia* 16: 159–95.

Singerman, Jerome E. (1986). *Under Clouds of Poesy: Poetry and Truth in French and English Reworkings of the 'Aeneid', 1160–1513* (New York and London).

Singleton, Charles S. (1968). *A Dictionary of Proper Names and Notable Matters in the Works of Dante*, by Paget Toynbee, revised by Charles S. Singleton (Oxford).

Singleton, Charles S., ed. and trans. (1970). *The Divine Comedy, Inferno*, 2 vols., Bollingen series, 80 (Princeton).

(1975). *The Divine Comedy. Paradiso*, 2 vols., Bollingen series, 80 (Princeton).

Skinner, Quentin (1978). *The Foundations of Modern Political Thought*, 2 vols. (Cambridge).

(1987). 'Sir Thomas More's *Utopia* and the Language of Renaissance Humanism', in *The Languages of Political Theory in Early Modern Europe*, edited by Anthony Pagden (Cambridge), 123–57.

Smalley, Beryl (1960). *English Friars and Antiquity in the Early Fourteenth Century* (Oxford).

Solodow, Joseph B. (1977). 'Ovid's *Ars amatoria*: the Lover as Cultural Ideal', *Wiener Studien*, n.s. 11: 106–27.

Southern, R. W. (1970). *Medieval Humanism and Other Studies* (Oxford).

(1979). Platonism, Scholastic Method, and the School of Chartres, The Stenton Lectures, 12 (Reading).

(1982). 'The Schools of Paris and Chartres', in Renaissance and Renewal in the Twelfth Century, edited by R. L. Benson and G. Constable (Oxford), 113–37.

Spearing, A. C. (1993). 'Canace and Machaire', Mediaevalia 16: 211–21.

Stahl, William H., trans. (1952). Macrobius. Commentary on the Dream of Scipio (New York).

Starkey, David (1981). 'The Age of the Household: Politics, Society and the Arts, c. 1350–c. 1550', in The Later Middle Ages, edited by Stephen Medcalf (London), 225–90.

Steele, Robert, ed. (1894). Lydgate and Burgh's Secrees of Old Philisoffres, EETS, e.s. 46 (London).

Stewart, H. F., E. K. Rand and S. J. Tester, trans. (1973). Boethius, The Theological Tractates and Consolation of Philosophy (Cambridge, Mass. and London).

Stillwell, Gardiner (1948). 'John Gower and the Last Years of Edward III', Studies in Philology 45: 454–71.

Stock, Brian (1972). Myth and Science in the Twelfth Century. A Study of Bernard Silvester (Princeton).

Stockton, E. W., trans. (1962). The Major Latin Works of John Gower (Seattle).

Strohm, Paul (1979). 'Form and Social Statement in Confessio Amantis and the Canterbury Tales', Studies in the Age of Chaucer 1: 17–40.

(1982). 'A Note on Gower's Persona', in Acts of Interpretation, The Text in its Contexts 700–1600. Essays on Medieval and Renaissance Literature in Honour of E. Talbot Donaldson, edited by Mary J. Carruthers and Elizabeth D. Kirk (Norman, Oklahoma), 293–8.

(1992). Hochon's Arrow. The Social Imagination of Fourteenth- Century Texts (Princeton).

Sulowski, Jan., ed. (1972). Radulphus de Longo Campo: in Anticlaudianum Alani commentum, Polska Akademia Nauk: Zakad historii nauki i techniki. Zróda do dziejów nauki i techniki, 13 (Wroclaw).

Taylor, Jerome, trans. (1961). The 'Didascalicon' of Hugh of St Victor (New York).

Trimpi, Wesley (1978). 'Ut Pictura Poesis', Traditio 34: 29–73.

(1983). Muses of One Mind: The Literary Analysis of Experience and its Continuity (Princeton).

Ullmann, Walter (1974). Principles of Government and Politics in the Middle Ages, third edn (London and New York).

Vasoli, C. (1961). 'La "Theologia apothetica" di Alano di Lilla', Rivista critica di storia della filosofia 16: 153–87.

Waszink, Jan H. (1962). Plato. 'Timaeus', a Calcidio translatus commentarioque instructus, Plato latinus, 4. Corpus platonicum medii aevi (Leiden and London).

Webb, C. C. I., ed. (1909). *Ioannis Sarisburiensis episcopi Carnotensis Policratici, sive de nugis curialium et vestigiis philosophorum libri VIII*, 2 vols. (Oxford).

(1929). *Ioannis Saresburiensis episcopi Carnotensis Metalogicon* (Oxford).

Weber, Robert (1969). *Biblia Sacra iuxta vulgatam versionem*, 2 vols. (Stuttgart).

Weisheipl, James A. (1965). 'Classification of the Sciences in Medieval Thought', *Mediaeval Studies* 27: 54–90.

Westra, Haijo Jan, ed. (1986). *The Commentary on Martianus Capella's 'De Nuptiis Philologiae et Mercurii' Attributed to Bernardus Silvestris*, Studies and Texts, 80 (Toronto).

Wetherbee, Winthrop (1969). 'The Function of Poetry in the *De Planctu Naturae*', *Traditio* 25: 87–125.

(1972). *Platonism and Poetry in the Twelfth Century: the Literary Influence of the School of Chartres* (Princeton, N.J.).

(1976). 'The Theme of the Imagination in Medieval Poetry and the Allegorical Figure "Genius"', *Medievalia et Humanistica* n.s. 7: 45–64.

(1986). 'Genius and Interpretation in the *Confessio Amantis*', in *Magister Regis, Studies in Honour of Robert Earl Kaske*, edited by Arthur Groos (New York), 241–60.

(1988). 'Philosophy, Cosmology, and the Twelfth-Century Renaissance', in *HTCWP*, 21–53.

(1991). 'Latin Structure and Vernacular Space: Gower, Chaucer and the Boethian Tradition', in *Chaucer and Gower: Difference, Mutuality, Exchange*, edited by R. F. Yeager, English Literary Studies, 51 (Victoria, B.C.), 7–35.

Wetherbee, Winthrop, trans. (1973). *The 'Cosmographia' of Bernardus Silvestris* (New York).

White, Hugh (1986). 'Langland's Ymaginatif, Kynde and the *Benjamin Major*', *Medium Aevum* 55: 241–8.

(1988). 'Division and Failure in Gower's *Confessio Amantis*', *Neophilologus* 72: 600–16.

(1989). 'Nature and the Good in Gower's *Confessio Amantis*', in *John Gower: Recent Readings. Papers Presented at the Meetings of the John Gower Society 1983–88*, edited by R. F. Yeager, Studies in Medieval Culture, 26 (Kalamazoo), 1–20.

Wieland, Georg (1982). 'The Reception and Interpretation of Aristotle's *Ethics*', in *The Cambridge History of Later Medieval Philosophy 1100–1600*, edited by Norman Kretzmann, Anthony Kenny and Jan Pinborg (Cambridge), 657–72.

Wilks, Michael (1963). *The Problem of Sovereignty in the Later Middle Ages* (Cambridge).

(1977). 'Alan of Lille and the New Man', in *Renaissance and Renewal in Christian History*, edited by Derek Baker (Oxford) (= *Studies in Church History*, 14), 137–57.

Willis, J., ed. (1970). *Ambrosii Theodosii Macrobii commentarii In Somnium Scipionis* (Leipzig).

Willner, Hans, ed. (1903). *Des Adelard von Bath Traktat 'De eodem et diverso'*, *BGPTM*, 4.1.

Wittig, Joseph (1972). '*Piers Plowman* B, Passus IX–XII: Elements in the Design of the Inward Journey', *Traditio* 28: 211–80.

Wright, Thomas, ed. (1856). *De triumphis ecclesiae libri octo* (London).

Yeager, R. F. (1989). 'Did Gower Write *Cento*?', in *John Gower. Recent Readings. Papers Presented at the Meetings of the John Gower Society, 1983–88*, edited by R. F. Yeager, Studies in Medieval Culture, 26 (Kalamazoo), 113–32.

  (1990). *John Gower's Poetic. The Search for a New Arion*, Publications of the John Gower Society, 2 (Cambridge).

  (1991). 'Learning to Read in Tongues: Writing Poetry for a Trilingual Culture', in *Chaucer and Gower: Difference, Mutuality, Exchange*, English Literary Studies, 51, edited by R. F. Yeager (Victoria, B.C.), 115–29.

Zeeman, Nicolette (1991). 'The Verse of Courtly Love in the Framing Narrative of the *Confessio Amantis*', *Medium Aevum*, 60: 222–40.

Ziolkowski, Jan (1985). *Alan of Lille's Grammar of Sex. The Meaning of Grammar to a Twelfth Century Intellectual*, Speculum Anniversary Monographs, 10 (Cambridge, Mass.).

General Index

Editors' (including editors of reference works) and translators' names have been omitted, except where I refer to substantial arguments in editions. If the reference is to a page number, and the name also appears in the notes to the same page, references to the note are not listed.

CAMBRIDGE STUDIES IN MEDIEVAL LITERATURE

General Editor: Professor Alastair Minnis, Professor of Medieval Literature, University of York

EDITORIAL BOARD

TITLES PUBLISHED